FINANCIAL SERVICES MARKETS AND REGULATIONS

ANIL AGASHE
Visiting Faculty in Management and Corporate Trainer

Himalaya Publishing House
MUMBAI • NEW DELHI • NAGPUR • BENGALURU • HYDERABAD • CHENNAI • PUNE • LUCKNOW • AHMEDABAD • ERNAKULAM • BHUBANESWAR • INDORE • KOLKATA • GUWAHATI

FIRST EDITION : 2008
SECOND REVISED EDITION : 2014

Published by : Mrs. Meena Pandey for **Himalaya Publishing House Pvt. Ltd.,**
"Ramdoot", Dr. Bhalerao Marg, Girgaon, **Mumbai - 400 004.**
Phone: 022-23860170/23863863, Fax: 022-23877178
E-mail: himpub@vsnl.com; Website: www.himpub.com

Branch Offices :

New Delhi : "Pooja Apartments", 4-B, Murari Lal Street, Ansari Road, Darya Ganj, New Delhi - 110 002. Phone: 011-23270392, 23278631; Fax: 011-23256286

Nagpur : Kundanlal Chandak Industrial Estate, Ghat Road, Nagpur - 440 018. Phone: 0712-2738731, 3296733; Telefax: 0712-2721215

Bengaluru : No. 16/1 (Old 12/1), 1st Floor, Next to Hotel Highlands, Madhava Nagar, Race Course Road, Bengaluru - 560 001. Phone: 080-32919385; Telefax: 080-22286611

Hyderabad : No. 3-4-184, Lingampally, Besides Raghavendra Swamy Matham, Kachiguda, Hyderabad - 500 027. Phone: 040-27560041, 27550139; Mobile: 09390905282

Chennai : No. 8/2, Madley 2nd Street, Ground Floor, T. Nagar, Chennai - 600 017. Phone: 044-28144004/28144005; Mobile: 09345345051

Pune : First Floor, "Laksha" Apartment, No. 527, Mehunpura, Shaniwarpeth, (Near Prabhat Theatre), Pune - 411 030. Phone: 020-24496323/24496333; Mobile: 09370579333

Lucknow : House No 731, Shekhupura Colony, Near B.D. Convent School, Aliganj, Lucknow - 226 022. Mobile: 09307501549

Ahmedabad : 114, "SHAIL", 1st Floor, Opp. Madhu Sudan House, C.G. Road, Navrang Pura, Ahmedabad - 380 009. Phone: 079-26560126; Mobile: 09377088847

Ernakulam : 39/176 (New No: 60/251) 1st Floor, Karikkamuri Road, Ernakulam, Kochi - 682011, Phone: 0484-2378012, 2378016; Mobile: 09344199799

Bhubaneswar : 5 Station Square, Bhubaneswar - 751 001 (Odisha). Phone: 0674-2532129, Mobile: 09338746007

Indore : Kesardeep Avenue Extension, 73, Narayan Bagh, Flat No. 302, IIIrd Floor, Near Humpty Dumpty School, Indore - 452 007 (M.P.). Mobile: 09301386468

Kolkata : 108/4, Beliaghata Main Road, Near ID Hospital, Opp. SBI Bank, Kolkata - 700 010, Phone: 033-32449649, Mobile: 09883055590, 07439040301

Guwahati : House No. 15, Behind Pragjyotish College, Near Sharma Printing Press, P.O. Bharalumukh, Guwahati - 781009, (Assam). Mobile: 09883055590, 09883055536

DTP by : Sudhakar Shetty (HPH Pvt. Ltd., Bhandup)

Printed at : Geetanjali Press Pvt. Ltd., Nagpur.

PREFACE

I am delighted that the Himalaya Publishing House is bringing out the revised edition of my book, "Financial Services Markets and Regulations".

I hope the students of the subject will find the book useful. I also hope that this book is useful to others who may be interested in this subject.

These markets are extremely dynamic by nature and things change very quickly. An effort has been made to be as up to date as possible about the regulations for these markets. However, I must add a note of caution — As regulations keep changing frequently the reader should keep a track on these regulations. The best way to do this is to visit the SEBI website and review the regulations there.

I am thankful to all for their cooperation in writing this book and also to the people who used the earlier edition.

I am grateful to Himalaya for publishing this revised edition.

The readers are encouraged to give their feedback/suggestions to me on my e-mail-agasheanil@gmail.com. This will help me to improve.

ANIL AGASHE

CONTENTS

1 INTRODUCTION TO CAPITAL MARKETS: "BACKGROUND"

◈ What are Capital Markets?

Capital market is generally understood as a market for long-term funds and investments in long-term instruments available in this market. Capital markets mean the market for all the financial instruments, short-term and long-term. It is a market for corporate securities like shares, debentures and bonds.

The capital market deals with capital. The market consists of companies needing money to finance their business and those who wish to invest money in these companies.

Capital markets deal in both, debt and equity. In these markets productive capital is raised and made available to the corporate. The Central and State governments raise large amounts of money every year. This, however, is not considered as a part of capital market operations. Capital market refers to all the institutes and mechanisms of raising medium and long-term funds, through various instruments available like shares, debentures, bonds, etc.

With the liberalization of the economy from early 90s, these markets have grown phenomenally in the last 20 years. Every year, private enterprises as well public sector enterprises raise thousands of crore of rupees from these markets. Of course, the underlying economic conditions play a major role in this exercise. When the economy is doing well, more companies approach the investors for investments. While when the economy **does badly** or is in a slow down mode, not many companies come to the markets and even if they come, the response from the investors in not very enthusiastic at such times. The capital market serves a very useful purpose by pooling the savings of individuals and making them available to the business world. Well-developed markets augment resources by attracting and lending funds on a global scale. The Global Depository and American Depository markets perform these functions for companies across the globe. A well-developed capital market can solve the problem of paucity of funds for the business enterprises. The rapid growth of corporate entities has been made possible by the growth of these markets. This is a global phenomenon.

Capital markets seem to be in news always and that how it should be! These markets are normally open for five days a week and the business is transacted at National Stock Exchange

(NSE) and Bombay Stock Exchange (BSE) from 9.30 a.m. to 3.30 p.m. everyday. Approximately ₹ 1 lakh crore of business is transacted daily. Out of this figure 75 to 80 per cent is in Futures and Options segment and the balance in cash segment. Most of the trade takes place on NSE.

These markets reflect the underlying strength or weakness of the economy. They are also largely influenced by the happenings in the world economy. In a globalised world, this is inevitable. Today money flows seamlessly in all free markets. Thus, we get money from all over the world in our markets and as a matter of fact Indian markets compete with other emerging markets to attract more and more international capital. In India, this capital mainly comes from **Foreign Institutional Investors (FII)** and **Private Equity Funds (PE).** Recently, the government has allowed foreign individual investors to invest in our markets through the Indian Mutual Funds. How this latest initiative will pan out only time will tell.

Major investors in most companies are their promoters. As many Indian companies are owned by families, these promoters hold majority of the equity in these companies. Promoters are allowed to hold up to 75 per cent of the paid-up capital in their companies. The balance is to be held by the non-promoters. Non-promoters include institutional holdings like that of FIIs, Mutual Funds, Banks and Insurance companies. Non-institutional holdings are by retail investors. The sad fact of our markets is that, these categories of investors hold not more than 15 per cent of the capital in most of the listed companies. Actually the number of individual shareholders population has decreased to 80 lakh from 2 crore earlier. This is a worrying trend. The equity cult instead of increasing is declining. It has been well established that equities over a longer period tend to give better returns than most other classes of investment. The Indian capital markets have given 15 per cent annualized return over the past 20 years and still common Indians are not investing in these markets. What is more surprising is gains made in these investments are tax free and still the attractiveness of these markets seems to be declining! Dividend income is tax free in the hands of the receiver and there in no capital gains tax on profits through capital appreciation if the security is held for more than 12 months! If the security is bought and sold within 12 months then the gains are taxed as short-term capital gains @ 15 per cent. The reality today is that common Indian is not benefiting from the growth of Indian economy, as they refuse to participate in these markets, while foreigners have invested close to $ 100 billion over the past twenty years and have made considerable profits due to the growth of our economy!

As incomes have grown since the opening of our economy, it was expected that the people's participation in stock markets will increase. Sadly that has not happened. Indians are still investing most of their savings in bank FDs. These instruments are mostly safe, in the sense, the risk of the capital vanishing is minimum except in some weak cooperative banks. Almost 65 per cent of savings are parked in banks. One reason for this is most Indians are risk averse and have traditionally invested in banks or have bought gold. Gold prices in India have almost always risen, creating a false impression that they will never fall. However, now if the international prices were to fall, Indian prices will also follow them, because there are neither any restrictions on gold imports nor are there ridiculously high import duties on the commodity. Till now, due to the depreciation of Indian rupee against dollar, the fall in world gold prices did not reflect in domestic prices. Now the situation is different. **As the exchange rate is fairly stable in a range**, any large fall in world gold prices will cause a fall in Indian prices as well. We have seen huge depreciation in the month of June.

The second reason is extremely worrying. Most Indians, even if they are well educated, are financially illiterate and ignorant. They also do not seem to be willing to make an effort to know things. There are many ways to educate one about financial matters. It is horrifying to realise that most employees of even big companies never try to read the financials of their own companies! Securities and Exchange Board of India conducts seminars to educate people on matters related to markets. One wonders how many take advantage of these.

Recently NGOs like 'Money Life Foundation' started by Mr. Debashish Basu and Ms. Sucheta Dalal are conducting free seminars in different cities on how to be safe while making investments. These seminars are receiving encouraging response everywhere. They have also now started live streaming of these seminars on their website. This will allow many more people to take advantage of these seminars even they cannot attend them themselves.

The third thing that is noticed, is that many people made investments in the markets at the wrong time and lost money and have thus sworn never ever to buy stocks. Such people generally blame the markets for their losses instead of analyzing their own mistakes that have caused the loss. They also do not accept the fact that they lost money because of their ignorance about these matters. (what **kind of mistakes? Ignorance? Clarification required here?) The most grave mistake was not understanding the financials of a company. The other was of course greed.**

It was also thought that people who do not understand how to directly invest in these markets would take the mutual fund route. However, there have been problems here as well. For one, there are many schemes in the market and the potential investors seem to be confused about how to go about making the right investment decisions. If it was hard enough to know which stocks to buy now it is equally confusing to choose a mutual fund scheme! Many of those who have invested in these funds have invested in debt funds! Mutual Funds have also failed to help these hapless investors by introducing new schemes **unnecessarily.** ***There is a tendency to introduce new schemes when markets are doing well. As a matter of fact these so-called new schemes are mere clones of the older ones!***

Many youngsters and even middle aged got attracted to investing in ULIPs of Insurance companies from 2004. It is worth recalling that, that was the time when markets had also started recovering after the lows of 2001-03, following the melt-down in world markets and the coming out of Ketan Parekh scam at home. In the euphoria of 2005-2007, these products sold like hot cakes. After the fall of the markets in 2008, the reality became clear. These were one of the most mis-sold products in our markets. Many investors are still in loss even though the markets have recovered from their low levels of 2008. This also turned the sentiments against investments in stock markets.

The other problem of investors is that many of them want to become rich quickly. This is not possible. Getting rich requires hard and intelligent work ethic. Investments are required to be long-term for them to deliver profits. Secondly, many are unable to control greed and then suffer because of this. **Others invest in IPOs only to sell on listing to get** some quick money. Sometimes this does not happen. We saw this during the much hyped Reliance Power IPO. Many lost money as the market price crashed on listing.

◆ Participants of Capital Markets

Capital market requires many intermediaries who are responsible to transfer funds from those who save to those who require these funds for investments. There are two important operations carried on in these markets.

1. Raising new capital, and
2. Trading in the securities already issued by the company.

The important participants of the capital market are:

1. The stock exchanges
2. Banks
3. The investment trusts and companies.
4. Specialized financial institutions or development banks
5. Mutual funds
6. Non-banking financial institutions
7. International financial investors and institutions.

The other participants are:

1. Individuals.
2. Corporates.
3. Governments.
4. Foreign funds, either institutional or individuals
5. Provident funds.
6. Financial institutions.

Many of these entities contribute to savings in the economy. Parts of these savings naturally flow in the capital markets. Individuals invest in these markets directly by investing in shares or debentures of companies, through bond issues of public sector units or through mutual funds. Corporate, who have more savings than their requirement for funds are also participants in these markets.

Indian stock markets before 1991 were not open for foreign investors. Even Indians were not very savvy about investing and unfortunately they are same today. The markets in those days were extremely narrow. It was said the markets worked mainly on inside information. Till 1988, there was no index that is the year when SENSEX came into being.

Late Dhirubhai Ambani is widely credited as the person who took the equity culture to the Indian middle-classes. It was his offerings from Reliance Industries which somehow got at least some Indians in making investments in stock markets. Today's generation probably knows this in a dramatic way having watched Mani Ratnam's film *"Guru"* rather than what Ambani actually did!

Indians for many generations believed that investing in stock markets was akin to gambling. This sentiment is still prevalent among a large number of people even now. This is one main reason of non-participation of a sizeable population in these markets.

However, many things about the markets changed rapidly in the last decade of the last century. Dr. Manmohan Singh unleashed unprecedented reforms in the Indian economy and the financial markets. The whole scenario changed dramatically. Companies were now given freedom as never before to raise large sums of money from the capital markets. The first decision was to abolish the office of Controller of Capital Issues (CCI) which had a stranglehold on companies that wished to raise money. The premium to be charged by the companies on their offerings had to be approved by this regulator. In a free market, such regulations were redundant. Securities and Exchange Board of India was formed in 1988 and after the abolition of CCI, SEBI became the market regulator. Though the requisite powers for this were not granted to the SEBI at one go, but over a period of time SEBI became the sole regulator of capital markets.

The mutual fund industry which was opened to nationalized banks, insurance companies was also opened for private sector as well as foreign funds in early 90s. It gave another channel to potential investors to participate in these markets.

Another major development was the establishment of National Stock Exchange (NSE) which is the first corporatized stock exchange of India. Dr. R.H. Patil and his team deserve all credit for creating a worldclass stock exchange which had made full use of information technology. Now NSE is counted amongst the best stock exchanges across the world. Creation of these markets helped make trade seamless across India as with the help of internet, it was possible to trade from anywhere. For India it was a huge step forward. Such market was obviously a pre-condition for attracting FIIs to our markets. They were used to the most sophisticated markets that they traded in all over the world and they would want the same kind of platform here. This market also made settlements faster and less risky. Bombay Stock Market (BSE) was notorious in this respect and settlement would get postponed for days if traders wished so. NSE brought in a lot of discipline to the market. The settlement cycle became regular and settlement of all trade became possible on a particular day unlike the practice that was followed at BSE where "A" group shares were settled separately and others separately. Different stock exchanges had different trading settlement cycles given undue advantage to big players. All this became history. Today, India is probably the only market where trades are settled **T+2.** SEBI has said that they would bring this to T+1 when banks across the country become technologically compliant. The time has probably come as banks can now transfer money on the Real Time Gross Settlement (RTGS) platform.

Bombay stock exchange refused for a long time to embrace technology as it was driven more by the interests of the traders and promoters rather than the investors. This cost them heavily in terms of turnover. Today, NSE accounts for 70 per cent plus trade in cash segment and up to 99 per cent trade in Futures and Options segment.

It is now being said that NSE has a stranglehold on trade and is making every effort to retain it by making sure that other stock exchanges are not given permission to start trading on their platform.

After the reforms in financial markets and freeing of the industries from unnecessary licensing controls, many companies enthusiastically looked at the markets to raise large sums of money. There was a general euphoria about the markets and the SENSEX scaled a level of 4,000 plus point in the early 90s. Harshad Mehta became the unofficial God of stock markets in India around this time and was named as the "Big Bull" of the market by the pink press. All his investments and pronouncements received unprecedented publicity in financial press. Soon it was realized that all this was a nightmare. *Times of India* exposed the illegal dealings of Mehta and his play in government securities and illegal possession of money that belonged to someone else but which Mehta was allowed to use to ramp up the markets through the *'Badla"* route. All hell broke around and the market crashed. Many first time investors suffered heavy losses as market prices had run far ahead of fundamentals. Indians came to face with free economy and its perils if markets are not regulated properly. This same story was to repeat again in early parts of twenty first century as another "Big Bull" Ketan Parekh ramped up prices using almost a similar *modus operandi* that was used earlier by Mehta. This once again exposed the inadequacies of SEBI and other regulatory authorities. What was most annoying in this episode was enough warnings were coming from the press about some wrong doings that were apparent and still no cognizance was taken by the powers. Markets crashed once again almost inevitably and once again greedy breed of so-called small investors who had invested their hard earned and sometimes borrowed money in pursuance of overnight profits saw their capital disappearing faster than their dreams of becoming rich.

In the past twenty years, the markets have gone through many phases of high-low. Sometimes this has happened due to the fluctuations in our own economy and other times international events have moved the markets. In early parts of liberalization, the euphoria combined with Harshad factor raised the markets to new heights. After the fall of Harshad, the markets also crashed. Then they were affected by the South East Asian crisis. Then we once again saw the markets doing well in late 90s as the world economy also did well. **Then came the fall first due to the dot com burst** and then the Ketan factor. The markets were completely down in 2003. Then came an unprecedented bull phase; that lasted till 2007 end or early 2008 on the back of Indian economy growing @8 per cent consistently and on account of liquidity in the world markets. Then came the sub-prime crisis in 2008 and the Indian markets were down in dumps so to say. The SENSEX fell from the dizzy highs of 21,000 levels to sub 8,000 levels as major investment banks suffered losses never seen before. Big names like Lehman Brothers, Merrill Lynch and AIG became history or had to be rescued by the US government by almost nationalizing them. Many banks also went bust. The European banks also suffered. Indian banks did not suffer much as the RBI under Dr. Y.V. Reddy made sure to protect them from toxic products and came out shining as a top regulator. But foreign investors who had burnt their fingers badly had no option but to book profits in India and pulled out close to $ 13 billion in the calendar year 2008 after having pumped in close to $ 35 billion in the earlier 3-4 years time. But the markets made a come back again the following year as the FIIs that had pulled money out poured in close to $17 billion in 2009.

Many Indian companies have raised large amounts from the market. Coal India last year raised about ₹ 15,000 crore from its issue. Earlier in 2008, Reliance Power had raised ₹ 10,000 crore through its IPO that was oversubscribed by whopping 74 times. This was one of the most talked about IPO of its time. However, the hype was short lived as the issue which was priced at ₹ 450 per share with five per cent discount offered to retail investors. On listing the shares traded at a premium for sometime but soon sunk at ended the day at a discount to the IPO price. There was widespread disappointment among the investors who suddenly started saying that the issue was overpriced! It is remarkable instance of hypocrisy that these same investors had found nothing wrong with the pricing when they applied for the same. We shall discuss this later.

As is seen in all bull phases, a lot of companies came to the market in the 2005-early 2008 with large issues. They had no trouble selling their issues as the gullible investors lapped them up with no concern either for the fundamentals of the companies or to the pricing of the issues in question. Many brokerage houses and real estate companies took full advantage of this and successfully placed their shares at very high valuations. However, it must be remembered that the retail investors alone cannot to be blamed for this. These companies had privately placed their shares with the Private Equity players at very high prices in pre-issue placements made by them, thereby setting the base price of their public offerings. Also since 50 per cent of the issue is reserved for the institutional investors and mutual funds and an additional reservation of 15 per cent is available to so-called High Net worth Individuals (HNIs), they set the trend for the retail investors in an IPO. Once retail investors see huge interest and investments by these categories they jump on the band wagon. There is obviously enough reason to believe that promoters, merchant bankers and the institutional investors act in concert on pricing. If a share gets listed at premium, many so-called long-term investors from Qualified Institutional Bidders (QIB) category are the ones who sell and walk away with profits. Others who buy at this stage looking at the premium of issue price are normally left with an egg on their faces. If one were to look back at issues made by Reliance Power, DLF, Unitech, Shobha Developers, Eddlewise, Motilal Oswal, Anand Rathi and others, this fact will be absolutely clear. Many of these companies suffered large fall in their share prices in the blood bath of 2008. And even as the market has recovered splendidly, since then, many of the companies named above and others who had overpriced their issues are trading below their IPO price! There is a lesson in all this for retail investors that euphoria is no reason to invest. The track record of promoters, past history of the company, past history of the group companies who may have raised money through public offerings, type of industry and its likely future, along with the grading of the issue needs to be considered before making the investment decision. It is another matter that many companies had received investment grading of 4 or 5 from the rating agencies for their issues.

What companies did to the investors was done equally enthusiastically by the mutual fund industry. As the markets were going up the New Fund Offerings from them also flooded the markets. They launched new schemes regularly and attracted investments on the premise that the markets will continue to move up at all times. Investors also believed this gleefully and kept investing in new schemes quite foolishly. Today, many of these schemes are still in negative and investors have not received any returns.

Insurance companies also jumped in the rising markets with all the enthusiasm. The lure of making quick money as shown on the template attracted many to invest in ULIP schemes which combined insurance with investments and hence attractive indicated returns that promised returns far in excess of what markets had returned in about 15 years! Many IT employees and professionals invested large amounts of money in these schemes lured by the false promises of wealth creation that were made. Having invested in haste and to gratify their greed they are now repenting in leisure. ULIPs will go down as one of the most mis-sold products in India.

Over the last 20 years, the Government of India has also used these markets effectively to earn large amounts of money for itself by divesting its stakes in Public Sector Enterprises popularly known as PSUs. For the fiscal 2012-13 a disinvestment target of ₹ 40,000 crore was envisaged but due to the slowdown of the economy it was not achieved. Finally the government was able to raise just more than half of this target. For the current year also the government expects to raise around ₹ 30,000 crore. What may help the government is the fact that according to SEBI guidelines all listed PSUs will have to have at least 10 per cent of public holding so that in companies where there is scope to do this the government will be doing this. There was also some confusion in open market sale of NTPC shares and the issue had to be salvaged by LIC. The NDA government actually was bold enough to even privatise companies like BALCO, Modern Foods, CMC and VSNL to name a few. Some of these are listed entities. In other cases like Coal India, most of the Nationalised banks, Maruti, ONGC, BHEL, Oil India, NTPC, NHPC, etc., the government used these markets to part sell their equity holding through IPOs and Follow on Offers to the public at large. Most of these issues were sensibly priced and the investors have made profits by participating in these issues. One issue where this is not true is the IPO of NHPC where years after disinvestment that was done at a price of around ₹ 34 per share, the market price is well below this price consistently. In most other issues, investors have made money. It must therefore be admitted that the government has not been excessively greedy in its pricing policies.

The government was expected to disinvest more in the fiscal 2011-12 and had budgeted ₹ 40,000 crore from such proceeds. But with markets volatile this has not come about. Now SEBI has allowed another route that is auctioning of shares and the government may take this route to divest stake in some of its companies. There is a talk that the government may take this route to divest 5 per cent of its equity from ONGC. However, this issue had a lot of confusion may be because of the fact that it was the first issue under this route and the participants were not familiar with the process.

Debt Markets

Indian debt markets are also sought to be made more vibrant. Recently the Reserve Bank of India has allowed the participation of individuals in the government securities markets, which till now were dominated by the banks, financial institutions and mutual funds. This move is likely to open new avenues for investment to individuals. The R.H. Patil committee on debt markets has submitted its reports and we are likely to see positive changes in these markets soon. Hopefully these markets will become as vibrant as the ones in the developed economies giving investors another avenue to park their money. However, it has to be admitted that the progress on this front has best been tardy and the problem of stamp duty that is different in different states has still not been addressed adequately. One sees very little activity in these markets and individual investors are not getting an opportunity to invest in good quality debt instruments. SEBI has made it mandatory to list all debt instruments in stock markets, but the trade is thin and retail participation is pathetic. Companies prefer to raise debt through private placements rather than through a public issue. This keeps retail investors out of the market. But it must be acknowledged that there is great demand for good quality debt paper by banks, FIIs and mutual funds and insurance companies. Private placement is also cheaper for the issuer. In 2011, we saw two very successful public issues from L&T Finance and Tata Capital that were lapped up by retail investors as both offered very attractive returns and came from well established and respected names. In June 11, Shriram Transport also made a hugely successful issue for ₹ 1,000 crore where many individual investors did not get allotment as it was on first-come-first-basis. However, more importantly, these three issues have once again proved that there is a large class of investors out there waiting for such issues. The industry does not seem to be tempted to use this route. One would have thought that in the era of rising interest rates where RBI has increased interest rates 10 times in past 18 months or so, companies would raise medium-term funds through this route to escape escalating interest costs.

We have also seen some debt issues from government finance companies like NHAI, IRFC and HUDCO which were in great demand as the interest on these bonds is going to be tax free. There was huge demand for these bonds. People in highest tax bracket will immensely benefit from these investments as a coupon rate of 8 per cent + for 10 years is very attractive indeed. This is so because by investing in these bonds they will generate tax free income for themselves.

The budget for 2003-04 had some good news for the capital markets. The finance minister had conceded the demand for the removal of income tax on dividend in the hands of the receiver. The companies now pay dividend distribution tax @ 15 per cent and the receiver will not be taxed on dividend income. Secondly, the finance minister had proposed that there shall be no capital gains tax on investments made in equity after 1.3.03 and held for one year. This provision also has been extended. However, Indian middle-class has failed to take advantage of these tax breaks. What this implies is that any gains made will be tax free for the investors.

One peculiar thing about Indian markets is that there actually are many stock markets across the country. Since most of the trading happens in NSE and BSE, it is really baffling that so many stock exchanges are still allowed to exist at all. Most of them hardly have any business. Essentially, these exchanges list regional companies who are not eligible to list on the two major exchanges and need an exchange. But a platform for such companies has already been created on BSE and I think these exchanges to be allowed to be either merged with the top two exchanges or they should be dissolved. The policy in this regard is not very clear as of now and many regional exchanges are just languishing with little or no activity as most companies have de-listed from these exchanges. Most regional exchanges are not functioning any more.

It is now mandatory that all exchanges have to be corporatized. Earlier the exchanges were working as trusts. However, we have still to see an exchange getting listed.

One of the major improvements of the markets is that we have now almost fully adopted dematerialization of shares and debt instruments. The facility has now been extended to the units of mutual funds as well. However, not many people have opted for this facility as far as units of mutual funds are concerned as those are in any case not held in physical form by the investors. It is heartening that as far as shares are concerned they are majorly held in this format. I believe that holding shares in De-mat form needs to be made **mandatory. (it is not mandatory now).** Right now the trading in secondary markets and allotment in IPOs is through De-mat accounts only. However, under the law an investor can hold shares in materialized form if he so wishes, not only that but he can re-materialise shares that he holds in the De-mat form. This facility has improved many other things as well. Now dividends are being credited directly to the bank accounts of the shareholders resulting in huge savings for all concerned and the convenience that it has offered is really great. It is really surprising that in spite of this one sees details of dividends outstanding in most companies' annual reports. From 2011 the companies have decided to send financial statements in electronic form unless requested for in form of hard copies. This is a good step because most retail investors hardly ever bother to read the financial statements of the companies. This is also eco-friendly thing to do.

The derivative markets have shown unbelievable growth in India in a short time. This market is being used by institutional investors mainly. Many retail investors have also being participating in them, but it must be understood that retail investors are required to be extremely cautious if they wish to participate in this market.

Even as the government has opened our markets to foreigners it has at the same time allowed the Indian companies to raise money from the international markets and the eligible companies have taken full advantage of this. The money is raised by issuing American Depository Receipts (ADR), Global Depository Receipts (GDR) and Foreign Currency Convertible Bonds (FCCBs). Today, many Indian companies who had issued FCCBs **pre-2008 in a bull market** crash find themselves in great trouble as the conversion price accepted at the time of issuance was much higher than the prevailing market price of those securities. Since the investors are not likely to accept conversion at those prices. This will mean that the companies will either have to renegotiate the conversion price: If they do this they will have to allot more shares than they had bargained for. This will dilute the stake of the promoters. The other option is to repay the money. Many weak companies will find this difficult as banks may not be keen to finance them and with interest rates on the upward cycle it is a catch twenty-two situation for many companies.

SEBI has also allowed foreign companies to raise money from the Indian markets by issuance of Indian Depository Receipts. (IDR). So far **only** Standard Chartered Bank plc. has raised money through this route. It is going to take a long time before other companies are likely to use this route.

Another important step initiated by SEBI is that it is going to allow Indian companies to issue equity simultaneously in the domestic and international markets. M.S. Verma committee recommended the **dual floatation in 2002**. It is recommended that the book running for both the floats should be done simultaneously. This will help settle the issue of pricing.

SEBI has also introduced Anchor investors in IPOs. These investors apply for the shares before the opening of the IPO and are obliged to hold the shares for thirty days post-allotment. It is felt that this will give confidence to investors and may reduce volatility in shares post-listing. SEBI has also mandated that on the opening day of the IPO only QIBs will be allowed to make offers. Other investors can put in their bids only from the second day. This will give an idea to retail investors as to how QIBs are looking at the IPO. **During the IPO on the day IPO opens for subscription only Institutional Investors are allowed to bid. The book opens for retail and HNI investors only from the second day. This is done so that these investors can know the response from the institutes to the issue and then take a call on whether to apply or not based on this information. If an issue receives good response from the institution then it is perceived that it an issue worth applying for!**

The bullish story of Indian market continued from 2004 to 2008. FIIs have pumped in $ 35-40 billion in our markets in these four years. One of the most heartening features in 2006 was the huge inflows in the equity mutual funds. This trend continued in 2007 as well. On top of that the markets also saw brisk activity in the PE space as these funds pumped in further $ 10-12 billions both in listed and unlisted companies. All this came to an abrupt halt in 2008 on the back of sub-prime crisis.

SEBI has also tried to bring in more transparency in the working of the listed entities by making the implementation of clause 49 of the listing agreement. It is further to the initiatives taken in the field of Corporate Governance practices. But overall Indian markets and companies are nowhere near the desirable levels of Corporate Governance best practices. In 2013, the government has passed the new Companies Act and has also passed a law giving more powers to SEBI.

Obviously since the markets were doing very well before 2008-09 and especially from 2006 to 2008 and the early part of 08-09, the amounts raised were substantial. The activity decreased from the second half of 08-09 in line with the market trends. Two major Rights issues of Tata Motors and Hindalco were undersubscribed in 08-09 and that affected the market sentiments.

So as can be seen a lot of things have happened in the markets over the past twenty years. But it must be realised a lot needs to be done. As things change in the business environment the market regulators have to be alert to make necessary changes in the markets as well.

Today we are facing many serious problems in our country. Our economy has grown by only around 5 per cent in the fiscal 2012-13. It is hoped that it will grow @ about 6 per cent in 2013-14. However, next year is election year. We have seen many scams that have erupted and have also seen the parliament not functioning for days. The legislative business thus has come to grinding halt unfortunately. We may have to wait for the elections to be over and a new government to be in place for the legislative business to resume. However, there is also the big risk that we may not have a state government post-elections and if that happens our problems will only get compounded.

Though the WPI has moderated to around 5 per cent CPI still is hovering around 10 per cent with food inflation remaining very high in spite of record food production of 255 Metric Tonnes last year! This has forced RBI to be conservative and it has not been able to cut interest rates aggressively.

The problem is being compounded by the fact that our exports have stayed at around $ 306 billion and imports have surged. High imports of gold have added to our current account deficit problems as well. The CAD is very high and that has put pressure on rupee. It is trading at its historical low of 59.90 in June 2013. It went down to almost 69 and is now reaching @ 62-62 levels.

With the revival of US economy in the last one year some FII money is going out of India. In last few months FIIs have taken out roughly $ 5 billion. This has put more pressure on rupee.

The Government of India has increased the maximum support price of foodgrains by almost 100 per cent in the last 6-7 years. This has put some money in the pockets of the rural population in spite of poor supply chain management of agriculture in the country. This new purchasing power can be seen in the fact that the FMCG sales are growing more in semi-urban and rural areas. Same seems to be story with white goods and mobile and two-wheeler sales that are being reported month-on-month.

The second thing that has given boost to rural incomes is the loan waiver of close to **₹ 72,000 crore of loans to farmers.** This also has increased the purchasing power of rural population.

Thirdly, the government has given a big boost to its own employees both at the Centre as well as in States by accepting the recommendations of the sixth pay commission that has increased salaries as much as 25 per cent. This has increased liquidity and people are spending this money.

With major global IT companies in India the wages in this sector have also increased substantially for the competent people especially to stop attrition. This has created a new class of consumers that seems to afford things at whatever price.

Private sector has also increased salaries even at the entry level and this has forced them to increase salaries at all levels.

Since the economy has been doing well and growing at a good space even in the bad years the business class also has made plenty of money in the last 2-3 years. This allows them to spend money.

In all this, it has been reported that India consumed 550 tonnes of gold last year! Is it any wonder?

RBI has been trying to fight inflation in the economy for the last couple of years which has been persistently around 9 per cent on the back of high oil and other commodity prices in the international markets and high food prices in the domestic markets. Government finances have also not been in good condition with budget deficit for 2011-12 that was budgeted to be 4.6 per cent is likely to be actually around 5.6 per cent on the back of slow down of the economy which is now likely to see growth rate of around 6 per cent against the predicted growth rate of around 8-8.5 per cent. Subsidy bill has increased many fold in the current financial year, the finance minister recently admitted that he is losing sleep over this issue! The RBI has increased interest rates consistently and has used REPO and REVERSE REPO rates for this purpose. This has made money expensive At the same time, interest rates on bank deposits have also gone up to about 9-9.5 per cent. The industries are therefore paying higher interest and that has impacted their profitability. New investments are not being planned as industries wait for the rates to come down. The government has projected budget deficit @ 4.8 per cent of GDP for 2013-14. The FM has said several times that he would not let the deficit exceed this limit. The inflation has declined to about 7 per cent and there is a hope that interest rates will not be increased any more. However, it is not known when the RBI will actually start cutting the interest rates. The IIP numbers have shown a lot of inconsistency. So the situation is serious and needs action urgently. The Repo rate now stands at 7.50 per cent and Reverse Repo is 6.50 per cent.

With European crisis deepening and no solution in sight, things may continue to be difficult. The standoff between US and European countries and Iran on nuclear issue, the oil prices have firmed up once again. **The US economy has still not stabilized.**

In India the government seems to be in what is referred to as "Governance Deficit" and "Policy Paralysis". It is also caught in the middle of various scams. The Commonwealth Scam, Adarsh Scam and the mother of all scams 'the 2G scam'. Added to this is the pressure put by the Civil society on the issue of Lokpal.

It really seems that the government is in paralysis and is not doing anything on the reforms front. In UPA–I there was a problem that the government was dependent on Left support for survival. That situation changed after 2009 elections. But since then no major reforms have come through. I believe that having Pranab Mukherjee as Finance Minister is a big mistake. He is not a natural reformer and he is involved in too many other things of the government that he probably does not have the time that is required to run the finance ministry.

The government is also facing the task of containing its own deficit that always has a big influence on all economies. Since 2008 crisis **it seems to me that** the government went overboard with their stimulus package and that has hurt government finances. The political lack of consensus means that even a sensible reform like the enactment of goods and services tax has got delayed. The FDI in Multibrand Retail is also hanging fire. Hopefully Direct Tax code (DTC) will come into effect in 2012, but it must be mentioned that this version is a far too diluted version of the first draft that was out when Chidambaram was the finance minister and the real man behind this bill.

What is encouraging is coming from the export front. Growth in exports has caused worry in 2012-13 and have reached only $800 bn. In the past 7 months of fiscal 2013-14, exports have grown @ 5 per cent and imports have contracted. The CAD is now projected to be around $60 bn a much desired improvement over the last year.

It must be kept in mind India is only one of the countries from the so-called emerging markets and the foreign funds go to all these markets to make investments. India is not the most preferred destination as of now. As a matter of fact in calendar year 2011, Indian markets are one of the worst performing markets amongst the emerging markets.

So we must keep reforming and growing economically to make investments in the markets worthwhile. It is important that we make all out efforts to attract Indian investors especially the middle-class to capital markets. Despite the tax advantage of investing in equities, this class has gone away from the markets in the recent past. Another blow is dealt by the provision in DST which proposes to take away tax exemptions on investments made in Equity Linked Schemes of Mutual Funds. So one attractive way to encourage taxpaying public to invest in markets; will not be available from the next year.

We must take urgent steps to broaden and deepen our debt markets in line with the Dr. R.H. Patil committee's recommendation in this regard. A debt market with depth is required to finance our infrastructure development.

So let's hope that the government does all that it needs to do for our economy and the reforms that are stalled get under way. However, it must be realised by the investors that they can make investments in fundamentally good companies whatever may be the state of the markets. The thing to be remembered is what one pays is price and what we are looking for is value.

For beginners who wish to invest money in capital markets, here are some things that they should consider and keep in mind. Also please be careful as to what believe from all that is dished out on business channels. Please remember nobody is going to give you free advice so that you could become rich without doing anything and just following their advice! Becoming rich requires intelligence especially if you are trying to be rich on someone else's performance. Getting rich is not easy, it requires hard work and it needs more intelligent work to remain rich!

1. **Invest in businesses you understand:** It is important for an investor to understand the business of a company before deciding to buy the shares of a company. This is important because otherwise various developments that take place in the sector in which that company operates and the peculiarities that every business has, will not become clear to him. Our investments have to be tracked frequently and the business environment for a particular sector or business can undergo changes that have an impact on the future performance of a company will bypass an investor who does not have the adequate knowledge of these matters.
2. **Always have pre-decided exit levels**: This means that we must cap our greed by setting a profit target by deciding how much appreciation is enough. Of course, there is a school of thought that suggests that companies who are doing well and in the view of the investors they have good future over the long-term; such companies' shares need not be sold but should be accumulated. Every individual has to make this decision for himself. Many investors have two kinds of portfolios. One is long-term where they follow the strategy of long-term investment and other where they put an exit level and exit that company once that level is reached.
3. **Never marry your scrip**: This means that when a company's future is uncertain and when it is doing badly it is better to get rid of that investment. Sometimes it so happens that the company is doing fine but its stock prices do not move up, in such situation if an investor believes that the price has reached its peak and more profits are no more a possibility, then he should quit and take his investment somewhere else.
4. **Do not look at the stock market every moment:** Some people have the habit of looking at prices on their laptops or TV screens. Your investment should be for a particular duration and that time limit must be clear in your mind before making the investment. Looking at prices constantly does not help but can only distract you from your work leading to mistakes being made. None of us has the power to change the price to our liking by looking at it, so why waste time?
5. **Average on the rise:** When one buys a share and its price falls there is a tendency to buy more shares so as to bring down the average price of acquisition. What people tend to forget is that by doing so they are putting more money in the scrip of a company that is not doing well! So if you want to average buy more shares of a company that is doing well and whose price is rising. The exception to this rule is when markets fall in an unprecedented manner as they did in 2008. In such situation even well performing companies will suffer a price loss; this then would be a good time to average on declines. But remember that the companies need to be very good.
6. **What goes up must come down:** This is golden rule of nature. What goes up will come down and what goes up too fast is likely to go down at double the speed. The other way is also possible for good companies. If they loose ground for sometime due to difficult business environment they can reverse the trend and start to go up.

7. **Churn your portfolio once every six months**: All investors have an obligation to watch their investments from time-to-time to see how they are performing. One can make a mistake and that mistake needs to be corrected. There is no investor in the world who does not buy a bad stock ever. So, if you have done it there is no shame. You must get out of it and minimize your loss. The shame would be not to accept the mistake and stick to or marry the stock and not get out of it!
8. **Diversify:** One needs to diversify one's portfolio. We cannot keep all our eggs in one basket. Diversification reduces the risk of a portfolio. It also gives us the advantage of having investments in different sectors. So if one sector is not doing well, the other sectors may compensate.
9. **Keep invested your profits:** One of the normal mistakes made by investors is that when they make profits in their investments they tend to spend this money. It is advised that all profits should be reinvested to get the long-term benefits of investments. When you book profits and spend them, your portfolio value decreases. Profits should be spent only when there is no other alternative.
10. **Never believe in tips:** Tips means sheer speculation. Nobody is going to give you tips so that you make money. Tips are good at race courses and even there, people lose money by betting on the basis of tips. Investing is not gambling if you do not want it to be.
11. **Invest for the long-term:** For best returns in the stock markets it is required to be a long-term investor. Long-term means minimum three years and depending on the performance of the company the longer horizon can be decided from time-to-time.
12. **Invest money you can afford to lose:** Does not mean that you should lose money. It means that if you were to lose money it should not make a difference to your present requirements. That means you are investing your surplus without expecting profits in the short-term and are willing to wait for profits to accrue over a period of time.
13. **Never try to earn profits overnight:** Earning profits is long-term thing. Very rarely one will be lucky make profits in a very short period of time. This may happen once in a lifetime. Do not believe stories of others who will tell you how they hit pay dirt in no time. Remember very few people talk honestly about the times when they have lost money.
14. **All shares cannot become ten baggers:** All investments that you make will not give fantastic returns.
15. **If possible try to stay away from the stock market:** If you think that you can't follow the above given "Pointers" on how to go about investing or if you do not believe in them, then you better stay away from stock markets.

    (any pointer required about the proper documentation/address change/nomination part? Share broker/adviser?)

2 SECURITIES AND EXCHANGE BOARD OF INDIA (SEBI)

The Securities and Exchange Board of India was set up on April 12, 1988, following the recommendations of the high-powered G. S. Patel Committee on Stock Exchange Reforms.

SEBI has a mandate to create an environment, which would facilitate mobilisation of adequate resources through the securities market. This environment would include rules and regulations, institutions and their inter-relationships, instruments, practices, infrastructure within an appropriate policy framework, should have an overall air of fairness. The market regulator must create confidence in the minds of the investors.

SEBI has to be responsive to the needs of three groups, which constitute the market:

(*a*) The issuers of securities

(*b*) The investors, and

(*c*) The market intermediaries.

It must be understood that all investors carry certain risk and it is for the investor to study and understand risks and choose his investments judiciously. SEBI cannot eliminate all such risks or the consequences of the risks. SEBI has the responsibility to regulate markets and the constituents of the market in such a way that the investors interests are well protected.

The role assigned to SEBI:

1. SEBI shall create a proper and conducive atmosphere required for raising money from the capital market. The atmosphere includes rules, regulations. Trade practices, customs and relations among institutions, brokers, investors and companies. SEBI is responsible for safeguarding the interests of small investors.
2. SEBI shall educate investors and make them aware of their rights in clear and specific terms.
3. SEBI shall create proper investment climate to enable corporate sector to raise industrial securities easily, efficiently and at affordable cost.

4. SEBI shall develop a proper infrastructure so that market automatically facilitates expansion and growth of business of middlemen like brokers, banks, merchant bankers, mutual funds, etc. So it will ensure that they provide efficient service to the constituents of the markets.
5. SEBI shall make more effective, the laws in the existing statues as far as they relate to the industrial securities, mutual funds, investments in Units, LIC saving plans, Chit funds, etc.
6. SEBI shall create the framework for more open, orderly and unprejudiced conduct in relation to takeover and mergers in the corporate sector to ensure fair and equal treatment to all the security holders and to facilitate such takeovers and mergers in the interest of efficiency by prescribing a mechanism for more orderly conduct.
7. It shall devise laws with unified set of objectives, single administrative authority and an integrated framework to deal with all the aspects of the securities market.
8. It shall introduce a system of two-stage disclosure at the time of initial issue and make compulsory of the companies to provide detailed information to all stock exchanges and investors on demand.
9. It shall work as an authoritative institution to see that the intermediaries are financially sound and equipped with professional and competent manpower.
10. It shall ensure that the rules are versatile and non-rigid to provide automatic and self-regulatory growth.
11. It shall establish effective inspection machinery, which is expected to act like an umpire.
12. It shall operate a security compensation fund in order to protect investors who suffer financial loss arising from the failure of a stockbroker to meet his contractual obligations.
13. It shall prohibit the malpractice prevailing in market such as insider trading, share cornering, etc.

The management of SEBI is under the management board headed by a chairman. The board consists of two members from amongst the officials of the finance and law ministries. One member shall be from amongst the officials of Reserve Bank of India. Two more board members are appointed by the Central government.

The general superintendence, direction and management of the affairs of the board vests in a Board of members, which may exercise all powers and do all acts and nothing which may be exercised or done by that Board.

The Chairman has the powers of general superintendence and direction of the affairs of the board and may also exercise all powers and do all acts and things which may be exercised or done by the Board. This provision makes the Chairman a very powerful person. Mr. U. K. Sinha is the Chairman of the SEBI at present. He has a lot of experience of the markets, with whom he dealt as Secretary in the Ministry of Finance. Mr. Sinha was the Chairman of UTI before his present appointment.

Functions of the Board

1. Regulating the business in stock exchanges and any other securities markets.
2. Registering and regulating the working of stock brokers, subbrokers, share transfer agents, bankers to an issue, trustees to trust deeds, registrars to the issue, merchant

bankers, underwriters, portfolio managers, investment advisor and such other intermediaries who may be associated with securities markets in any manner.

3. Registering and regulating the working of mutual funds.
4. Promoting and regulating self-regulatory organization.
5. Prohibiting fraudulent and unfair trade practices.
6. Promoting investor's education and training of intermediaries of the securities market.
7. Prohibiting insider trading in securities.
8. Regulating substantial acquisition of shares and takeover of companies.
9. Calling for information from, undertaking inspection, conducting, inquiring and audits of the stock exchanges and intermediaries and self-regulatory organisations in the securities market.

No stock broker, subbroker, share transfer agent, banker to an issue, trustee of trust deed, registrar to an issue, merchant banker, underwriter, portfolio manager, investment advisor and such other intermediary who may be associated with securities market buy, sell or deal in securities except under, and in accordance with the conditions of a certificate of registration obtained from the Board.

Every application for registration shall be in such manner and on payment of such fees as may be determined by regulations.

The board may, by order, suspend or cancel a certificate or registration in such manner as may be determined by regulation.

◈ SEBI and Individual Investor

The investors in the past have suffered at the hands of inefficient stock exchanges and greedy and unprofessional brokers. SEBI was to look after the investors suffering from any problems. The investor today can look forward to redressal of his grievances through SEBI. However, it must be admitted that SEBI's track record in this respect is patchy.

Normally investors have complaints of the following nature:

1. Delays in refund of application money.
2. Delay in receipt of dividend and/or interest warrants. (This has been largely taken care of as most payments are now made through the ECS system)
3. Delay in receiving the maturity value of fixed deposits or debentures on redemption.
4. Delay in receipt of share and debenture certificates after allotment. (This problem has also got dealt with, with the dematerialization of shares and debentures)

SEBI receives many such complaints regularly and tries to redress all such grievances. SEBI has from time-to-time pulled up companies against whom the complaints are received and has also initiated action against the defaulting companies.

SEBI has encouraged the registration of investors associations in various parts of the country to organize investors into an effective force for protection of their own interests.

Some of the actions taken by SEBI can be summarized as below:

- The introduction of screen-based trading.
- Improvement in the IPO process. The process is now required to be completed much faster. The companies are now required to list the shares within 14 days of the closing of the issue.

- The ban on Badla.
- The dematerialization of shares.
- The method of postal ballots so that small investors views are heard.
- The book building process in buyback of shares by the companies.
- The capital adequacy norms for brokers.
- Introduction of Futures and Options in the market.

Some of the important achievements of SEBI are:

1. Proper disclosure to investors through investors through prospectus made mandatory. The Red herring prospectus today gives a lot of information about the company, its promoters, past record and the details of the project for which the funds are being raised. It also contains the disclosure of both internal and external risks that the company foresees.
2. **Guidelines for merchant bankers:** These are discussed in the chapter on "Merchant Banking".
3. Advertising code for mutual funds.
4. **Mutual funds are required to publish balance sheets:** To make sure that the investors get information on the performance of their Mutual Funds in which they invest their money.
5. **Takeover code formulated:** A new code has just been released by SEBI after taking into account the experience of the earlier one.
6. Portfolio management service guidelines issued.
7. Guidelines on insider trading.
8. Registration of stockbrokers and subbrokers.

   SEBI has underlined following obligations for the brokers:

   (*a*) Entering into an agreement with his client or with subbroker and client

   (*b*) Maintenance of separate books of accounts and records for clients

   (*c*) Maintenance of money of clients in a separate account and their own money in a separate account.

   (*d*) Issue of daily statement of collateral utilization to clients

   (*e*) Appointment of compliance officer

   (*f*) Issue of contract note to his client within 24 hrs of the execution of the contract.

   (*g*) Delivery/payment to be made to the client within 24 hrs of payout.

   (*h*) Other duties as specified in the SEBI (Stock Brokers and Subbrokers) Rules, 1992.

   SEBI has also notified Rights and Obligations of an investor:

   (*a*) Before entering into a contract with the broker, ensure that he is registered with SEBI.

   (*b*) Satisfy yourself about the credentials of the broker by asking for information/ documents supporting his claims.

   (*c*) Keep a documentary proof of having made deposit of money or securities with the broker.

(*d*) Before activating your trading account, obtain clear idea from your broker about all brokerage, commissions, fees and other charges which will be levied on your trades.

(*e*) Furnish details in full as are required by the broker as required in "know your client" (KYC) norms.

(*f*) Ensure that a contract note is issued by the broker which contains complete records of every transaction within 24 hrs of the execution of the contract.

(*g*) In case payout of money and/or securities is not received on the next working day after date of payout, follow-up with the concerned broker for its release. If it is not released within five working days, ensure to lodge a complaint immediately with the Investors' Grievance Cell of the exchange.

(*h*) Ensure to receive a complete 'Statement of Accounts' for both funds and securities settlement every quarter.

9. **Underwriting made mandatory:** This is like an insurance against the failure of a issue. This is discussed in detail in the chapter on "Merchant Banking".

10. **ASBA facility for investors:** This was launched a few years back making applying for IPO easy for all categories of investors. ASBA means" Application Supported by Blocked Amount". Under this facility an investor can apply for IPO/rights issue online or óthe rwise without actually having to make payment till the allotment of shares is done to him. The amount is thus blocked in his account with the bank at the time of application and only if he gets allotment then the requisite amount is debited to his account and transferred to the designated account. Thus the investor continues to get interest on the amount. Earlier investors had to pay the entire amount with his application and the money would not earn him any interest as it left his account for a period of three to four weeks. This is an extremely useful feature. The regulation allows five applications per account.

    It is useful for the issuers as well as they are spared the trouble of refunding money to unsuccessful applicants.

11. SEBI has introduced Fast Track Issues (FTI). They work as follows:

    SEBI has introduced FTI in order to enable well established and compliant listed companies satisfying certain specific entry norms/conditions to access Indian Primary Market in a time effective manner. Such companies can proceed with FPOs/Right Issues by filing a copy of RHP/Prospectus with the RoC or the Letter of Offer with designated SE, SEBI and Stock Exchanges. Such companies are not required to file Draft Offer Document for SEBI comments and to Stock Exchanges.

    Entry norms for companies seeking to access Primary Market through FTI's in case aggregate value of securities including premium exceeds ₹ 50 lakh:

    (*i*) The shares of the company have been listed on any stock exchange having nationwide terminals for a period of at least three years immediately preceding the date of filing of offer document with RoC/SE;

    (*ii*) The "average market capitalisation of public shareholding" of the company is at least ₹ 10,000 crore for a period of one year up to the end of the quarter preceding the month in which the proposed issue is approved by the Board of Directors/ shareholders of the issuer;

(*iii*) The annualized trading turnover of the shares of the company during six calendar months immediately preceding the month of the reference date has been at least two per cent of the weighted average number of shares listed during the said six months period;

(*iv*) The company has redressed at least 95 per cent of the total shareholder/investor grievances or complaints received till the end of the quarter immediately proceeding the month of the date of filing of offer document with RoC/SE.

(*v*) The company has complied with the listing agreement for a period of at least three years immediately preceding the reference date;

(*vi*) The impact of auditors' qualifications, if any, on the audited accounts of the company in respect of the financial years for which such accounts are disclosed in the offer document does not exceed 5 per cent of the net profit/loss after tax of the company for the respective years.

(*vii*) No prosecution proceedings or show cause notices issued by the Board are pending against the company or its promoters or whole-time directors as on the reference date; and

(*viii*) The entire shareholding of the promoter group is held in dematerialised form as on the reference date.

12. **SEBI has made grading for IPOs mandatory:** Companies who wish to make issues have to obtain grading for their issues from the recognized Credit Rating Agencies. The grading is given on the scale of 0 to 5. Grading up to 3 is indicates low grading and can be considered as non-investment grading. Higher grading indicates higher safety and lesser risk for the investors.

However, I have my own doubts about the efficiency of this process. Many issues that are graded high have destroyed the wealth of the shareholders post-listing. The biggest of these was Reliance Power issue! We have also seen the fate of highly rated issues of Wockhardt Hospitals and EMMAR-MGF that had to be withdrawn after having been opened, due to pathetic response from the investors!

◈ What SEBI does with its power?

The SEBI exercises power under Section 11 and 11B of SEBI Act, 1992 and 17 other regulations.

- It can ask any intermediary or market participant for information.
- It can inspect books of depository participants, issuers or beneficiary owners.
- It can suspend or cancel a certificate of registration granted to a depository participant or issuer.
- It can request the RBI to inspect books of a banker to an issue and suspend or cancel the registration of the banker to an issue.
- It can suspend or cancel certificate issued to the custodian of securities.
- It can suspend or cancel registration granted to foreign institutional investors.
- It can investigate and inspect books of accounts and records of insiders. (The case of Tata Finance.)
- It can investigate an acquirer, a seller or merchant banker for violating the takeover norms. (The case of Grasim's takeover bid on L&T and the sale of shares of L&T by

Reliance to Grasim. You can also refer to the attempted takeover case of Bombay Dyeing by Bajoria. Also refer to Sterlite Industry's attempt on Indal.)

- It can suspend or cancel the registration of a merchant banker.
- It can investigate the affairs of mutual funds, their trustees and asset management companies.
- It can investigate any person dealing in securities on complaint of contravention of trading regulation.
- It can suspend or cancel the registration of errant portfolio managers.
- It can cancel the certificate of registrars and share transfer agents.
- It can cancel the certificate of brokers who fail to furnish information of transactions in securities or who furnish false information.

Let us take a look at some of the actions taken by SEBI under powers granted to it:

The Securities and Exchange Board of India (SEBI) has recently barred several directors and officials of Bharatiya Global Infomedia (BGIL) from the capital market as part of its crackdown on irregularities in the initial public offerings (IPOs) of seven companies. It has also prohibited Almondz Global Securities, the lead manager from taking up any new assignment.

In July 2011 BGIL raised ₹ 55 crore, at a price of ₹ 82 per share with the stated objective of purchasing offices (₹ 9.89 crore), investment in a digital post-production studio (₹ 22 crore), expanding its R&D centre (₹ 6.56 crore), repayment of bank borrowings (₹ 2.69 crore) and for long-term working capital (₹ 5 crore).

It was the brazen manipulation of the BGIL shares on the listing day that caught the regulator's eye. The shares, which were listed on 28 July, 2011 at ₹ 81.90, on the Bombay Stock Exchange (BSE), rose to ₹ 83 and soon began to slide, plunging to ₹ 29.90 at close. This kind of movement is unusual to say the least and any such movements should be actually noticed by the concerned stock exchange and reported to the regulator.

A SEBI investigation revealed that rigging its share price was just one of its many acts of mischief. Wrong disclosures in its prospectus (which is a legal document), misutilisation of IPO proceeds and other violations soon tumbled out.

What SEBI found in its investigation was rigging was not the only thing wrong with this company. It was found that disclosures were incorrect, and there was also mis-utilisation of IPO proceeds. The most shocking fact was the track record of Chairman and M.D. Rakesh Bhatia who it was found was involved in the past with other questionable entities. He was Promoter and M.D. of a company called SRG(Infotech) that made an IPO in 1994 and the shares of that company are trading at rupee one now! He was also the promoter and chairman of SRG Financial and Management when it came out with its IPO in 1996. The company doesn't seem to exist today. Subsequently, he became the managing director of Visesh Infosystems, currently known as Visesh Infotechnics, which came up with an IPO in 1999, and quit in 2004. It is surprising that his association with various companies with whom was associated at the time of IPO and then subsequently quitting those companies was not noticed either by Merchant Bankers and the Regulators. However, it is unbelievable that these entities had no information regarding this.

BGIL had also claimed to have spent ₹ 2.50 crore to purchase offices at Mumbai and Noida, however documents revealed that the money was advanced to Dhanmangal Developers of Kolkata, about which there was no mention in the prospectus. Worse, there was no move to set up offices in Mumbai or Noida.

SEBI rules require promoters to disclose a list of relatives of the promoters for the purpose of insider trading rules. BGIL conveniently omitted to disclose several of these, with the intention that property deals could be done through them to siphon-off IPO funds. For instance, the company signed up to acquire property from Gadeo Electronics owned by Richa Mittal (95 per cent stake in the partnership firm) and R.K. Mittal (5 per cent). The latter is the father of BGIL's director Sanjeev Kumar Mittal. But the prospectus said: "Mrs. Richa Mittal is wife of Mr. Rajeev Mittal and a resident of A-147-148, Sector 55, Noida, Uttar Pradesh, and not related to our company, our Promoters/Directors or Promoter Group Companies". Rajeev Mittal, the husband, is the brother of Mr. Sanjeev Mittal but the relationship was falsely concealed.

A bigger problem, from the investors' perspective is the concealment of significant borrowings. BGIL's borrowing through inter-corporate deposits (ICDs) amounted to around 60 per cent to its total liabilities — of this, ₹ 7 crore was not revealed in the prospectus and amounted to a 100 per cent jump on current liabilities. Instead, the prospectus brazenly lied and said: "Our company has not raised any bridge loan against the proceeds of the present issue".

The above facts also point towards another hazard. It shows that the Merchant Bankers managing issues do not do their compliance work properly and even SEBI is found wanting in its process of giving go ahead to issues without making sure that all disclosures are counter checked and information is verified by them as well. Thus questions need to be raised on the sanctity of the whole process and the investors need to be cautious while investing money in unknown companies and promoters.

SEBI has investigated many cases of market manipulation and price rigging. In certain cases it awarded the maximum penalty of suspension of registration and cancellation of registration of the intermediary. The company involved is denied access to capital market for the stipulated period, and criminal prosecution recommended. (The cases of Videocon, Sterlite and BPL). However, many of SEBI's decisions are successfully challenged by the affected companies in the tribunal and many decisions have been overturned by the tribunal. This reflects poorly on SEBI's investigations and in building a sound case against the offenders. Many times the decisions are reversed because of this.

◈ SEBI Guidelines for Issue of Debt Instruments

SEBI regulates the issuance of debt instruments like debentures by the companies. SEBI also regulates the issuance of Indian Depository Receipts issued by foreign companies to raise money from Indian markets. SEBI has formulated the guidelines for both these instruments.

A company offering Convertible/Non-convertible debt instruments through public offer have to comply with the following guidelines:

1. Credit rating for these instruments is mandatory, irrespective of maturity or conversion period. The credit rating has to be disclosed in the offer document.
2. For an issue equal to or greater than ₹ 100 crore two ratings from two different credit ratings have to be obtained.
3. If rating is obtained from two different credit rating agencies is obtained all ratings including the unaccepted rating shall be disclosed.
4. All the credit ratings obtained during the past three years preceding the public or rights issue of debt instrument for any listed security of the issuer company shall be disclosed in the offer document.
5. In case of issue of debentures with maturity of more than 18 months the issuer shall appoint a Debenture Trustee. The name of this trustee shall be disclosed in the offer

document. A trust deed shall be executed by the issuer company in favour of the debenture trustees within six months of the closure of the issue. Trustees shall be vested with the requisite powers for protecting the interest of debentureholders.

6. The merchant banker shall along with draft offer document, file with SEBI certificates from the bankers that the assets on which security is to be created are free from any encumbrances and the necessary permission has been obtained or a no-objection certificate from financial institutions or banks for a second or *pari passu* charge in cases where assets are encumbered.
7. Trustees shall obtain a certificate from the company's auditors in respect of utilisation of funds during the implementation period of the project. In the case of debentures for working capital, certificate shall be obtained at the end of each accounting year.
8. A company has to create Debenture Redemption Reserve (DRR) in case of issue of debentures with a maturity period of more than 18 months.
9. DRR shall be treated as a part of General Reserve for consideration of bonus issue proposals.
10. A company shall create DRR equivalent to 50 per cent of the amount of debenture issue before debenture redemption commences. Drawal for this reserve is permissible only after the company has actually redeemed 10 per cent of the debenture liability.
11. In case of new companies, distribution of dividends shall require approval of the trustees to the issue and the lead institution if any. Dividends may be distributed out of profit of particular years only after transfer of requisite amount to reserves.
12. The security shall be created within six months from the date of issue of debentures. If for any reason the company fails to create charge within 12 months from the date of issue of debentures the company shall be liable to pay 2 per cent penal interest to debentureholders. If security is not created even after 18 months, a meeting of the debentureholders shall be called within 21 days to explain the reasons thereof and the date by which the security shall be created.
13. In case no charge is created for debentures maturing in less than 18 months, the issuer company shall ensure compliance with the provisions of the companies (Acceptance of Deposit) Rules, 1975 as unsecured debentures/bonds are treated as "Deposits" for the purpose of these rules.
14. In case of rollover of debentures without the change of interest rate following conditions will be followed:
    (*a*) An option shall be compulsorily given to debentureholders to redeem the debentures as per the terms of offer.
    (*b*) Rollover shall be done only in cases where debentureholders have sent their consent for rollover. Non-receipt of consent shall not be considered as consent.
    (*c*) Before the rollover fresh credit rating will have to be obtained.
    (*d*) A fresh trust deed has to be executed.
15. In case of conversion of instruments into equity capital by listed company, value of which exceeds ₹ 50 lakh and whose conversion price was not fixed at the time of issue; holders of such instruments shall be given a compulsory option of not converting into equity capital. Conversion can be done only in cases where instrument holders have sent their positive consent and not on the basis of non-receipt of their negative reply.

◈ SEBI Guidelines for Issuance of Indian Depository Receipts (IDRs)

Issues by foreign companies in India (Indian Depository Receipts)(IDRs)

This sub-section attempts to cover the basic concepts and questions related to issuance of Indian depository receipts (IDRs) by foreign companies. For full particulars of laws governing primary markets, please refer to the Acts/Regulations/Guidelines appearing in the Legal Framework Section.

1. Whether a foreign company can access Indian securities market for raising funds?

Yes, a foreign company can access Indian securities market for raising funds through issue of Indian Depository Receipts (IDRs).

2. What is an Indian Depository Receipts (IDRs)?

An IDR is an instrument denominated in Indian rupees in the form of a depository receipt created by a Domestic Depository (custodian of securities registered with the Securities and Exchange Board of India) against the underlying equity of issuing company to enable foreign companies to raise funds from the Indian securities markets.

3. Which are all the legislations governing IDRs?

Central government notified the Companies (Issue of Indian Depository Receipts) Rules, 2004 (IDR Rules); pursuant to the Section 605 A of the Companies Act. SEBI issued guidelines for disclosure with respect to IDRs and notified the model listing agreement to be entered between exchange and the foreign issuer specifying continuous listing requirements.

4. Who is eligible to issue IDRs?

The eligibility criteria given under IDR Rules and Guidelines are as under:

The foreign issuing company shall have pre-issue paid-up capital and free reserves of at least US$ 50 million and have minimum average market capitalization (during the last three years) in its parent country of at least US$ 100 million;

- A continuous trading record or history on a stock exchange in its parent country for at least three immediately preceding years;
- A track record of distributable profits for at least three out of immediately preceding five years; listed in its home country and not been prohibited to issue securities by any Regulatory Body and has a good track record with respect to compliance with securities market regulations. The size of an IDR issue shall not be less than ₹ 50 crore.

5. Which intermediaries are involved in issuance of IDRs?

- Overseas Custodian Bank is a banking company which is established in a country outside India and has a place of business in India and acts as custodian for the equity shares of issuing company against which IDRs are proposed to be issued in the underlying equity shares of the issuer is deposited.
- Domestic depository who is a custodian of securities registered with the as SEBI and authorised by the issuing company to issue Indian Depository Receipts;
- Merchant Banker registered with SEBI who is responsible for due diligence and through whom the draft prospectus for issuance of the IDR is filed with SEBI by the issuer company.

6. Whether the draft prospectus for IDRs has to be filed with SEBI as in case of domestic issues?

Yes. Foreign issuer is required to file the draft prospectus with SEBI. Any changes specified by SEBI shall be incorporated in the final prospectus to be filed with Registrar of Companies.

7. Whether IDRs can be converted into underlying equity shares?

IDRs can be converted into the underlying equity shares only after the expiry of one year from the date of the issue of the IDR, subject to the compliance of the related provisions of Foreign Exchange Management Act and Regulations issued thereunder by RBI in this regard.

8. Who is responsible to distribute the corporate benefits to the IDR holders?

On the receipt of dividend or other corporate action on the IDRs, the Domestic Depository shall distribute them to the IDR holders in proportion to their holdings of IDRs.

10. Whether there are any other requirements for investing in IDRs

Yes. IDRs can be purchased by any person who is resident in India as defined under FEMA. Minimum application amount in an IDR issue shall be ₹ 20,000.

- Investments by Indian companies in IDRs shall not exceed the investment limits, if any, prescribed for them under applicable laws
- In every issue of IDR —
  (i) At least 50 per cent of the IDRs issued shall be subscribed to by QIBs;
  (ii) The balance 50 per cent shall be available for subscription by non-institutional investors.

◈ Consent Orders and SEBI

SEBI has also started the controversial practice of "Consent Orders" .In this the accused company can negotiate a settlement with the regulator without admitting its offence and pay the fine that is imposed on it. Many companies have availed of this method. Recently Reliance Power case was settled like this.

Here are some of the instances of cases dealt with by this procedure:

Anil Ambani and four ADAG officials: This consent order is dt. 14.1.2011. The case related to Reliance Infra and RNRL who were alleged to have violated rules relating to foreign portfolio investment by routing money through foreign borrowings into the market including buying shares of some group companies. SEBI negotiated personal liability on Anil Ambani and the four officials and they paid ₹ 50 crore as settlement charges. They were restricted from investing in listed company's stocks.

The second instance involves Merrill Lynch Capital Markets. This order is dt. 13.5.201. SEBI had pulled up the company for the stock market crash of 2004. The charge was that most of the trade was on behalf of its hedge fund clients. A penalty of ₹ 60 lakh was imposed.

On 23.1.2008 Rakesh Agarwal case was settled with a fine of ₹ 48 lakh. ABS Industries MD Rakesh Agarwal was accused of violating the insider trading norms as he had bought his own firm's shares from the market prior to the takeover deal between ABS and Bayer.

On June 9th, 2011 the case against Reliance Securities (formerly Reliance Money) was settled. The firm was accused of having violated SEBI's code of conduct for brokerages on at least 20 counts during April 2007 to March 2009. The company was debarred from taking new clients for 45 days from the date of the order and it was directed to spend ₹ 1 crore on investors awareness programme. The company also paid ₹ 25 lakh as settlement charges.

Till March 2011 SEBI had received 2,296 consent applications of which it allowed 1,012 applicants to settle various cases. SEBI has so far collected ₹ 190 crore as settlement fees.

This process cuts down on time and costs in settling cases but it has its own problems as well. It is felt that this mechanism is effective where there is failure to comply with technical requirements. Some legal experts believe that serious offences should not be encouraged to be settled through consent. It is also felt that this procedure requires more transparency and the entire order must be shared with the investors.

The consent process involves many stages. Once the settlement terms are agreed upon by the regulator and the entity involved they are placed before an independent advisory committee. This committee examines the terms set and then recommends them for going ahead or rejects it and suggests modifications. Based on this report two whole-time directors of SEBI pass the final order that is binding on the applicant and can only be challenged by a third party investor who feels aggrieved by the order.

◈ Insider Trading Regulations of SEBI

As per the regulations insider means any person who is or was connected with the company or is deemed to be so connected and who is reasonably expected to have access, by virtue of such connection to unpublished price sensitive information, in respect of such securities of such company. A person is deemed to be a connected person if such a person is a group company or any subsidiary, an official of stock exchange or stock brokers, merchant banker or a director or an official of the company, banker of the company, or relatives of any of the persons mentioned above.

If such persons have access to the unpublished price sensitive information and are proved to have used it for personal gain or profits or price manipulation, they are liable to be penalised under these regulations.

Here is how SEBI defines insiders:

"Connected person" means any person who —

(*i*) Is a director, as defined in clause (13) of Section 2 of the Companies Act, 1956 (1 of 1956), of a company, or is deemed to be a director of that company by virtue of sub-clause (10) of Section 307 of that Act, or

(*ii*) Occupies the position as an officer or an employee of the company or holds a position involving a professional or business relationship between himself and the company [4][whether temporary or permanent] and who may reasonably be expected to have an access to unpublished price sensitive information in relation to that company:

[5][*Explanation*: For the purpose of clause (*c*), the words "connected person" shall [6][mean] any person who is a connected person six months prior to an act of insider trading.

"Dealing in securities" means an act of [7][subscribing,] buying, selling or agreeing to [8][subscribe,] buy, sell or deal in any securities by any person either as principal or agent;

"Insider" means any person who,

(*i*) Is or was connected with the company or is deemed to have been connected with the company and is reasonably expected to have access 10[***] to unpublished price sensitive information in respect of securities of 11[a] company, or (*ii*) has received or has had access to such unpublished price sensitive information;]

"Person is deemed to be a connected person", if such person —

(*i*) Is a company under the same management or group, or any subsidiary company thereof within the meaning of sub-section (1B) of Section 370, or sub-section (11) of Section 372, of the Companies Act, 1956 (1 of 1956) or sub-clause (g) of Section 2 of the Monopolies and Restrictive Trade Practices Act, 1969 (54 of 1969) as the case may be; or

[12][(*ii*) is an intermediary as specified in Section 12 of the Act, Investment company, Trustee Company, Asset Management Company or an employee or director thereof or an official of a stock exchange or of clearing house or corporation;]

(*iii*) Is a merchant banker, share transfer agent, registrar to an issue, debenture trustee, broker, portfolio manager, Investment Advisor, sub-broker, Investment Company or an employee thereof, or is member of the Board of Trustees of a mutual fund or a member of the Board of Directors of the Asset Management Company of a mutual fund or is an employee thereof who have a fiduciary relationship with the company;

(*iv*) Is a Member of the Board of Directors or an employee of a public financial institution as defined in Section 4A of the Companies Act, 1956; or

(*v*) Is an official or an employee of a Self-regulatory Organisation recognised or authorised by the Board of a regulatory body; or

(*vi*) Is a relative of any of the aforementioned persons;

(*vii*) Is a banker of the company.

"Price sensitive information" means any information which relates directly or indirectly to a company and which if published is likely to materially affect the price of securities of company.

Explanation: The following shall be deemed to be price-sensitive information:

(*i*) Periodical financial results of the company;

(*ii*) Intended declaration of dividends (both interim and final);

(*iii*) Issue of securities or buyback of securities;

(*iv*) Any major expansion plans or execution of new projects.

(*v*) Amalgamation, mergers or takeovers;

(*vi*) Disposal of the whole or substantial part of the undertaking;

(*vii*) and significant changes in policies, plans or operations of the company;]

(*i*) "Relative" means a person, as defined in Section 6 of the Companies Act, 1956 (1 of 1956);

As we can see above SEBI has put in place an elaborate definition of who is an insider and what is to be considered as sensitive information.

However, many observers believe that Indian markets are majorly driven by the insiders. We have seen many stock prices get manipulated especially in small-cap and mid-cap segments. As the floating stock of these companies is limited such manipulations are easy a even small orders can have a huge impact on their prices.

◆ Qualified Institutional Placements (QIP)

Companies are allowed to use this route to raise capital quickly and without having to spend a lot of time and money. The process of FPO and Right Issues is lengthy and expensive. Companies are allowed to raise a maximum five times of net worth in a financial year from all sources.

QIP issue has to be managed by a SEBI approved Merchant Banker. The Merchant Banker has to file a certificate of Due Diligence with SEBI before the issue and certify that all legal requirements have been complied with. The merchant banker shall file a copy of the placement document and post-issue details with SEBI within thirty days of the allotment, for record purpose.

The issue can be of equities or any other instrument that is convertible into equities. As far as the convertibles are concerned they need to be converted in maximum sixty months after the issue.

◆ Guidelines for Issuance of QIP

1. The company who needs to raise the capital through the QIP are required to issue a minimum of 10 per cent of the securities issued under the scheme to mutual fund.
2. It is mandatory for the company to ensure that there are at least two allottees, if the size of the issue is up to ₹ 250 crore and at least five allottees if the company is issuing securities above ₹ 250 crore.
3. Pursuant to the QIP scheme, the securities may be issued by the issuer at a price that shall not be lower than the higher of the average of the weekly high and low of the closing prices of the related shares quoted on the stock exchange (i) during the preceding six months; or (ii) the preceding two weeks.
4. The aggregate of proposed placement under the QIP scheme and all previous placements made in the same financial year by the company shall not be more than five times the net worth of the issuer as per the audited balance sheet of the previous financial year.
5. The securities allotted pursuant to the QIP scheme shall not be sold by the allottees for a period of one year from the date of allotment, except on a recognized stock exchange.
6. This provision allows the allottees an exit mechanism on the stock exchange without having to wait for a minimum period of one year, which would have been the lock-in period if they had subscribed through a preferential allotment.

◆ Institutional Placement Programme (IPP)

Under this new scheme the regulator will allow promoters of companies wanting to bring down their holding to 75 per cent as mandated by offering fresh shares through this new route. The regulation mandates that all listed companies must have 25 per cent non-promoter holding to be eligible to be listed entities by June 2013. However they promoters are not allowed to take the QIP route for this. They will now be allowed to do this through IPP route. It is possible that the government which is sure to miss its disinvestment target of ₹ 40,000 crore for the fiscal 2011-12 may use this route to issue fresh equity.

According to this proposal promoters can also now sell their shares through the stock exchange by auction method. In such transaction that are known as Offer for Sale (OFS) promoters are expected to declare a floor price above which all interested investors will have to apply.

SEBI is investing the insider-trading angle in the case of Tata Finance. The inquiry is being conducted against the Ex-M.D. Mr. Pendse, and the Ex-director Mr. Talaulikar. Recently SEBI has imposed a fine of ₹ 2 lakh on Mr. Talaulikar.

◈ Participatory Notes issued by FIIs

Participatory notes (commonly known as P-notes) are instruments used by foreign funds and investors who are not registered with the Securities and Exchange Board of India (SEBI) but are interested in taking exposure in Indian securities. Participatory notes are generally issued listed overseas by the associates of India-based foreign brokerages and domestic institutional brokerages. They are, in fact, offshore derivative instruments issued by foreign institutional investors and their sub-accounts against underlying Indian securities. Participatory notes are issued where the underlying assets are securities on the Indian bourses.

There have been lots of concerns about this instrument. It was banned for sometime and the FIIs were told to liquidate all such notes in a specific time period. However after the crash of 2008 this decision was reversed as FII flow in the markets dried up. At the government level security concern regarding these notes was raised. It was feared that illegal money stashed by Indians abroad was flowing through these notes. It was also feared that the drug money or terrorist funds also may be coming in through this route. RBI has now made it mandatory for the issuing FIIs to disclose the names of the beneficiaries to the regulated as and when asked for.

In January 2012 SEBI has allowed foreign individual investors, pension funds and trusts to directly invest in Indian equities markets. The equity markets after inflows of $ 29 billion in 2010 saw net outflow of $ 500 million in 2011. The SENSEX shed about 25 per cent of its value in year 2011 making one of the worst performing markets in this year. The move by SEBI is to try and attract more money in our markets and needs to be welcomed. The direct entry would make KYC compliance easier for the regulators. At present a foreign investor wishing to invest in our markets has to be registered as a sub-account of an FII, which in turn has to apply to SEBI on behalf of sub-accountholder. This deters many investors from investing in our markets. The new move is to get over this problem.

The government has allowed certain foreign investors to invest in Indian mutual funds. This scheme has come in force from 15th January, 2012.

◈ Anchor Investors

In another significant decision, the SEBI board has allowed allocation of up to 30 per cent of shares in a public issue to Anchor Investors (AIs) — who will be treated as qualified institutional buyers (QIBs). The minimum size of application by AIs would be ₹ 10 crore and would have to pay 25 per cent of the amount on application and the balance 75 per cent within 2 days of the date of closure of the public issue.

"There will be a lock-in period of 30 days on the shares allotted to these investors from the date of allotment. No person related to the promoter or promoter group or the book running lead managers can apply as Anchor Investor", SEBI said. If the IPO issuer can find Anchor Investors, it indicates that the company enjoys good reputation and its public offer could be a success. The SEBI move on Anchor Investors has come at a time when an estimated ₹ 40,000 crore is being eyed by public sector firms through IPOs or rights issues and about ₹ 20,000 crore by private sector public offers.

◆ SEBI sets guidelines for offer-for-sale by promoters

The Securities and Exchange Board of India (SEBI) has laid down comprehensive guidelines for promoters seeking to offload stake via offer-for-sale (OFS).

The guidelines incorporate all representations and suggestions received from marketmen.

Thursday's OFS guidelines replace all the three SEBI circulars dated February 1, February 23 and February 27.

◆ Norms

SEBI has mandated that the OFS facility would be available only on the NSE and the BSE.

OFS can be used by promoters of companies who wish to attain minimum public shareholding of 25 per cent by June 2013.

Eligible promoters should not have bought or sold the company shares 12 weeks before and should not buy or sell shares 12 weeks after the OFS.

Within this cooling off period of plus-12 weeks, promoters can sell through OFS or institutional placement programme (IPP) with a gap of two weeks between successive offers, said SEBI.

This is also applicable to promoters who had already offered shares through OFS/IPP.

All non-promoter entities are eligible to buy under the OFS. The offer size will be a minimum of ₹ 25 crore or that amount which enables the promoter to achieve a minimum public shareholding of 25 per cent in a single tranche.

The advertisement and offer expenses related to the OFS shall be borne by the seller (promoter).

◆ No part cancellation

OFS can be withdrawn before opening and another offer can be made by the promoter only after a cooling off period of 10 trading days.

The seller cannot cancel the offer when bidding is on. In case of insufficient demand at or above the floor price, the seller has the choice to either conclude the offer or cancel it in full.

The seller may also choose to conclude or fully cancel the offer in case of default in settlement.

Floor price is the minimum price at which the seller wishes to sell a share.

SEBI has directed exchanges to amend by-laws rules and regulations; notify member brokers and disseminate the circular on their websites. This has since been implemented.

Let us now take a look at some cases where SEBI was involved:

◆ MS Shoes

This case happened in 1995. The company was allowed to raise capital of ₹ 699 crore from the public. The issue opened on February 14 for fully convertible debentures, convertible in equity at a premium of ₹ 189 per share. The market price of the share on that day was ₹ 509. However this price was cum-rights, which means that post-issue price per share would be much lower than this and so the comparison between the two prices was not really fair from the point of view of the investors. The company failed to disclose this fact to the public. When this fact came to the notice of SEBI, it asked the company to make a public statement in the press stating the price ruling was sum-rights price. On 13th February the company did the needful. However the TV advertisements continued to compare the issue price of ₹ 199, with the market price of ₹ 509. In view of this SEBI asked the company to give the option to the investors to the effect that any allottees who wishes to get the money refunded, can make the application within 20 days from the date of receipt of the allotment letter.

It was soon realised that the MS Shoes issue was undersubscribed, and thus it led to devolvement on the underwriters. But they refused to put the money, saying that the company had closed the issue on the earliest closing date, indicating that the issue was oversubscribed. The liability of the underwriters was estimated to be ₹ 500 crore.

SEBI then initiated action against the company and its managing director and also handed over the case to CBI. CBI's investigations reveled that the company and its MD Pawan Sachdeva could be charged with criminal breach of trust, complicity with SEBI officials, dishonest intentions and concealment of facts in the issue. The complicity of SEBI officials was that they allowed Sachdeva 30 days of time waiver to bring in ₹ 130 crore towards his share or rights.

SEBI in this case failed to enquire into all omissions and commissions in the prospectus and in investigating the promoter's track record for personal honesty, integrity and dependability.

In 2001 a case of rigging and short selling based on insider trading, was noticed in the case of the proposed merger of UTI Bank with GTB. The merger had to be called off due to the intervention of RBI and SEBI. It is alleged that the scam-tainted broker Ketan Parekh was involved in this case. The mass short selling in these companies took place in April 2001 when the merger talks were on. The short selling was alleged to be masterminded by the bears led by the erstwhile President of BSE Anand Rathi. These activities were investigated by SEBI and action was taken against Rathi, who was forced to resign from his post, and brokerage houses including CSFB, Nirmal Bang and First Global were debarred from undertaking brokerage business. Madhavpura Mercantile Cooperative Bank was also involved in all this as the bank had issued a pay order worth ₹ 150 crore on behalf of Ketan Parekh, though he had no money in his account, and the pay order bounced when it was presented for clearing.

◈ Ketan Parekh Scam

Ketan Parekh was a broker in the market. He was a serious investor; who had a good market research team working with him and they were investing in fundamentally strong companies, which had low capital base and therefore low floating stock. Ketan Parekh used to buy such stocks and accumulate these shares over a period of time. This would drive the market prices of these stocks. Parekh would then sell at a handsome profit. He would reinvest in these stocks at lower levels. In short he was trading in these stocks, buying at low prices and selling when the prices went up and earned profit. Ketan had his favourite stocks like Global Tele, Zee Telefilms and Himachal Futuristic. The ten stocks in which he was mostly investing came to be known as K-10 stocks. It was alleged that the UTI and some other mutual funds were actually using this K-10 index instesd of the official stock market indices like the sensex to determine their investments in the stock markets.

All this operation required huge funds. Where did he get these?

1. He had a line of credit sanctioned to him by banks against the security of the shares that he purchased. The two banks whose involvement has come to light are GTB and Madhavpura Cooperative Bank Ltd.

2. It is alleged that the companies in which he was investing and thus helping these companies market price going up, were also funding his operations. This is case of clear nexus between him and the promoters of some companies at least. Zee Telefilms had in fact funded him and has accepted that the company gave funds to him.

Ketan Parekh used Kolkata stock exchange for his buying operations, because surveillance here was weak and he could indulge in unofficial Badla through the local brokers. This kept him away from the limelight of Mumbai.

By January 1999 the stock markets had started bubbling with excitement, as the sensex went up by 700 points in just three months. The K-10 stocks were in the forefront of this rally and the market seemed to be taking its clues from these very stocks. The international markets were also doing well at this time. The US markets were upbeat on the new economy stocks and the flavour of the market seemed to be what were known as the ICE stocks, *viz.*, Information Technology, Communications and Entertainment. On the day the union budget was presented on 28th of February the BSE sensex was at the unprecedented level of 6000 points. The budget was welcomed whole-heartedly by most.

However just two days later the scenario changed for the worst. The news of unsavoury dealing of Ketan Parekh started coming out. The American markets, which were nervous since December on the persistent fears of meltdown in Dot com sectors, were also falling. The celebrated K-10 stocks started loosing value much faster than the other stocks and the banks that had lent money to him started getting nervous as there safety margins were being eroded at a very fast rate. They started asking the broker to either pledge more shares or repay the money. He now had to sell his shares, cut losses and pays the banks or he had to take the gamble of holding on and hoping for the revival of the market. He made a fatal mistake of holding on. He sold some of his favorite stocks but invested this money in some of his other favourite stocks. In short his greed got better of his professional judgement. He also blocked his funds in some companies through the route of private placements.

All this meant that he now had severe liquidity problems. His 70 brokers in Kolkata stock exchange started feeling the heat, as he could not meet his obligations in Badla trades. Around 70 brokers defaulted on this exchange. They together had an obligation of ₹ 700 crore.

In Mumbai another drama was unfolding as the bear cartel headed by the Mumbai stock exchange President Mr. Anand Rathi was trying to go after him. It is alleged that Rathi passed on sensitive information of the market to his friends in the cartel, helping them to dump the Parekh favourite stocks, pushing him in the corner. Anand Rathi was forced to quit his post by SEBI and investigations were launched against him.

It was at this time that Madhavpura Bank episode exploded when they issued a pay order of ₹ 150 crore on his behalf to Bank of India. This pay order bounced as Madhavpura Bank had no funds to clear it. As a matter of fact this was a case of a blatant fraud. A bank cannot issue a pay order unless the buyer of the pay order deposits the money. In this case Parekh did not deposit the money. The bank already had an exposure of ₹ 840 crore. It is also believed that Parekh was using the brokerage firm owned by the Madhavpura Bank's Chairman's son to put through his transactions.

We now should take a look at the role of the regulators in this scam. RBI was unable to detect the mal practices that were taking place. There was also the problem of dual control on cooperative banks, by RBI and cooperative department. It should be noted that only after this incident RBI was entrusted with the complete responsibility of inspecting the cooperative banks. RBI till then was inspecting these banks every two years. It was reported that in the last such inspection conducted by RBI, nothing untoward was found.

There is hardly any doubt that SEBI also failed as the market regulator. It was very late in the date an investigation was conducted in the role of the bear cartel.

Even now it is alleged that Ketan Parekh is still active in the markets and SEBI is turning a blind eye to his activities. Also one hardly hears of any progress on the various cases that are filed against him. All cases in different scams from Harshad Mehta, CRB or Ketan Parekh need to be dealt with expeditiously. This is a great failure of Indian judicial system and shows a lack of commitment from the government of India as well.

This delay has proved costly in terms of the dwindling investor population in our country. People who have suffered due to various scams and the inability of the regulators to safeguard their interests have turned away from the markets for good.

◈ Tata Finance

The scam in Tata Finance came to light on 12th April, 2001 when a person named Shankar Sharma circulated a letter on the Dalal Street stating that the company is in deep financial trouble. This happened just before the company's Rights Issue.

The company's MD Pendse commenced extensive share market operations through its subsidiary company Nishkalp at the end of 1999. The portfolio mostly consisted of the famous K-10 stocks.

Tata's have accused Dilip Pendse of embarking upon carry forward transactions between December 2000 and March 2001 in these stocks, which led to a loss of ₹ 300 million in the last quarter of fiscal 2001. The total loss suffered by Nishkalp is estimated to be ₹ 480 crore. Pendse is accused of cheating, falsification of accounts, forgery and criminal breach of trust in the FIR filed against him and other employees of the company. The FIR also alleges that the funds were siphoned off for personal benefit. Pendse is accused of having given ICDs to the tune of ₹ 5 billions to Nishkalp for these transactions.

Pendse is held responsible for breaching the prudential norms of RBI that are applicable to NBFCs on two counts namely that he failed to maintain the capital adequacy ratio of 12 per cent and lending over 25 per cent of the company's net worth to a single entity, *i.e.*, Nishkalp in this case.

SEBI suspects insider trading in the case of Chairman of Nishkalp Mr. Talaulikar's selling of his personal holding of 1,00,000 shares of Tata Finance. It is suspected that he used inside information, as he knew that the company's shares would take a beating on the brouses, once the information of Nishkalp's losses becomes public. It is alleged that Talaulikar devised an ingenious way of transferring funds of ₹ 7 million from Nishkalp to the concerned share broker with a request to back date the sale contract to September 6th, 2000 that is six months before the rights issue opened for subscription, when the price of the share was ₹ 69/-. But SEBI has found that the shares were transferred from the respective accounts of members to broker's de-mat account only in the first week of April 2001. In May 2001 when Talaulikar realised that a detailed investigation was being planned by the Tatas to probe the Nishkalp affairs, he immediately reversed the transaction and sold the shares at the prevailing market price of ₹ 34. He returned to the broker a sum of ₹ 3.5 million, which in turn was returned to Nishkalp.

SEBI has hinted at a possible nexus between former Tata Finance MD Pendse and Suzlon Energy and its affiliate Sarjan Securities, which purchased 75,000 TFL shares in March 2001. Sulzon supplied wind mills to Tata Group of companies and it will not be surprising that on account of obligations to Pendse, shares were purchased by Sarjan at a price of ₹ 91 much higher than the market price of ₹ 40. Incidentally Sulzon gave ₹ 5 crore to Sarjan for purchase of 6,18,000 shares. According to the SEBI report Tata Finance purchased about 13 windmills from Suzlon while Khuda Gawah Investments and Nalini Properties, purchased one windmill each. During 2000-01, TFL purchased these at a cost of ₹ 350 crore. Pendse had proposed to buy these as a tax-planning measure. The connection between Pendse and Sarjan has been established in the SEBI report as follows: Pendse's wife Anuradha, his associate Anjali Beke, Nalini Properties and Ajudi Properties and Investments sold 2,90,000 shares of TFL in a off-market deals to brokers and they in turn sold the shares to India Emerging Companies and Sarjan Securities. In this connection SEBI has commenced investigation against stock brokers Jhunjhunwala Stock Brokers Pvt. Ltd., and Malini Sanghvi Securities Pvt Ltd. for violation of the code of conduct for the market intermediaries, insider trading and unfair trade practices.

◈ The saga of L&T, Reliance and Grasim

On November 18, 2001, Reliance announced its decision to sale its 10.5 per cent holding in L&T to Grasim for ₹ 306 per share. The price of L&T till then was languishing somewhere around ₹ 150. Some people think that it was due to the fact that the indecision on the demerger of its cement division was one of the main reasons for this. The company was talking about the demerger for a very long time but no concrete decision and action was coming forth. The stock rose to ₹ 208 on the day the deal was announced. The question uppermost in the minds of many analysts was who was buying the stock and did these entities or persons had any inclination about the sale by Reliance. In short there was suspicion of insider trading.

Mr. Kirit Somaya a Member of Parliament complained to SEBI that just before the deal was concluded Reliance had increased its stake in L&T from 6.62 per cent to 10.5 per cent. During the period October 8, 2001 to November 9, 2001 Reliance bought 1.95 per cent of L&T's equity, then again between November 12 to November 15 it bought another 0.17 per cent of the capital. This means just three days before the sale of its stake to Grasim Reliance was buying the L&T stock in the market.

On March 31, 2001 Reliance held 6.62 per cent of L&T equity. However, after September 11, 2001 when the BSE Sensex had touched a 10-year low of around 2,600, Reliance says it had 'used the opportunity of the then prevailing low and attractive prices to consolidate our equity share holding in L&T, thereby strengthening our position to make an open offer for L&T, if and when considered appropriate at any point of time in the future'.

Reliance's response to SEBI contains an interesting little table, which lists its sale and purchase of L&T shares since April 1, 2001 when it had held 6.62 per cent of the equity. Then in May, June and July 2001 it sold large quantities of the scrip (0.04 per cent, 1.81 per cent and 0.78 per cent of its stake, respectively, in those months) again in October 2001 it sold another 0.08 per cent of its stake. Its holding had thus dropped to just 3.92 per cent by October 1, 2001.

This large-scale selling would have had a negative impact on the price. Then, all of a sudden in October 2001 Reliance turned buyer. It picked up a hefty 6.17 per cent stake in L&T in under a month and took its total holding to 10.09 per cent. The entire lot was off-loaded on to Grasim at a huge premium on November 18, making a fantastic profit for Reliance. In other words, Reliance is a clear beneficiary of the upward and downward movement of L&T's share price.

This raises another issue. If Reliance's share had fallen below 5 per cent and later increased to 10 per cent, did it inform SEBI, as required under the takeover regulations? It seems that it did not. Both the stock exchanges have confirmed that Reliance has not intimated them of the fluctuation in its shareholding. Had it done so, SEBI would have been alerted to Reliance's large-scale market activity in the L&T scrip and probably monitored it more closely. Even otherwise, failure to inform SEBI under regulation 15A is punishable with a ₹ 5,00,000 fine. But that is less than an insignificant punishment. As a matter of fact Reliance was later on fined this amount and quickly paid the fine. This fine was subsequently refunded to the company!

The real puzzle is if Reliance was holding just about 4 per cent in October, and if Grasim was interested in buying into L&T, then why did Grasim not acquire the shares in the open market at a price that was much lesser than the price it paid to Reliance to acquire its stake?

Sucheta Dalal the famous columnist in one of her columns on this issue says that Grasim's deal with Reliance also included the clause that the Ambani brothers would step down as non-executive directors from the board of L&T post-acquisition of their stake by Grasim. According to her Grasim's deal with Reliance included the clause that the Ambani brothers would step down as non-executive directors of L&T and Reliance would agree not to 'acquire or deal in L&T shares' either directly or through its associates or subsidiaries for a minimum period of five years. Interestingly, the L&T management seems to be a quiet approver of all that went on and quickly took the Birlas on board.

◆ IPO Scam

The Indian stock markets were rocked by what is now known as IPO scam. This scam was perpetuated during the IPOs of various companies by some people who opened a lot of De-mat accounts and used these accounts to make many applications in the IPOs of IDFC, YES Bank, etc. The main perpetuator of this scam was Roopalben Panchal. However there is reason to believe that she was the front and the actual scamsters were some other influential people.

Two months after the IPO scam was discovered, the Central Bureau of Investigation (CBI) had arrested many of the key players involved in it — Deepak Panchal, Parag Jhaveri, Jayesh Khandwalla and Dhiren Vora, all from Ahmedabad. However, Roopalben Panchal, who was supposed to have cornered almost 50 per cent of retail shares through multiple demat accounts in IDFC IPO, had gone missing. Tired of being on the run, she listened to her mother's advice and surrendered before the CBI on 13th March, to cooperate for investigation in the scam.

The real brain behind the scam is said to be Deepak Panchal who found Roopalben to be a convenient front. With Roopalben's husband Naresh Panchal not doing too well in his business, and two teenage kids to look after; Roopalben was easily persuaded to assist Deepak.

Three months after the scam was detected, life has gone back to normal for most of the accused. The CBI, which had filed a case of criminal conspiracy against them, released them in early March.

The premises of Deepak Panchal, Sugandh and Rajan Dapki in March — their offices — are deserted. But market sources allege that Panchal's men are now persuading people to rent their identity details for ₹ 1,500 a month. He is said to be operating from his friend's office, where he has kept his database of fictitious accounts.

Though he is supposed to have dreamt up the scheme, he could never have manipulated the system without the help of brokers and financiers. The fact that it remained undetected for quite sometime points to the complicity of other players.

◆ The Panchals and their Associates

Brokers in Ahmedabad say that Deepak Panchal has been in the business of arranging multiple/bogus applications for investing in stock markets since 1983. His wife Devangi and her sister Roopalben probably became actively involved in his schemes almost from the start. They had been persuading their relatives and friends to open a bank account through them, and later on the de-mat accounts also, when paperless trading was introduced in the late 1990s. They would offer a token amount of ₹ 200-300 in return to the people who agreed to open these accounts. But soon, Panchal realised that there was a limit to the number of accounts that could be opened in this manner.

To increase the scale of his business, Panchal needed more de-mat and bank accounts. While he could create fictitious names, for photographs he persuaded a photo shop to run a free photo campaign for the public. Being aware that 'thrifty' Gujaratis go out of the way to avail such offers, at least 100 people would queue up every day to get their free photos. By using these photographs, Panchal created a database of both fictitious and genuine investors over a period of time.

Market sources point out that Panchal's business achieved scale when he met Dhiren Vora a few years back. Vora is known to be a big operator in Ahmedabad and runs several investment firms like H. Nyalchand Financial Services (HNFS). Large corporates, including a large media house based in Ahmedabad, are said to be his clients. This is not the first time that Vora has come under SEBI's lens either. In February 2000, SEBI had warned HNFS for non-compliance of norms. Again, in January 2004, SEBI had banned Vora and his two firms, HNFS and Park Light Rolling, on charges of price manipulation.

An appeal in the Securities Appellate Tribunal (SAT) revoked his ban, and Vora was back in business within five months. Fellow brokers say that Vora wants to be the dominant operator. Vora appears to have had easy access to big funds and he is supposed to have persuaded Panchal to change the scale of what was essentially a small-scale operation till then.

Fortuitously for the players concerned, the primary market had started showing signs of revival after several years in the dumps. And, thus, began the game of cornering shares in the retail quota of IPOs.

Apart from Panchal and Vora, there was a third major player in the operation: Parag Jhaveri of Sugandh Estate. Sugandh allegedly collected money from financiers and investors and applied for allotment in the IPOs through a host of friends and relatives. On allotment or refund, these friends passed back the shares or money to Sugandh, who then passed it on to the financiers and investors.

With the markets booming, it made sense to try and corner a big chunk of shares from the retail quota at the IPO and sell them immediately on listing. This meant quick and hefty profits.

To understand why Panchal & Co. dreamt up their little scheme, one needs to first understand regulations that govern IPOs. In any IPO, 35 per cent of the issuing company's shares are reserved for the retail investor. One qualifies as a retail investor if the application amount is not more than ₹ 1 lakh (this limit was ₹ 50,000 during the YES Bank IPO). That's why, an individual, who doesn't qualify as an institutional investor but wants to apply for a large chunk of the IPO shares, has every incentive to try and get around the regulation limit of ₹ 1 lakh per retail investor. (The limit has since been increased to ₹ 2,00,000).

In the YES Bank IPO, Panchal applied through 6,315 de-mat accounts for 1,050 shares each. In the IDFC issue, he used 27,000 de-mat accounts to apply for 1,400 shares each.

These de-mat accounts were opened with Karvy DP at various times beginning June 2003. As the SEBI order points out, majority of the IPO applications through these de-mat accounts had common bank accounts with two branches of Bharat Overseas Bank — 6,315 accounts in Mumbai and 27,000 accounts in Ahmedabad. The address for communication in most of the accounts was Deepak Panchal's office at Shaswat Building in Ahmedabad.

◈ Roopalben Panchal

Calculations show that an amount of ₹ 30 crore in YES Bank and ₹ 129 crore in IDFC was made available to Deepak Panchal. Where did he get this money from? According to market sources, almost 40-50 per cent came from broker financiers, including an Ahmedabad-based media house that has routed the money as a short-term advance to one of the brokers involved in the scam. The rest of it was arranged through IPO financing from banks. In essence, Panchal and gang were merely acting as middlemen for various others who were interested in getting a larger portion of the shares under the retail investor quota. The share allotment was completed by 5th July, 2005 in YES Bank and 5-6 August in IDFC issue. Within 1-2 days of each allotment, the shares were transferred from all the above de-mat accounts to Roopalben Panchal's de-mat account. In all, she received 5 per cent of the total retail allotment in YES Bank and a whopping 50 per cent of IDFC.

Few days prior to listing, Roopalben transferred these shares to the broker-financiers and their firms and to her family members including Deepak Panchal and his wife.

Apparently, the transfers were made on the basis of the funding provided by them. In YES Bank, one day prior to listing, the majority of share transfer was made to private companies namely Seer Finlease, Excell Multitech, Zenet Software and Taurus Infosys. It is alleged that Dhiren Vora controlled these entities. These entities, in turn, sold all the shares on the listing day.

The stakes were high in the IDFC issue. The largest beneficiaries were the above mentioned four private companies that got an aggregate of 22 lakh shares from Roopalben and Sugandh Estate. They sold 17.84 lakh shares on the listing day. Assuming that these entities paid ₹ 34 per share for shares they sold, they stood to make a profit of ₹ 5 crore. The rest of the 4,45,000 shares were transferred to Lok Prakashan, its promoters and their family members. Lok Prakashan is the publishing house of Gujarat Samachar, the largest selling vernacular paper in the state.

Roopalben also transferred shares to her five family members who sold shares on listing day. Their profits would have been to the tune of ₹ 6 crore. Also, Roopalben and Sugandh transferred shares to broker financiers like Jayesh Khandwala, Rajan Dapki and Gautam Jhaveri. And most of them could have pocketed a 100 per cent gain by selling off on listing day.

It was a network of financiers, brokers and people who only lent their names for application, money-lenders who worked on an unprecedented scale in Ahmedabad. But there were equally sharp minds doing similar activities in Mumbai. In IDFC, one Purshottham Budhwani got 12.63 lakh shares (8 per cent of the IDFC allotment) from 4,748 de-mat accounts held with Karvy-DP and Pratik DP. Here again, the addresses and bank accounts of majority of these accounts were the same. Budhwani sold a major chunk of his holding at ₹ 61-64 on listing. Their game indeed wasn't restricted to these two IPOs only. For instance, as per the SEBI order, Budhwani had been doing similar operations in the majority of IPOs that came out in 2005.

HOW THE SCAM WORKED

◈ The Facilitators

Panchal or Budhwani couldn't have carried on the business on such a scale without some help. Had the banks and the depository participants (DPs) carried out even a cursory check, the scam would have been caught early on. Banks like Bharat Overseas, Vijaya and HDFC facilitated account opening and funding. And the DPs were reckless in opening de-mat accounts. The banking and depository regulations are silent on the number of accounts that can be opened by an individual. But if a bank gets applications for opening 14,000 accounts or a DP gets 1,500 applications in a single day, and most of them coming from a common address, it is hard to believe that this would have gone through without a hitch without some help at least. As per the SEBI order, the Panchals opened 14,000 de-mat accounts with Karvy DP over two days. All of them had a bank account with the same branch of the Bharat Overseas Bank in Ahmedabad. The account numbers were in serial order too.

Karvy DP, which had opened the maximum number of accounts for the Panchals and Sugandh, has the following explanation: these accounts carried valid documentation proofs and there was no ground for rejection. Further, there is no regulation that says that it has to reject any application because of common address, as investors either tend to give their employers' address, or a funding bank will provide its address on all the applications it has funded.

That is a valid stand to take but the sheer scale of the accounts being opened should have triggered off some sort of inquiry within the system. During 2003 to 2005, Deepak Panchal also opened nearly 12,000 de-mat accounts with as many as 2,700 in just one day.

Had Karvy carried out even a fairly basic check after receiving all these applications in a single day, there would have been reasonable grounds to expand the investigation.

Twelve thousand individuals can't possibly reside nor have their office in a tiny three-room office in a commercial building. This was, after all, the Panchal office and the address from which all these applications emanated.

Karvy squarely puts the blame on the banks. A senior Karvy official had said: "If a customer brings a bank document as proof, then we have no ground to suspect or reject him". The market participants are not inclined to be charitable about Karvy, though. They say that Karvy has always been aggressive in chasing customers for opening de-mat accounts and has often gone out of its way to faciliate opening of accounts for clients. As banks require an introducer to open an account, often, Karvy had acted as an introducer and also arranged for the IPO financing from the same bank.

Even more than the slip at Karvy's end, it is difficult to understand how the banks didn't spot anything amiss. Bharat Overseas, Vijaya Bank, HDFC Bank and many others clearly didn't adhere to the 'know your customer' (KYC) rules while opening these accounts and extending loans for the IPO.

◆ The Onlookers

Apart from banks and DPs, there are a host of intermediaries involved in an IPO process. In any IPO, application forms move from syndicate members to bankers and then to the registrar. The merchant bankers are also responsible for the issue management. The registrar does the final job of preparing the basis for allotments along with the issuer and the merchant banker. The depositories, NSDL and CDSL, maintain a database of all DPs and credit the shares to successful allottees. The fact that none of these intermediaries could figure out that half of the IDFC shares reserved for retail investors were actually going to applicants with the same address points to serious problems in the checks and balances they follow.

Equally difficult to understand is why SEBI took so long to figure out that a scam was taking place. All these de-mat accounts were at least two years old, so why didn't SEBI's spot audits detect these fictitious DP accounts? Since December, SEBI has been inspecting the role of all these intermediaries, but it hasn't been able to pin down the responsibility on any of the intermediaries except DP. The blame game seems to be on.

In its YES Bank order, SEBI held that the depositories (in particular NSDL) as a self-regulatory organization (SRO), failed to detect the operations of Karvy DP. In a strongly worded seven-page response, NSDL argued that it's not an SRO as per SEBI's definition. For its role in the IPO process, the letter said: "The role of the depository in an IPO is limited to the extent of electronically evidencing ownership of the successful allottees based on details given by the registrar". However, in the IDFC order, SEBI retaliated stating that depositories and DPs have an agent-principal relationship, thus pinning the liability on the former for the conduct of DPs.

Merchant bankers, on the other hand, argue that they just oversee and ensure that all parties involved in the issue are doing their job correctly. Enam Financials, DSP Merrill Lynch, Kotak Investment Bank and SBI Capital Markets were the merchant bankers for the YES Bank and IDFC issue. "If a SEBI-registered DP acknowledges that a particular application is unique, then how can I say that it's not unique?" points out one of them.

"The registrar weeds out multiple applications if the name, age, father's name, DP ID and address in any two applications are the same. In this case, it seems that only the address was common. So there was no ground for rejection", says another.

The problem, says an industry insider, is that no one is interested in scrutinizing applications too carefully when markets are booming. "When the primary market started picking up, in a race to get oversubscription in IPOs, merchant bankers choose to ignore the quality of sub-brokers who were bringing in maximum applications."

Further, if the broking community in Ahmedabad is to be believed, Karvy's role as the registrar needs maximum scrutiny. After all in an IPO, the registrar does the tail end of the job. It keys in all the demographic details that the syndicate member and bankers don't capture. So was there a possibility of tracing these accounts? Sources also say the Panchals and others had a whiff of the number of shares allotted before the credits were made into the de-mat accounts. Further, they also point out that in one of the two IPOs, instead of sending out refunds to individual applicants, the registrar prepared a single refund order for Deepak Panchal. In fact, as the SEBI order points out, in the IDFC issue, 25 applicants who transferred shares to Roopalben had not even provided any details of the bank account or the payment mode in their application forms.

However, Karvy's claim so far has been that the applications were valid from the registrar's point of view and the entire processing of IPO applications is followed by a concurrent audit from external auditors.

◆ The Reformers

Three months after the scam, the required action from the regulators had not been forth coming. The RBI showed its promptness by levying fines on 10 banks, which didn't adhere to KYC and IPO funding norms. It is not clear whether it has carried out any inspection or audit of these banks — after all, large cheque payments or issue of so many cheque leaves simply can't go unnoticed by the internal audit systems of a bank. To push IPO financing, many banks, especially in Ahmedabad, are recklessly opening bank and de-mat accounts.

SEBI, on its part, has been finding ways to eliminate benami de-mat accounts and to bring in a system of identifying individual investors with a unique number. But what about the penal action against the entities involved in the scam as well as the intermediaries that facilitated it?

As of now, only Roopalben and Sugandh Estate have been debarred from stock market transactions. But the brokers and financiers, who ultimately made the killing, are restrained only from the IPO market. Some among them have have had a history of being warned or penalised by SEBI.

There hasn't really been any strict action yet against the intermediaries. As per SEBI's initial findings, Karvy DP had actively colluded with the likes of Panchal and Budhwani.Yet, Karvy has just been restricted from opening any new de-mat accounts until it verifies genuineness of all its multiple de-mat accounts. Also, there seem to be no action against other two DPs, ING Vysya Bank and HDFC Bank. These DPs had opened 600 accounts for Budhwani.

However, SEBI has asked depositories to inspect if any of their DPs' have more than 20 de-mat accounts bearing a common address. If any such accounts are found, then the genuineness of such accountholders has to be verified. Well anyone can escape this test, if he has 10 de-mat accounts with a CDSL-registered DP and 10 with the NSDL.

The regulator has also made the permanent account number (PAN) an additional proof of identity for de-mat accountholders. But even PAN numbers are found to be bogus. Reportedly, there are 1 million bogus PAN numbers in circulation. As the demand for PAN numbers has now gone up; you won't get it for free in a place like Ahmedabad now. In fact, it was sold for as much as ₹ 500. Therefore even the PAN number doesn't stand as a proof for a genuine person.

The MAPIN committee formed in 2005 and chaired by Jagdish Capoor, chairman of HDFC Bank and former RBI deputy governor had said that UIN will not achieve the desired results. It stated that if a fraudster cannot be traced through a broker, de-mat account, bank account or PAN number, then there is no guarantee that he will be traceable with UIN. "It should be recognised that benami entities can be created under the biometrics-based system and that the biometrics-based system is also not error-free."

Meanwhile, an Ahmedabad-based activist observes that there is no hope of such scams stopping in the near future. "In every broker's office in the city, the security guard, the peon, the receptionist and the family members will have a de-mat and a bank account in their name." Hemantsingh Jhala claims that SEBI has just scratched the surface of the datamine of Panchal.

◆ Other IPOs that may have been affected by the scam:

- Suzlon Energy IPO: ₹ 1,496.34 crore (September 23-29, 2005)
- Key operators used 21,692 fictitious accounts to corner 3, 23,023 shares which is equal to 3.74 per cent of the total number of shares allotted to retail individual investors.
- Jet Airways IPO: ₹ 1,899.3 crore (Feb. 18-24, 2005)
- Key operators used 1,186 fake accounts for cornering 20,901 shares which is equal to 0.52 per cent of the total number of shares allotted to retail investors.
- National Thermal Power Corporation IPO ₹ 5,368.14 crore (Oct 7-14,2004).
- 12,853 different accounts were used for cornering 27,50,730 shares representing 1.3 per cent of the total number of shares allotted to retail investors.
- Tata Consultancy Services IPO: ₹ 4,713.47 crore 14,619 'benami' accounts were used to corner 2,61,294 shares representing 2.09 per cent of the total shares allotted to retail individual investors.

◆ The Case of Reliance Power IPO

2008 saw the IPO of Reliance power. It was a much anticipated event and the offering was the largest till that date seen in the Indian markets. This was also the first offering from

ADAG Group led by Anil Ambani and was the first group company to hit the markets after the split in the group. The IPO size was ₹ 10,000 crore and it was oversubscribed to the tune of 72 times creating another record in our markets. It is alleged that over 2,00,000 de-mat accounts were opened in a record time just before the issue opened for subscription. The issue was priced @ ₹ 450 with a 5 per cent discount thrown in for the retail investors.

There was huge frenzy surrounding this issue. The grey market was reportedly very active with premium on listing being quoted in these markets. The bet was on a listing price of anywhere between ₹ 700 and ₹ 800.

Most investors were very enthusiastic about the offer and did not understand that the company had no established cash flow to service the huge equity base that had. It was very clear that it would take the company at least 5 years to start making meaningful profits. The rating agencies joined the party or rather added fuel to the spirits of the investors by giving grading of 5 on 5 for the issue. The institutional investors also gave thumps up to the issue by putting in large bids.

On the day of reckoning that is the day of listing there was a lot of pomp and show as Anil Ambani sound the bell to commence trading! The scrip did open at a premium but by the end of the trading hours was trading well below the issue price. The smiles on the faces of successful allottees had got wiped off. People who were hoping to make a killing post-listing were lying around brutally hurt. The market had taken the right road for once. The unstable international conditions and the first signs of the financial turmoil that was to grip the US and the rest of the world had started to make their presence felt. The so-called small investors had burnt their fingers once more. Their greed had triumphed over financial knowledge. Financial illiteracy had once again claimed more victims.

Anil Ambani then did what he does best. He is a master of Financial Engineering and he took the advantage of the letter of the law and once more killed the spirit of the law. His holding in the company stood at 90 per cent post-issue. ADAG Group held 45 per cent while Reliance Infrastructure the other promoter held another 45 per cent. Anil came out with a fantastic scheme saying that he will issue bonus shares to all successful applicants to the issue and thereby bring down their acquisition cost!. This was astounding. He also announced that the promoters will not be eligible for this bonus issue The shareholders of Reliance Infra rose in revolt led by the institutional investors and said that their company should not be made to forgo this offer on the whims of the promoter Anil Ambani. Anil had no choice now. He said the bonus shares will be issued to all except the ADAG Group and the shares to be thus issued will be from the shares held by ADAG Group and not an issuance of additional shares!

This whole sordid goings on and the unique way in which this whole thing was handled have raised many serious issues as far as I can see. I am listing below such issues:

1. Is it correct to make a bonus issue favouring only some shareholders?
2. Are investors really have an option of refusing shares issued to them as bonus?
3. Should a company be allowed to issue bonus shares when its commercial operations are not underway and when it is not making any money?
4. This may pass-off as a scheme of capital restructuring but is it correct to allow it?
5. What happens tomorrow when the company starts making money and then a resolution is passed saying that only the ADAG should be allotted bonus shares to compensate them for their loss?

Many more questions can arise in future if some other company also tries to do this. It also needs to be noted that even after the issue of bonus shares in this bizarre manner the investors continued to make a loss on their initial investment. Many investors complained after the shares were allotted and listed that the issue was overpriced! This argument is untenable at this late stage. Investors have to decide if the pricing is right or not before they invest and not after the listing. This is sheer hypocrisy. If one thinks that the issue is overpriced then one should not apply for the same!

◆ Wockhardt Hospitals and EMAAR-MGF IPO Withdrawal

The IPOs of both these companies opened for subscription in February 2008. Both IPOs together were to raise approximately ₹ 8,000 crore. Both issues were priced very aggressively. However soon after the opening both companies found that there was very little response to their offering both from the institutional as well as retail investors. Both the companies revised the price of their issues downwards and also extended the offer period. It may be noted that both these issues were given high grading by the Credit Rating Agencies. Ultimately both the companies withdrew their issues due to the poor demand!

This withdrawal raises many questions. The managements of both the companies blamed the prevailing market conditions. The markets were coming off the peak that it had scaled. The first rumblings of the sub-prime crisis in the US had started appearing.

Secondly, a huge amount of the investors was still locked in the Reliance Power IPO which had received subscription of close to ₹ 72,000 crore! However this fact was well known to all concerned that the refunds from this mega offer will not have reached the investors at the time of the opening of these two issues and the Merchant Bankers could have differed the date of opening for this. But they were so confident and arrogant that they did not do so but took umbrage in this after their issues bombed!

Nobody was also willing to accept the fact that both the offers were probably highly over priced and that actually was the reason why the response was timid. In a bull market bad issues also get good valuations and in such markets companies and Merchant Bankers try to make issues at very high prices. Many issues actually sail through in such circumstances. Both these companies had been hoping for the same thing to happen to their issues but fortunately for investors it did not.

The other issue is why are underwriters not made to pay for the unsubscribed portion of the issue? The whole purpose of underwriting is to make sure that the issue gets subscribed even if the response from the investors is not adequate. However in India we follow the soft underwriting route which allows them to get scot free from their obligations. I think this must be seriously looked at. This defeats the purpose of underwriting itself.

I also believe that once an issue is opened for subscription then the issuer should not have the right to change the price band. They should also not be allowed to extend the issue by changing the closing date. Current regulations however allow this. I believe that this is unfair and the current regulations need to be re-looked.

Mutual funds are a very important constituent of the capital markets. Investors who are not capable of investing their money directly in the stock markets are expected to take this route. Since mutual funds are managed by experts it is believed that the retail investors are better-off putting their money through them. This also allows them automatic diversification of their portfolio.

◈ What is a Mutual Fund?

Depending upon the risk profile, one should look at investing some part of the savings in the stock market. But direct investing puts a person at great risk. So, the next best alternative is going for 'mutual fund'.

One can define a mutual fund as a trust that pools in the savings of investors who have a common financial goal. Mutual funds issue units to investors, which represent equitable rights in the assets of the mutual fund. Mutual fund by its nature are supposed to be diversified, *i.e.*, its assets are invested in many different securities.

Mutual funds invest the money in stocks, bonds or money market securities or combination of these. These investments will be made according to the objective of the fund.

These are professionally managed on the behalf of the unitholders and each investor holds a *pro rata* share of the portfolio entitled to any profits when the securities are sold, but subject to any losses as well. There are number of schemes of mutual fund and all of them have different characters and objectives. Nowadays it has become difficult for investors to chose a fund for investing their money as there are about 35 Mutual Fund Houses in India that offer thousands of schemes. Investors thus need to be clear about the objective of investment and chose the right and suitable scheme. Fortunately data on the performance of different schemes including the returns generated by them over different timelines is available. Mutual fund scheme rankings are also being published to help the investors chose the right scheme. But it has to be kept in mind as said in the MF advertisements, "Past performance is no guarantee for future performance".

A lot of churning has happened in this industry in the past 10 years or so. The failure and winding up of US 64 scheme of UTI was a big event. Since then some consolidation has happened in the industry. Some new funds have entered while some have staggered along with pathetic performance. How they manage to continue is a mystery and why SEBI allows them to continue is another mystery. Some foreign fund houses that had entered India with a lot of enthusiasm have quit having failed to make any mark here. The latest casualty appears to be one of the biggest funds in the world Fidelity that is planning to sell-off its Indian business and is reportedly searching for a buyer.

◈ Mutual Fund Conceptual Framework

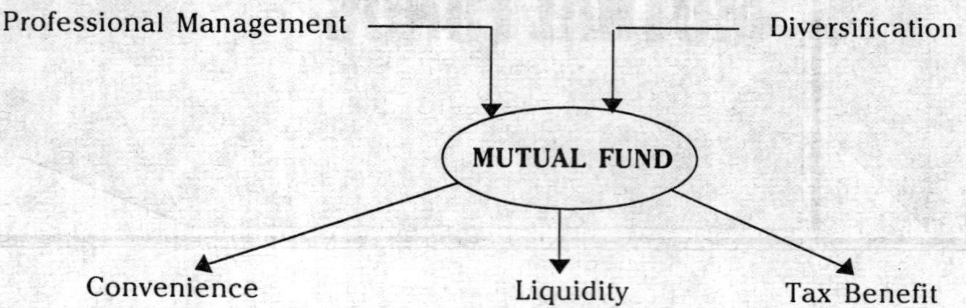

◈ Regulators of the Mutual Fund

- SEBI
- RBI
- MOF
- CLB
- STOCK EXCHANGE
- PUBLIC TRUSTEE OFFICE

ROLE OF REGULATORS

◈ SEBI

- Apex body to regulate capital market activities
- All mutual funds have to be registered with them
- SEBI guidelines govern mutual fund operations, investments, income-expense accounting, and disclosures for investor protection

◈ RBI

- Dual supervisory role in mutual fund regulation
- *Bank owned mutual fund:* RBI and SEBI both jointly regulate mutual funds

  SEBI — market related and investor related

  RBI — issues regarding ownership of AMC, fund mergers, capital adequacy for assured returns
- *Money Market Mutual Fund* guidelines were formulated in 1995. Bank institutions and private sector were allowed to set up money market mutual fund.

Ministry of Finance

- Supervises both RBI and SEBI.
- Plays the role of appellate authority for disputes in SEBI guidelines

Company Law Board, Department of Company Affairs, Registrar of Company

- CLB is the apex regulatory authority under Company's Act. CLB is a body specially constituted by the Central government for carrying out judicial proceedings with respect to company affairs. CLB has the legal standing of a civil court, and may call for inspection of documents, enforce attendance.
- Overall responsibility for formulating and modifying regulations relating to companies lies with the DCA.
- ROC ensures that AMC or the Trustee Company as the case may be is in compliance with all Companies Act provision. All AMC accounts and records are filed with the ROC. He plays the role of watchdog.

Office of Public Trustee

- The Board of Trustees or the Trustee Company is accountable to the Office of Public Trustee.
- The Office reports to the charity commissioner.

Self-regulatory Organizations (SRO)

- SROs are the organizations, which group market participants and have been granted some powers to regulate their own members. E.g., Stock Exchange regulating its broker under overall supervisory by SEBI.
- SROs regulate admissions, set code of conduct, rules and by-laws.
- Every Trade Associations is not necessarily a SRO.
- Investment company plays the role as industry association for mutual funds in USA. AMFI is not a SRO as on date.
- Stock Exchange is a SRO supervised by SEBI.

Who can invest?

- Banks and insurance companies
- Primary Dealers
- Provident Funds
- Trusts
- Mutual Funds
- Foreign Institutional Investors
- Corporates and NBFCs
- Retail Investors

◈ Non-residents including

- Non-residents Indians
- Overseas Corporate Bodies

◈ Foreign Institutional Investors registered with SEBI can invest in mutual fund.

◈ Investor's Rights and Obligations

- Right in beneficial ownership of the assets.
- Right to get dividend
- Right to get information from trustees
- Right to receive dividend warrants within 42 days
- 75 per cent of the unitholders can terminate the AMC.
- Right to inspect major documents
- Fundamental attributes of a closed end fund can be changed by 75 per cent consent.
- Right to receive financial statement, personal statement.

◈ Investor Obligation

- Offer Document
- Financial Statement
- Due diligence certificate from compliance officer.
- Advantages of mutual fund

◈ Portfolio Diversification

Normally mutual funds invest in well-diversified portfolio. As each investor is a part owner of all fund's assets, so he can invest in diversified portfolio even with a small amount. This is the biggest advantage for an investor as he indirectly owns a diversified portfolio even though his individual investment is pretty small. This is something he cannot easily achieve by investing directly in the market as the corpus available to him is limited.

◈ Professional Management

The investment management skills along with the needed research into available investment options ensure a much better return than what an investor can manage on his own. Theoretically it is true but in practice this is not true always. There are many funds in the market that do not perform anywhere near their own benchmarks. Investors therefore have to watch the performance of the funds in which they invest and take appropriate decisions as to whether to stay invested or get out of the scheme which is not performing satisfactorily.

◈ Reduction or Diversification of Risk

Diversification reduces risk of loss as compared to investing directly in one or two shares or debentures or other instruments. When an investor invests directly then the risk of loss is his own. But if he invests in well-diversified securities then loss is automatically shared with the other investors. This because all stocks owned by a fund need not do badly at the same time. Due to this the risk gets reduced. However, when overall market sentiments are not bullish this does not hold true. In a situation like the one that prevailed in 2001-03 or more recently in 2008, when the markets went down heavily even the well managed funds would suffer. Investors in such times tend to panic and sell-off their investments in bad markets out the fear that the markets would go down further. If the entire market is getting affected then it is better to sit tight and hold on to the investments in good schemes as they will bounce back once the markets stabilize and start moving up once again. It is because of this that investors should refrain from investing in NFOs of funds that are launched at the height of the Bull Run.

◈ Reduction of Transaction Cost

A direct investor bears all the costs of investing such as brokerage or custody of securities, but if he goes through a fund he has the benefit of economies of scale, less cost due to large volume. This is not completely true as AMCs charge a fee to the fund for managing it. In some cases these fees are very stiff and that increases the cost of the investors. It is therefore advisable to see the expense ratio of a scheme before investing in it. Fund houses also bear Security transaction tax on each deal made on the market, thus a fund manager who shuffles his portfolio often will end up paying huge amount of STT the burden of which has to be borne by the investor.

◈ Liquidity

An investor can liquidate the investment by selling the units to the fund if open-ended or selling them in the market if the fund is close-ended.

◈ Convenience and Flexibility

Here investor can easily transfer his holdings from one scheme to the other, get updated information and so on.

Mutual fund industry is also rocked by some scandals from time-to-time. There have been schemes of mutual funds, which are run almost like portfolio management schemes. SEBI found out that some schemes seemed to have been devised for such a purpose itself. A leading MF in its discloser recently has shown one investor accounting for 90 per cent of the assets under management. The minimum number of investors per scheme is now proposed to be 20 and maximum investment by a single investor is capped at 25 per cent of the corpus and has set a timeframe for existing schemes to comply with this rule. UTI has since foreclosed some of its schemes in lie with these regulations. Bajaj Auto has taken the UTI to court against this foreclosure. It will be interesting to see what stand the courts will take in this matter.

However, it is believed that norms for funds need to be tightened further. In today's conditions having just 20 investors per fund and corpus of just ₹ 25 crore is ridiculous. This can lead to complications and manipulation of the scheme itself. It is believed that this guideline needs to be revised upwards substantially. A fund must have at least 2,500 investors and the minimum corpus should be at least ₹ 250 crore to make a scheme worthwhile. Also it must be made mandatory that schemes currently not complying to these conditions should be asked to merge them with the other schemes of the MF with the consent of the unitholders. Alternatively investors should be given the option of withdrawing from such schemes at NAV.

There has also been the problem of dividend stripping that is getting a lot of attention. The growth schemes, which are designed to allow capital appreciation to the investors, have declaring dividends and bonuses. It has also been found that many funds are declaring in advance the dates on which the dividends will be declared and releasing advertisements asking investors to invest before the date and take immediate dividends. This is a new trend.

Economic Times had reported in April 04 that some funds whose NAV is below par have declared dividends! Dividend stripping involves investors entering a scheme shortly before a dividend is announced. Investors enjoy tax-free dividends and book a short-term capital loss as the value of the MF units decline after the dividend is announced. These losses are offset against some other capital gains. The budget for 2004-05 has incorporated amendments to stop the practice of dividend stripping by increasing the holding period to 9 months.

Indian MFs are also reported to have learnt from their American counterparts the art of indulging in late trading that has become a global practice, which has sparked off a major investigation in the U.S. Late trading refers to the practice of buying and selling shares after the close of market hours, but at the closing price of the day. Recently some Indian funds were found to be allowing large investors to enter funds after the cut-off timing. This was done to allow these investors to take advantage of price-sensitive information announced by companies after the close of the markets. SEBI is now planning to take action against both these practices of dividend stripping and late trading deals.

After the crash of markets in 2008 the inflows in equity schemes showed a marked decline. The situation did improve in 09 and 10. However, 2011 has not been good for the funds as investors have pulled out money from equity schemes due to the volatility in the markets.

In the scenario increasing interest rates witnessed in Indian economy, debt funds have done better. The returns from these funds have been good and the risk is less. These funds have tended to generate better post-tax returns than the bank fixed deposits as dividends are tax exempt in the hands of the receivers and interest of bank deposits is taxable. So even though debt funds have to pay dividend distribution tax their returns have been better than bank deposits. Many investors in high tax bracket have put money in these schemes.

The Fixed Maturity Plans (FMPs) have also become very popular. These are essentially debt schemes. The maturity profile of the securities in which the funds invests its corpus is similar to the maturity profile of the scheme itself. These schemes are also more tax efficient than bank deposits, as they offer indexation benefits, and therefore investors who have excess funds and do not have a problem of locking them up for a fixed period of time have found these schemes very attractive. One disadvantage of these schemes is that it lacks liquidity and getting out of it before maturity is thus almost impossible. It is better to invest in these schemes when interest rates are high as they are in 2012. Right now we are probably at the peak of interest rate cycle and the rates may start to come down in the next fiscal. So now is the right time to investing these products to lock-in on high returns.

◆ Systematic Transfer Plans

Another comparatively new product that has been introduced is called "Systematic Transfer Plans" (STP). Many people today invest money in chosen fund schemes through the popular Systematic Investment Plans (SIP). In this way investors manage the risk related to stock markets better. Now STP and SIP can be used together. What investors can do is park fairly large amount of money in a STP fund that invests in debt instruments and then transfers a fixed amount every month as in SIP to an equity scheme of their choice. One can use STP to transfer money into several schemes of one's choice. When an investor puts money in the primary scheme which is either debt or income scheme he earns a better return that he would earn by parking his money in a bank savings account.

Some STP funds allow investors to use a flexible approach. The investor invests more money when markets are down so the NAV is less, in the same way when markets are doing well pushing up the NAV fewer amounts is transferred in the equity schemes. The other advantage is in falling markets one can opt for reversal of investments in the sense that funds are withdrawn from equity schemes and parked in a debt fund.

Expert advice that to avoid switching costs one should activate the STP only when one's primary scheme has completed one year after the initial investment as there may be an exit load if money is withdrawn before this period.

In March 06 Reliance Mutual Fund created history in the Indian mutual fund industry when it collected a record amount of ₹ 5,700 crore in its New Fund Offering "Reliance Equity Fund". It is reported that a record one million investors participated in this offer, which also is a record. Reliance has claimed that they were able to collect such a large amount due to their innovating marketing of this scheme. They marketed this scheme in smaller towns are rural areas. The problem in such cases is that the Fund Manager is under pressure to find right investment avenues for such a large corpus in a short period of time. This can make him investments that may prove to be very risky. Generating returns of such a large corpus can thus become problematic.

This goes to show that there are a lot of investors spread across India who need to bring into the mutual fund. What is lacking on the part of the mutual funds is that they are not willing to do the hard work of educating the investors in smaller areas and then sell the various schemes to them. Reliance has made the beginning and hopefully their success will encourage other mutual funds also to take this route.

Indian mutual funds have assets under management worth ₹ 7,00,000 crore and the total investor population is in the region of three crore.

The budget 2006 has allowed mutual funds to invest $ billion cumulatively every financial years in markets abroad. Earlier this limit was $ 1 billion with many restrictions on where to invest. All restrictions have now been removed. It remains to be seen if the industry takes advantage of this in the coming years if not months. Funds will have to do a lot of research if they are going to make investments abroad. It will interest to also see if Indian investors will invest in funds which are willing to take this route. This limit has since been raised to $2 billion per year.

However, it has been observed that not many funds are investing money in markets abroad. It is understandable because between 2003 to 08 Indian markets were in the bull phase and were giving great returns and thus there was no need to take the risk of investing in foreign markets. Post-2008 most markets have shown high volatility while Indian markets rebounded in 2009 and 2010. 2011 was not very good but then the markets in Europe and US were more volatile on the back of continuing economic crisis there.

One had thought that foreign funds present in India may take up such investments because they already are present in these markets. However one has not seen this happening. Some funds both foreign owned and Indian floated schemes to invest in foreign markets but the response from investors has been not very good and the said schemes have also not performed well.

TERMS USED IN MUTUAL FUND BUSINESS

◆ Portfolio

Portfolio is the group of securities that the fund managers plan to invest. The fund manager can change the composition of securities. The combined statement of all investments can thus be called portfolio of a fund.

◆ Asset Management Company (AMC)

The AMC is formed by a group of trustees, which is managed by the board of directors. In India each fund house has its own AMC, though it can use services of any AMC that is eligible to handle the business. Many insurance companies have used the services of MF AMCs to manage the funds that they generated from their ULIP schemes as they themselves did not have the knowledge of investing.

AMC is required to have worth of not less than 10 crore.

Every Mutual Fund on behalf of the unitholders sets up an Asset Management Company (AMC) or assigns its fund to a AMC for managing its funds. The AMC invests on behalf of the respective schemes. Regular expenses like Custodial fees, Cost of dividend warrants, registrar fees, AMC fees are borne by the individual schemes. However, these regular expenses cannot exceed 3 per cent of the assets of a scheme in a year.

Investors need to track these fees carefully. When expense ratio of a fund is high it means that the investors are burdened with these costs and that adversely affect their returns from the schemes. When investors are judging the performance of a scheme they need to take a look at these figures. In most funds the expense ratio is maintained around 2 per cent. However, in passive schemes meaning schemes that need have to be managed very actively on day-to-day basis the expense ratio needs to be lower. Such schemes are basically like Exchange Traded Funds.

◆ Net Asset Value (NAV)

The net asset value of the fund is the cumulative market value of the assets fund net of its liabilities. In other words, if the fund is dissolved or liquidated, by selling off all the assets in the fund, this is the amount that the unitholders would collectively own. This gives rise to the concept of net asset value per unit, which is the value, represented by the ownership of one unit in the fund. It is calculated simply by dividing the net asset value of the fund by the number of units. However, most people refer to the 'NAV per unit 'as 'NAV', ignoring the "per unit". All sale and purchase transactions are done at this value. One can also make out the performance of a scheme by comparing the NAV at which an investor bought the fund and the NAV ruling at any given time. However, it must be kept in mind that in dividend payout schemes the NAV declines to the extent of dividend paid.

◆ Calculation of NAV

The most important part of the calculation is the valuation of the assets owned by the fund. Once it is calculated, the NAV is simply the net value of assets divided by the number of units outstanding.

Asset value is equal to:

Sum of market value of shares/debentures liquid assets/cash held, if any Dividends/ interest accrued — Current liabilities — Expenses accrued but not paid.

$$\text{NAV} = \frac{\text{Asset value of the fund}}{\text{No. of units outstanding}}$$

◆ Load

Some asset management companies (AMCs) levy service charges for allowing subscribers entry into or exit from mutual fund schemes. The service charge is termed as entry/exit load and such schemes are called "load" schemes. SEBI has abolished the entry load for all funds.

However, some funds still charge Exit load in some schemes if one were to leave the scheme before the completion of certain period.

With the vibrancy of capital markets in India and the returns available in these markets, it was natural that more and more people wanted to enter these markets. However, during the bad times in stock markets and the small investors did suffer heavy losses, mainly because of their lack of knowledge about the working of these markets. These investors also are unable to spread the risks across securities and are carried away by market gossip, rather than the knowledge that is essential to make investments in these markets. The mutual funds are the natural answer to many of these problems. It is thought to be much better for the investors to invest in capital markets, through the mutual funds. Professional portfolio managers, who can spread the risks inherent in these investments, manage the mutual funds. The small investors thus get to invest their money in many companies as, members of the funds, something they are unable to do, due to their limited resources.

Until 1987 UTI was the only mutual fund in India. This was the year when public sector banks' subsidiaries were allowed to start the mutual funds, followed by the state run insurance companies. The early entrants in this field were led by State Bank, Canara Bank, Bank of India and Life Insurance Corporation and General Insurance Corporation. Post-1992, mutual funds sponsored by other public and private sector financial institutions, corporates in collaboration with foreign investment and fund managers, and foreign institutional investors emerged on the scene.

Mutual funds are defined by SEBI regulations as funds established in the form of a trust to raise money through the sale of units — that is, the interest of the unitholders in a scheme, which consists of each unit representing one undivided share in the assets of a scheme to public under one/more scheme for investing in securities including money market instruments consisting of commercial papers, commercial bills, etc. According to the procedure laid down by SEBI, mutual funds have to be registered with SEBI. The application for registration together with a non-refundable fee should be made in the prescribed form.

A mutual fund can be constituted in the form of a trust and the instrument of trust should be in the form of a deed, duly registered under the Indian Registration Act, executed by the sponsor in favour of the trustees named in the instrument.

Trustees mean the Board of trustees or the Trustee company who hold the property of the mutual fund in trust for the benefit of the unitholder.

◆ Asset Management Company (AMC)

The AMC appointed by the trustees with the prior approval of the SEBI would be responsible for floating schemes for the mutual fund after approval of the same by the trustees and the managing the funds mobilised under various schemes, in accordance with the provisions of the trust deed and SEBI regulations.

It cannot undertake any other business other than the management of mutual funds and activities as financial consultants and like, as long as they are not in conflict with the fund management activity itself without the prior approval of the trustees and SEBI.

The AMC has to ensure that no offer document of a scheme, key information memorandum, annual results is issued without the trustee's prior approval, and disclose the basis of calculating the repurchase price and NAV of the various schemes of the mutual fund in the scheme particulars and disclose the same to the investors at such intervals as may be specified by the trustees and SEBI.

The Trustees have the right to obtain all information concerning the operations of the various schemes of the funds managed by the AMC. The AMC has to submit a quarterly report on the functioning of the schemes of the mutual fund to the trustees or at such intervals as may be required by the trustees or SEBI.

India's capital market regulator SEBI has introduced some changes in the regulations with respect to mutual fund management rules to allow a single fund manager to manage multiple funds as long as at least 70 per cent of the portfolio values of the funds have similar assets. A less than 70 per cent similarity in the portfolios of two funds will require an asset management company (AMC) to appoint two fund managers.

The Securities and Exchange Board of India, or SEBI, said, "AMCs will appoint separate fund managers for each separate fund managed by it unless the investment objectives and assets allocations are the same and the portfolio is replicated across all the funds managed by the fund manager".

Going by the new norms, if the portfolio values of two funds match 70 per cent or more, the two funds can be managed by a single fund manager and the AMC will have to ensure that the fund manager does not take opposite positions in the funds at any point of time. As a matter of compliance, whenever a fund manager is common across funds or schemes, AMCs will be required to disclose the returns of all such mutual, pension and offshore fund schemes every month on their websites and in all advertisements of such schemes. SEBI has also said that if the difference between the annual returns of such schemes managed by the same fund manager is more than 10 per cent, it will have to be explained to the trustees of the AMC and disclosed on the website.

In a separate note, SEBI has mandated that from 30th September, 2011 all debt securities maturing in 60 days or later will have to be valued on a mark-to-market, or MTM, basis. MTM is an accounting practice of valuing a financial assets in accordance with its current market value and not on the price at which it was bought.

The trustees have the power to dismiss the AMC under specific events with the approval of SEBI. They also have the right to obtain from the AMC such information as is considered necessary by them.

Where the trustees have reason to believe that the conduct of business of the mutual fund is not in accordance with the SEBI regulations and the fund scheme, they should forthwith take such remedial steps as are necessary by them and immediately inform the SEBI of the violation and the action taken by them.

The trustees must obtain consent of the unitholders:

- Whenever required to do so by SEBI.
- Whenever required to do so on the requisition made by three-fourths of the unitholders of any scheme.
- When the majority of the trustees decide to wind up or prematurely redeem the units.
- When a change is proposed to be made in the fundamental attributes of a scheme.

The trustees are also governed by a code of conduct.

◈ Constitution of AMC

The AMC has to fulfil certain criterions for grant of approval by SEBI as follows:

- An existing AMC should have a sound track record, reputation and fairness in transactions.
- The directors should have adequate professional experience in finance and financial service related field.
- The board of directors of AMC must have at least 50 per cent independent directors.
- The chairman of AMC should not be trustee of any mutual fund.
- The AMC must have net worth of ₹ 10 crore.
- No director of AMC other than an independent director can hold the office as director in another AMC.
- Any change in controlling interest of the AMC can be only with the prior approval of trustees, SEBI and the unitholders.
- AMC cannot act as a trustee of any mutual fund or undertake any other business activities expect activities in the nature of portfolio management services, etc.
- The mutual fund should appoint a custodian to carry-out the custodial services for the schemes and send intimation of the same to SEBI within fifteen days of the appointment.

TYPES OF SCHEMES OFFERED BY THE MUTUAL FUNDS

◈ Open-ended vs. Close-ended Schemes

An open-ended scheme is a scheme, in which an investor can buy and sell units on daily basis; the scheme has a perpetual existence and a flexible, ever-changing corpus. The investors are free to buy and sell any number of units, any point of time, at prices that are linked to the NAV of the units. In these schemes the investor can invest or disinvest any amount, any time after the initial lock-in period. These schemes are extremely liquid and the funds announce sale and repurchase prices from time-to-time. These are not listed in stock exchanges and can be only bought and sold to the mutual fund.

A close-ended scheme is one in which, the subscription period for the mutual fund remains only for the specific period, called the redemption period. At the end of this period, the entire corpus is disinvested and the proceeds distributed to the various unitholders. Thus, after final distribution, the scheme ceases to exist. However, such schemes can be rolled over with the approval of the unitholders. They can be listed on the stock exchanges.

◈ Pure Growth Schemes

A pure growth scheme aims at generating long-term capital appreciation for the investors. The objective is achieved by investing a substantial portion of the corpus in high growth equity shares or other equity-related instruments of corporate bodies. The dividend can be declared and distributed as and when the boards of trustees approve it but the principal remains capital appreciation.

◈ Pure Income Schemes

Their aim is to generate and distribute regular income to the investors. This is done by investing a substantial portion of the corpus in high-income yield/fixed income instruments, such as debentures, bonds and so on. Declaration of regular dividends is the main objective of the scheme.

◆ Balanced Schemes

The aim of these schemes is both, to distribute regular income and also provide capital to the investors by balancing the investments of the corpus between the high growth equity shares and the regular income earning securities.

◆ Equity Linked Savings Scheme: (Tax Saving Scheme)

These are schemes, which also offer tax rebates to the investors under the Income Tax Act, under Section 80 (C), which entitles an investor rebate in income tax up to a maximum investment of ₹ 1,00,000 per annum. When EET regime will come into force, as it will shortly, this scheme will become more attractive as investments in equities is exempt from all taxes.

However, the new proposed Direct Tax Code bill proposes to delete ELSS from the ambit of tax exemptions available under Section 80 C. This has caused uncertainty about his product. The inflows which were as high as ₹ 5,000 crore in 2007 on the back of raging bull markets have fallen substantially in the last two years as markets corrected and have been volatile. Thus in 2010 these funds collected only ₹ 1,366 crore and 2011 the collection further dropped to ₹ 1,003 crore.

Recently CRISIL the rating agency has come out strongly in favour of ELSS, they said.

"Our analysis shows that ELSS gave 26 per cent and 22 per cent annualised returns over three and ten years, respectively, *vis-a-vis* 8-9 per cent offered by traditional tax saving investment products such as PPF and NSC."

Investments in an equity-linked savings scheme (ELSS) of a mutual fund have yielded higher returns compared to other instruments like PPF and NSC in the last few years, a report by CRISIL has said.

CRISIL added that interest on employee's provident fund (EPF) for 2011-12 was slashed to 8.25 per cent from 9.5 per cent in the previous year and thus ELSS can act as a strong alternative to investors.

Though the traditional debt products are considered to be relatively safer bet as they are not affected by volatility, they are unable to generate higher inflation-adjusted returns in the long run.

The PPF accounts fetched 8.12 per cent over the last ten years and in the similar period, the NSC gave an interest of 9.10 per cent. The average inflation over the past ten years stood at 6.05 per cent.

"ELSS is not only an attractive option to save tax, but also helps create wealth over the long run. ELSS as a category has outperformed the Nifty 500 across three and ten years. With average inflation around 7 per cent over the past three years, top CRISIL-ranked ELSS gave an inflation adjusted return of 14 per cent, which is significantly higher than returns offered by other tax saving products", CRISIL's senior director Mukesh Agarwal said.

The rating agency, however, cautioned that the ELSS investment requires some amount of market risk and had to cherry pick those schemes which have performed consistently well.

"Since investments in ELSS are subject to market risks, investors must take into consideration their age and risk-taking abilities. The investment horizon should be more than five years for higher inflation-adjusted returns."

(***Source:*** CRISIL)

There are two types of mutual funds according to the investment target:

◈ Debt-oriented Schemes

This type of schemes invest most of the funds in fixed income instruments like debentures of the private sector companies, public sector bonds, Government securities and money market instruments, the balance is invested in equity shares. Given the portfolio composition of such schemes, a reasonably firm indication is provided about the returns investors can expect from schemes.

In this category one may find that some schemes invest only in debt while some others may have a limited exposure to stocks.

A new category has emerged in this in the past few years. These are known as Fixed Maturity Funds (FMP). These schemes invest only in debt instruments that are rated high and the maturity of these instruments are close to the maturity of the fund itself. These schemes are offered across maturities. Investors can put in their money if they perceive that they can afford to lock-up their funds till the maturity of the scheme. One disadvantage of these funds is that they are almost illiquid till maturity and thus there is a risk that if money is urgently required for something it will be difficult to get it out of these schemes easily. However they score over the bank deposits in a sense that post-tax return offered by them could be higher than the bank FDs. These schemes are subject to Dividend Distribution Tax but the income accrues as dividend to the investors and is thus tax-free in his hands.

◈ Equity-oriented Schemes

As against the debt-oriented schemes, these schemes invest the bulk of their funds in equity shares and in fixed income avenues. These schemes are good for investors who have appetite for risk but do not know how to invest in individual stocks by themselves. These schemes also offer them diversification of their risks and allow them exposure across sectors. The fund managers can pick stocks in sectors that they believe are likely to better in future and get out of sectors that are not performing well.

◈ Sector Funds

As the name suggests, sector funds specialise in the stock of single industry or market sector. The fund's portfolio is invested among a handful of stocks in the same industry and thus these can be regarded as aggressive funds. Such schemes concentrate their investments in the specified sector/industry such as Pharma/IT/FMCG, etc. They also focus on Government securities. The diversification is lower in the case of these funds and hence the risk borne by the investor is higher. These sector fund buyers are likely to be more sophisticated and look for a balance between the diversification of a conventional fund and the narrow focus of buying shares in an individual company.

◈ Money Market Mutual Funds

These are designed as a conduit through which the investors can earn market related yield on the money market instruments. They have to operate within the framework of RBI guidelines.

It has been a year now since the government has allowed domestic mutual funds to invest in the foreign equity markets; principal MF has become the first mutual fund to launch a global equity scheme. They are in the process of launching the Principal Global Opportunities Fund, which is opening for subscription in February 2004.

Under the guidelines issued by the RBI the domestic funds are allowed to invest in foreign companies, which have more than a 10 per cent stake in listed Indian companies. The regulations also stipulate that there will be a cap of $ 1 billion on the MF industry's overseas investments and an individual MF investments and an individual MF investments limit of ₹ 200 crore.

The fund is an innovative concept that will allow investors to diversify their investments in blue-chip global equities for the first time.

◈ Tax Treatment of Mutual Funds

Income of notified mutual funds authorised by SEBI is exempt from tax provided 90 per cent of the profit of a mutual fund is mandatorily distributed to the unitholders.

Units of mutual funds held for a continuous period of 12 months preceding the date of sale/transfer/redemption/repurchase are treated as long-term capital assets and taxed at 10 per cent capital gain tax.

No discussion on mutual funds is ever complete without the mention of Unit Trust of India. The fund has gone through one crisis after the other in the recent past. Many investors in the fund's flagship scheme US 64 have suffered losses. There were almost 2 crore investors in this scheme. The government had to bail out this scheme first in 1998, by investing close to ₹ 3,500 crore. The bigger crisis came three years later, when the fund suspended sale and repurchase in this scheme and also expressed its inability to pay any dividend for the first time in its history. These proposals were later rolled back and another bail out had to be worked out.

After the crisis of 1998 a committee was appointed under the chairmanship of Mr. Deepak Parekh, which suggested many fundamental changes in the working of the fund. All suggestions were not implemented before the crisis of 2001. Since then many more investigations in the working of India's largest and oldest mutual fund have been conducted including by a Joint Parliamentary Committee.

The mutual fund industry is going through exiting times these days. Many public sector and private sector banks who are active in mutual fund industry are restructuring their AMCs by inviting foreign funds to participate in their AMCs by investing in the equity of these companies. IDBI has recently decided to disinvest in favour of their foreign partners Principal. State Bank of India is also looking for a partner for its AMC.

Many Indian companies are already running their mutual fund schemes in partnerships with foreign collaborators. HDFC and ICICI have both got such tie-ups.

On the other hand some foreign mutual funds like Zurich have sold out their India operations to HDFC. Fidelity has sold its operations to L&T mutual fund. UTI has acquired the mutual fund of ILF&S.

In the future mutual funds are likely to introduce innovative products for the investors. There is already an application filed with the SEBI, by HDFC, to start a scheme related to Real Estate markets. However these funds have failed to take-off as yet.

On 27th March, 2012, Fidelity mutual fund has sold its India business to L&T mutual fund. Fidelity had announced that it would be selling its Indian assets as a part of its restructuring plan worldwide. Over the years many foreign funds have bought stakes in Indian mutual funds as well. The following table gives some of those deals.

Target	Acquirer	%stake	Deal value in $ millions
Reliance	Nippon Life	26	286
IDFC	Natixis	25	61.1
UTI	T-Rowe Price	26	142.4
LIC	Nomura	35	62.8
Can Bank	Robaco	49	26.1
Bank of Baroda	Pioneer	51	NA
Sundaram	BNP	49.9	22
SBI	SocGen	37	35
IDBI	Principal Financial	50	20

There are strong rumours in the market that the South Korean MF Mirae is also planning to sell of its business in India in the near future.

It is difficult to say if this association has helped these funds in improving their performance. As a matter of fact in UTI the partners have been at logger heads many times and they have differed on many issues including the top level appointments. This may be due to the fact that the owners of UTI are government institutions and some of them have their own mutual fund subsidiaries as well.

The truth of the matter is plain and simple. Many foreign funds came to India without proper preparation and on the basis of wrong assumptions about the Indian markets. Once they launched operations here they found the conditions very different than what they had thought. Thus many foreign funds never came to terms with the Indian markets. Many of them were left with no alternative but to sell-off their business in India. Many of these funds had tried to go it alone in India and found it tough.

Securatisation is a new product for Indian markets, and this is likely to open up newer opportunities for mutual funds as well as, for investors.

Indian investors will have to look towards mutual funds as investors seek to increase their returns on investments. This is going to be a major challenge for the industry, as they must strive to give the investors, better returns than the average return available and to provide capital appreciation in equity-oriented schemes.

◆ Regulatory Aspects

The asset management company shall launch no scheme unless the trustees approve such scheme and a copy of the offer document has been filed with the Board.

Every mutual fund shall along with the offer document of each scheme pay filing fees.

The offer document shall contain disclosures which are adequate in order to enable the investors to make informed investment decision including the disclosure on maximum investments proposed to be made by the scheme in the listed securities of the group companies of the sponsor. A close-ended scheme shall be fully redeemed at the end of the maturity period. "Unless a majority of the unitholders otherwise decide for its rollover by passing a resolution".

The mutual fund and asset management company shall be liable to refund the application money to the applicants:

(*i*) If the mutual fund fails to receive the minimum subscription amount referred to in clause (a) of sub-regulation (1);

(*ii*) If the money is received from the applicants for units are in excess of subscription as referred to in clause (b) of sub-regulation (1).

The asset management company shall issue to the applicant whose application has been accepted, unit certificates or a statement of accounts specifying the number of units allotted to the applicant as soon as possible but not later than six weeks from the date of closure of the initial subscription list and or from the date of receipt of the request from the unitholders in any open-ended scheme.

◈ Rules Regarding Advertisement

The offer document and advertisement materials shall not be misleading or contain any statement or opinion, which are incorrect or false.

◈ Investment Objectives and Valuation Policies

The price at which the units may be subscribed or sold and the price at which such units may at any time be repurchased by the mutual fund shall be made available to the investors.

◈ General Obligations

Every asset management company for each scheme shall keep and maintain proper books of accounts, records and documents, for each scheme so as to explain its transactions and to disclose at any point of time the financial position of each scheme and in particular give a true and fair view of the state of affairs of the fund and intimate to the Board the place where such books of accounts, records and documents are maintained.

The financial year for all the schemes shall end as of March 31 of each year. Every mutual fund or the asset management company shall prepare in respect of each financial year an annual report and annual statement of accounts of the schemes and the fund as specified in Eleventh Schedule.

Every mutual fund shall have the annual statement of accounts audited by an auditor who is not in any way associated with the auditor of the asset management company.

◈ Procedure for Action in Case of Default

On and from the date of the suspension of the certificate or the approval, as the case may be, the mutual fund, trustees or asset management company, shall cease to carry on any activity as a mutual fund, trustee or asset management company, during the period of suspension, and shall be subject to the directions of the Board with regard to any records, documents, or securities that may be in its custody or control, relating to its activities as mutual fund, trustees or asset management company.

◈ Restrictions on Investments

A mutual fund scheme shall not invest more than 15 per cent of its NAV in debt instruments issued by a single issuer, which are rated not below investment grade by a credit rating agency authorized to carry-out such activity under the Act. Such investment limit may be extended to 20 per cent of the NAV of the scheme with the prior approval of the Board of Trustees and the Board of Asset Management Company.

A mutual fund scheme shall not invest more than 10 per cent of its NAV in unrated debt instruments issued by a single issuer and the total investment in such instruments shall not exceed 25 per cent of the NAV of the scheme. All such investments shall be made with the prior approval of the Board of Trustees and the Board of Asset Management Company.

No mutual fund under all its schemes should own more than ten per cent of any company's paid-up capital carrying voting rights.

Such transfers are done at the prevailing market price for quoted instruments on spot basis.

The securities so transferred shall be in conformity with the investment objective of the scheme to which such transfer has been made.

A scheme may invest in another scheme under the same asset management company or any other mutual fund without charging any fees, provided that aggregate inter-scheme investment made by all schemes under the same management or in schemes under the management of any other asset management company shall not exceed 5 per cent of the net asset value of the mutual fund.

The initial issue expenses in respect of any scheme may not exceed six per cent of the funds raised under that scheme.

Every mutual fund shall buy and sell securities on the basis of deliveries and shall in all cases of purchases, take delivery of relative securities and in all cases of sale, deliver the securities and shall in no case put itself in a position whereby it has to make short sale or carry forward transaction or engage in badla finance.

Every mutual fund shall, get the securities purchased or transferred in the name of the mutual fund on account of the concerned scheme, wherever investments are intended to be of long-term nature.

Pending deployment of funds of a scheme in securities in terms of investment objectives of the scheme a mutual fund can invest the funds of the scheme in short-term deposits of scheduled commercial banks.

No mutual fund scheme shall make any investment in;

(*i*) Any unlisted security of an associate or group company of the sponsor; or

(*ii*) Any security issued by way of private placement by an associate or group company of the sponsor; or

The listed securities of group companies of the sponsor which is in excess of 30 per cent of the net assets [of all the schemes of a mutual fund]

No mutual fund scheme shall invest more than 10 per cent of its NAV in the equity shares or equity related instruments of any company. Provided that, the limit of 10 per cent shall not be applicable for investments in index fund or sector or industry specific scheme.

A mutual fund scheme shall not invest more than 5 per cent of its NAV in the equity shares or equity related investments in case of open-ended scheme and 10 per cent of its NAV in case of close-ended scheme.

Recently SEBI has made some sweeping changes in the guidelines for Mutual Funds. Some such changes are as below:

First, for New Fund Offers (NFOs): They will **be open only for 15 days**. (ELSS funds will continue to stay open for up to 90 days).

(2) NFOs **can only be invested at the close of the NFO period**. Earlier, Mutual funds would keep an NFO open for 30 days, and the minute they received their first cheque, the money would be directly invested in the market; creating a skewed accounting for those that entered later since they get a fixed NFO price. The market regulator has corrected this by extending Application Supported by Blocked Amount (ASBA) to mutual funds. This has become effective starting July 1st, 2011.

(3) **Dividends can now only be paid-out of actually realized gains. Impact:** It will reduce both the quantum of dividends announced, and the measures used by MFs to garner investor money using dividend as a carrot to entice new investors. However it has been observed that even now funds are announcing dividends and the record date is later thus investors can buy the units of the fund for which dividend has been declared and receive it within days of its announcement. This practice must be stopped. The record date needs to be the same as the declaration of dividend.

(4) Equity mutual funds have been asked to play a **more active role in corporate governance** of the companies they invest in. This will help mutual funds become more active and not just that, they must reveal, in their annual reports from next year, what they did in each "vote". SEBI has now made it mandatory for funds to disclose whether they voted for or against moves (suggested by companies in which they have invested) such as mergers, demergers, corporate governance issues, appointment and removal of directors. MFs have to disclose it on their website as well as annual reports. This is an important change. In the past it was observed that MFs were silent spectators at the AGMs when they should be in the forefront to protect the interests of minority shareholders as they represent thousands of such shareholders due to their investments in mutual fund schemes that own these shares on their behalf.

(5) Equity funds were allowed to charge 1 per cent more as management fees if the funds were "no-load"; but since SEBI has banned entry loads, **this extra 1 per cent has also been removed.**

(6) SEBI has also asked mutual funds to **reveal all commission paid to its sponsor or associate companies, employees and their relatives.**

(7) **Regarding the Fund-of-fund (FOF):** The market regulator has stated that information documents that Asset Management Companies (AMCs) have been entering into revenue sharing arrangements with offshore funds in respect of investments made on behalf of fund-of-fund schemes create conflict of interest. Henceforth, AMCs shall not enter into any revenue sharing arrangement with the underlying funds in any manner and shall not receive any revenue by whatever means/head from the underlying fund.

However, everything is not fine with the MF industry. The investors have taken out a lot of funds in the last one year. The assets under management that had risen to ₹ 7 lakh crore have retreated as investors' appetite seems to be on decline. We have witnessed negative trends even in popular SIP route. There are many investors who have got hurt by investing in wrong schemes and at wrong times. Many investors had rushed to invest in NFOs at the peak of the bull run in the markets. Many of these schemes have failed to give any returns to their investors in the volatile market conditions of today. This has shaken the confidence of many investors. SEBI banned entry load and also severely curtailed commissions paid to brokers for selling MF schemes. Many intermediaries thus have stopped selling MF products as they do not find it rewarding. Many have found selling Insurance products more rewarding, have shifted to that space. Indian investors are not used to paying for financial advice as they have got it free till date. SEBI wants investors to pay a fee to Certified Financial Planners who are expected to give financial investment advice to their clients. It is going to take a long time before investors warm up to this idea. As a matter of fact Indian investors are used to getting 'incentives" from the intermediaries. Many intermediaries like insurance agents, PPF agents or brokers selling MFs were regularly passing on part of the commissions that they received to their investors. Though this practice has been declared illegal it seems that it is still thriving.

◈ The Case of US-64

No discussion on the subject of mutual funds in India can be complete without a discussing the US-64 problem, which rocked our financial markets a couple of years back.

US-64 was the first scheme floated by UTI and was by far the most popular scheme, as is evident from the fact that almost 2 crore investors had put their money in this scheme. The reason was quite obvious; the scheme had given very good returns to the investors. This scheme was designed as a debt-oriented one so that regular dividend could be paid to the investors. In the early 90s Indian stock markets were reaching dizzying heights at the height of Harshad Mehta led frenzy. During this time UTI top brass under the chairmanship of Mr. Pherwani change the composition of this scheme to make it equity biased as opposed to debt, as returns in stock markets were phenomenal. Around the same time the Government of India under its disinvestment programme started selling its stake in the public sector units. UTI was one of the major buyers of these equities. However the prices of these shares in the stock markets did not make this investment very profitable. UTI it is alleged made many investments in unsustainable projects under political pressure. Many of these shares were bought at a high premium under the free pricing regime, and companies with dubious background issued these. During all these years UTI refused to be brought under the SEBI regulations for mutual funds. It also refused to disclose its portfolio and the NAV of the units. UTI also started to feel the heat of competition as private sector mutual funds started eating away its market share steadily.

The crunch came in 1998, when the government had to bail out UTI by providing an amount of almost ₹ 3,500 crore to make the shortfall. This was done by buying back the PSU shares originally sold to the fund.

◈ High Level Expert Committee

In October 1998, UTI constituted a High Level Expert Committee under the chairmanship of Deepak Parekh to undertake a comprehensive review of the functioning of US-64 to strengthen the scheme and to recommend measures for sustaining investor confidence.

The terms of reference of the High Level Expert Committee were as under:

1. Review of the objectives, features and structure of the scheme in the context of its role in the mobilisation of domestic savings and investment in the capital market.
2. Review of the policies of the scheme relating to pricing and income distribution, having regard to the profile of existing investors of the scheme.
3. Review of the policies and procedures about the portfolio composition of the scheme, as well as the asset management process.

The High Level Expert Committee submitted its report on February 25, 1999 and the full report was made public on May 18, 1999. Of the 19 recommendations made by the Committee, 13 recommendations had been implemented and 3 recommendations were in the process of implementation. The remaining 3 recommendations on which action still remains to be taken are:

1. US-64 should be NAV driven.
2. There should be a separate Asset Management Company for US-64 with an independent board.
3. The number of trustees should be increased by the addition of 5 trustees.

4. Implementation of the last two recommendations had to be kept pending as they needed an amendment of the UTI Act.

The Committee had the following terms of reference:

1. To review the competitive positioning of UTI in the light of the second generation reforms in the financial sector.
2. The emerging development in the area of mutual fund business and regulation as well as the trend towards broader financial services companies.
3. Globalisation of the Indian financial services sector.
4. The confidence of investors in financial organisation of different sizes and strengths.
5. Obligations of UTI to the existing unitholder under UTI Act and the implications of any change in this context and progress of implementation of recommendations of the Deepak Parekh Committee.
6. To recommend appropriate follow-up action plans including amendments to connected legislation for enabling UTI to fully meet with the Mutual Fund Regulations of SEBI and enhancing the competitive positioning of UTI.
7. The Committee had several meetings and had almost concluded its deliberations when the UTI Board, at its meeting held on 2nd July, 2001 announced that it had suspended the sale and repurchase operations in the US-64 scheme till December 31, 2001. This created an immediate outcry and loss of confidence of unitholders in UTI and demands for government intervention and support. To meet the demands for liquidity and some amount of safety for small unitholders, UTI announced on 15th July, 2001 that unitholders would be offered an option for repurchase up to 3,000 units out of their aggregate holdings during the period up to 31st May, 2003 at prices which would progressively increase from ₹ 10 to ₹ 12 per unit. It was also announced that US-64 would be made NAV driven from 1st January, 2002. The reason for the suspension of sale and repurchase operations was stated to be the fact that in April 2001 and May 2001.
8. US-64 faced massive redemptions aggregating to ₹ 426 crore and ₹ 3,767 crore respectively at the then repurchase prices which were later admitted to be well above the Net Asset Value of the units of the scheme. Sales and repurchase in the scheme had been stopped with effect from 1st June, 2001 for closure of books prior to payment of dividend for the year ended 30th June, 2001.

◆ Malegam and Tarapore Committees

The Malegam Committee was appointed in July 2000 by the UTI's board of trustees to review the recommendations of the Deepak Parekh Committee and to recommend follow-up action plans to enable UTI to fully meet with the mutual fund regulations of SEBI and enhancing the competitive positioning of UTI. The last bit was generally perceived as a politely couched euphemism for chalking out a blueprint for converting the UTI into a professionally-run mutual fund.

Interestingly, the Malegam Committee report has been passed on to the Joint Parliamentary Committee (JPC) probing the March 2001 stock scam, without it even being discussed by the UTI's board of trustees. Neither has it been vetted by the Finance Ministry as the UTI board is yet to forward the report to the Ministry for its views.

The Finance Ministry has its nominee now — Dr J. Bhagwati, Joint Secretary (Capital Markets and ECB) — on the board of trustees of UTI.

The Malegam Committee's (whose report is available on UTI's website) recommended a single asset management company to control all of UTI's 73 domestic schemes. It asked for all the schemes to be valued and pointed out that several of its 25 assured return schemes also had a shortfall between the NAV and return assured to investors. Most importantly, it suggested a way to get UTI out of the clutches of government by inducting a strategic partner who would hold a 60 per cent stake in the AMC.

◈ Tarapore Committee Report

The Tarapore Committee Report once again confirmed that UTI's problems were largely due to shady and doubtful investments, bailout of chronic industrial defaulters such as the Essar Group and others and investment in a variety of volatile software scrips and stocks pushed by stockbroker Ketan Parekh. The Tarapore panel, which comprised a former CBI chief, top central banker and a nationalised bank chairman — asked that its findings be sent to pre-investigative body for further inquiry. S.S. Tarapore (a former Deputy Governor of the Reserve Bank of India) who headed the committee has argued in an interview to the *Financial Express* that it was not "suitably empowered" and had to "rely on documents placed before it by the UTI" and was also unable to questions the regulators and the counter parties to several transactions with UTI.

◈ Joint Parliamentary Committee

A JPC was appointed in the wake of Ketan Parekh scandal and the troubles at UTI. They both had a definite link though it must be made clear that UTI had many other problems that were swept under the carpet from time-to-time without rectifying them.

The composition of JPC reflects the individual strength of political parties in parliament proportionately and hence clearly the ruling coalition will have majority in such committees and hence it is clear that such committees will never put the blame on its own minister. in charge of the concerned departments.

The JPC naturally gave a clean chit to the Finance Minister Mr. Yashvant Sinha and blamed the Finance Secretary Ajit Singh, UTI Chairman Subramaniam and IDBI the principal contributor to UTI for the decline of US-64 in particular and the UTI in general. It also recommended an enquiry in the affairs of UTI by SEBI and Department of Company Affairs. It seemed to have completely ignored the fact UTI management had repeatedly refused to come under the purview of SEBI and this was not objected to or overruled by the government. Finally when UTI agreed to abide by SEBI regulations it kept US-64 away from SEBI's jurisdiction. This was a clear indication that the management of UTI knew that everything was not right about the scheme. In this UTI was supported by the Finance Ministry and as such it cannot escape the blame in this whole matter.

Some of the observations of the committee are as follows:

"SEBI appears to have done nothing particularly substantive": monitoring and regulating the massive inflow of some ₹ 50,000 crore from abroad into the stock market; the mismatch between the primary and secondary stock market; the mismatch between the huge number of listed scrip and the small number of actively traded scrip; the rise in private placements to the detriment of the primary market; and "negligence" in checking whether bull operators were overtly or covertly obtaining bank funding. Little wonder then that fraudsters had a field day deceiving investors while the government prided itself on the "feel good factor" which pervaded the stock market.

- "It was SEBI's job", says the JPC, "to ferret out the irregularities and defuse them before they blew up. This was the primary job of SEBI which they failed to do on time." Thus, SEBI failed "to analyze why the BSE index reached a phenomenal high in February 2000".

  "Absence of an investigation when the BSE index unusually rose contrary to the fundamentals of the stock markets represents the failure of the regulator. Had steps been taken by the regulator at the relevant time, perhaps the phenomenal rise could have been contained and the defaults avoided. The regulator should have known that regulation of the market could only be provided through constant vigil and in cooperation with other regulatory authorities."

- On the securities scam, the committee blamed tainted big bull Ketan Parekh for his price manipulations in the securities market in connivance with some banks and corporate houses.

  "When stock markets were rising, there was general lack of concern to see that such a rise should be in consonance with the integrity of the market and not the consequence of manipulation or other malpractice. On the other hand, when the markets went into a steep fall, there was concern all over."

  "The scam does not lie in the rise and fall of prices in the stock market but in large scale manipulations like the diversion of funds, fraudulent use of bank funds, use of public funds by institutions like the Unit Trust of India (UTI), violation of the risk norms on the stock exchanges and banks, and use of funds coming through overseas corporate bodies to transfer stock holdings and stock market profits out of the country."

- THE RBI's performance as the regulator of the banking system was no better than SEBI's as the regulator of the stock market. The JPC have severely indicted the RBI for a whole host of deficiencies, including failure to "effectively supervise" urban cooperative banks notwithstanding "the huge increase in the number of UCBs, the huge size of their deposits and their increasing involvement, overtly and covertly, in stock market operations well before the scam". The scam would not have occurred if SEBI or the RBI or both, or the High Level Coordination Committee chaired by the RBI Governor and serviced by the Ministry had been a little alert to what was going wrong when the going was apparently good. That the Finance Ministry did next to nothing to chivvy the regulators is testimony alike to the incompetence and impotence of the Ministry and the Minister who headed it.

◆ UTI Crisis — Recommendations of the Deepak Parekh Committee

1. Initial contributors to UTI should infuse permanent funds of at least ₹ 500 crore.
2. The PSU portfolio should be transferred at book value to a Special Unit Scheme (SUS-99) to be subscribed for by GoI by the issue of dated GoI securities.
3. US-64 should make a strategic sale of its significant equity holdings by negotiation to the highest bidder to ensure fetching the best value for the unitholder.
4. (*a*) The investment sub-limit of ₹ 10,000 for tax benefit on Equity Linked Savings Schemes should be removed and benefit should be extended to US-64 and all schemes investing more than 50 per cent in equity.

   (*b*) Income distributed by US-64 and schemes investing more than 50 per cent in equity should be exempt from tax.

5. New schemes for investing in growth stocks in IT, Pharma and FMCG sectors should be launched, to be subscribed for by banks.
6. The size of the UTI Board should be increased to 15, with additional five members being co-opted by the Board.
7. (*a*) Trustees should assume higher degree of responsibility and exercise greater authority.
   (*b*) The remuneration of Trustees should be increased and their attendance record be published in the Annual Report.
8. There should be a separate Asset Management Company for US-64 with an independent Board of Directors.
9. (*a*) Chinese walls should be created by appointing separate and independent fund managers for each scheme.
   (*b*) Inter-scheme transfers must be based on independent decisions and requirements of concerned fund managers and at market determined prices.
10. (*a*) There should be an independent fund manager for US-64 with full responsibility and accountability.
    (*b*) The fund manager should be helped by a strong research team and the research capability should be strengthened.
11. (*a*) Investment/disinvestment decisions should be based on research analysts' recommendations who should have the authority and responsibility of making the recommendations.
    (*b*) The fund manager should have the final authority and responsibility in decision making based on his perception of the market and research inputs.
12. The focus on small investors should be strengthened and the lilt towards corporate investors reduced.
13. (*a*) US-64 should be NAV driven within three years.
    (*b*) If at the end of the three years period, the repurchase price and the NAV are not in line, the Trust will be left with no alternative but to seek GoI support once again the provide the difference between the NAV and the repurchase price. Only a clear commitment from the GoI to stand by US-64 till it finally assumes the character of a NAV driven scheme will instill the required confidence in the US-64 investors.
14. The spread between sale and repurchase prices should be gradually increased to deter short-term investors.
15. (*a*) The dividend distribution policy needs to follow a more conservative approach to build-up sufficient reserves during periods of good performances.
    (*b*) As a rule, dividends need to be curtailed when there is inadequate income.
16. The rate of return offered to investors needs to be reviewed on a periodic basis. The yield offered on US-64 is excessively high as compared to other comparable instruments.
17. The composition of the portfolio needs to be changed to provide for more weightage to debt consistent with the objectives of the scheme.
18. The operations of US-64 should be brought under SEBI purview at the earliest.

19. An independent professional firm should be commissioned for a detailed review of asset management processes including back office, inter-scheme transfer and investor servicing.

In 2001 UTI was rocked with even more serious trouble when in June it decided to suspend sale and purchase of units and also decided for the first time in its history that the fund will pay no dividend for that year. UTI was found to be in some way involved with the Ketan Parekh saga which was unfolding around the same time. There was also the proposed merger of UTI Bank with Global Trust Bank, which had to be called-off, as GTB's involvement in Ketan Parekh affair became clear.

Finally the government had to come to the rescue of UTI once again. It decided the scheme will pay a dividend of 10 per cent and the scheme will be made NAV based. It also decided to buy the units held by small investors at a premium to the NAV, which will go up by 10 paisa every month peaking in May 2003 to ₹ 12 per unit. It was decided that 5,000 units per holder would be eligible to be sold under this rescue package.

The scheme has become NAV based now and UTI itself has been split into two. The government decided to offer tax-free bonds to the unitholders of this scheme who wish to quit the scheme in May 2003. It is expected that many investors will opt for this switchover, as this will offer them a good return.

In February 2004 UTI-I has sought the permission of SEBI to prematurely close and assured plans. Among these schemes are four long-term full assurance schemes with remaining maturities ranging between 18 and 22 years. These schemes were launched with an assured return of 13-14 per cent. However, due to the present market conditions the schemes are getting returns much below what has been promised. This has been partly due to the fact that some of the investments made by UTI have turned into Non-performing Assets.

The current shortfall in these schemes is expected to be around ₹ 8,000 crore. If these schemes are not foreclosed, then the government will have to pick-up the tab for making good the difference.

However, all is now well with UTI mutual fund. The existing AMC manages only the good schemes and all bad or irregular schemes were transferred to a special unit called UTI-I. All those schemes have been terminated. The tax-free bonds issued to the erstwhile US-64 holders will be liquidated without any difficulty on the due date. Due to the sustained bullishness witnessed in the stock markets over the last few years the value of the shares held by UTI has gone up enormously, thus the government will not have to bail out UTI by infusion of funds.

CRISIL's RATINGS OF MUTUAL FUNDS

◆ CRISIL Mutual Fund Ranking – Brief Methodology

CRISIL Mutual Fund Ranking is the relative performance ranking of mutual fund schemes within the peer group. The basic eligibility criteria for inclusion in the ranking universe are two-years NAV history (one-year for Liquid, Ultra Short Term Debt, Index and Debt-short funds and five-year inclusion for the Consistent Performers), assets under management in excess of category cut-off limits and complete portfolio disclosure. The ranking is done based on the following parameters:

◆ Superior Return Score

The Superior Return Score (SRS) is the relative measure of the return and the risk for the schemes compared to their peer group. It is computed for Equity Oriented Categories, Equity

Linked Saving Schemes (ELSS), Debt, Balance, Monthly Income Plan (Aggressive and Conservative) and Gilt categories for a two-year period. The weightage for the four six monthly periods starting from the latest are 32.5 per cent. 27.5 per cent, 22.5 per cent and 17.5 per cent respectively. In case of the consistent Mutual Fund Performers for Equity, Balanced and Debt categories, the SRS is calculated for a period of five years, with separate one year periods weighted differentially with the most recent period having the highest weightage.

◈ Mean Return and Volatility

Mean return and volatility are considered separately in case of Liquid, Ultra short-term Debt and Debt short-term schemes for a one year period. Mean return is average of daily return on fund NAV for the latest one year period and the volatility is the standard deviation of these returns. The weightage for the four quarterly periods starting from the latest are 32.5 per cent, 27.5 per cent, 22.5 per cent and 17.5 per cent respectively. In case of the Consistent Mutual Fund Performers for the Liquid category, mean return and volatility are calculated for a period of five years, with separate one year periods weighted differentially with the most recent period having the highest weightage.

◈ Portfolio Concentration Analysis

Concentration measures the risk arising out of improper diversification. Diversity score is used as the parameter to measure industry concentration and company concentration for equity securities. In case of debt papers, the industry concentration is analyzed only for any/over exposure in sensitive sectors which is arrived at based on CRISIL's assessment of the prospects for various sectors and company concentration will have an individual issuer specific limit of 10.0 per cent.

◈ Liquidity Analysis

It measures the ease with which the portfolio can be liquidated. In case of equities, liquidity is calculated by taking the average of last three months impact cost published by stock exchanges. Gilt liquidity is measured by analysing the market turnover, days traded and size of trade in any security for a three months period for that security. Corporate Debt Liquidity is computed by classifying each security into three categories — Liquid, Semi-liquid and Illiquid and then evaluating a fund's exposure to each such category.

◈ Asset Quality

Asset quality measures the probability of default by the issuer of a debt security to honour the debt obligation in time. CRISIL penalizes lower rated securities to a higher level in its analysis.

◈ Modified Maturity/Average Maturity

Modified duration/Average Maturity are considered across all debt categories except liquid to capture the interest rate risk of the portfolio. Lower the value better it is.

◈ Downside Risk Probability (DRP)

DRP measures the probability of the investment getting lower returns than short tenor risk-free securities. It measured by assessing the number of times a fund's return falls below the risk-free return over the period of analysis. The risk-free return is taken as the 91-day T-Bill yield over the period.

◆ Asset Size

It is considered only for Ultra short-term Debt and Liquid categories to take into account the effect of large fund flows on the funds' performance and ability of the funds to manage such flows optimally. Higher the asset size better it is.

◆ Tracking Error

This is used only for index funds. The tracking error is an estimation of the variability in a fund's performance *vis-à-vis* the index that it tracks. Lower the tracking error better it is.

◆ Historic CRISIL Mutual Fund Performance

Historic CRISIL mutual fund performance is considered only for the consistent category. Quarterly mutual fund ranks during the five years period of analysis are weighted with separate one year periods weighted differentially with the most recent period having the highest weightage.

◆ CRISIL Mutual Fund Ranking Category Definitions

Category	*Interpretation*
CRISIL Fund Rank 1	Very Good performance in the category (Top 10 percentile of universe)
CRISIL Fund Rank 2	Good performance in the category
CRISIL Fund Rank 3	Average performance in the category
CRISIL Fund Rank 4	Below average performance in the category
CRISIL Fund Rank 5	Relatively weak performances in the category.

(*Source:* CRISIL website)

ANNEXURE

ASSETS UNDER MANAGEMENT OF VARIOUS MUTUAL FUNDS AS ON 31-3-2013

Mutual Funds	*Dec. 2012*	*March 2013*	*Change*	*% Change*
HDFC Mutual Fund	101,393	101,720	328	0.32
Reliance Mutual Fund	90,636	94,580	3,944	4.35
ICICI Prudential Mutual Fund	81,394	87,835	6,441	7.91
Birla Sun Life Mutual Fund	76,890	77,046	157	0.20
UTI Mutual Fund	70,638	69,450	–1,188	–1.68
SBI Mutual Fund	53,311	54,905	1,594	2.99
Franklin Templeton Mutual Fund	40,869	41,564	696	1.70
Kotak Mahindra Mutual Fund	31,773	35,361	3,589	11.29
IDFC Mutual Fund	30,002	32,886	2,884	9.61
DSP BlackRock Mutual Fund	30,838	32,342	1,505	4.88
Tata Mutual Fund	19,742	19,897	155	0.79
Deutsche Mutual Fund	18,037	18,114	77	0.43
JP Morgan Mutual Fund	13,300	15,856	2,556	19.22
Sundaram Mutual Fund	14,595	14,871	276	1.89
Religare Invesco Mutual Fund	14,025	14,202	177	1.26

Axis Mutual Fund	10,550	12,114	1,564	14.82
L&T Mutual Fund	12,064	11,169	–895	–7.42
Canara Robeco Mutual Fund	7,513	8,851	1,338	17.81
JM Financial Mutual Fund	7,467	7,411	-55	–0.74
Baroda Pioneer Mutual Fund	5,406	7,303	1,897	35.10
LIC NOMURA Mutual Fund	6,882	7,185	303	4.40
IDBI Mutual Fund	6,256	6,249	–7	–0.11
PRINCIPAL Mutual Fund	4,955	5,573	618	12.47
HSBC Mutual Fund	5,347	5,230	–117	–2.19
Peerless Mutual Fund	4,721	4,875	153	3.25
Goldman Sachs Mutual Fund	4,786	4,800	14	0.29
Taurus Mutual Fund	4,177	4,732	555	13.28
BNP Paribas Mutual Fund	3,216	3,726	510	15.85
Union KBC Mutual Fund	3,012	3,118	106	3.51
Morgan Stanley Mutual Fund	2,539	2,660	121	4.78
Indiabulls Mutual Fund	2,553	2,639	86	3.38
Pramerica Mutual Fund	2,038	2,592	554	27.20
BOI AXA Mutual Fund	661	1,104	443	66.98
PineBridge Mutual Fund	1,164	1,099	-65	–5.60
ING Mutual Fund	933	993	60	6.41
Mirae Asset Mutual Fund	527	540	13	2.45
Motilal Oswal Mutual Fund	588	539	-50	–8.47
Quantum Mutual Fund	252	280	28	11.02
Daiwa Mutual Fund	537	266	-271	–50.46
Edelweiss Mutual Fund	242	259	17	6.86
Escorts Mutual Fund	230	255	25	10.90
Sahara Mutual Fund	287	254	-34	–11.70
IIFL Mutual Fund	198	210	12	6.01
Total	**7,86,544**	**8,16,657**	**30,114**	

From the table above we can see that there are 44 Fund Houses in India. This is far too many. It can be observed that many of these funds have very small amounts under their management. The rationale of such funds being in operation needs to be questioned. The large number of funds and schemes does not help the investors to decide where to invest. It is time for SEBI to look at the regulations regarding individual schemes and increase the threshold for minimum investors and minimum amount to be collected in a NFO.

◆ Introduction to Money Markets

The money market is a market for overnight to short-term funds, and for short-term money and financial asset, that are close substitutes for money. Short-term in Indian context means a period up to one-year. Close substitute for money means any financial asset, which can be quickly converted into money.

The major participants in this market are the commercial banks, the other financial intermediaries, large corporates and the Reserve Bank of India. The RBI plays a major role and occupies a strategic position in these markets. It influences the availability and cost of credit. The objectives of these markets are to provide:

1. A mechanism for evening out short-term surpluses and deficiencies.
2. A focal point of central bank intervention for influencing liquidity in the economy.
3. A reasonable access to the users of short-term funds to meet their requirements at realistic cost.

In the money market the operations are for short duration as compared to capital markets. There is large number of participants in money market. The depth of this market depends on the number of participants. This is wholesale market. The volumes here are very large, and therefore there is a need for professionals to operate in these markets. Trading here is conducted mainly on telephones, followed by written confirmation from both the parties.

PARTICIPANTS IN MONEY MARKETS

◆ Discount and Finance House of India Ltd.

The RBI jointly with the public sector banks and the all-India financial institutions set up the Discount and Finance House of India Ltd., as an autonomous financial intermediary. It was conceived with the main objective of increasing the transactions of the money market assets. The main function of DHFI is to smoothen the short-term liquidity imbalances by developing an active secondary market. DHFI participates in call/notice/term money markets both as borrower and lender, and purchased and sold T-bills, commercial bills, commercial paper and certificate of deposits.

With an objective to strengthen the infrastructure of fixed income securities market in India, Discount and Finance House of India (DFHI) was incorporated by Reserve Bank of India (RBI) along with other Public Sector Banks (PSBs) and All-India Financial Institutions (FIs) under the Companies Act, 1956, on March 8, 1988. After receiving certificate of commencement of business on April 25, 1988, the company started its operation with an initial paid-up capital of ₹ 100 crore (RBI – ₹ 51 crore, PSBs – ₹ 33 crore and FIs – ₹ 16 crore). However, in order to broadbase the activity of the company, the paid-up capital was subsequently increased to ₹ 150 crore in 1989-90 and further to ₹ 200 crore during 1991-92.

DFHI since its inception has been actively trading in all the money market instruments (*viz.*, call/notice/term money, commercial bills, treasury bills, certificate of deposit and commercial paper) and its business turnover has grown progressively over the years. With effect from the year 1992-93, DFHI has been authorised to deal in Dated Government Securities also. After the company was accredited as a Primary Dealer (PD) in February 1996, its operations have increased significantly particularly in Treasury Bills and Dated Government Securities.

Meanwhile, over a period of time RBI took a policy decision to divest their shareholdings in favour of the existing shareholders. Thus State Bank of India (SBI) became the major shareholder and DFHI became a subsidiary of SBI from 31.03.2003.

SBI Gilts Ltd., a subsidiary of SBI and established in the year 1996 was also an active participant in the market and one of the top five PDs. As both the companies were engaged in the same line of business, it was decided to merge SBI Gilts Ltd., with DFHI Ltd., in April 2004. Accordingly, from June 2004 the name of the merged entity was changed to SBI DFHI Ltd.The shareholding pattern of the company underwent a change as under:

Institutions	*Percentage of Shareholding*
State Bank Group	**67.01**
Nationalised Banks	**22.46**
All-India Financial Institutions/Private Banks	**5.84**
Asian Development Bank	**4.69**
	100.00

◈ Primary Dealers

The objectives of PD's include:

- Strengthening the infrastructure in the government securities market including money markets, to make them vibrant.
- To ensure the development of underwriting and market making for government securities.
- To improve the secondary market trading system.

◈ Money Market Instruments

1. "T" Bills
2. Commercial Paper (CP)
3. Certificates of Deposits (CDs)

4. Money Market Mutual Funds
5. Repos and Reverse repos market.

T-bills were introduced to stabilise the money markets. They are sold on the basis of fortnightly auction, but the amount, however is not specified in advance. These bills have been instrumental in reducing the net RBI credit to the government. They have become extremely popular due to their higher yield coupled with liquidity and safety and are being used as benchmark. They have also widened the money market and provided an innovative outlet for the surplus funds.

◈ 14 days Intermediate T-bills

The participants in these bills are State governments, foreign central banks, and specified bodies. These are non-transferable and are issued only in book entry forms and would be redeemed at par.

◈ Instruments in Money Markets

◈ Commercial Paper Market

Following the acceptance of Vaghul committee recommendations, RBI allowed the issue of CPs in 1989.

- The CP is a short-term negotiable instrument, consisting of usance primary notes with a fixed maturity, indicating the short-term obligation of an issuer. Companies as a means of raising short-term debt issue CPs. It is issued on a discount to face value basis but can also be issued in interest bearing form. The issuer promises the buyer a fixed amount at a future date but pledges no assets.
- A CP, as a short-term financial instrument, has several advantages to the issuer. It involves very little documentation. It is flexible in terms of maturity. It is unsecured. There are no limitations on the end-use of the funds used in this manner. They are negotiable and transferable instruments and are highly liquid.
- The participants in this market are the corporate bodies, banks, mutual funds, UTI, LIC, GIC and others who have surplus funds and are on a lookout for opportunities for short-term investments. The DFHI also operates both in the primary and secondary markets for CPs by quoting its bid and offering prices.

The CP market is fairly popular these days; however a secondary market in these is yet to develop.

◈ RBI Guidelines for Issuance of CPs

◈ Who can Issue Commercial Paper (CP)?

1. Corporates, primary dealers (PDs) and satellite dealers (SDs), and the all-India financial institutions (FIs) that have been permitted to raise short-term resources under the umbrella limit fixed by Reserve Bank of India are eligible to issue CP.
2. A corporate would be eligible to issue CP provided: (*a*) the tangible net worth of the company, as per the latest audited balance sheet, is not less than ₹ 4 crore; (*b*) company has been sanctioned working capital limit by bank/s or all-India financial institution/s; and (*c*) the borrowal account of the company is classified as a Standard Asset by the financing banks/institutions.

This effectively leaves out smaller companies from the issuance of these instruments. Note that a company that has no working capital borrowings is also not eligible to issue CPs.

◆ Rating Requirement

3. All eligible participants shall obtain the credit rating for issuance of commercial paper from either the Credit Rating Information Services of India Ltd., (CRISIL) or the Investment Information and Credit Rating Agency of India Ltd., (ICRA) or the Credit Analysis and Research Ltd., (CARE) or the FITCH Ratings India Pvt. Ltd., or such other credit rating agency (CRA) as may be specified by the Reserve Bank of India from time-to-time, for the purpose. The minimum credit rating shall be P-2 of CRISIL or such equivalent rating by other agencies. The issuers shall ensure at the time of issuance of CP that the rating so obtained is current and has not fallen due for review.

◆ Maturity

4. CP can be issued for maturities between a minimum of 15 days and a maximum up to one year from the date of issue.

◆ Denominations

5. CP can be issued in denominations of ₹ 5 lakh or multiples thereof. Amount invested by single investor should not be less than ₹ 5 lakh (face value).

◆ Limits and the Amount of Issue of CP

6. CP can be issued as a "standalone" product. The aggregate amount of CP from an issuer shall be within the limit as approved by its Board of Directors. Banks and FIs will, however, have the flexibility to fix working capital limits duly taking into account the resource pattern of companies' financing including CPs.
7. An FI can issue CP within the overall umbrella limit fixed by the RBI, *i.e.*, issue of CP together with other instruments, *viz.*, term money borrowings, term deposits, certificates of deposit and inter-corporate deposits should not exceed 100 per cent of its net owned funds, as per the latest audited balance sheet.
8. The total amount of CP proposed to be issued should be raised within a period of two weeks from the date on which the issuer opens the issue for subscription. CP may be issued on a single date or in parts on different dates provided that in the latter case, each CP shall have the same maturity date. Every CP issue should be reported to the Chief General Manager, Industrial and Export Credit Department (IECD), Reserve Bank of India, Central Office, Mumbai through the Issuing and Paying Agent (IPA) within three days from the date of completion of the issue, incorporating details as per Schedule II.
9. Every issue of CP, including renewal, should be treated as a fresh issue.

◆ Who can act as Issuing and Paying Agent (IPA)?

10. Only a scheduled bank can act as an IPA for issuance of CP.

◆ Investment in CP

11. CP may be issued to and held by individuals, banking companies, other corporate bodies registered or incorporated in India and unincorporated bodies, Non-resident Indians (NRIs) and Foreign Institutional Investors (FIIs). However, investment by FIIs

would be within the limits set for their investments by Securities and Exchange Board of India (SEBI).

◈ Mode of Issuance

12. CP can be issued either in the form of a promissory note (Schedule I) or in a dematerialised form through any of the depositories approved by and registered with SEBI. As regards the existing stock of CP, the same can continue to be held either in physical form or can be demateralised, if both the issuer and the investor agree for the same.
13. CP will be issued at a discount to face value as may be determined by the issuer.
14. No issuer shall have the issue of Commercial Paper underwritten or co-accepted.

◈ Preference for Dematerialised Form

15. While option is available to both issuers and subscribers, to issue/hold CP in dematerialised or physical form, issuers and subscribers are encouraged to prefer exclusive reliance on dematerialised form of issue/holding. Banks, Financial Institutions, PDs and SDs are advised to invest and hold CPs only in dematerialized form, as soon as arrangements for such dematerialisation are put in place.

◈ Payment of CP

16. The initial investor in CP shall pay the discounted value of the CP by means of a crossed account payee cheque to the account of the issuer through IPA. On maturity of CP, when the CP is held in physical form, the holder of the CP shall present the instrument for payment to the issuer through the IPA. However, when the CP is held in de-mat form, the holder of the CP will have to get it redeemed through the depository and receive payment from the IPA.

◈ Stand-by Facility

17. In view of CP being a 'standalone' product, it would not be obligatory in any manner on the part of banks and FIs to provide standby facility to the issuers of CP. Banks and FIs would, however, have the flexibility to provide for a CP issue, credit enhancement by way of standby assistance/credit backstop facility, etc., based on their commercial judgement and as per terms prescribed by them. However, these should be within the prudential norms as applicable and subject to specific approval of the Board.

◈ Procedure for Issuance

18. Every issuer must appoint an IPA for issuance of CP. The issuer should disclose to the potential investors its financial position as per the standard market practice. After the exchange of deal confirmation between the investor and the issuer, issuing company shall issue physical certificates to the investor or arrange for crediting the CP to the investor's account with a depository. Investors shall be given a copy of IPA certificate to the effect that the issuer has a valid agreement with the IPA and documents are in order (Schedule III).

◈ Role and Responsibilities

19. The role and responsibilities of issuer, IPA and CRA are set out below:

(a) Issuer

With the simplification in the procedures for CP issuance, issuers would now have more flexibility. Issuers would, however, have to ensure that the guidelines and procedures laid down for CP issuance are strictly adhered to.

(b) Issuing and Paying Agent (IPA)

(*i*) IPA would ensure that issuer has the minimum credit rating as stipulated by the RBI and amount mobilised through issuance of CP is within the quantum indicated by CRA for the specified rating.

(*ii*) IPA has to verify all the documents submitted by the issuer, *viz.*, copy of board resolution, signatures of authorised executants (when CP in physical form) and issue a certificate that documents are in order. It should also certify that it has a valid agreement with the issuer (Schedule III).

(*iii*) Original documents verified by the IPA should be held in the custody of IPA.

(c) Credit Rating Agency (CRA)

(*i*) Code of Conduct prescribed by the SEBI for CRAs for undertaking rating of capital market instruments shall be applicable to them (CRAs) for rating CP.

(*ii*) Further, the credit rating agency would henceforth have the discretion to determine the validity period of the rating depending upon its perception about the strength of the issuer. Accordingly, CRA shall at the time of rating, clearly indicate the date when the rating is due for review.

(*iii*) While the CRAs can decide the validity period of credit rating, CRAs would have to closely monitor the rating assigned to issuers *vis-a-vis* their track record at regular intervals and would be required to make its revision in the ratings public through its publications and website.

21. Fixed Income Money Market and Derivatives Association of India (FIMMDA), as a self-regulatory organisation (SRO) for the fixed income money market securities, may prescribe, for operational flexibility and smooth functioning of CP market, any standardised procedure and documentation that are to be followed by the participants, in consonance with the international best practices. Till such time, the procedures/ documentations prescribed by IBA should be followed.

22. Violation of these guidelines will attract penalties prescribed in the Act by the RBI and may also include debarring from the CP market.

◈ Non-applicability of Certain Other Directions

23. Nothing contained in the Non-banking Financial Companies Acceptance of Public Deposits (Reserve Bank) Directions, 1998 shall apply to any non-banking financial company (NBFC) insofar as it relates to acceptance of deposit by issuance of CP, in accordance with these guidelines.

◈ Certificate of Deposits

A CD is a document title to a time deposit and can be distinguished from the conventional time deposit in respect of its free negotiability and hence marketability.

CD's are a marketable receipt of funds deposited in a bank for a fixed period at a specified rate of interest. They are bearer instruments and are readily negotiable.

As per the RBI scheme, the CD can be issued only by scheduled commercial banks at a discount rate from the face value, and the discount rate can be freely determined. It means that there is no restriction on the rate of interest that can be paid to a depositor.

The CD can be issued to individuals, corporates, companies, trust funds, association and so on. The NRI's can also subscribe to them, but only on non-repatriable basis.

The banks are required to maintain the usual SLR and CRR on the issue price of CDs, nor buy them back prematurely. They are freely transferable by endorsement and delivery after 45 days from the date of issue, and are in the form of usance promissory note payable on a fixed date without any grace period. The maturity period of CDs is 3-12 months. However, six all-India financial institutions are allowed to issue CDs with maturity of one to three years.

GUIDELINES OF RBI FOR ISSUANCE OF CERTIFICATES OF DEPOSITS

1. Introduction

Certificate of Deposit (CD) is a negotiable money market instrument and issued in dematerialised form or as a Usance Promissory Note against funds deposited at a bank or other eligible financial institution for a specified time period. Guidelines for issue of CDs are presently governed by various directives issued by the Reserve Bank of India (RBI), as amended from time-to-time. The guidelines for issue of CDs, incorporating all the amendments issued till date, are given below for ready reference.

2. Eligibility

CDs can be issued by (*i*) scheduled commercial banks {excluding Regional Rural Banks and Local Area Banks}; and (*ii*) select All-India Financial Institutions (FIs) that have been permitted by RBI to raise short-term resources within the umbrella limit (prescribed in paragraph 3.2 below) fixed by RBI.

3. Aggregate Amount

3.1 Banks have the freedom to issue CDs depending on their funding requirements.

3.2 An FI can issue CD within the overall umbrella limit prescribed in the Master Circular on Resource Raising Norms for FIs, issued by DBOD and updated from time-to-time.

4. Minimum Size of Issue and Denominations

Minimum amount of a CD should be ₹ 1 lakh, *i.e.*, the minimum deposit that could be accepted from a single subscriber should not be less than ₹ 1 lakh, and in multiples of ₹ 1 lakh thereafter.

5. Investors

CDs can be issued to individuals, corporations, companies, trusts, funds, associations, etc. Non-resident Indians (NRIs) may also subscribe to CDs, but only on non-repatriable basis, which should be clearly stated on the certificate. Such CDs cannot be endorsed to another NRI in the secondary market.

6. Maturity

6.1 The maturity period of CDs issued by banks should not be less than 7 days and not more than one year, from the date of issue.

6.2 The FIs can issue CDs for a period not less than one year and not exceeding three years from the date of issue.

7. Discount/Coupon Rate

CDs may be issued at a discount on face value. Banks/FIs are also allowed to issue CDs on floating rate basis provided the methodology of compiling the floating rate is objective, transparent and market-based. The issuing bank/FI is free to determine the discount/coupon rate. The interest rate on floating rate CDs would have to be reset periodically in accordance with a pre-determined formula that indicates the spread over a transparent benchmark. The investor should be clearly informed of the same.

8. Reserve Requirements

Banks have to maintain appropriate reserve requirements, *i.e.*, cash reserve ratio (CRR) and statutory liquidity ratio (SLR), on the issue price of the CDs.

9. Transferability

CDs in physical form are freely transferable by endorsement and delivery. CDs in de-mat form can be transferred as per the procedure applicable to other de-mat securities. There is lock-in period for the CDs.

9. Trades in CDs

All OTC trades in CDs shall be reported within 15 minutes of the trade on the FIMMDA reporting platform.

10. Loans/Buybacks

Banks/FIs cannot grant loans against CDs. Furthermore, they cannot buyback their own CDs before maturity. However, the RBI may relax these restrictions for temporary periods through a separate notification.

◈ Money Market Mutual Funds

To enable the small investors to participate in the money market, a money market mutual fund is a conduit through which they can earn market related yield.

MMMFs invest the funds collected from the investors in instruments like: (*a*) Treasury bills and Government securities. (*b*) Call/Notice money, (*c*) Commercial bills, (*d*) Commercial paper, (*e*) Certificate of deposit.

They are free to determine the extent of their investments in each of the above instruments; in accordance with the guidelines laid down by the RBI.

◈ Repos and Reverse Repos

Repo/ready forward/purchase (buyback) transactions/deal is an agreement between a seller and buyer stipulating the sale and later repurchase of securities at a particular price and a date. It is essentially a short-term loan to the seller with securities issued as collateral. Similarly, the buyer purchases securities with an agreement to sell the same to the seller on an agreed date in future at a prefixed price. For the buyer of the securities it is a reverse repo deal.

In a standard ready forward transaction (repo) when a bank, sells securities to another bank, it simultaneously enters into a contract with the latter to repurchase them at a predetermined date and price in future. Both sale and repurchase prices are determined prior to entering in a deal.

◆ Revised Scheme of Liquidity Adjustment Facility

Under this scheme both Repo and Reverse Repo operations are conducted everyday. The maximum period for Repo transactions is seven days while for Reverse Reop it is overnight only.

The transactions are conducted at a fixed rate. RBI sets these rates periodically. RBI however has a right to conduct these transactions at variable rates depending on the conditions prevailing in the markets.

All Scheduled Commercial Banks (excluding Regional Rural Banks) and Primary Dealers (PDs) having Current Account and SGL Account with Reserve Bank, Mumbai will be eligible to participate in the Repo and Reverse Repo auctions. Bids are received for a minimum amount of ₹ 5 crore and in multiples of ₹ 5 crore thereafter. Repos and Reverse Repos are undertaken in all SLR-eligible transferable Government of India dated Securities/Treasury Bills. A margin is uniformly applied in respect of the above eligible securities. The amount of securities offered or tendered on acceptance of a bid for ₹ 100 will be ₹ 105 in terms of face value.

Securities held by the Reserve Bank on behalf of participants in RC SGL account and credit balance in the RRC SGL account will be counted for SLR purpose and a certificate is issued to banks by the Reserve Bank on a daily basis.

◆ Bills Rediscounting Scheme

Many banks offer bills discounting as a means of working capital finance. In this scheme the banks discount sales bills raised by the supplier on the buyer and this bill is accepted for payment by the buyer. This is a better way of financing working capital than giving cash credit facilities that are difficult to monitor and are open for mis-use.

Bills discounting is a post-sales activity. The seller sells goods to the buyer on credit. However he is not interested in blocking his money during the credit period granted by him. He thus asks his bank to lend this money to him through the mechanism of Bills Discounting.

Under this scheme the bank either discounts or purchases the bill from its client. It pays to the client the present value of the bill. The difference between the bill amount and the present value is the income of the discounting bank. On the due date the discounting bank is supposed to get the bill amount form the buyer, thus completing the transaction.

In view of providing liquidity to the banking system RBI allows banks to rediscount these outstanding bills with itself and introduces liquidity in the markets. The bans thus get the present value of the discounted bills from RBI and are in a position to lend this money short-term.

Thus this scheme is very useful for all concerned.

◆ Securities Trading Corporation of India Ltd. (STCI)

The RBI has set up STCI in 1994, with an authorised capital of ₹ 500 crore. The objective is to promote a secondary market in Government securities.

Its operations extend to dated Government securities, Treasury Bills, in borrowing and lending in call money markets.

◈ Market Stabilisation Bonds

Due to the immense inflow of the foreign exchange in India the RBI has to issue bonds to suck out this excess liquidity from the markets. This helps RBI to maintain stability in the Forex markets. However, this borrowing adds the government's borrowing.

The government has therefore decided to launch new bonds from fiscal 2004-05 named Market Stabilisation Bonds. The borrowings arising of this new series are not meant to finance expenditure in excess of current revenues. These bonds will be used only to suck out the excess liquidity from the market. This has been done on the advice of a working group formed by the RBI.

The RBI will hold the amounts raised through bonds in a separate account. These borrowings will add to the government's debt, the move will not impact the fiscal, except to the extent of the cost of servicing the interest on these bonds. The maturity of these bonds the timing of their launch will be decided by the RBI in consultation with the government. The tenor could be matched with the expected outflows based on RBI's assessment. There will be put and call options available on these bonds. It is expected that these bonds will be actively traded in the markets.

Introduction to Merchant Banking

Merchant banks are a very important factor in the capital markets. They have a big role to play especially, in placing equity in the primary markets, through the Initial Public Offers route.

Public money or savings play a vital role in financing many big projects. Thousands of crore are raised every year from the markets either through equity or debt from the market. The merchant banks play a crucial role in helping the corporates raise money from these markets.

The SEBI issued guideline for the merchant bankers in April 1990.

With the passage of time the role of merchant bankers has enlarged to a great extent. It is mandatory for companies raising money from the capital markets whether equity or debt to appoint merchant bankers for this purpose. For the buyback of shares also the companies will need to appoint merchant bankers to oversee the entire process.

One of the major areas where these entities will henceforth a major role is in the space of mergers and acquisitions. They will especially play a hugh role in hostile takeovers. This activity is relatively new in India but it is bound to grow in the coming years. We have already witnessed mega deals through this route. The proposed acquisition of Sahara Air by Jet Airways is one such deal.

Internationally merchant bankers are known as investment bankers mainly on account of their role valuing companies for possible takeovers and advising companies who are in the market for acquisitions. These bankers also help raise money for these takeovers.

Following the globalisation of the Indian economy we have witnessed that many Indian companies are now acquiring companies abroad. We have already seen companies like Tata Motors, TISCO, VSNL, Reliance, Bharat Forge and Dr. Reddy's, to name a few acquiring companies abroad. Many more Indian companies will be in this field from now on. All these companies will need merchant bankers to help them in this endeavour.

Activities of Merchant Bankers

The merchant banks undertake following activities:

1. Project finances advice
2. Project appraisal.
3. Capital restructuring
4. Issue management.
5. Loan syndication.
6. Foreign currency finances.
7. Investment management.
8. Mutual funds.
9. Lease finance.
10. Bills discounting.
11. Mergers and acquisitions.
12. Working capital finance.
13. Government consents.
14. Arranging fixed deposits.
15. Corporate counselling.
16. Underwriting.
17. Non-resident investments.
18. Restructuring of sick units.
19. Hire purchase.
20. Money market operations.

We shall now take a look at some of the activities that are undertaken by the merchant bankers.

Issue Management

The merchant bankers help corporates to raise money from the markets through the issue of shares, debentures, bonds, etc. They are designed as managers to the issue. Their main business is to attract public money to capital issues.

They usually render the following services:

1. Drafting of prospectus and getting it approved from the stock exchanges.
2. Obtaining consent/acknowledgement from SEBI.
3. Appointing bankers, underwriters, brokers, advertisers, printers, etc.
4. Obtaining the consent of all the agencies involved in the public issue.
5. Holding road shows, to sell the issue. These shows are held for the analysts, brokers and institutional investors. The purpose of these shows is to answer queries from these people about the company and the project for which the funds are being raised.
6. Deciding the pattern of advertising.

7. Deciding the branches where application money should be collected.
8. Deciding the dates of opening and closing of the issue.
9. Obtaining the daily report of application money collected at various branches.
10. Obtaining subscription to the issue.
11. After the close of the issue, obtaining consent of stock exchange for deciding basis of allotment, etc.

The merchant bankers help the companies to determine their capital structure.

◈ Corporate Advisory Services Relating to the Issue

In India the company, now freely decides the pricing of issues with valuable inputs from the merchant bankers, who have to sell the issue at the decided price. The pricing of the issue especially in a public issue is very important. The pricing has to be such that the investors will be attracted to invest in the issue at that price; at the same time the company should get the premium that is looking for. After all, the premium can play a very big role in deciding the company's capital structure, as larger the premium lesser will be the requirement for borrowed funds.

The promoter also needs to decide whether to go in for a fresh issue or go for a rights issue. However, this will depend mainly on the quantum of funds that the company needs to raise. The success of the issue is dependent on the selection of the right type of security. In this matter, the expert advice of the merchant bankers is of immense importance.

In the issue management the merchant bankers have to coordinate the various agencies to the issue. The success of the issue depends on the cooperation of all the agencies involved.

The merchant bankers offer following services during the public issues:

1. Preparing an action plan and budget for the total expenses for the issue.
2. Preparation of application to SEBI and assistance in obtaining the consent from SEBI.
3. Drafting of the prospectus.
4. Selection of underwriters, brokers, etc.
5. Selection of bankers to the issue.
6. Selection of advertising agency for publicity.
7. Obtaining approval of the institutional underwriters and stock exchanges for publication of the prospectus.

Companies are free to appoint one or more agencies as managers to an issue. SEBI guidelines insist that all issues should be managed by at least one authorised merchant banker, functioning either as the sole or lead manager to the issue. Ordinarily, not more than two merchant bankers should be associated as lead managers, advisors and consultants to a public issue. In issues of over ₹ 100 crore, the number could be up to a maximum of four.

The responsibilities of merchant bankers in management of public issues are many. Some of these are:

We have seen that many unscrupulous promoters have raised money from the market. This has hurt the investors a lot and has also made investors nervous about stock market investments. This in turn affects the functioning of stock markets both the primary and the secondary markets. It is therefore necessary that merchant bankers are satisfied with the viability of the project, which they can then sell to the investors with confidence. It is therefore important for the reputation of merchant bankers, to only associate themselves with good issues.

It has also been observed that many agencies associated with an issue tend to make tall claims about the promoters, the projects and the profitability, etc. The merchant bankers should act as the custodians of the investors' money and this puts a lot of responsibility on them. To discharge this function the merchant bankers have to exercise due diligence independently by verifying the contents of the prospectus and the reasonableness of the views expressed therein. Though they do not have to sign the prospectus, they have to give a certificate to that effect to SEBI.

It is the responsibility of the merchant bankers to get the securities listed on all the stock exchanges mentioned in the prospectus. It can be especially true of companies, who cannot list their shares listed on either NSE or BSE, but promise listing on several regional stock markets, but actually list them only on one or two exchanges.

Non-receipt of refund orders and allotment advice within the stipulated period is a most common complaint of the investors. With the introduction of de-mat accounts the complaints about allotment have surely gone down. It is the responsibility of the lead managers/merchant bankers to ensure timely refunds and allotment of securities to the investors.

The merchant bankers have to certify that they have verified everything and that they believe it to be true. This assures the investing public about the safety of their investment. The precautions by the merchant bankers would ensure that all the fake companies, whose intention is to defraud the investors, do not have access to the market.

◈ Underwriting

Underwriting is like insurance against the failure of an issue. It is a guarantee to the issuing the company, that the money that it requires for its project will definitely be raised. It means that even if the issue is not fully subscribed to by the public, the underwriters will make-up the short fall.

Underwriting involves the underwriter agreeing to subscribe directly, or to procure subscription for the unsubscribed portion of the issue, which is not taken up. For the risk that the underwriter takes, he is paid commission. When there is more than one underwriter to an issue the liability is shared by them on *pro rata* on the basis of amounts underwritten by them.

Underwriting is a device that ensures the success of new issues. New companies entering the markets for the first time, always face number of problems in raising funds from the market. One of the biggest problems of course that the company is not well known to the investors and many of them will be unwilling to invest their money in such ventures. Many a time even existing companies may find it difficult to raise money, due to some reasons. Issuing companies therefore approach different underwriters with a request to underwrite the issue.

Underwriters on their part need to satisfy themselves about the viability of the project and also about the integrity of the promoters of the company. It must be noted that when an issue is undersubscribed, the underwriters will pick the shares and only if the project is good enough, then in future they can sell the shares in the market and get not only their money back, but can also make a decent profit as well.

The issues, which are backed by well known underwriters, may receive a high premium from the investing public. This gives some sort of comfort level to the investors. Underwriting assures both the issuing company as well as the investing public that the issue will be a success.

It is obligatory for the merchant bankers to accept a minimum 5 per cent underwriting in the issue subject to a ceiling. By taking underwriting in an issue managed by them, they show their full commitment to the issue that they are managing. The SEBI has made it mandatory for issuing companies to underwrite all issues.

Given below are the guidelines for IPOs

◈ Public Issue

What are the eligibility norms for an unlisted company for making a public issue?

An unlisted company has to satisfy the following criteria to be eligible to make a public issue

(*i*) Pre-issue net worth of the company should not be less than ₹ 1 crore in last three out of last five years with minimum net worth to be met during immediately preceding two years and

(*ii*) track record of distributable profits for at least three (3) out of immediately preceding five (5) years and

(*iii*) The issue size (*i.e.*, offer through offer document + firm allotment + promoters' contribution through the offer document) shall not exceed five (5) times its pre-issue net worth.

In case an unlisted company does not satisfy any of the above criterions, it can come out with a public issue only through the book-building process. In the book-building process the company has to compulsorily allot at least sixty per cent (60 per cent) of the issue size to the Qualified Institutional Buyers (QIBs), failing which the full subscription monies shall be refunded.

What are the eligibility norms for a listed company for making a public issue?

A listed company is eligible to make a public issue if the issue size (*i.e.*, offer through offer document + firm allotment + promoters' contribution through the offer document) is less than five (5) times its pre-issue net worth.

If the issue size is more than or equal to five times of pre-issue net worth, then the listed company has to take the book-building route and allot sixty per cent (60 per cent) of the issue size to the Qualified Institutional Buyers (QIBs), failing which the full subscription monies shall be refunded.

For details refer Chapter II of SEBI (DIP) Guidelines and relevant clarifications issued subsequently.

Are there any restrictions on pricing by companies?

The companies can freely price their equity shares. However they have to give justification of the price in the offer document/letter of offer.

What are the requirements regarding promoter's contribution and lock-in?

In case of an Initial Public Offer (IPO), *i.e.*, public issue by unlisted company, the promoters have to necessarily offer at least 20 per cent of the post-issue capital.

In case of public issues by listed companies, the promoters shall participate either to the extent of 20 per cent of the proposed issue or ensure post-issue shareholding to the extent of 20 per cent of the post-issue capital.

In case of any issue of capital to the public the minimum contribution of promoters shall be locked-in for a period of three years, both for an IPO and public issue by listed companies.

In case of an IPO, if the promoter's contribution in the proposed issue exceeds the required minimum contribution, such excess contribution shall also be locked-in for a period of one year.

In case of a public issue by a listed company, participation by promoters in the proposed public issue in excess of the required minimum percentage shall also be locked-in for a period of one year as per the lock-in provisions as specified in guidelines on preferential issue.

Beside the above, in case of IPO the entire pre-issue share capital, *i.e.*, paid-up share capital prior to IPO and shares issued on a firm allotment basis along with issue shall be locked-in for a period of one year from the date of allotment in public issue.

What is the basis of allotment?

In case of oversubscription in a fixed price issue the allotment is done in marketable lots, on a proportionate basis (for details refer to clause 7.6.1 of DIP guidelines).

In case of a book-building issue, allotment to Qualified Institutional Buyers and Non-institutional buyers are done on a discretionary basis. Allotment to retail investors is done on a proportionate basis as per provisions of Clause No. 7.6.1 of guidelines.

How does one come to know of issues on offer and from where can one get copies of the draft offer document?

Every week SEBI issues press releases for information of the public, details of offer documents filed with SEBI and observations issued. Details can be obtained from the "Primary Market" page of the SEBI website. The draft offer document can also be purchased from the SEBI office where the document is filed on payment of ₹ 100 by way of DD drawn in favour of SEBI. The draft offer document/letter of offer remains posted on SEBI website for a period of 21days from the date of filing the same to SEBI and can also be downloaded from there.

From where does one get the application forms and the prospectus?

Application form can be obtained from the lead manager and brokers to the issue. The application forms are also generally available at collecting bankers. Name and addresses of the lead manager are available in the prospectus/letter of offer.

Can the public give their comments/complaints on the Issuer company or others connected with the issue?

Yes, the objective of making offer document public is to invite public comments. The comments should be given within 21 days of the filing of the draft offer document with SEBI.

Where does one complain in case of wrong/non-disclosures/mis-statement in the offer document?

The Primary Market Division in SEBI.

Within how many days an investor should receive the refund order/allotment advice?

Despatch of refund orders/allotment advice is to be within 2 working days of finalisation of the basis of allotment.

Companies are required to finalise the basis of allotment within 30 days from the closure of the issue in case of a fixed price issue and within 15 days from the closure of the issue in case of a book-building issue or else they are liable to pay interest @ 15 per cent p.a.

In case of non-receipt of the refund order/share certificate/allotment advise what is the course of action available to the investor?

The investor should give his complaint in writing to the lead manager/registrar/Investor Grievance Cell of SEBI.

Within how many days should the company get its securities listed after the issue?

The post-issue lead manager ensures that all steps for completion of the necessary formalities for listing and commencement of trading at all stock exchanges where the securities are to be listed are taken within 7 working days of finalisation of basis of allotment.

From where can I get the addresses of the companies and details of change of names, etc.?

From the stock exchanges and Registrar of Companies.

What is Book-building?

SEBI guidelines define book-building as a process undertaken by which a demand for the securities proposed to be issued by a corporate body is elicited and built up and the price for such securities is assessed for the determination of the quantum of such securities to be issued by means of a notice, circular, advertisement, document or information memoranda or offer document.

What is the main difference between offer of shares through book-building and offer of shares through normal public issue?

Price at which securities will be allotted is not known in case of offer of shares through book-building while in case of offer of shares through normal public issue, price is known in advance to investor. In case of book-building, the demand can be known everyday as the book is built. But in case of the public issue the demand is known at the close of the issue.

What is minimum number of days for which bid should remain open in book-building?

Book should remain open for minimum of five days.

Can open outcry system be used for book-building?

No. As per SEBI, only electronically linked transparent facility is allowed to be used in case of book-building.

Is the issue pricing for placement portion and net offer to public the same?

Yes.

What is the floor price in case of book-building?

Floor price is the minimum price at which bids can be made.

Can the individual investor use book-building facility for making an application?

Yes.

Can the bidder revise his bids?

Yes.

What proof can bidder request from trading member for entering bids?

A bidder can request for a transaction registration slip as the proof of his/her having entered the bid. Whenever trading members into the system enters a bid, a unique transaction registration slip is automatically generated. Transaction registration slip gives details regarding number of shares bidded for, price, the client name, etc.

Is it possible to enter bids less than floor price?

No. The system automatically rejects the bids if price is less than floor price.

Merchant bankers have to be careful about the pricing of an issue. In the IPO of Reliance Power in 2008 this came to the centre stage. The issue was oversubscribed @ a price of ₹ 450 with 5 per cent discount to retail investors. The general impression that had got created was that the post-listing price would be around ₹ 700, in reality the price fell below issue price on the day of listing. Many investors had applied for the IPO hoping to make a decent profit on listing. This did not happen and panic spread in markets leading to unwinding of positions by many players pulling the price down further.

It must be understood here that the company was unlikely to make sufficient profits in the first five years of its operations as power projects have long gestation period and are extremely capital-intensive. The realization seemed to have dawned on the investors only after the listing. This has been seen in many issues. The company and merchant bankers tend to aggressively price some issues that are backed by good past record. This is what happened here. The name Reliance was a respected name in the market and some investors had blind faith in the name. What they did not realise was this the first issue from the group after the split between the brothers. Many did not take this into account at all.

What happened later was bizarre to put it mildly. Anil Ambani offered to give bonus shares to investors who had bought shares in the IPO and had seen the valued of their investments deteriorate rapidly post-listing. A bonus was declared and given, effectively bringing down the purchase value of shares by the investors. This must be the first case where a company that had no revenue and hence no profit was allowed to make a bonus issue! The regulators did not interfere and let the issue go through. What was more stunning was that Anil Ambani himself gave up his entitlement of bonus as a shareholder and bonus shares were allotted from his shares in the company thus bringing down his holding in the company post-bonus issue! All this is unprecedented.

Another thing that is seen at times is companies that are planning to go public in near future make a preferential allotment to Private Equity players at a sizeable premium. This sets the premium for the public offering indirectly. This also increases the company's net worth and paid-up capital. Thus the company can now make a much larger offering. It has been observed by market watchers that these funds sell-off their shares immediately after the listing making huge profits in the process. This is being done regularly and no action has been forthcoming wither SEBI or the CLB.

Corporate Services

This kind of services can be of following nature:

They provide guidance in area of diversification. They appraise projects for their clients. They help ailing companies to appraise their technology and processes, and assessing their requirements and restructuring their capital base. They also interact with banks and financial institutions for rehabilitation of these industries. They also monitor the rehabilitation of these schemes.

The area of corporate counselling is vast which covers any matter worth the benefit for a corporate unit, involving financial aspects, government regulations, policy changes and the business environment.

Project Counselling

These relate to project finance and broadly cover the study of the project and offering advisory assistance on the viability of the project and the steps for the implementation. This will also involve the study of the technical feasibility of the project. They also help in preparation of the project report.

Loan Syndication

This involves the preparation and submission of applications to the financial institutions and banks. They help finalise the cost of the project. They also help in the estimation of working capital requirements. Finally the funding for the project is to be tied-up with various lenders, who will take exposure in funding the total cost of the project.

Merchant bankers need to possess following qualities:

They must have knowledge and information about the various aspects of the capital markets, trends prevailing in the markets and the psychology of the investors.

They must have the ability to evaluate and analyse various aspects concerning, the formation of an industrial project and affecting the viability and the profitability of the project.

Integrity and maintenance of high professional standards are necessary for their success.

Due to the new developments in capital markets, the needs of the corporate clients are changing rapidly. For this they must be more involved with the clients and must update their knowledge.

SEBI Guidelines for Merchant Bankers

They have to obtain an authorisation from them SEBI and strictly adhere to the guidelines laid down.

They should have necessary expertise, good financial standing, maintain high degree of professional integrity and fairness in their transactions and take greater responsibility in disclosures about issues and post-issue allotments and refunds.

It is expected they would ensure that the company abides by the various requirements relating to disclosures, listing of instruments, etc.

◆ Categories of Merchant Bankers

Due to the nature and range of activities of the merchant bankers, and their responsibilities toward SEBI, investors, and the issuers of the securities, it has been decided to have the following three categories of merchant bankers.

Merchant bankers in this category must have a minimum net worth of ₹ 1 crore, in II category the net worth requirement is ₹ 50 lakh, and for category three the net worth requirement is ₹ 20 lakh. Initial authorisation fee for the three categories is ₹ 5 lakh, ₹ 3 lakh and ₹ 1 lakh.

For issues up to ₹ 50 crore, the number of lead managers will not exceed two, for issues above ₹ 50 crore and up to ₹ 100 crore the maximum number will be three and for issues above ₹ 100 crore the number can go up to a maximum of four. There is no limit fixed for the number of co-managers. The company and the lead managers are free to decide the number.

ANNEXURE

◈ Guidelines for Listing

Listing means admission of securities to dealings on a recognised stock exchange. The securities may be of any public limited company, Central or State government, quasi-governmental and other financial institutions/corporations, municipalities, etc.

The objectives of listing are mainly to:

- provide liquidity to securities;
- mobilize savings for economic development;
- protect interest of investors by ensuring full disclosures.

The Bombay Stock Exchange (BSE) has a dedicated Listing Department to grant approval for listing of securities of companies in accordance with the provisions of the Securities Contracts (Regulation) Act, 1956, Securities Contracts (Regulation) Rules, 1957, Companies Act, 1956, Guidelines issued by SEBI and Rules, Bye-laws and Regulations of BSE.

BSE has set various guidelines and forms that need to be adhered to and submitted by the companies. These guidelines will help companies to expedite the fulfilment of the various formalities and disclosure requirements that are required at various stages of

- Public Issues
- Initial Public Offering
- Further Public Offering
- Preferential Issues
- Indian Depository Receipts
- Amalgamation
- Qualified Institutional Placements

A company intending to have its securities listed on BSE has to comply with the listing requirements prescribed by it. Some of the requirements are as under:

I. Minimum Listing Requirements for New Companies

II. Minimum Listing Requirements for Companies already listed on other Stock Exchanges

III. Minimum Requirements for Companies Delisted by BSE seeking relisting on BSE

IV. Permission to Use the Name of BSE in an Issuer Company's Prospectus

V. Submission of Letter of Application

VI. Allotment of Securities

VII. Trading Permission

VIII. Requirement of 1 per cent Security

IX. Payment of Listing Fees

X. Compliance with the Listing Agreement

XI. Cash Management Services (CMS) — Collection of Listing Fees

[I] Minimum Listing Requirements for New Companies

The following eligibility criteria have been prescribed effective August 1, 2006 for listing of companies on BSE, through Initial Public Offerings (IPOs) and Follow-on Public Offerings (FPOs):

1. Companies have been classified as large cap companies and small cap companies. A large cap company is a company with a minimum issue size of ₹ 10 crore and market capitalization of not less than ₹ 25 crore. A small cap company is a company other than a large cap company.

(*a*) In respect of Large Cap Companies

(*i*) The minimum post-issue paid-up capital of the applicant company (hereinafter referred to as "the Company") shall be ₹ 3 crore; and

(*ii*) The minimum issue size shall be ₹ 10 crore; and

(*iii*) The minimum market capitalization of the company shall be ₹ 25 crore (market capitalization shall be calculated by multiplying the post-issue paid-up number of equity shares with the issue price).

(*b*) In respect of Small Cap Companies

(*i*) The minimum post-issue paid-up capital of the company shall be ₹ 3 crore; and

(*ii*) The minimum issue size shall be ₹ 3 crore; and

(*iii*) The minimum market capitalization of the company shall be ₹ 5 crore (market capitalization shall be calculated by multiplying the post-issue paid-up number of equity shares with the issue price); and

(*iv*) The minimum income/turnover of the company shall be ₹ 3 crore in each of the preceding three 12-months period; and

(*v*) The minimum number of public shareholders after the issue shall be 1,000.

(*vi*) A due diligence study may be conducted by an independent team of Chartered Accountants or Merchant Bankers appointed by BSE, the cost of which will be borne by the company. The requirement of a due diligence study may be waived if a financial institution or a scheduled commercial bank has appraised the project in the preceding 12 months.

2. For all companies:

(*a*) In respect of the requirement of paid-up capital and market capitalization, the issuers shall be required to include in the disclaimer clause forming a part of the offer document that in the event of the market capitalization (product of issue price and the post-issue number of shares) requirement of BSE not being met, the securities of the issuer would not be listed on BSE.

(*b*) The applicant, promoters and/or group companies, shall not be in default in compliance of the listing agreement.

(*c*) The above eligibility criteria would be in addition to the conditions prescribed under SEBI (Disclosure and Investor Protection) Guidelines, 2000.

[II] Minimum Listing Requirements for Companies Already Listed on Other Stock Exchanges

The listing norms for companies already listed on other stock exchanges and seeking listing at BSE, made effective from August 6, 2002, are as under:

1. The company shall have a minimum issued and paid-up equity capital of ₹ 3 crore.
2. The company shall have a profit making track record for the preceding last three years. The revenues/profits arising out of extra ordinary items or income from any source of non-recurring nature shall be excluded while calculating the profit making track record.
3. Minimum net worth shall be ₹ 20 crore (net worth includes equity capital and free reserves excluding revaluation reserves).
4. Minimum market capitalisation of the listed capital shall be at least two times of the paid-up capital.
5. The company shall have a dividend paying track record for at least the last three consecutive years and the dividend should be at least 10 per cent in each year.
6. Minimum 25 per cent of the company's issued capital shall be with Non-promoter shareholders as per Clause 35 of the Listing Agreement. Out of above Non-promoter holding, no single shareholder shall hold more than 0.5 per cent of the paid-up capital of the company individually or jointly with others except in case of Banks/ Financial Institutions/Foreign Institutional Investors/Overseas Corporate Bodies and Non-resident Indians.
7. The company shall have at least two years listing record with any of the Regional Stock Exchanges.
8. The company shall sign an agreement with CDSL and NSDL for de-mat trading.

[III] Minimum Requirements for Companies Delisted by BSE Seeking Relisting on BSE

Companies delisted by BSE and seeking relisting at BSE are required to make a fresh public offer and comply with the extant guidelines of SEBI and BSE regarding initial public offerings.

[IV] Permission to Use the Name of BSE in an Issuer Company's Prospectus

Companies desiring to list their securities offered through a public issue are required to obtain prior permission of BSE to use the name of BSE in their prospectus or offer for sale documents before filing the same with the concerned office of the Registrar of Companies.

BSE has a Listing Committee, comprising of market experts, which decides upon the matter of granting permission to companies to use the name of BSE in their prospectus/offer documents. This Committee evaluates the promoters, company, project, financials, risk factors and several other aspects before taking a decision in this regard.

Decision with regard to some types/sizes of companies has been delegated to the Internal Committee of BSE.

[V] Submission of Letter of Application

As per Section 73 of the Companies Act, 1956, a company seeking listing of its securities on BSE is required to submit a Letter of Application to all the stock exchanges where it proposes to have its securities listed before filing the prospectus with the Registrar of Companies.

[VI] Allotment of Securities

As per the Listing Agreement, a company is required to complete the allotment of securities offered to the public within 30 days of the date of closure of the subscription list and approach the Designated Stock Exchange for approval of the basis of allotment.

In case of book-building issues, allotment shall be made not later than 15 days from the closure of the issue, failing which interest at the rate of 15 per cent shall be paid to the investors.

[VII] Trading Permission Top

As per SEBI Guidelines, an issuer company should complete the formalities for trading at all the stock exchanges where the securities are to be listed within seven working days of finalization of the basis of allotment.

A company should scrupulously adhere to the time limit specified in SEBI (Disclosure and Investor Protection) Guidelines 2000 for allotment of all securities and dispatch of allotment letters/share certificates/credit in depository accounts and refund orders and for obtaining the listing permissions of all the exchanges whose names are stated in its prospectus or offer document. In the event of listing permission to a company being denied by any stock exchange where it had applied for listing of its securities, the company cannot proceed with the allotment of shares. However, the company may file an appeal before SEBI under Section 22 of the Securities Contracts (Regulation) Act, 1956.

[VIII] Requirement of 1 per cent Security

Companies making public/rights issues are required to deposit 1 per cent of the issue amount with the Designated Stock Exchange before the issue opens. This amount is liable to be forfeited in the event of the company not resolving the complaints of investors regarding delay in sending refund orders/share certificates, non-payment of commission to underwriters, brokers, etc.

[IX] Payment of Listing Fees

All companies listed on BSE are required to pay to BSE the Annual Listing Fees by 30th April of every financial year as per the Schedule of Listing Fees prescribed from time-to-time.

◈ What is a Rolling Settlement?

What is the difference between a rolling settlement and the prevailing weekly settlement?

A rolling settlement is one in which trades outstanding at the end of the day have to be settled (payments made for purchases or deliveries in the case of sale of securities) at the end of the settlement period.

In a T+5 rolling settlement, a transaction entered into Monday has to be settled on the fifth working day, which will be the subsequent Monday, when either payin or payout takes place.

As opposed to this, in a weekly settlement, the transactions made during any of the five trading days are permitted to be squared up — or purchases offset against sales — during the same settlement period.

Only those transactions, which are outstanding at the end of the last trading day, are required to be settled by payments or deliveries.

Internationally, most developed countries follow the rolling settlement system. For instance, both the US and UK follow a rolling settlement (T+3) system, and the German stock exchanges follow a T+2 settlement cycle.

In India we are presently following the settlement cycle of T+3. It has been proposed by SEBI that from April 1st, 2003 T+2 will come in force, with the intention of finally moving towards T+1 settlement cycle.

What are the advantages of rolling settlements?

In rolling settlements, payments are quicker than in the weekly settlements. Thus, investors benefit from increased liquidity. For example, in a rolling settlement system, investors would receive the payments on the fifth day after the sale. The National Stock Exchange was the first to introduce rolling settlements in the country.

Rolling settlements could not be introduced earlier because India did not have depositories. Rolling settlements necessarily require electronic transfers of funds and de-mat facilities in respect of securities being traded. This is because handling large volumes of paper on a daily basis is extremely difficult for the clearing houses of stock exchanges.

It is only now that India has adequate facilities for electronic delivery of shares (de-mat shares), which facilitates trading and clearing large volumes on a daily basis. However, transfer of funds in India still takes two to three days, as all banks are not yet connected electronically with all their branches.

India is probably the only market where settlement is done on T+2 basis. As a matter of fact SEBI is thinking of moving to T+1 basis. With Real Time Gross Settlement (RTGS) system now available across banking system it is quite feasible to move on to this method.

One thing needs to be greatly appreciated and which is not in that Indian markets have seen almost seamless transactions for past many years. This is a great achievement. We have rarely seen the system not functioning or mal-functioning. The people who trades have hardly complained about the settlement process as shares and money is gets transferred regularly without any problem.

DEREVATIVES IN STOCK MARKETS

◈ Index Futures

THE Securities and Exchange Board of India (SEBI) has recently taken a decision to expand trading in derivatives to options on stock market indices and on individual stocks. The risk containment and software related issues are being worked out.

Index futures have recently made their entry into Indian markets and even though the volumes are still small these are picking up. When you buy or sell an index future, you take a view on what the index (say the sensex) will be at some point in the future.

Simply put, derivatives allow investors to trade in instruments derived from the cash market, where typically buyers take delivery on payment of cash. Such instruments — futures and options — allow investors to hedge their risk or even take speculative positions.

How can you hedge using these instruments?

This is how it works: if you feel the market is going to fall and the value of your portfolio is going to diminish you take a position on the futures market.

If it rises, then even though there is a loss on the futures position, the underlying cash portfolio rises and this help risk minimisation. It is for this reason that indices, which mirror closely a very wide basket of stocks, prove successful in index futures trading.

What is a futures contract?

A futures contract is an agreement between a buyer and a seller for the purchase and sale of a particular asset at a specific future date. The asset in the case of index futures is an index — it could be the S&P CNX Nifty index or the BSE30 sensex.

With passage of time, several more indices are going to be allowed to be traded on the futures markets. In a futures contract, the price at which the asset would change hands in the future is agreed upon at the time of entering into the contract. A futures contract involves an obligation on both the parties to fulfil the terms of the contract.

What is the period for which a futures position could be taken?

Currently, both the stock exchanges have come out only with three contracts: one month, two month and three month contracts each of which expires on the last Friday of the respective month. More flexibility is expected to be introduced as index futures catches up.

What are options?

Options are contracts which go a step further than futures contracts in the sense that they provide the buyer of the option the right, without the obligation, to buy or sell a specified asset at an agreed price on or up to a particular date.

For acquiring this right, the buyer has to pay a premium to the seller. The seller on the other hand, has the obligation to buy or sell that specified asset at that agreed price. This makes options more of an insurance product where the downside risk is covered for the payment of a certain fixed premium.

So the loss would be minimised to the extent of the premium paid, like in an insurance product.

An option is a contract, which gives the buyer the right, but not the obligation, to buy or sell specified quantity of the underlying assets, at a specific price on or before a specified time. The underlying asset may be physical commodities like wheat, cotton, gold, oil or financial instruments like equity stocks, stock index, bonds, etc.

Example, an investor buys a call option to purchase equity shares of BSES Ltd., at the end of 30 days at a price of ₹ 200 at a premium of ₹ 10. If the market price of the share on the day of expiry is say ₹ 230, the investor will exercise the option and buy the share at ₹ 200 and earn ₹ 20 per share (₹ 230 – ₹ 200 – ₹ 10). On the other hand, if the market price falls to say ₹ 170, then the investor will not exercise the option, and the maximum loss to him will be only ₹ 10 being the option premium paid. Thus the losses are limited while the profits are unlimited.

While the American style option can be exercised on or before the expiration date, the European style option can be exercised only on the expiration date.

What is a call or put option?

The right to buy is called a call option while the right to sell is called a put option. The buyer of the call option can call upon the seller of the option and buy from him, the underlying instrument, at any point in time on or before the expiry date by exercising his option at the agreed price.

The seller of the option has to fulfil the obligation on exercise of the option. The right to sell is called the put option where the buyer of the option can exercise his right to sell the underlying instrument to the seller of the option, at the agreed price.

The technical group of SEBI has decided that stocks to be eligible for options trading should meet the following criteria.

The market capitalisation during the preceding six months and average free float market capitalisation (non-promoter holding in the stock) should not be less than ₹ 750 crore.

The stock should appear in the list of top 200 scrips based on the average daily volume during the preceding six months which should not be less than ₹ 5 crore in the underlying cash market.

The stocks should be traded at least 90 per cent of the trading days during the preceding six months.

Non-promoter holding in the company should be at least 30 per cent.

The ratio of daily volatility of the stock *vis-a-vis* daily volatility of index should not be more than four, at any time during the preceding six months.

It must be made clear here that trading in derivatives is not easy and should not be indulged in by people who are not well versed in the way the system operates. Many have suffered losses in these markets all over the world. This platform is best for institutional investors as opposed to individual investors. Many experts' advice retail investors to stay away from these markets.

Derivatives are actually to be used as a hedging tool to minimize potential losses. However for the past many years they are being aggressively used for speculative activities. This has created havoc in many markets across the world. The US economic crisis of 2008 was largely due to the misuse of this product in the mortgage markets. Warren Buffett once called derivatives "Weapons of mass destruction". 2008 proved how prophetic his words turned out to be!

◈ Depository and Dematerialisation

Shares were traditionally held in physical or paper form. This method has its own inherent weaknesses like loss/theft of certificates, forged/fake certificates, cumbersome and time-consuming procedure for transfer of shares, etc. Therefore, to eliminate these weaknesses, a new system called Depository System has been established.

A depository is a system, which holds your shares in the form of electronic accounts in the same way a bank holds your money in a saving account.

Depository system provides the following advantages to an investor:

- Your shares cannot be lost or stolen or mutilated.
- You never need to doubt the genuineness of your shares, *i.e.*, whether they are forged or fake.
- Share transactions like transfer; transmission, etc., can be effected immediately.
- Transaction costs are usually lower than that in the physical segment.
- There is no risk of bad delivery.
- Bonus/Rights shares allotted to you will be immediately credited to your account.
- You will receive the statement of account of your transactions/holding periodically.

When the investor decides to have the shares in electronic form, one should approach Depository Participants (DP) who is an agent of the depository and open an account. The investor should surrender his share certificates in physical form and the DP will arrange to get them sent to and verified by the company and on confirmation credit his account with an equivalent number of shares. This process is known as dematerialisation. The investor can always reverse this process if he so desires and get his shares converted into paper form. This process is known as rematerialisation.

Share transactions like sale or purchase and transfer/transmission, etc., in the electronic form can be effected in a much simpler and faster way. All one needs to do is that after confirmation of sale/purchase transaction by the broker, one should approach one's DP with a request to credit/debit one's account for the transaction. The depository will immediately arrange to complete the transaction by updating your account. There is no need for separate communication to the company to register the transfer.

Due to the advantages of dematerialisation of shares, it is advisable that all investors should switch over to this system. As a matter of fact all securities in the group on both BSE and NSE are transacted only in dematerialised form. SEBI has also permitted companies making initial public offering to allot share only in this form.

Many investors in India now hold shares in this form only. However the charges by banks are a major concern. Maintaining an account costs anything between ₹ 300-500 per annum and one has to pay a charge for every transaction in account. There has been a demand from activists that the maintenance charges of these accounts should be borne by the listed companies. The argument is that these companies have saved a lot of money due to this system as they now do not have to print and send dividend warrants to the shareholders. This has resulted in a sizeable cost savings for them and thus they can now bear the account maintenance charges. It is believed that there are only about 80 lakh investors actively investing in markets and the number of accounts would be more than this. Thus the financial burden on 6,000 plus listed companies would not be much. We can obviously make institutional investors to pay for their accounts as they do not need this facility.

The new initiative now is to not to send to the shareholders the printed bulky Annual Reports. Under "Green Initiative" companies have now decided to send annual reports in electronic form. This is a good initiative. It is environmentally friendly and will also reduce the costs of the companies a great deal. It is a fact that most shareholders do not bother to read these reports at all. Most of those who read do not completely understand them. Shareholders can a get a hard copy on request, thus those make this request, companies are required to send them a hard copy.

◈ The National Securities Depository Ltd. (NSDL)

IDBI, UTI and the NSE to provide electronic depository facilities for stock traded in the equity and debt market promote NSDL. NSDL has been registered with SEBI and was launched on November 7, 1996 as India's first depository to facilitate trading and settlement of securities in dematerialised form. Settlement of securities in dematerialised form will eliminate problems that are normally associated with settlement through physical certificates, like tearing/mutilation of share certificates due to careless handling, loss of certificates in the post or delays with registrars, problems of bad delivery of shares. Cases of forgery of certificates get eliminated in the electronic trading system. Settlement of trades will be faster and hassle-free leading to shorter settlement cycles.

◈ Depository

A depository is an organization where the securities where the securities of a shareholder are held in the electronic form at the request of the shareholder through the medium of a depository participant.

A depository is a bank of securities.

The depository can legally transfer beneficial ownership, which a custodian cannot.

The main objective of a depository is to minimise paperwork involved with the ownership, trading and transfer of securities.

◈ Facilities Offered by NSDL

1. Enable surrender and withdrawal of securities to and from the depository.
2. Rolling settlement — Electronic form.

3. Effect settlement of securities traded on the exchanges.
4. Carry-out settlement of trades not done on the stock exchanges.

◆ Non-voting Shares (NVS)

Shareholders have two rights (a) dividend, and (b) voting rights. In case of non-voting shares one right gets excluded, *i.e.*, the shareholder looses the right to vote, even though he is the member of the company and may attend the annual general meeting of the company. They usually are not entitled to rights or bonus issues of shares of the concerned company.

NVS therefore have to be more attractive than those that carry full voting rights are. This can be done in two ways: (a) by giving discount on the issue price, and (b) by giving higher dividend on these shares.

Theoretically these shares will quote at a discount to the price of normal shares.

Industry needs resources for modernization, expansion and new projects. But raising funds by way of equity has an inherent danger of losing control to others. The ability to raise debt has its own limitations. NVS can provide a way out to companies to garner equity without dilution of the promoters' stake and control.

There can always be investors who would prefer a higher return, rather than right to vote. It is evident that very few shareholders actually turn up for the annual general meetings of the companies. As is evident from the recent experience of voting through postal ballot, it reinforces the view that many shareholders are not really interested in the affairs of the company or wish to participate in the affairs of the company.

◆ Differential Voting Rights (DVR)

This is a scheme that is slightly different from the earlier one. In India we follow the principal of one share one vote. This means that a shareholder's votes are equal to the number of shares that he holds.

Under this scheme the voting rights are not one share one vote but the shareholders have lesser votes as compared to the number of shares that they hold. For example, Tata Motors has issued this type of shares. Under their scheme a shareholder has one vote for every ten shares that he holds. However, these shareholders get extra five per cent dividend than what the equity shareholders are paid. This compensation is paid to them for sacrificing their voting power. It must be acknowledged that most retail investors hardly ever exercise their voting rights. So if they were to give up or are willing to have lesser voting rights than normal they can be rewarded with additional dividend. This is also beneficial for the promoters as even though they raise more capital the dilution of their voting rights is minimal under this scheme.

In spite of the advantages this scheme has still not caught on and very few companies like Gujarat NRE Coke have used it. Hopefully in future we will see more such issues from companies.

◆ Bonus Debentures of HLL

Recently Hindustan Lever one of the most respected companies in India has come out with a unique product called Bonus Debentures. This is the first time that such a product has been introduced and promises to be a popular product in future.

The scheme, formulated under Sections 391 to 394 of the Companies Act, entails issue and allotment of bonus debentures of the face value of ₹ 6/- each, in the ratio of one fully paid debenture of ₹ 6/- each for every rupee one equity share held in the company on a record date to be fixed by the Board after the scheme is sanctioned by the Bombay High Court. The debentures would be secured, and redeemable at par in two equal instalments on the second and third anniversary of the issue. Shareholders can trade on the debentures post-allotment, since they would be listed on the NSE and the BSE. The debentures would carry an interest rate of 9 per cent per annum payable annually. The debentures would be considered as a 'deemed dividend' under the provisions of the Income Tax Act. HLL would bear and pay, in addition, dividend distribution tax at 10.2 per cent on the issue from the General Reserves.

The issue and allotment of the debentures will account for approximately ₹ 1,320 crore from the General Reserves. The dividend distribution tax will account for about ₹ 135 crore from the General Reserves. Thus a total amount of approximately ₹ 1,455 crore would be utilised from HLL's General Reserves of ₹ 1,609 crore (as at December 31, 2000).

HLL will now make necessary applications to the Bombay High Court for its directions for convening a meeting of shareholders to seek their consent.

HLL decided to issue bonus debentures to enhance the efficiency of the balance sheet in the context of excess cash carried for several years. The scheme will significantly increase HLL's Return on Net Worth and reduce the cost of capital.

The scheme is equitable to each and every shareholder, including the parent company, Unilever, because every shareholder receives one debenture each for every equity share held in the company. The scheme is predicated on improving the efficiency of HLL's balance sheet, while benefiting all shareholders.

HLL had evaluated other options to deal with the issue of surplus cash. A cash dividend was ruled out because under the Companies Act, a company can pay dividend out of General Reserves, within specified limits, only when it has incurred a loss or there is inadequacy of profits, neither of which is the case with HLL. In the circumstances, a special dividend could have been paid only under a court scheme. The proposed bonus debentures scheme has the benefit of retaining access to the cash for exploiting any business opportunity that may come up within a defined timeframe of three years, while at the same time unlocking value to the shareholders immediately.

A buyback would not have been equitable to every shareholder, because not all shareholders would have diluted their holdings. Apart from this, a buyback would need to be staggered over a period of at least three years, and would have accounted for only fewer than 3 per cent of HLL's equity.

HLL also rejected the option of invoking Section 100 of the Companies Act reducing the face value of its rupee one shares to a lower amount, and returning the differential amount to shareholders with a suitable premium. Besides being tedious and administratively cumbersome, there was no benefit in altering the basic share capital structure of the company.

Bonus shares were not considered because it would have merely implied conversion of General Reserves into equity shares without any underlying outflow of cash, the basic issue being addressed by this scheme. Bonus shares would also involve permanent increase in the company's equity capital. In the case of a bonus issue, HLL would have continued to have cash and capital in excess of needs, with the attendant dilution of Return on Net Worth/ Return on Capital.

Hence, the proposed issue of bonus debentures came up as the most viable route to improve the efficiency of HLL's balance sheet, while benefiting all shareholders. Payment of interest on debentures would lead to a marginal dilution in earnings, but it is estimated that the dilution would be in the order of about 40 paisa per share in the first year of implementation. However, in real terms, shareholders would now have two streams of cash flow — one by way of dividend on shares and the other by debenture interest/redemption.

The scheme contemplates that small debentureholders — holding less than 1,000 debentures — who are original allottee can tender their debentures to the company at any time on a first-come-first-serve basis for repurchase at par. This facility would be available to a maximum extent of ₹ 100 crore in any year.

The company is also in discussion with its merchant bankers (HSBC), to lead a consortium of banks and financial institutions to formulate a scheme under which debentureholders could sell their debentures to them soon after their allotment should they wish to do so within a defined timeframe. The company has been advised that sale/redemption of debentures at par (₹ 6/- per debenture) will not attract any capital gains tax in the hands of the shareholder, being a deemed dividend; HLL will pay dividend distribution tax at 10.2 per cent on this distribution. Interest on the debentures will be taxable on receipt in the normal course.

HSBC, which assisted the company in formulating the bonus debentures scheme, has been appointed as the merchant bankers for the scheme.

The Bonus Debenture does not in any way impair HLL's capability to make capital investments to fund the growth of existing businesses, enter into new businesses or to execute a large acquisition should such an opportunity arise. Even after the proposed restructuring of the General Reserves by issue of debentures by way of deemed dividend out of the General Reserves, HLL would have a strong balance sheet. This would enable it to make significant acquisitions should such opportunities arise. The reduction of the General Reserves is thus not expected to impact HLL's ability to exploit longer-term growth opportunities. In fact should opportunities come for profitable investment in core businesses, a balance sheet, which is appropriately geared, would be desirable from the point of view of HLL and its shareholders and would be in line with an optimal financial structure by way of debt-equity ratio which is efficient and in keeping with well accepted and prudent norms of financial management.

A few years ago Colgate Palmolive did something different to take out cash from its books. The company under a scheme approved by its shareholders as well as the high court as required by the company law decided to restructure its capital by reducing the face value of shares from ₹ 10 to rupee one. The company paid ₹ 9 to every shareholder and thus distributed cash to reduce its cash balance that it could not invest anywhere else. Since the EPS of the company did not change; this had no adverse impact of its share price. Theoretically its share price should have come down by at least ₹ 9.

◆ E-trading

One of the most revolutionary things to happen at the end of the twentieth century is obviously the revolution in communication through the internet. The Net has become the way future business is heading towards. It is therefore no surprise that the Net has made a big difference in the way stock markets around world will function in future.

Developments like screen based trading in the place of traditional trading ring and the dematerialisation of the shares have played a big role in making E-trading a reality. Without these developments E-trading would not be as effective as it is now.

Due to this new innovation one can now operate in the stock market from the privacy of one's home or office. The transactions can be put through in a matter of few minutes, to one's satisfaction. This method guarantees complete secrecy in the transactions.

Various portals like Indiainfoline, Sharekhan, ICICI, Capital markets have come up in the last few years. These portals are full of information about almost 5,000 companies listed on the stock exchanges. This enables the investors to study the companies' performance, before making investment decisions. They also provide latest information concerning the companies, which is essential for the investors to make decisions. TV channels like CNBC also contribute a great deal in this effort by reporting latest happenings along with the necessary analysis by experts and by telecasting live the investor meets, allowing investors to get first hand information from the various company's officials.

On January 31, 2000 SEBI, cleared the guidelines for Net based trading. The trading platform was created through VSAT operational since 1994. The investors were now free to trade directly through their stockbrokers from the comfort of their homes.

◈ The Pre-conditions for Trading on Net are:

- A P.C. with net connection.
- A registered account with a broker.
- A de-mat account.
- An account with a bank with payment gateway or online banking facility.

◈ How to Trade Online

- Log on to the broker's website.
- Register yourself as a client.
- Fill in the client broker agreement on stamp paper.
- Log on to the broker's site using secure user ID and password.
- The markets watch page will show real time data.
- Trade shares directly by entering the symbol of the securities.
- The brokers' server will check the limit in the online and the de-mat account for the number of shares. And execute the trade.
- Usually the order is executed in about 20 seconds and you get the confirmation.
- The broker will send one e-mail confirmation and printed contract by mail.
- On the settlement day the de-mat and bank accounts will automatically get debited and credited.

◈ Stock Lending Mechanism

This scheme was introduced by SEBI in 1997, to make capital market active by putting idle stocks to work. The scheme became operational in 1999. The National Securities Clearing Corporation Ltd., (NSCCL) is the first Approved Intermediary (AI) to implement this scheme.

All clearing members are eligible to participate in this scheme. All lending and borrowing transactions are backed by 100 per cent collateral. The NSCCL bears all risks attached with these transactions. The investors willing to lend/borrow securities approach their broker participant for putting through securities lending transaction.

This transaction involves two parties one who is willing to lend and the other who wishes to borrow securities at market related rates. The lender gets the benefit of a reasonable return called lending fee for parting with the securities for a specified time. The lender is assured of getting equivalent the relevant securities by the NSSCL on the settlement date. If the borrower fails to return the securities on the settlement date, the NSCCL has powers to carry-out an auction, buy the shares on behalf of the lender and return them to him.

This scheme has so far failed to take-off in a significant manner. With the introduction of Derivative products, many investors seem to prefer, to deal in those products.

◈ Employees Stock Options Plan (ESOP)

There is a story that says that when Microsoft decided to go public it was not because the company wanted money, but due to the fact the employees wanted to cash their ESOPs, something that they could not do unless the company was listed. Hence Microsoft went public!

ESOPs is said to be the recipe to make employees millionaires apparently at no cost to the employer. This phenomenon is relatively new in India and the IT industry was the first to adopt it wholeheartedly on the experience in the American markets. The distinguishing feature of ESOPs is that the reward is linked with the increase in the prices of shares of the company. But the other point that is being increasingly faced by employees is what if the stock prices decline, below the price at which they bought these options in the first place? Today this is the reality in India. ESOPs are granted in the form of shares directly allotted, stock options, stock appreciation rights, etc., and each of these can have many variants.

A stock option is a right, but not an obligation, of the option holder to acquire the shares of a company during the specified period, at a predetermined price.

ESOPs represent one of the methods of giving part ownership of the company to the employees whereby they can work for and take part in the prosperity of the company. It is expected that when an employee becomes a part owner of the company, his motivational level would increase. This scheme is also a step towards achieving the social objectives of the company. This is an incentive to the employee. The scheme comes with the rider of Lock-in Period. This means that the employees after exercising the option are not allowed to sell these shares for sometime as stipulated by the company, and usually also cannot create a charge on them.

◈ SEBI Guidelines

Stock options can be issued under two methods, (*a*) Employee's Stock Option Scheme (ESOS), (*b*) Employee Stock Purchase Scheme (ESPS).

There has to vesting period during which the employees have to hold on to the option, but cannot apply for the shares. After this there is the exercise period during which the option can be exercised. After this is the lock-in period during which these shares cannot be sold.

There are extensive disclosure requirements that need to be fulfilled. The promoters are not allowed to take part in this scheme. The scheme also needs to be ratified by the shareholders before it can be implemented. The approval has to be in the form of a special resolution passed by the AGM.

Under the corporate governance practices the scheme has to be implemented through a Compensation Committee of the Board of Directors of the company. This committee must have majority of independent directors.

Considerable freedom has been granted to the companies as regards the manner in which the scheme can be designed and implemented.

The option granted to the employees is non-transferable.

The schemes are available only to the employees and the non-promoter directors of the company.

These guidelines are applicable only to the listed companies. This however does not mean that companies that are not listed cannot offer this scheme to their employees.

There is no limit either of quantity or as a percentage of capital or the shares or stock options issued under any scheme.

Under the ESPS the shares can be allotted without any waiting period.

A certificate has to be obtained from the auditors of the company stating that the scheme has been implemented in accordance with the SEBI guidelines and in accordance with the resolution passed in the AGM.

◈ Sweat Equity

The Company's Act says that "Sweat Equity Shares" means equity shares issued by the company to employees or directors at a discount or for consideration other than cash for providing know-how or making available rights in the nature of intellectual property rights or value additions by whichever name called.

The following are the essential features of this instrument:

A. The term is restricted to equity shares only and no other type of shares or other instruments can be issued as sweat equity.

B. Such equity shares may be issued at a discount or for such consideration other than cash, as has been specified.

All companies can issue sweat equity as per the guidelines issued by SEBI. Unlisted companies also have to follow the guidelines applicable for them, while issuing sweat equity.

The issue of sweat equity shares has to be authorised by a special resolution passed by the AGM.

The resolution should specify the number of shares, current market price, and consideration, if any and the class or classes of directors or employees to whom such equity shares are to be issued. Upper limit needs to be mentioned for number of shares.

◈ London Stock Exchange – AIM

AIM is world's leading market for smaller, growing companies from all over the world. Since its launch in 1995 about 2,100 companies from all across the world have got listed on this market. Its success is built on the basis of its simple regulatory environment that has been specifically designed keeping in mind the requirements of smaller companies. One will find many kinds of companies on AIM some of which may be financed by Venture Capitalists, while others may be more established companies that are trying to expand.

Reasons why companies are attracted to this market could be summed up as follows:

Unlike most other markets AIM does not stipulate minimum criterion in relation to company's size, track record or a set number of shares in the public hands. All prospective companies will need to nominate an advisor from the AIM's approved register who will ensure that the company is eligible to be listed on this exchange.

Listing on this exchange allows companies to raise funds with initial floatation and also more floatation later on.

Create a market for the company's shares, broadening its shareholders base and potentially given its existing shareholders exit option.

Raise its profile with a view to expanding its operations into new overseas markets.

Raise money for acquisitions.

◈ Years of Euphoria and the Downfall

The Indian stock markets were on a roll between 2005 to early 2008. FII's poured in roughly $ 35 billion in Indian equities in this period. The Private Equity firms probably brought in another $ 20 billion. The markets saw hectic activity in IPOs as well. Large amounts of money were raised. The economy was booming and GDP was growing @9 per cent+. This is always a dangerous time for markets and retail investors. This is so because many companies and their merchant bankers become greedy and take advantage of illiteracy of investors on one hand and their greed and belief that in a bull market the quality of issues does not matter. So issues get overpriced and they get lapped up by unthinking investors. As long as markets are high they can make money by selling on listing. However many of them fall prey when markets correct or fall as happened after January 08.

It would be interesting for you to look at the valuations at which shares of real estate companies like DLF, Unitech, Shobha Developers, etc. In the euphoria the investors bought these shares. The prices in the secondary market went up but the greed prevented these shareholders from booking profits. They were sure that the markets will continue to rise. Today many of these companies have lost more than 50 per cent of its issue price and the investors have lost money big time in these companies. Now they say markets are a bad place to invest.

The brokerage houses like Edelweiss, Religare, Anand Rathi and Motilal Oswal also raised money at very high rates. There share prices have met with the similar fate. One really fails to understand why should there be any speculation in these shares at all!

Now the markets are volatile again due to many factors like euro crisis, our own economy slowing down. If the markets keep going down then there will be opportunities to buy good stocks. At this point of time many people will not buy fearing that the markets would go down further. It has to be understood that buying good stocks when markets are in decline is the right thing to do.

Most people lose money because they buy at the wrong time. When markets are going up too fast for no other reason except that there is too much of liquidity, it is the worst time to buy. Secondly, investors buy wrong stocks. An investor must do a lot of study before buying stocks and most have no idea as to how it is done.

Investors do not seem to learn their lessons by and large. We had seen this in 2001-03 when markets crashed following the Dotcom burst in US and the arrest of Ketan Parekh in India. For two years markets were in turmoil and good stocks were available at cheap rates but only smart investors bought. Others who had lost money by following the so-called Ketan's to became so afraid that they refused to buy even the best Indian companies at ridiculously low prices. The same thing happened in 2008 as well. As the market fell from 21,000 to less than 8,000, investors forgot that it is the right time to buy! Now again we are seeing the markets going down and the same behaviour pattern may get repeated.

Some smart and intelligent investors have also started to build their portfolios by doing SIP in specific stocks. What they do is they choose say five companies and buy one share of these per month irrespective of price. Some research done shows; that this is a great strategy of investment and does give good returns.

❋ ❋ ❋

7 STOCK EXCHANGES

Stock Exchanges play a very important role in the economy of a country. Many developed countries have vibrant stock exchanges. India has two main stock exchanges the 100+ years old Bombay Stock Exchange (BSE) and the latest and one of the most savvy exchanges in the world the National Stock Exchange (NSE). There are many other smaller regional exchanges of no significance and their existence is not even warranted. NSE is the most modern exchange in India and has acquired almost a monopoly status. Almost 75 per cent of daily cash turnover and 99 per cent of derivative market turnover takes place on NSE! BSE in comparison has fallen way behind. Some other exchanges like MCX who wish to start stock trading have been thwarted by the regulator SEBI consistently. Some critics believe that the regulators are actually favouring NSE by doing this and the matter has gone to the court.

◈ Introduction to Securities Contract Regulation Act

Section 4 of the Securities contracts (Regulation) Act, 1956 defines the term Stock Exchange as; an association, organization or a body of individuals, whether incorporated or not, established for the purpose of assisting and controlling the business of buying, selling and dealing in securities. A stock market can operate only if it is recognised by the government under the SCRA. The recognition is granted under Section 3 of the Act by the Central government, Ministry of Finance, Stock Exchange Division.

The government has far-reaching powers under this Act.

- It can grant and withdraw the recognition, approval or change of by-laws.
- Call for periodical returns.
- Conduct inquiries against the members when required.
- Directing the stock exchange to make certain rules.
- Supersede or suspend the Governing Board of the Exchange.
- Impose any other conditions or regulations for trading.

◈ Introduction to Stock Exchanges

Some stock exchanges in India are voluntary non-profit making associations, while some others are joint stock companies limited by shares, while some others are companies limited by guarantee.

The government is now moving towards demutilisation of all the stock exchanges. Demutilisation would mean that the ownership and management of the stock exchanges would be separated. It is decided that the stock exchanges will now be joint stock companies. Both NSE and BSE are corporate entities now. The BSE is likely to make ownership public by issue of shares, which can be listed and traded. This has been talked about for a long time but nothing has come about.

Without an efficient stock exchange, the savings of the community, which are essential for economic progress, would not be available for the business community. It provides for a mechanism in buying and selling the securities. It assists in reasonably correct evaluation of securities in terms of their real worth. In evaluating the prices on the exchange, the operators take into account all the relevant factors, present and prospective, concerning the particular enterprise and industry. It is because of this the price of one company's share is different than the other company's share price. This price difference can be attributed to the difference between the profitability and the future prospects of the two companies.

Stock exchanges constitute a market for trading in the existing listed securities and they also facilitate listing of new securities for trading. They also provide a reasonable degree of safety and fair dealings to the investors.

The stock markets are affected by practically anything, especially in India. Mr. Armstrong an authority on stock markets says, "The winds that play upon stock exchanges is as varying and inconsistent as those that blow upon the ocean are. They are frequently just as disturbing."

Basically two sets of factors affect the stock exchanges, one is known as fundamental factors and other is technical factors. The fundamental factors are related to the industry and are economic and financial in nature. The technical factors are related to techniques of stock evaluation methods.

The governing body of a recognised stock exchange has wide powers and is the decision making body of the exchange. It has the power, subject to governmental approval, to make, amend and suspend the operation of the rules, by-laws and regulations of the exchanges. It also has complete jurisdiction over all members and in practice, its power of management and control is almost absolute. The governing body has the power to admit and expel members, to warn, censure, fine and suspend members.

SEBI has over the years initiated many reforms in the working of the stock markets. We shall now take a quick look at some of these actions.

It has initiated measures to prohibit unfair trade practices, manipulation of prices, misleading statements and other fraudulent practices to induce sales or purchases of securities with a view to influence the prices and make undue profits or gains out of such practices.

The lock-in period for preferential allotment was removed for all categories except for promoters. The disclosure norms and responsibilities of merchant bankers were tightened and revised guidelines were issued for ESOPs.

The entry norms were tightened for companies who were making initial public offerings. It was decided that a company should have a track record of dividend payment for a minimum of three years out of the immediately preceding five years, to be eligible for listing on the stock exchanges. However, a manufacturing company, whose issue and project have been appraised by a public financial institution or a bank, which has also participated in its funding, may make public issue to get its shares listed on a stock exchange.

It has been announced that the allotment process must be completed within 14 days from the closure of the issue. For any delay the company has to pay interest @15 per cent to the investors.

The limit for aggregate investment of FIIs, NRIs, and OCBs, etc., was raised to 30 per cent. It has since been revised to 40 per cent or beyond if the AGM passes a resolution to this effect.

The RBI has permitted the banks to invest in the capital market up to 5 per cent of their incremental deposits. This ceiling of 5 per cent also includes any loans to stockbrokers against shares and debentures and advances to individuals against such securities.

IMPORTANCE AND OPERATIONS OF DEPOSITORIES

What is a depository?

Depository is an organization, which holds securities of investor in electronic form at the request of the investor through a registered Depository Participant. It also provides services related to transactions in securities.

How is a depository similar to a bank?

It can be compared with a bank, which holds the funds for depositors. A Bank - Depository Analogy is given in following table:

BANK DEPOSITORY — AN ANALOGY

Bank	*Depository*
• Holds funds in an account	• Hold securities in an account
• Transfers funds between accounts on the instruction of the accountholder	• Transfers securities between accounts on the instruction of the accountholder.
• Facilitates transfers without having to handle money	• Facilitates transfers of ownership without having to handle securities.
• Facilitates safekeeping of money	• Facilitates safekeeping of shares.

How many depositories are registered with SEBI?

At present two depositories, *viz.*, National Securities Depository Limited and Central Depository Services (I) Limited are registered with SEBI.

Who is depository participant?

A Depository Participant (DP) is an agent of the depository through which it interfaces with the investor. A DP can offer depository services only after it gets proper registration from SEBI. A depository can be compared with a bank, like-wise a DP may be compared with a branch of a Bank.

- What is the minimum net worth is required for a depository?
- The minimum net worth stipulated by SEBI for a depository is ₹ 100 crore.
- What are the benefits of availing depository services?

Benefits are enumerated below:

- A safe, convenient way to hold securities;
- Immediate transfer of securities;
- No stamp duty on transfer of securities;
- Elimination of risks associated with physical certificates such as bad delivery , fake securities, delays, thefts, etc.;
- Reduction in paperwork involved in transfer of securities;
- Reduction in transaction cost;
- No odd lot problem, even one share can be sold;
- Nomination facility;
- Change in address recorded with DP gets registered with all companies in which investor holds securities electronically eliminating the need to correspond with each of them separately;
- Transmission of securities is done by DP eliminating correspondence with companies;
- Automatic credit into de-mat account of shares, arising out of bonus/split/consolidation/ merger, etc.

From the year ending March 2012 companies have decided on Green Initiative and have decided to send Annual Reports by e-mail instead of sending printed copies.

ACCOUNT OPENING

How can services of a depository be availed?

To avail the services of a depository you require to open an account with any of the depository participant of any depository.

How can one open an account?

First an investor has to approach a DP and fill up an account opening form. The account opening form must be supported by:

Proof of Identity: Signature and photograph of investor must be authenticated by an existing de-mat accountholder or by investor's bank. Alternatively, one can submit a copy of a valid Passport, voters ID card, driving license or PAN card with photograph.

Proof of Address: A copy of ration card/passport/voter ID/PAN card/driving license/bank passbook as proof of address. (Investor should carry original documents for verification by an authorized official of the depository participant, under his signature.)

Further investor has to sign an agreement with DP in a depository prescribed standard format, which detail investor's and DPs rights and duties. DP should provide investor with a copy of the agreement and schedule of charges for your future reference.

The DP will open investors' account in the system and give an account number, which is also called BO ID (Beneficiary Pwner Identification Number).

What should be done if address of the investor changes?

Investor should immediately inform his/her DP, who in turn will update the records. This will obviate the need of informing different companies.

Can multiple accounts be opened?

Yes. An investor can open more than one account in the same name with the same DP and also with different DPs.

Does the investor have to keep any minimum balance of securities in his accounts?

No.

Is it necessary to have account with the same DP as broker has?

No. Depository/DP can be chosen by investor as per convenient irrespective of the DP of the broker.

Can an investor open a single account for securities owned in different ownership patterns such as securities owned individually and securities owned along with others?

No. The de-mat account must be opened in the same ownership pattern in which the securities are held in the physical form. Example, if one share certificate is in your individual name and another certificate is jointly with some other, two different accounts would have to be opened.

What is required to be done if one has physical certificates with the same combination of names, but the sequence of names is different, *i.e.*, some certificates with 'A' as first holder and 'B' as second holder and other set of certificates with 'B' as first holder and 'A' as the second holder?

In this case one may open only one account with 'A' and 'B' as the accountholders and lodge the security certificates with different order of names for dematerialisation in the same account. You will fill up an additional form called "Transposition cum de-mat" form. This would help you to effect change in the order of names as well as dematerialise the securities.

Whether investors can freeze or lock their accounts?

Investors can freeze or lock their accounts for any given period of time, if so desired. Accounts can be frozen for debits (preventing transfer of securities out of accounts) or for credits (preventing any movements of hindrances into accounts) or for both.

Find out what happened in the recent scam relating to multiple de-mat accounts.

◈ Dematerialisation — Process and Operation

What is dematerialisation?

Dematerialisation is the process by which physical certificates of an investor are converted to an equivalent number of securities in electronic form and credited into the investor's account with his/her DP.

How can one convert physical holding into electronic holding, *i.e.*, how can one dematerialise securities?

In order to dematerialise physical securities one has to fill in a DRF (De-mat Request Form) which is available with the DP and submit the same along with physical certificates one wishes to dematerialise. Separate DRF has to be filled for each ISIN no. The complete process of dematerialisation is outlined below:

- Surrender certificates for dematerialisation to your depository participant.
- Depository participant intimates depository of the request through the system.
- Depository participant submits the certificates to the registrar.
- Registrar confirms the dematerialisation request from depository.
- After dematerialising certificates, registrar updates accounts and informs depository of the completion of dematerialisations.
- Depository updates its accounts and informs the depository participant.
- Depository participant updates the account and informs the investor.

What is an ISIN?

ISIN (International Securities Identification Number) is a unique identification number for a security.

Can odd lot shares be dematerialised?

Yes, odd lot share certificates can also be dematerialised. Actually under this process there is nothing like an odd lot.

Do dematerialised shares have distinctive numbers?

Dematerialised shares do not have any distinctive numbers. These shares are fungible, which means that all the holdings of a particular security will be identical and interchangeable.

Can transfer-cum-dematerialisation be done simultaneously?

Yes. After the company/registrar has transferred the shares in one's name they will request one to let them know whether one wishes to receive them in electronic mode. In case one opts to receive in electronic mode one should inform the company/registrar through one's DP within 30 days of the date of option letter failing which company or registrar can dispatch the certificates and the securities shall be credited to one's account. This facility is offered only for those scrips for which the Issuer Company has agreed to provide this facility.

Can one's electronic holdings be converted back into physical certificates?

Yes. The process is called rematerialisation. If one wishes to get back your securities in the physical form one has to fill in the RRF (Re-mat Request Form) and request your DP for rematerialisation of the balances in your securities account. The process of rematerialisation is outlined below:

- One makes a request for rematerialisation.
- Depository participant intimates depository of the request through the system.
- Depository confirms rematerialisation request to the registrar.
- Registrar updates accounts and prints certificates.
- Depository updates accounts and downloads details to depository participant.
- Registrar dispatches certificates to investor.

◈ Trading/Settlement

What is the procedure for selling dematerialised securities?

The procedure for buying and selling dematerialised shares is similar to the procedure for buying and selling physical shares. The difference lies in the process of delivery (in case of sell) and receipt (in case of purchase) of securities.

In case of purchase:

The broker will receive the securities in his account on the payout day.

The broker will give instruction to its DP to debit his account and credit investor's account.

Investor will give 'Receipt Instruction to DP' for receiving credit by filling appropriate form. However one can give standing instruction for credit into one's accounts that will obviate the need of giving Receipt Instruction every time.

In case of sell:

You will give delivery instruction to DP to debit one's account and credit your broker's account. Such instruction should reach to your DP's office at least 24 hours before the pay-in otherwise DP will accept the instruction only at your risk.

What is delivery instruction slip (DIS)? What precautions do one need to observe with respect to delivery instruction slips?

To give the delivery instruction to DP one has to fill one form called Delivery Instruction Slip (DIS). DIS may be compared to cheque book of a bank account. The following precautions are to be taken in respect of DIS:

Ensure and insist with DP to issue DIS book; do not use loose slips.

Ensure that DIS numbers are pre-printed and DP takes acknowledgement for the DIS booklet issued to the investor.

Ensure that your account number [client id] is pre-stamped.

If the account is a joint account, all the jointholders have to sign the instruction slips. Instruction cannot be executed if all jointholders have not signed.

Avoid using loose slips.

Do not leave signed blank DIS with anyone, *viz.*, broker/subbroker.

Keep the DIS book under lock and key when not in use.

If only one entry is made in the DIS book, strike out remaining space to prevent misuse by any one.

Investor should personally fill in target account id and all details in the DIS.

◈ Corporate Benefits

Is it possible to get securities allotted in public offering directly in the electronic form?

Yes, it is possible to get securities allotted to in public offerings directly in the electronic form. In the public issue application form there is a provision to indicate the manner in which an investor wants the securities allotted. He has to mention the BO ID and the name and ID of the DP on the application form. Any allotment made will be credited into the BO account.

How are cash corporate benefit such as dividend/interest received?

The concerned company obtains the details of beneficiary holders and their holdings as on the date of the book closure/record date from depositories. The payment to the investors will be made by the company through the ECS (Electronic Clearing Service) facility, wherever available. Thus the dividend/interest will be credited to your bank account directly. Where ECS facility is not available dividend/interest will be given by issuing warrants on which your bank account details are printed. The bank account details will be those, which you would have mentioned in your account opening form or changed thereafter.

How would one receive non-cash corporate benefit such as bonus, etc.?

The concerned company obtains the details of beneficiary holders and their holdings as on the date of the book closure/record date from depositories. Your entitlement will be credited by the company directly in one's depository accounts.

Who should be contacted in case of discrepancies in corporate benefits?

In case of discrepancies in corporate benefits, one can approach his/her DP or the company/ its R and T agents.

◆ Pledging

Can one pledge dematerialised securities?

Yes. In fact, pledging dematerialised securities is easier and more advantageous as compared to pledging physical securities.

What should one do to pledge electronic securities?

The procedure is as follows:

- Both investor (pledgor) as well as the lender (pledgee) must have depository accounts;
- Investor has to initiate the pledge by submitting to DP the details of the securities to be pledged in a standard format;
- The pledgee has to confirm the request through his/her DP;
- Once this is done, securities are pledged;
- All financial transactions between the pledgor and the pledgee are handled as per usual practice outside the depository system.

How can one close the pledge after repayment of his loan?

After one has repaid the loan, one can request for a closure of pledge by instructing the DP in a prescribed format. The pledgee on receiving the repayment will instruct his DP accordingly for the closure of the pledge.

Can one change the securities offered in a pledge?

Yes; if the pledgee [lender] agrees, one may change the securities offered in a pledge.

Who would receive the corporate benefits on the pledged securities?

The securities pledged are only blocked in the account of pledgor in favour of the pledgee. The pledgor would continue to receive all the corporate benefits.

◈ Transaction Statement

How does one know that the DP has updated the account after each transaction?

The DP gives a transaction statement periodically, which will details current balances and various transactions made through the depository account. If so desired, DP may provide the transaction statement at intervals shorter than the stipulated ones, probably at a cost. A format of statement of transactions is reproduced as Annexure.

At what frequency does one receive transaction statement from DP?

Transaction statement is received from DP once in a quarter. If a transaction has been carried out during the quarter, the statement is received within fifteen days of the transaction.

What is to be done if there are any discrepancies in transaction statement?

In case of any discrepancy in the transaction statement, one can contact his/her DP. If the discrepancy cannot be resolved at the DP level, one should approach depository.

Whom should one contact in case of any complaint/problem/query?

In case of any complaint/problem/query one may first contact DP. If DP is unable to solve complaint/problem/query one should approach concerned depository. If one is not satisfied one may approach SEBI. One may also approach SEBI directly.

What is a custodian?

A custodian is basically an organisation, which helps registers and safeguards the securities of its clients.

What is the role of a custodian?

Besides safeguarding securities, a custodian also keeps track of corporate action, *i.e.*, collecting dividends, rights shares, bonus shares and other activities on behalf of its clients.

Introduction to National Stock Exchange

NSE was set up by IDBI and other financial institutions with paid equity capital of ₹ 25 crore. It started operations in wholesale debt market in June 1994 and in equity in November 1994. The wholesale debt market or money market segments cater to banks, FIs, etc., to encourage high value transactions in PSU bonds, units of UTI, Treasury bills, Government securities and call money.

In January 2007 some of the original promoters of NSE have divested their stakes from the equity of this exchange in favour of foreign companies. The NYSE has acquired a stake of 5 per cent for a consideration of $ 115 million, while Goldman Sachs, Soft Bank, Asian Infrastructure Fund and General Atlantic have bought another 15 per cent by paying $ 125 million each. These investors have valued NSE in the region of $ 2 to 2.5 billion. The sellers were ILF&S 5 per cent, IFCI 7 per cent, GIC 2 per cent, ICICI Bank 5 per cent and PNB 1 per cent. The total value of this deal is around $ 450 million.

There is no trading floor in this exchange. The trading is screen based, meaning that brokers are connected to the exchange by PC terminals. This makes trading very transparent and it is also cost-effective. The investment counters can be spread wide in the country un the electronic network. The companies who wish to list their shares on this exchang have a minimum paid capital of ₹ 10 crore. The settlement cycle on this excha present T+3. This is likely to become T+2 by April, and sometime in near future it w

T+1. This will mean that transactions on the exchange will be much faster, and sellers will get their money and buyers get their securities very quickly.

NSE admits members separately to the wholesale debt market segment and capital market segment. Only corporates members are admitted on the debt market segment, whereas individuals and firms are eligible for membership in capital market segment.

The exchange also has capital adequacy norms for both the segments. For WDM this requirement is ₹ 2 crore, while for stock market the requirement for individuals and registered firms is ₹ 75 lakh and for corporate bodies it is ₹ 100 lakh.

NSE does not look at membership as a property right that can be traded upon. The members do not have to pay any membership fee at the time of becoming members; they pay only an annual subscription fee.

The exchange provides facility of screen based trading with automated order matching. The system is order-driven and conceals the identity of all parties. The trading system operates on a price time priority. All orders received are sorted out with the best-priced order getting the first priority for matching, *i.e.,* the best buy order matches the best sell order. Within similar priced orders, they are sorted on time, *i.e.,* the one that came in earlier than the other, get the priority. The matching of the orders is done by the computers, thus making the whole process transparent, objective and fair.

When an order does not find a match it remains in the system and is displayed to the whole market, till a fresh order comes in or this pending order is cancelled.

This trading system is very flexible, and this enables the investors to place several time, price and volume related orders. The system provides complete market information online. All key information is updated on a real time basis. Due to this it is possible for the investor to know the actual position of the market, before placing the order. Investors can also know the status of their orders almost as soon as they are placed.

◈ Wholesale Debt Market

WDM or money market is a market where pure debt instruments such as Government securities, Treasury bills, public sector bonds, corporate debentures, commercial paper, certificates of deposits, etc., are traded.

- A few large usually institutional investors and a very high volume of trade dominate this segment.
- The exchange has set up systems to contain market risk by ensuring that the primary responsibility of settlements rests with the participants. The exchange authorities closely monitor the settlements. Every participant sets up counterparty exposure limits, which are automatically adjusted each time a trade takes place.
- Trades on this market are settled on the basis of trade-for-trade, *i.e.,* each transaction is settled individually. Each trade has a settlement date specified upfront at the time of order entry and is used as a matching parameter. The actual settlement of funds and securities are effected directly between participants.
- Gilt securities are immobilized with the RBI and they maintain a book entry of holders. The RBI through book entry adjustments affects all transfers in these securities.
- Recently the RBI has allowed the individuals to buy and sell Government securities. It will be interesting to see how this market develops in the coming days.
- The government has now allowed the Securitized paper to be listed and traded. Once this starts then we may see a lot of activity in these markets.

◈ Stock Market Indices

Everyone talks about Sensex, whenever the talk turns to stock markets. This is a way in which the movements on stock markets are known. Sensex going up or down and the reasons thereof are matters of hot debate. Let us now take a look as to how the Sensex is constructed.

In order to enable the market participants, analysts, etc., to track the various ups and downs in the Indian stock market, the BSE introduced in 1986 an Equity Stock Index called BSE-SENSEX that subsequently became the barometer of the movements of the share prices in the Indian stock market. It is a "Market Capitalization-Weighted" index of 30 component stocks representing a sample of large, well established and leading companies. The base year is 1978-79. The Sensex is widely reported in both domestic and international markets through print and electronic media.

Sensex is calculated using a market capitalization-weighted method. As per this method, the level of index reflects the total market value of all 30 component stocks from the different industries related to a particular base period. The total market value of a company is determined by multiplying the price of its stock by the number of shares outstanding. Statisticians call an index of a set of combined variables (such as price and number of shares) a composite index. An indexed number is used to represent the results of this calculation in order to make the value easier to work with and track over time. It is much easier to graph a chart based on indexed values than one based on actual values. World over majority of the well known indices are constructed using market capitalisation-weighted method.

In practice, the daily calculation of SENSEX is done by dividing the aggregate market value of the 30 companies in the index by a number called the Index Divisor. The divisor is the only link to the original base period value of the Sensex. The divisor keeps the index comparable over a period of time and is the reference point for all the index maintenance adjustments.

While choosing the companies for inclusion in the Sensex many criterions are used. The market capitalisation, the volume of shares traded on a daily average is two important criterions. The Sensex must also represent industries across the spectrum. Before the 90s no company representing the ICE stocks, *viz.*, Information Technology, Communication and Entertainment did not form a part of the Sensex companies. However now they are an integral part of the Sensex. This is the reflection of today's reality. The stock exchanges keep changing the composition of the Sensex from time-to-time so that they can take out companies who no longer are eligible to be in the Sensex, by those who are now more important. The companies are given a weightage in the Sensex individually. Any change in the value of these companies affects the Sensex, taking it up with high weightage companies' share value goes up and it goes down when share values of these companies dips. It must be understood that the change in the value of Sensex does not indicate change in the share value of all companies listed on the exchange, in the same proportion. Out of the total turnover recorded on the stock exchange the index companies contribute mainly to the volume and the value.

This is the snap shot of companies that were part of the Sensex as on 8th December 2006 along with the respective weightage allotted to different companies in the Sensex. The table also gives the market capitalisation of these companies on that date.

Sensex **08 Dec. 17:30**

Company Name	*Last Price*	*Mkt Cap (₹ cr)*	*Weight*
ACC		20,690.28	1.17%
BHEL		64,518.74	3.65%
Bajaj Auto	2,649.20	26,804.61	1.52%
Bharti Airtel	633.20	120,038.26	6.80%
Cipla	246.50	19,159.21	1.09%
Dr. Reddy's Labs	775.30	11,902.41	0.67%
Grasim	2,758.05	25,288.56	1.43%
Guj Ambuja Cement	141.00	19,183.76	1.09%
HDFC	1,550.05	38,718.70	2.19%
HDFC Bank	1,085.05	34,161.71	1.94%
HLL	233.80	51,590.31	2.92%
Hero Honda	743.75	14,852.69	0.84%
Hindalco	179.60	20,821.03	1.18%
ICICI Bank	876.70	78,344.54	4.44%
ITC	184.95	69,528.25	3.94%
Infosys	2,197.25	122,118.76	6.92%
Larsen	1,451.55	40,715.98	2.31%
Maruti Udyog	932.40	26,938.90	1.53%
NTPC	151.65	125,042.40	7.08%
ONGC	840.55	179,782.72	10.18%
Ranbaxy Labs	387.50	14,441.35	0.82%
Reliance	1,267.80	176,669.20	10.01%
Reliance Comm	447.30	91,455.85	5.18%
Reliance Energy	555.05	11,829.78	0.67%
SBI	1,353.50	71,234.71	4.04%
Satyam	456.70	29,977.79	1.70%
TCS	1,176.15	115,098.04	6.52%
Tata Motors	866.80	33,399.54	1.89%
Tata Steel	482.40	28,001.87	1.59%
Wipro	577.05	82,942.28	4.70%

◆ Sensex Calculation Methodology

Sensex is calculated using the "Free-float Market Capitalization" methodology. As per this methodology, the level of index at any point of time reflects the Free-float market value of 30 component stocks relative to a base period. The market capitalization of a company is determined by multiplying the price of its stock by the number of shares issued by the company. This market capitalization is further multiplied by the free-float factor to determine the free-float market capitalization.

The base period of Sensex is 1978-79 and the base value is 100 index points. This is often indicated by the notation 1978-79=100. The calculation of Sensex involves dividing the free-float market capitalization of 30 companies in the index by a number called the Index Divisor.

The divisor is the only link to the original base period value of the Sensex. It keeps the index comparable over time and is the adjustment point for all index adjustments arising out of corporate actions, replacement of scrips, etc. During market hours, prices of the index scrips, at which latest trades are executed, and used by the trading system to calculate Sensex every 15 seconds and disseminated in real time.

◈ Dollex-30

BSE also calculates a dollar-linked version of Sensex and historical values of this index are available since its inception. (For more details click **'Dollex series of BSE indices'**).

UNDERSTANDING FREE-FLOAT METHODOLOGY

◈ Concept

Free-float methodology refers to an index construction methodology that takes into consideration only the free-float market capitalization of a company for the purpose of index calculation and assigning weight to stocks in index. Free-float market capitalization is defined as that proportion of total shares issued by the company that are readily available for trading in the market. It generally excludes promoters' holding, government holding, strategic holding and other locked-in shares that will not come to the market for trading in the normal course. In other words, the market capitalization of each company in a free-float index is reduced to the extent of its readily available shares in the market.

In India, BSE pioneered the concept of free-float by launching BSE TECk in July 2001 and BANKEX in June 2003. While BSE TECk Index is a TMT benchmark, BANKEX is positioned as a benchmark for the banking sector stocks. Sensex becomes the third index in India to be based on the globally accepted free-float methodology.

◈ Major Advantages of Free-float Methodology

- A free-float index reflects the market trends more rationally as it takes into consideration only those shares that are available for trading in the market.
- Free-float methodology makes the index more broad-based by reducing the concentration of top few companies in index. For example, the concentration of top five companies in Sensex has fallen under the free-float scenario thereby making the Sensex more diversified and broad-based.
- A free-float index aids both active and passive investing styles. It aids active managers by enabling them to benchmark their fund returns *vis-à-vis* an investable index. This enables an apple-to-apple comparison thereby facilitating better evaluation of performance of active managers. Being a perfectly replicable portfolio of stocks, a free-float adjusted index is best suited for the passive managers as it enables them to track the index with the least tracking error.
- Free-float methodology improves index flexibility in terms of including any stock from the universe of listed stocks. This improves market coverage and sector coverage of the index. For example, under a full-market capitalization methodology, companies with large market capitalization and low free-float cannot generally be included in the Index because they tend to distort the index by having an undue influence on the index movement. However, under the free-float methodology, since only the free-float market capitalization of each company is considered for index calculation, it becomes possible to include such closely held companies in the index while at the same time preventing their undue influence on the index movement.

- Globally, the free-float methodology of index construction is considered to be an industry best practice and all major index providers like MSCI, FTSE, S&P and STOXX have adopted the same. MSCI, a leading global index provider, shifted all its indices to the free-float methodology in 2002. The MSCI India Standard Index, which is followed by Foreign Institutional Investors (FIIs) to track Indian equities, is also based on the free-float methodology. NASDAQ-100, the underlying index to the famous Exchange Traded Fund (ETF) — QQQ is based on the free-float methodology.

◆ Definition of Free-float

Share holdings held by investors that would not, in the normal course come into the open market for trading are treated as 'Controlling/ Strategic Holdings' and hence not included in free-float. In specific, the following categories of holding are generally excluded from the definition of free-float:

- Holdings by founders/directors/acquirers which has control element
- Holdings by persons/bodies with "Controlling Interest"
- Government holding as promoter/acquirer
- Holdings through the FDI Route
- Strategic stakes by private corporate bodies/individuals
- Equity held by associate/group companies (cross-holdings)
- Equity held by Employee Welfare Trusts
- Locked-in shares which would not be sold in the open market in normal course.

The remaining shareholders would fall under the free-float category.

◆ Maintenance of Sensex

One of the important aspects of maintaining continuity with the past is to update the base year average. The base year value adjustment ensures that replacement of stocks in index, additional issue of capital and other corporate announcements like 'rights issue', etc., do not destroy the historical value of the index. The beauty of maintenance lies in the fact that adjustments for corporate actions in the index should not *per se* affect the index values.

The Index Cell of the exchange does the day-to-day maintenance of the index within the broad index policy framework set by the Index Committee. The Index Cell ensures that Sensex and all the other BSE indices maintain their benchmark properties by striking a delicate balance between frequent replacements in index and maintaining its historical continuity. The Index Committee of the exchange comprises of experts on capital markets from all major market segments. They include academicians, fund-managers from leading mutual funds, finance-journalists, market participants, independent governing board members, and exchange administration.

◆ Online Computation of the Index

During market hours, prices of the index scrips, at which trades are executed, are automatically used by the trading computer to calculate the Sensex every 15 seconds and continuously updated on all trading workstations connected to the BSE trading computer in real time.

◆ Adjustment for Bonus, Rights and Newly Issued Capital

The arithmetic calculation involved in calculating Sensex is simple, but problem arises when one of the component stocks pays a bonus or issues rights shares. If no adjustments were made, a discontinuity would arise between the current value of the index and its previous value despite the non-occurrence of any economic activity of substance. At the Index Cell of the exchange, the base value is adjusted, which is used to alter market capitalization of the component stocks to arrive at the Sensex value.

The Index Cell of the exchange keeps a close watch on the events that might affect the index on a regular basis and carries out daily maintenance of all the 14 indices.

- **Adjustments for Rights Issues:**

  When a company, included in the compilation of the index, issues right shares, the free-float market capitalisation of that company is increased by the number of additional shares issued based on the theoretical (ex-right) price. An offsetting or proportionate adjustment is then made to the Base Market Capitalisation (see 'Base Market Capitalisation Adjustment' below).

- **Adjustments for Bonus Issue:**

  When a company, included in the compilation of the index, issues bonus shares, the market capitalisation of that company does not undergo any change. Therefore, there is no change in the Base Market Capitalisation, only the 'number of shares' in the formula is updated.

- **Other Issues:**

  Base Market Capitalisation Adjustment is required when new shares are issued by way of conversion of debentures, mergers, spin-offs, etc., or when equity is reduced by way of buyback of shares, corporate restructuring, etc.

- **Base Market Capitalisation Adjustment:**

  The formula for adjusting the Base Market Capitalisation is as follows:

  $$\text{New Base Market Capitalisation} = \text{Old Base Market Capitalisation} \times \frac{\text{New Market Capitalisation}}{\text{Old Market Capitalisation}}$$

  To illustrate, suppose a company issues right shares which increases the market capitalisation of the shares of that company by say, ₹ 100 crore. The existing Base Market Capitalisation (Old Base Market Capitalisation), say, is ₹ 2,450 crore and the aggregate market capitalisation of all the shares included in the index before the right issue made is, say ₹ 4,781 crore. The "New Base Market Capitalisation " will then be:

  $$\frac{2{,}450 \times (4{,}781 + 100)}{4.781} = ₹\ 2{,}501.24 \text{ crore}$$

  This figure of ₹ 2,501.24 will be used as the Base Market Capitalisation for calculating the index number from then onwards till the next base change becomes necessary.

◈ Sensex — Scrip Selection Criteria

The general guidelines for selection of constituents in Sensex are as follows:

1. **Listed History:** The scrip should have a listing history of at least 3 months at BSE. Exception may be considered if full market capitalisation of a newly listed company ranks among top 10 in the list of BSE universe. In case, a company is listed on account of merger/demerger/amalgamation, minimum listing history would not be required.

2. **Trading Frequency:** The scrip should have been traded on each and every trading day in the last three months. Exceptions can be made for extreme reasons like scrip suspension, etc.
3. **Final Rank:** The scrip should figure in the top 100 companies listed by final rank. The final rank is arrived at by assigning 75 per cent weightage to the rank on the basis of three-month average full market capitalisation and 25 per cent weightage to the liquidity rank based on three-month average daily turnover and three-month average impact cost.
4. **Market Capitalisation Weightage:** The weightage of each scrip in SENSEX based on three-month average free-float market capitalisation should be at least 0.5 per cent of the Index.
5. **Industry Representation:** Scrip selection would generally take into account a balanced representation of the listed companies in the universe of BSE.
6. **Track Record:** In the opinion of the committee, the company should have an acceptable track record.

◆ Index Review Frequency

The Index Committee meets every quarter to discuss index related issues. In case of a revision in the index constituents, the announcement of the incoming and outgoing scrips is made six weeks in advance of the actual implementation of the revision of the Index.

HISTORY OF REPLACEMENT OF SCRIPS IN SENSEX

Date	*Outgoing Scrips*	*Replaced by*
01.01.1986	Bombay Burmah	Voltas
	Asian Cables	Peico
	Crompton Greaves	Premier Auto.
	Scinda	G.E.Shipping
03.08.1992	Zenith Ltd.	Bharat Forge
19.08.1996	Ballarpur Inds.	Arvind Mills
	Bharat Forge	Bajaj Auto
	Bombay Dyeing	BHEL
	Ceat Tyres	BSES
	Century Text.	Colgate
	GSFC	Guj. Amb. Cement
	Hind. Motors	HPCL
	Indian Organic	ICICI
	Indian Rayon	IDBI
	Kirloskar Cummins	IPCL
	Mukand Iron	MTNL
	Philips	Ranbaxy Lab.
	Premier Auto	State Bank of India
	Siemens	Steel Authority of India
	Voltas	Tata Chem

16.11.1998	Arvind Mills G. E. Shipping IPCL Steel Authority of India	Castrol Infosys Technologies NIIT Ltd. Novartis
10.04.2000	I.D.B.I. Indian Hotels Tata Chem Tata Power	Dr. Reddy's Laboratories Reliance Petroleum Satyam Computers Zee Telefilms
08.01.2001	Novartis	Cipla Ltd.
07.01.2002	NIIT Ltd. Mahindra & Mahindra	HCL Technologies Hero Honda Motors Ltd.
31.05.2002	ICICI Ltd.	ICICI Bank Ltd.
10.10.2002	Reliance Petroleum Ltd.	HDFC Ltd.
10.11.2003	Castrol India Ltd. Colgate Palmolive (India) Ltd. GlaxoSmithKline Pharma. Ltd. HCL Technologies Ltd. Nestle (India) Ltd.	Bharti-Tele-Ventures Ltd. HDFC Bank Ltd. ONGC Ltd. Tata Power Company Ltd. Wipro Ltd.
19.05.2004	Larsen & Toubro Ltd.	Maruti Udyog Ltd.
27.09.2004	Mahanagar Telephone Nigam Ltd.	Larsen & Toubro Ltd.
06.06.2005	Hindustan Petroleum Corp. Ltd. Zee Telefilms Ltd.	National Thermal Power Corpn. Ltd. Tata Consultancy Services Ltd.
12.06.2006	Tata Power Ltd.	Reliance Communication Ventures Ltd.

Currently following companies are part of Sensex as on May 2012:

Scrip Code	*Company*	*Close Price*	*No.of Shares (normal)*	*Full Mkt. Cap. (₹ crore)*	*Free-float Adj. Factor*	*Free-float Mkt. Cap (₹ crore)*	*Weight in Index (%)*
500325	RELIANCE		3,274,550,412		0.55	127,150.79	9.34
500875	ITC LTD		7,818,424,300		0.7	126,013.45	9.26
500209	INFOSYS LTD		574,230,001		0.85	119,087.98	8.75
500010	HOUSING DEVE		1,473,851,251		1	96,574.10	7.1
500180	HDFC BANK LTD		2,346,630,905		0.8	94,982.23	6.98
532174	ICICI BANK LTD		1,152,795,747		1	90,413.77	6.64
532540	TCS LTD		1,957,220,996		0.3	73,149.18	5.37
500510	LARSEN & TOUBRO		612,398,899		0.9	64,612.37	4.75
500112	STATE BANK OF INDIA		671,044,838		0.4	55,175.99	4.05
500312	ONGC CORP. LTD		8,555,490,120		0.25	54,263.20	3.99
500696	HIND UNI LTD		2,160,879,033		0.5	46,102.35	3.39
500570	TATA MOTORS		2,691,486,150		0.7	43,935.82	3.23
532454	BHARTI AIRTEL		3,797,530,096		0.35	40,153.18	2.95
500520	MAHINDRA & MAHINDRA		613,974,839		0.75	30,009.56	2.2

500470	TATA STEEL		971,214,779		0.7	27,387.77	2.01
507685	WIPRO LTD.		2,458,733,486		0.25	25,174.36	1.85
532555	NTPC LTD		8,245,464,400		0.2	24,225.17	1.78
524715	SUN PHARMA		1,035,550,385		0.4	23,506.99	1.73
532977	BAJAJ AUTO		289,367,020		0.5	21,890.62	1.61
533278	COAL INDIA		6,316,364,400		0.1	20,319.74	1.49
532286	JINDAL STEEL		934,833,818		0.45	18,570.71	1.36
500182	HEROMOTOCO		199,687,500		0.5	18,341.30	1.35
500103	BHEL		2,447,600,000		0.35	18,156.91	1.33
532155	GAIL INDIA		1,268,477,400		0.4	16,360.82	1.2
500087	CIPLA LTD.		802,921,357		0.65	16,160.60	1.19
532500	MARUTI-SUZUKI		288,910,060		0.5	15,983.23	1.17
500440	HINDALCO IN		1,918,607,775		0.7	15,673.11	1.15
500400	TATA POWER		2,373,072,360		0.7	15,540.06	1.14
500900	STERLITE IND		3,360,704,478		0.45	14,230.90	1.05
532868	DLF LIMITED		1,698,385,719		0.25	7,846.54	0.58

With the advent of technology the trading in stocks is now possible from anywhere in the country. This meant that many regional stock exchanges lost business. These stock exchanges had many large companies listed on their platform. However, they started delisting their shares from these exchanges as their shares could be traded either on BSE or NSE. Some small companies, those were not eligible for getting listed on these two exchanges had to be listed on these regional stock exchanges.

BSE has now launched a market to list Small and Medium Enterprises (SME). NSE has also unveiled similar platform. BSE platform is called BSE SME platform.

A study group appointed by the Prime Minister in 2007 had recommended establishment of a separate platform for the SMEs so that they could access funds through the stock markets. SEBI has also laid down the necessary regulation for the creation of such a platform.

Following are the benefits to SMEs of this exchange:

◈ Access to Capital

These companies may require small amount of capital in the initial phases and are unable to list themselves on the leading national exchanges due to their listing requirement being out of their reach. This exchange hoped will offer them a suitable platform for raising resources.

◈ Increased Visibility and Prestige

A listed company enjoys better visibility and carries certain prestige. This helps it in its business. For companies doing well financially this helps attract more diverse set of investors to fulfil their capital requirement.

◈ Attracting Venture Capitalists

A listed entity finds it easier to attract VC funds for investments. VCs require a vibrant market. They also need an exit route. A listing on stock market provides this.

◈ Liquidity to Shareholders

Shareholders will be hesitant to invest money even in a promising venture if they do not have an exit opportunity. The listing provides this.

◈ Ability to Offer ESOPs

Listing makes it possible for the management to offer Employee Stock Options to its employees. If the stock in not listed there will be no incentive for employees to opt for ESOPs and they may not be able to get capital gains from such offerings by the company.

The guidelines give emphasis on the following:

- The post-issue face value should not exceed ₹ 25 crore.
- The minimum application and trading lot size shall not be less than ₹ 1 lakh.
- The existing members would be eligible to participate on this exchange.
- The issues will be 100 per cent underwritten and the merchant bankers will have to underwrite 15 per cent themselves.

SEBI has compulsorily mandated market making for all scrips listed and traded on SME exchange.

The obligations for market makers are as follows:

- The merchant bankers to the issue will undertake market making through a stock broker who is registered as market maker with the SME exchange.
- The merchant bankers shall be responsible for the market making for a minimum period of three years.
- The market makers are required to provide two way quotes for 75 per cent of the time in a day. The same shall be monitored by the exchange.
- There will not be more than five market makers for scrip.
- Market makers will compete with other market makers for better price discovery.
- The exchange shall prescribe the minimum spread between bid and ask prices.
- During the compulsory market making period, the promoter holding shall not be eligible for the offering to market makers.
- Market maker shall be allowed to deregister by giving one month notice to the exchange.
- Trading system may be either order-driven or quote-driven.

The application and trading lot size is being kept at ₹ 1,00,000 so as to curtail the entry of retail investors. It has also been stated that the minimum depth shall be of one lakh rupees and at any point of time it cannot go below that amount. The investors holding with value less than ₹ 1,00,000 shall be allowed to offer their holding to the market maker in one lot. However, in functionality the market lot will be subject to revival after a stipulated time.

One will have to wait and see how successful this exchange is going to be going forward. However, the past experience has not been very encouraging. Hopefully this time it will be successful. However, it is difficult to see how retail investors could be attracted towards this market. Companies that will be listed here will naturally have no past history. Investors are likely to perceive and quite rightly that smaller companies will be highly risky investments.

The NSE also has its own index called NSE-NIFTY, comprising 50 companies. BSE also has an index called BSE-100. This is a broader index than the Sensex.

There are various other indexes popular on the stock exchanges, which reflect various industries like Pharma, IT, FMCG, etc.

Let us now take a look at the trading and settlement of BSE:

◈ Trading and Settlement

(a) Trading

The exchange, which had an open outcry trading system, had switched over to a fully automated computerized mode of trading known as BOLT (BSE online Trading) System. Through the BOLT system the members now enter orders from Trader Work Stations (TWSs) installed in their offices instead of assembling in the trading ring. This system, which was initially both order- and quote-driven, was commissioned on March 14, 1995. However, the facility of placing of quotes has been removed w.e.f., August 13, 2001 in view of lack of market interest and to improve system-matching efficiency. The system, which is now only order-driven, facilitates more efficient processing, automatic order matching and faster execution of orders in a transparent manner.

Earlier, the members of the exchange were permitted to open trading terminals only in Mumbai. However, in October 1996, the exchange obtained permission from SEBI for expansion of its BOLT network to locations outside Mumbai. In terms of the permission granted by SEBI and certain modifications announced later, the members of the exchange are now free to install their trading terminals at any place in the country. The expansion of BOLT network was inaugurated by Shri P. Chidambaram the then Finance Minister, Government of India on August 31, 1997.

In order to expand the reach of BOLT network to centres outside Mumbai and support the smaller Regional Stock Exchanges, the exchange has, as on June 30, 2002, admitted subsidiary companies formed by 13 Regional Stock Exchanges as its members. The members of these Regional Stock Exchanges work as subbrokers of the member-brokers of the exchange.

The objectives of granting membership to the subsidiary companies formed by the Regional Stock Exchanges were to reach out to investors in these centres via the members of these Regional Exchanges and provide the investors in these areas access to the trading facilities in all scrips listed on the exchange.

Trading on the BOLT system is conducted from Monday to Friday between 9:55 a.m. and 3:30 p.m. The scrips traded on the exchange have been classified into 'A', 'B1', 'B2', 'F' and 'Z' groups. The number of scrips listed on the exchange under 'A', 'B1 ', 'B2' and 'Z' groups, which represent the equity segment, as on June 30, 2002 was 172, 563,1923 and 3044 respectively. The 'F' group represents the debt market (fixed income securities) segment, wherein 748 securities were listed as on June 30, 2002. The 'Z' group was introduced by the exchange in July 1999 and covers the companies which have failed to comply with listing requirements and/or failed to resolve investor complaints or have not made the required arrangements with both the depositories, *viz.*, Central Depository Services (I) Ltd., (CDSL) and National Security Depository Ltd., (NSDL) for dematerialization of their securities by the specified date, *i.e.*, September 30, 2001. Companies in "Z" group numbered 3,000 as on June 30, 2002. Of these, 1,385 companies were in "Z" group for not complying with the provisions of the Listing Agreement and/or pending investor complaints and the balance companies were on account of not making arrangements for dematerialization of their securities with both the depositories. 1,615 companies have been put in "Z" group as a temporary measure till they make arrangements for dematerialization of their securities. Once they finalize the arrangements for dematerialization of their securities, trading and settlement in their scrips would be shifted to their respective erstwhile groups.

The Exchange has also the facility to trade in "C" group which covers the odd lot securities in 'A', 'B1', 'B2' and 'Z' groups and Rights renunciations in all the groups of scrips in the equity segment. The exchange, thus, provides a facility to market participants of online trading in odd lots of securities and Rights renunciations. The facility of trading in odd lots of securities not only offers an exit route to investors to dispose of their odd lots of securities but also provides them an opportunity to consolidate their securities into market lots.

The 'C' group can also be used by investors for selling up to 500 shares in physical form in respect of scrips of companies where trades are to be compulsorily settled by all investors in de-mat mode. This scheme of selling physical shares is compulsory in de-mat scrips is called as Exit Route Scheme.

With effect from December 31, 2001, trading in all securities listed in equity segment of the exchange takes place in one market segment, *viz.*, Compulsory Rolling Settlement Segment.

◈ Permitted Securities

The exchange has since decided to permit trading in the securities of the companies listed on other stock exchanges under "Permitted Securities" category which meet the relevant norms specified by the exchange. Accordingly, to begin with the exchange has permitted trading in scrips of five companies listed on other stock exchanges w.e.f. April 22, 2002.

◈ Computation of Closing Price of Scrips in the Cash Segment

The closing prices of scrips are computed on the basis of weighted average price of all trades in the last 15 minutes of the continuous trading session. However, if there is no trade during the last 15 minutes, then the last traded price in the continuous trading session is taken as the official closing price.

◈ Compulsory Rolling Settlement (CRS) Segment

With a view to introduce the best international trading practices and to achieve higher settlement efficiency, as mandated by SEBI, trades in all the equity shares listed on the exchange in CRS segment were to be settled on T+5 basis w.e.f. December 31, 2001. SEBI has further directed the stock exchanges that trades in all scrips should be settled on T+2 basis. Accordingly, all transactions in all groups of securities in the equity segment and fixed income securities listed on the exchange are settled on T+2 basis.

Under a rolling settlement environment, the trades done on a particular day are settled after a given number of business days rather than settling all trades done during a period at the end of an 'account period'. A T+3 settlement cycle means that the final settlement of transactions done on T or trade day by exchange of monies and securities, occurs on third business day after the trade day.

The transactions in securities of companies which have made arrangements for dematerialization of their securities by the stipulated date are settled only in de-mat mode on T+2 on net basis, i.e., buy and sale positions in the same scrip are netted and the net quantity is to be settled. However, transactions in securities of companies, which have failed to make arrangements for dematerialization of their securities or/are in "Z" group, are settled only on trade to trade basis on T+3, *i.e.*, the transactions are settled on a gross basis and the facility of netting of buy and sale transactions in a scrip is not available. For example, if one buys and sells 100 shares of a company on the same day which is on trade to trade basis, the two positions will not be netted and he will have to first deliver 100 shares at the time of payin of securities and then receive 100 shares at the time of payout of securities on the same day. Thus, if one fails to deliver the securities sold at the time of payin, it will be treated as a shortage and the position will be auctioned/ closedout.

In other words, the transactions in scrips of companies which are in compulsory de-mat are settled in de-mat mode on T+3 on netting basis and the transactions in scrips of companies, which have not made arrangements for dematerialization of their securities by the stipulated date or are in "Z" group for other reasons, are settled on trade-to-trade basis on T+3 either in de-mat mode or in physical mode.

The settlement of transactions in 'F' group securities representing Fixed Income Securities is also on Rolling Settlement Cycle of T+3 basis.

The following tables summarizes the steps in the trading and settlement cycle for scrips under CRS:

Day	***Activity***
T	• Trading on BOLT and daily downloading of statements showing details of transactions and margins at the end of each trading day. • 6A/7A entry by the member-brokers.
T+1	Confirmation of 6A/7A data by the custodians. Downloading of securities and funds obligation statement by members.
T+3	Payin of funds and securities by 11:00 a.m. and payout of funds and securities by 2:00 p.m.
T+4	Auction on BOLT.
T+5	Auction payin and payout.
*6A/7A	A mechanism whereby the obligation of settling the transactions done by a member-broker on behalf of a client is passed on to a custodian based on his confirmation.

Thus, the payin and payout of funds and securities takes places on the third working day of the execution of the trade.

The Information Systems Department of the exchange generates the following statements, which can be downloaded by the members in their back offices on a daily basis.

(*c*) Statements giving details of the daily transactions entered into by the members.

(*d*) Statements giving details of margins payable by the members in respect of the trades executed by them.

The settlement of the trades (money and securities) done by a member on his own account or on behalf of his individual, corporate or institutional clients may be either through the member himself or through a SEBI registered custodian appointed by him or the respective client. In case the delivery/payment is to be given or taken by a registered custodian, he has to confirm the trade done by a member on the BOLT system through 6A-7A entry. For this purpose, the custodians have been given connectivity to BOLT system and have also been admitted as members of the clearing house. In case a transaction is not confirmed by a registered custodian, the liability for payin of funds or securities in respect of the same devolves on the concerned member.

The introduction of settlement on T+3 basis has resulted in reduction in settlement risk, provided early receipt of securities and monies to buyers and sellers respectively and brought Indian capital markets at the international standard of settlements.

(b) Settlement

Payin and Payout for 'A', 'B1', 'B2', 'C', "F" & 'Z' group of securities.

As discussed earlier, the trades done by members in all the securities in CRS are now settled by payment of money and delivery of securities on T+3 basis. All deliveries of securities are required to be routed through the Clearing House, except for certain off-market transactions which, although are required to be reported to the exchange, may be settled directly between the members concerned.

The Clearing House is an independent company promoted jointly by Bank of India and Stock Exchange, Mumbai for handling the clearing and settlement operations of funds and securities on behalf of the exchange. For this purpose, the Clearing and Settlement Dept. of the exchange liaises with the Clearing House on a day-to-day basis.

The Information Systems Department (ISD) of the Exchange generates Delivery and Receive Orders for transactions done by the members in A, B1, B2 and F group scrips after netting purchase and sale transactions in each scrip, whereas Delivery and Receive Orders for "C" and "Z" group scrips are generated on trade-to-trade basis, *i.e.*, without netting of purchase and sale transactions in a scrip.

The Delivery Orders provide information like scrip, quantity and the name of the receiving member to whom the securities are to be delivered through the Clearing House. The money statement provides scripwise/itemwise details of payments/receipts for the settlement. The Delivery/Receive Orders and money statements can be downloaded by the members in their back offices.

The bank accounts of members maintained with the eight clearing banks, *viz.*, Bank of India, HDFC Bank Ltd., Global Trust Bank Ltd., Standard Chartered Bank, Centurion Bank Ltd., UTI Bank Ltd., ICICI Bank Ltd., and IndusInd Bank Ltd., are directly debited through computerized posting for their settlement and margin obligations and credited with receivables on accounts of payout dues and refund of margins.

The securities, as per the Delivery Orders issued by the exchange, are required to be delivered by the members in the Clearing House on the day designated for securities payin, i.e., on T+3 day. In case of the physical securities, the members have to deliver the securities in special closed pouches (supplied by the exchange) along with the relevant details (distinctive numbers, scrip code, quantity, and receiving member) on a floppy. The data submitted by the members on floppies is matched against the master file data on the Clearing House computer systems. If there are no discrepancies, then a scroll number is generated by the Clearing House and a scroll slip is issued. The members can then submit the securities at the receiving counter in the Clearing House.

◆ Auto D.O. Facility

Instead of issuing Delivery Out instructions for their delivery obligations in a settlement/ auction, a facility has been made available to the members of automatically generating Delivery Out (D.O.) instructions on their behalf from their CM pool accounts by the Clearing House w.e.f., August 10, 2000. This Auto D.O. facility is available for CRS (Normal and Auction) and for trade-to-trade settlements. This facility is, however, not available for delivery of non-*pari passu* shares and shares having multiple ISINs. The members wishing to avail of this facility have to submit an authority letter to the Clearing House. This Auto D.O facility is currently available only for Clearing Member (CM) Pool accounts/Principal Accounts maintained by the members with National Securities Depository Ltd., (NSDL) and Central Depositories Services Ltd., (CDSL).

◈ De-mat Payin

The members can effect de-mat payin either through Central Depository Services (I) Ltd., (CDSL) or National Securities Depository Ltd., (NSDL) In case of NSDL, the members are required to give instructions to their Depository Participant (DP) specifying settlement no., settlement type, effective payin date, quantity, etc. The securities are transferred to the Pool Account. The members are required to give delivery-out instructions so that the securities are considered for payin.

As regards CDSL, the members give payin instructions to their DP. The securities are transferred by the DPs to the Clearing Member (CM) Principal Account. The members are required to give confirmation to their DP, so that securities are processed towards payin obligations. Alternatively, the members may also effect payin from the clients' beneficiary accounts for which they are required to do break-up on the front end software to generate obligations and settlement IDs.

The Clearing House arranges and tallies the securities received against the receiving memberwise report generated on the payin day. This process is called securities payin. Once this reconciliation is complete, the bank accounts of members with eight clearing banks having payin obligations are debited on the scheduled payin day. This procedure is called Payin of Funds. Once the payin of securities and funds is complete, the Clearing House arranges for payout of securities and funds. As regards payout of securities, in case of de-mat securities, the same are credited in the Pool Account of the members or the Client Accounts as per the client details submitted by the members. In case of Physical securities, the receiving members are required to collect the same from the Clearing House on the payout day. The bank accounts of the members having payout of funds are credited by the Clearing House with the Clearing Banks. This process is referred to as Payout of Funds. In case of rolling settlements, payin and payout of both funds and securities is completed on the same day.

The settlement schedules are drawn by the exchange in advance on a quarterly basis and circulated to the market participants. The settlement schedules have been strictly adhered to by the exchange and there has been generally no case of clubbing of settlements or postponement of payin and payout during the last over six years.

The exchange is also maintaining a database of fake/forged, stolen, lost and duplicate securities in physical form with the Clearing House so that distinctive numbers submitted by members in case of physical securities on delivery may be matched against the database to weed out bad paper from circulation at the time of introduction of such securities in the market. This database has also been made available to the members so that delivering and receiving members can check the entry of fake, forged and stolen shares in the market.

Here are some of the systems that have been put in place:

◈ Trade Guarantee Fund (TGF)

While approving the proposal of the exchange for expansion of BOLT terminals to cities other than Mumbai, SEBI had, *inter alia*, stipulated that the exchange should introduce a system of guaranteeing settlement of trades or set up a Clearing Corporation to ensure that market equilibrium is not disturbed in case of payment default by any member.

The exchange has accordingly formulated a scheme to guarantee settlement of bonafide transactions of members, which form part of the settlement system. The exchange has constituted a Trade Guarantee Fund with the following objectives:

To guarantee settlement of bonafide transactions of members of the exchange *inter-se* which form part of the stock exchange settlement system, so as to ensure timely completion of settlements of contracts and thereby protect the interest of investors and the members of the exchange to inculcate confidence in the minds of secondary market participants generally and global investors particularly, to attract larger number of domestic and international players in the capital market.

To protect the interest of investors and to promote the development of and regulation of the secondary market. The scheme has come into force with effect from May 12, 1997. The scheme is managed by the Defaulters' Committee, which is a Standing Committee constituted by the exchange, the constitution of which is approved by SEBI. The temporary refundable advances for a stipulated period are given by the Defaulters Committee from the Trade Guarantee Fund to the members to meet their settlement obligations subject to certain conditions. During the period of advance, the BOLT TWSs of the members are kept deactivated. If a member fails to repay the advance within the stipulated period, he is declared a defaulter by the Governing Board on the basis of the recommendations of the Defaulters Committee.

All active members are required to make an initial contribution of ₹ 10,000 in cash to the fund and also contribute rupee 0.225 for every ₹ 1 lakh of gross turnover in all the groups of scrips by way of continuous contribution which is debited to their settlement account. The active members are required to maintain a base minimum capital of ₹ 10 lakh each with the exchange. This contribution has also been transferred to the fund and has been treated as refundable contribution of members. Each member is also required to provide to the fund a bank guarantee of ₹ 10 lakh from a scheduled commercial bank as an additional contribution to the fund. Thus, the initial contribution to the TGF of about ₹ 170 crore has been contributed by the exchange as well as members in the manner discussed above. The total corpus of the fund as on June 30, 2002 was ₹ 919.54 crore.

The creation of TGF has eliminated counterparty risk so that if a member is declared a defaulter, other members who had dealing with him during the settlement(s), do not suffer as was the case in the past. The creation of TGF has, thus, ensured smooth completion of settlements at the exchange.

◈ Brokers' Contingency Fund (BCF)

The exchange has set up a Brokers' Contingency Fund (BCF) with a view: to make temporary refundable advance(s) to the members facing temporary financial miss-match as a result of which they may not be in a position to meet their financial obligations to the exchange in time; to protect the interest of the investors dealing through members of the exchange by ensuring timely completion of settlement; and to inculcate confidence in the minds of investors regarding safety of bonafide transactions entered into on the exchange. The scheme has come into force with effect from July 21, 1997. The fund is managed by a committee appointed by the governing board.

The exchange has contributed a sum of ₹ 9.51 crore to the corpus of the fund. All the active members are required to make an initial non-refundable contribution of ₹ 1,000 to the fund and also contribute rupee 0.075 for every one lakh rupees of gross turnover by way of continuous contribution which is debited to their settlement account. Further, 5 per cent of the surplus remaining in the account of the defaulters after meeting all their liabilities in the exchange is credited to this fund before handing over the surplus to them. The members are eligible to get advance(s) from the fund up to a maximum of ₹ 25 lakh. The corpus of the fund as on June 30, 2002 was ₹ 32.75 crore. Thus, by creation of the BCF, an effort has been made that the settlement cycles at the exchange are not affected due to the temporary financial problems faced by the members. This, it is presumed, would help in increasing the credibility of the stock exchange settlement system.

◈ Surveillance

One of the objectives of the exchange is to promote and inculcate honourable and just practices of trade in securities transactions and to discourage malpractices.

The surveillance function at the exchange has assumed greater importance in the last over six years. SEBI had directed the stock exchanges in August 1995 to set up a separate the Surveillance Department with staff exclusively assigned to surveillance functions. The exchange has accordingly set up a separate Surveillance Department to keep a close watch on price movement of scrips, detect market manipulations like price rigging, etc., monitor abnormal prices and volumes which are not consistent with normal trading pattern and keep a watch on the exposure of the members. The Position Monitoring section of the Surveillance Dept. monitors exposure of the members on a daily basis as described in Para 10(e) above. The functions of price monitoring and investigations have been entrusted to the Surveillance Department where large variation in the prices as well as volumes of scrips is scrutinized and appropriate actions are taken.

The scrips which reach new high or new low and companies which have high turnover are watched. Also the prices and volumes in the newly listed scrips are monitored. In case certain abnormalities are noticed, then circuit filters are reduced to make it difficult for the price manipulators to increase or push down the prices of scrip within a short period of time. The exchange imposes special margin in the scrips where it is suspected that there is an attempt to ramp up the prices by creating artificial volumes. In cases, where there is excessive volatility or sudden spurt in volume or where the net deliverable quantity is insignificant, the settlement of the trades in the scrip, as a surveillance measure, may be shifted on a trade-to-trade basis. In cases where the abnormal movements continue despite the aforesaid measures, trading in the scrip is suspended.

Detailed investigations are conducted in cases where price manipulation is suspected and disciplinary action is taken against the members concerned, if warranted. Where any scrip has been suspended for more than three days, a detailed investigation report is prepared and sent to SEBI for further investigation/action, if any.

The exchange has developed an Online Real Time (OLRT) Surveillance System known as BSE Online Surveillance System (BOSS) which was commissioned from July 15, 1999 with the main objectives of detecting potential market abuses at nascent stage to reduce the ability of the market participants to influence the price and volumes of the scrips traded at the exchange, improve the risk management system and to strengthen the self-regulatory mechanism at the exchange. Under this system, alerts are generated by the system on-line, in real time, based on certain pre-set parameters like the price and volume variation in scrips, members taking unduly large positions not commensurate with their financial position or having concentrated position(s) in one or a few scrips, etc. The system also generates online and offline exception reports for settlement related information.

This system includes databases such as company profile, members' profile and historical database of turnover and price movement in scrips, members' turnover, their payin obligations, etc. The alerts generated by the system during the trading hours are analyzed and corrective action based on further investigations is taken in such cases.

The Surveillance Department also liaises with the Compliance Officers of the companies to obtain the comments of the companies on various price sensitive corporate news pertaining to them which appear daily in the leading financial newspapers. The comments received from the companies on such newspaper reports are immediately disseminated to the market to enable the investors to take informed decisions.

◈ Circuit Filters

The exchanges as per the directions from SEBI, are required to apply Circuit Filters on all scrips traded in Rolling Settlements at 20 per cent of the closing price of the scrips on the previous day. However, in the Rolling Settlement Scenario, since the trading horizon is only one day, the application of these Circuit Filters may pose high settlement default risk, when a market participant is not able to square-off his speculative trading position, as the scrip may have hit the Circuit Filter. Therefore, in all 54 scrips, which form part of the Sensex and Nifty or in which derivative products like stock options and futures are available, no circuit filters are applicable w.e.f. July 2, 2001. In other words, the prices of these scrips can have free fall or increase within a day.

However, in view of the market developments that took place in September, 001, SEBI has directed the exchanges to impose daily circuit filter of 10 per cent on these 54 scrips. Accordingly, these 54 scrips have daily circuit filter of 10 per cent and the remaining scrips in CRS have a daily circuit filter of 20 per cent.

◈ Market Wide Circuit Breakers

It may be noted that Circuit Filters at individual scrip level help to restrict the excessive movements of indices as well. In the revised scenario, where there are supposed to be no Circuit Filters on the scrips forming part of popular indices or in which derivative products are available, there is a need to contain such excessive market movements in indices like Sensex and Nifty. Therefore, in order to contain large market movements, SEBI has mandated that the Market Wide Circuit Breakers (MWCB) which at 10-15-20 per cent of the movements in either BSE Sensex or NSE Nifty, whichever is breached earlier, would be applicable. This would provide cooling period to the market participants and enable them to react to the market movements. The trading halt on all stock exchanges would take place as under:

In case of a 10 per cent movement of either index, there would be a 1-hour market halt if the movement takes place before 1:00 p.m. In case the movement takes place at or after 1 p.m.but before 2:30 p.m., there will be a trading halt for half an hour. In case the movement takes place at or after 2:30 p.m., there will be no trading halt at the 10 per cent level and the market will continue trading.

In case of a 15 per cent movement of either index, there will be a 2-hour market halt if the movement takes place before 1:00 p.m. If the 15 per cent trigger is reached on or after 1:00 p.m. but before 2 p.m., there will be 1-hour halt. If the 15 per cent trigger is reached on or after 2:00 p.m., the trading will halt for the remainder of the day.

In case of a 20 per cent movement of the either index, the trading will halt for the remainder of the day.

The above percentages are required to be translated by the exchanges into absolute points of the index variation on a quarterly basis, i.e., based on the closing index on the last trading day of the quarter and advised to the market participants in advance. Based on these absolute points, market wide circuit breakers are applied for the next quarter. The Market Wide Circuit Breakers at a national level have been introduced in the Indian markets for the first time. This is on the lines of the system prevailing in the US markets.

◈ Redressal of Investors' Grievances and Arbitration Procedure

The investors dealing in the primary and secondary markets may have grievances against various intermediaries like issuers, member-brokers, etc. The exchange has set up a separate cell to redress the grievances of investors against the companies as well as its own members. The exchange also assists in arbitration process both between investors and members *inter-se.* Investors' grievances against companies. The Investor Services Cell forwards the complaints of investors to the concerned companies and directs them to resolve the same within 15 days.

A copy of the letter sent to a company is also forwarded to the complainant. If a company fails to resolve the investors complaints and the total number of pending complaints against it exceed 25 and if the complaints are pending for more than 45 days, a show-cause notice is issued to the company. After issue of show-cause notice if there is no response from a company for 7 days, the scrip of the company is suspended from trading till grievances are resolved.

Further, the Registrars and Transfer Agents and officials of some of the companies visit the exchange to interact with investors as well as members on a regular basis. In spite of these efforts, if a company fails to resolve complaints, then the scrip is shifted to "Z" group. A "Z" category company means that it has not complied with various provisions of the Listing Agreement including non-resolution of investors' complaints or has not made requisite arrangements with both the depositories for dematerialization of their securities. By transferring companies to the "Z" group, the exchange tries to caution the potential investors to be more careful in their investments in scrips of such companies. In order to prevent price manipulation, the trades in "Z" group scrips, as stated earlier, are settled on trade-to-trade basis w.e.f. February 5, 2001.

Thus, by transferring companies to "Z" group, exchange attempts to put a pressure on the companies to ensure compliance with various requirements of the Listing Agreement, redress investor's grievances and arrange for dematerialization of their securities.

◈ Investors' Grievances Against Member-brokers of the Exchange

The exchange handles complaints of investors against members and SEBI registered sub-brokers affiliated to members of the exchange. The complaints of investors are forwarded by the exchange to the concerned members to settle/clarify the matter within 3/7 days from the receipt of the letter. If no reply is received from a member within the specified period, a reminder is sent to him. In case a member fails to submit a clarification/settle the complaint, penalties as prescribed by the exchange from time-to-time are levied on the members and the members may also render themselves liable for further action as provided under the Rules, Bye-laws and Regulations of the Exchange. In order to resolve the complaints expeditiously, the exchange has set up a Investors Grievance Redressal Committee (IGRC) consisting of six members which includes two retired High Court Judges as its members. Both the investors and members present their case before the committee and the committee after hearing both the parties, tries to settle the matter through the process of conciliation. In case a member fails to implement the decision of the IGRC, then the matter is considered for taking further action against the member including referring the matter to the Disciplinary Action Committee.

◈ Complaints of Member's *Inter-se*

In case of the complaints of members against other members of the exchange they are required to lodge complaints against other members in the prescribed format, in duplicate, along with the necessary proof in support of the same. In order to resolve the complaints of members *inter-se*, a Brokers' Consultative Committee has been appointed by the Governing Board. This committee consists of two members of the exchange. Whenever the complaints are received, the same are immediately put before the committee. The committee after hearing both the members gives an award and if a member against whom award has been given fails to implement the same then a show cause notice is issued to him. In spite of this, if a member does not implement the award, then the Investors' Service Cell directly debits the settlement account of the member in the Clearing House and credits the other member's account with the amount of the arbitration award.

◈ Resolution of Complaints Through Arbitration

With a view to ensuring speedy and effective resolution of claims, differences and disputes between non-members and members and member's *inter-se*, the exchange has laid down a set of procedures for arbitration thereof. These procedures are duly embodied in the Rules, Bye-laws and Regulations of the Exchange, which have been duly approved by the Government of India/SEBI, under the Securities Contracts (Regulation) Act, 1956.

Under the Rules, Bye-laws and Regulations of the Exchange, in-house arbitration machinery has been provided to decide on: dispute between members' *inter-se*; and dispute between non-members (clients/investors) and members of the exchange.

All contracts of sale and purchase of securities entered into by the members are subject to Mumbai jurisdiction and any dispute arising in respect of such contracts are necessarily required to be submitted for arbitration. However, complaints from non-members (clients/investors) against members and complaints of embers *inter-se* are in the first case generally scrutinized by the exchange. For the purpose of scrutiny, documentary proof like contract notes, bills, statement of accounts and relevant documentary proof are called for from the parties. If required, personal meetings of the parties are also arranged in cases where issues to be resolved are of a complicated nature. As a last resort, where there are claims and counter-claims and the matter cannot be easily resolved by the intervention of the exchange officials, the parties are advised to file an arbitration reference.

◈ Arbitration Committee

The provisions relating to Arbitration Committee, which deals with arbitration between members *inter-se* are laid down in the Bye-laws Nos. 282 to 315 of the Rules, Bye-laws and Regulations of the exchange.

Three-tier arbitration machinery has been provided in the exchange to decide on disputes between members. All claims, complaints, differences and disputes between members arising out of or in relation to any bargains, dealings, transactions or contracts are subject to arbitration and are deferred to the Arbitration Committee. The Arbitration Committee is appointed by the Governing Board every year. For the year 2001-2002, the Governing Board has appointed 23 members of the exchange as members of the Arbitration Committee.

◈ Lower Bench Arbitration

A Committee of three arbitrators from the Arbitration Committee is constituted by the Secretary of the Arbitration Committee to look into such disputes if the value of the claim exceeds ₹ 25,000, while only one arbitrator will hear the dispute if the value is up to ₹ 25,000.

A member filing an arbitration reference is required to attach a coupon of ₹ 100 along with his arbitration application. Both the applicant and the respondent or their authorized representatives are required to be present in the arbitration meetings. After hearing the parties, the arbitrators give the award.

◆ Full Bench Arbitration

An aggrieved member, who is not satisfied with the award of the Lower Bench Arbitration Committee, may file an appeal before the Full Bench of the Arbitration Committee within seven days from the date of receipt of the award by him provided the sum involved in the award is not less than ₹ 50,000. (It is proposed to increase this amount to ₹ 1,00,000). A member, who desires to file an appeal before the Full Bench of the Arbitration Committee, is also required to deposit the amount of the award or shares as stated in the Lower Bench award with the exchange along with a fee of ₹ 500. The deposit amounts are retained with the exchange until the case is decided by the Full Bench/Governing Board. In the Full Bench Arbitration meetings, all the members of the Arbitration Committee hear the appeal except those arbitrators who gave the award in the lower bench. Quorum of the Full Bench consists of one-third of its members.

◆ Appeal Before the Governing Board

An aggrieved member, who is not satisfied with the award of the Full Bench Arbitration Committee, may prefer an appeal before the Governing Board provided the claim amount/ award of the Full Bench Arbitration Committee is not less than ₹ 1,00,000. (It is proposed to increase this amount to ₹ 5,00,000). An appeal should be filed within seven days from the date of the award of the Full Bench Arbitration Committee by paying a fee of ₹ 700 and also by depositing the award amount/shares as stated in the award with the Stock Exchange. The Governing Board is the final appellate authority in the case of arbitration between members. Beyond this level, there is normally no appeal provision but in exceptional situations the Governing Board may permit a member to make a further appeal to a Court of Law.

The exchange has amended bye-laws relating to Client v/s. Member Arbitration in conjunction with Arbitration and Conciliation Act, 1996, passed by the Government of India. This has become effective from August 29, 1998. Under the amended bye-laws, in case the value of the disputed claim is less than ₹ 10 lakh, then only one arbitrator is appointed and if the claim value is ₹ 10 lakh or more, then there are three arbitrators for the case one appointed by the applicant, one by the respondent and third by the exchange. Under the amended bye-laws after getting the arbitration award, the aggrieved party may request for rectification to the arbitration tribunal for any typographical/computational/arithmetical or any other error of a similar nature, if any, occurred in the award within fifteen days from the receipt of the award. Similarly, the aggrieved party may within fifteen days of the receipt of the award file an appeal to an appeal bench challenging the award of the Arbitral Tribunal. Appeal against the award of the Arbitral Tribunal is heard and decided by an Appeal Bench constituted by the exchange consisting of five arbitrators out of which three are non-member arbitrators. The judgement of the appeal bench is by a majority and is binding on both the parties.

An arbitration award passed by the Arbitral Tribunal/Appeal Bench becomes a decree after expiry of 90 days from the date of receipt of the award by the concerned parties, if the same is not challenged under Section 34 of the Arbitration and Conciliation Act, 1996 and the same can be executed under Civil Procedure Code, 1908 as if it were a decree of a Court. The cases of non-implementation of arbitration awards by the active members are placed before the Disciplinary Action Committee of the Exchange for action against the members concerned after issuing a show cause notice to them.

An award against a defaulter is forwarded by Investors Service Cell to the Defaulters Committee (DC). If the case has been filed within six months of a member having been declared a defaulter, the Defaulters' Committee after satisfying itself about genuineness of the claim, recommends to the Trustees of the Customers' Protection Fund to release the award amount or ₹ 10 lakh, whichever is lower. After the approval of the Trustees, the amount is disbursed to the clients, who have obtained the award against the defaulters.

◈ Investors' Protection Fund

In accordance with the guidelines issued by the Ministry of Finance, Government of India, the exchange has set up an Investor Protection Fund (IPF) on July 10, 1987 to meet the claims of investors against defaulter members.

The fund is managed by the trustees appointed by the exchange.

The members at present contribute to this fund rupee 0.15 per ₹ 1 lakh of gross turnover, which is debited to their general charges account. The stock exchange contributes on a quarterly basis 2.5 per cent of the listing fees collected by it. Also the entire interest earned by the exchange on 1 per cent security deposit kept with it by the companies making public/rights issues is credited to the fund. As per the SEBI directive, auction proceeds in certain cases, where price manipulation/rigging was suspected, have been impounded and transferred to the fund. Also, the surplus lying in the account of the defaulters after meeting their liabilities on the exchange is released to them after transferring 5 per cent of the surplus amount to this fund.

The maximum amount presently payable to an investor from this fund in the event of default by a member is ₹ 10 lakh. This has been progressively raised by the exchange from ₹ 5,000 in 1988 to the present level and is the highest among the stock exchanges in the country.

The arbitration award obtained by investors against defaulters is scrutinized by the Defaulters Committee, a Standing Committee constituted by the exchange, to ascertain their genuineness, etc. Once the Defaulter Committee is satisfied about genuineness of the claim, it recommends to the Trustees of the Fund for release of the award amount or ₹ 10 lakh, whichever is lower. After the approval of the Trustees of the Fund, the amount is disbursed to the clients of the defaulters from the Investor Protection Fund.

◈ Listing of Securities

Listing means admission of the securities to dealings on a recognized stock exchange. The securities may be of any public limited company, Central or State Government, quasi-governmental and other financial institutions/corporations, municipalities, etc.

The objectives of listing are mainly to:

- Provide liquidity to securities;
- Mobilize savings for economic development;
- Protect interest of investors by ensuring full disclosures.

The Listing Department of the exchange grants approval for listing of securities of companies in accordance with the provisions of the Securities Contracts (Regulation) Act, 1956, Securities Contracts (Regulation) Rules, 1957, Companies Act, 1956, guidelines issued by SEBI and Rules, Bye-laws and Regulations of the exchange.

A company intending to have its securities listed on the exchange has to comply with the listing requirements prescribed by the exchange, which are as under:

◈ New Companies

- Category I (for companies with post-issue equity capital of ₹ 10 crore and above)
- Post-issue capital of ₹ 10 crore, and
- Post-issue net worth of ₹ 20 crore

The project/activity of the applicant company must have been appraised by a financial institution as described in Section 4(a) of the Companies Act, 1956 or Sate Finance Corporation or Scheduled Commercial Bank with a paid-up capital of ₹ 50 crore or Category I Merchant with a net worth of ₹ 10 crore.

All the above conditions are expected to be complied with by the companies seeking listing at the exchange. However, the Listing Committee has the discretion to waive the requirement at serial (iii) above after considering the merits of the case.

Category II (for companies with post-issue equity capital of ₹ 5 crore and above, but less than ₹ 10 crore)

- Post-issue capital of ₹ 5 crore, and
- Post-issue networth of ₹ 20 crore

The minimum market capitalization should be of ₹ 50 crore. (The capitalization will be calculated by multiplying the post-issue subscribed number of Equity Shares with the Issue Price)

The project/activity of the applicant must have been appraised by a financial institution as described in Section 4(a) of the companies Act, 1956 or Sate Finance Corporation or Scheduled Commercial Bank with a paid-up capital of ₹ 50 crore or Category I Merchant with a net worth of ₹ 10 crore.

All the above conditions are expected to be complied with by the companies seeking listing at the exchange. However, the Listing Committee has the discretion to waive the requirement at serial (iv) above after considering the merits of the case.

◈ Minimum Public Offer

As per Rule 19(2) (b) of the Securities Contracts (Regulation) Rules, 1957, securities of a company can be listed on a stock exchange only when at least 10 per cent of each class or kind of securities is offered to the public for subscription subject to the following conditions.

Minimum twenty lakh securities are offered to the public (excluding reservation, firm allotment and promoters' contribution).

The size of the offer to the public, *i.e.,* the offer price multiplied by the number of securities offered to the public at (i) above is minimum ₹ 100 crore and the issue was made only through book-building method with allocation of 60 per cent of the issue size to the qualified institutional buyers as specified by SEBI.

If a company does not fulfil the aforesaid conditions, it shall offer at least 25 per cent of each class or kind of securities to the public.

For this purpose, the term "offered to the public" means only the portion offered to the public and does not include reservations of securities on firm or competitive basis. SEBI may, however, relax this condition on the basis of recommendations of stock exchange(s), only in respect of a Government company defined under Section 617 of the Companies Act, 1956.

◈ Companies Listed on Other Stock Exchanges

For companies listed on other stock exchanges and seeking listing on this exchange, the threshold limit is ₹ 3 crore of minimum issued equity capital. Further, the following conditions have to be fulfilled:

- Profit track record for the last three years;
- The company should have minimum net worth of ₹ 20 crore (net worth includes equity capital + free reserves, excluding revaluation reserves)
- Minimum market capitalisation of ₹ 20 crore, based on average price of last six months;
- Trading for a minimum 50 per cent of the total trading days during the same six months on any stock exchange;
- Minimum average volume traded per day during the last three complete months should be 1,000 shares and minimum five trades per day;
- 25 per cent of the issued capital should be with public (including body corporate) and minimum 15 shareholders per ₹ 1 lakh of capital in the public category.
- The company should be agreeable to sign an agreement with CDSL and NSDL for de-mat trading.
- Companies delisted by this exchange seeking relisting on this exchange. The companies once delisted by this exchange can seek relisting only after they make public offer and comply with all the guidelines issued by SEBI and the exchange in this regard.
- Minimum number of shareholders.
- The public offer should result in a wide distribution of shares among the general public and there should be minimum 25 per cent/10 per cent (as applicable) of a company's issued capital with the public (inclusive of corporate bodies).
- Permission to use the name of the exchange in an Issuer Company's prospectus.

The exchange has started a procedure in terms of which the companies fulfilling the requirements as discussed above and desiring to list their securities offered through public issues are required to obtain its prior permission to use the name of the exchange in their prospectus or 'offer for sale' documents before filing the same with the concerned office of the Registrar of Companies. The exchange has formed a "Listing Committee" (formerly known as "Prospectus Scrutiny Committee") to analyze draft prospectus/offer documents of the companies in respect of their forthcoming public issues of securities and decide upon the matter of granting them permission to use the name of "The Stock Exchange, Mumbai" in their prospectus/ offer documents. The committee evaluates the promoters, company, project and several other factors before taking decision in this regard.

◈ Submission of Letter of Application

As per Section 73 of the Companies Act, 1956, a company seeking listing of its securities on the exchanges is required to submit a Letter of Application to all the stock exchanges where it proposes to have its securities listed before filing the prospectus with the Registrar of Companies.

◈ Allotment of Securities

As per the listing agreement, a company is required to complete allotment of securities offered to the public within 30 days of the date of closure of the subscription list and approach the Regional Stock Exchange, i.e., Stock Exchange nearest to its Registered Office for approval of the basis of allotment.

The companies, as per the requirements of listing agreement, are required to send allotment advices/refund orders within 30 days from the date of closure of the issue. If the same are not despatched to the investors within 30 days from the date of closure of the subscription list, the company is required to pay interest at the rate of 15 per cent per annum on the delayed refund orders from the 31st day.

◈ Allotment Letters/Certificates and Trading Permission

Now new companies have to issue shares in de-mat only. The companies seeking listing of their securities on the exchange are required to ensure and take all steps for completion of the normal formalities for listing and commencement of trading at all stock exchanges where the securities are to be listed within seven working days of finalisation of basis of allotment.

The companies are required to scrupulously adhere to the time limit of ten weeks from the date of closure of the subscription list for allotment of all securities and despatch of Allotment Letters/Share Certificates as required under Section 73 of the Companies Act, 1956 and for obtaining the listing permissions of all the exchanges whose names are stated in its prospectus or offer documents. In the event of listing permission to a company being denied by any stock exchange where it had applied for listing of its securities, it cannot proceed with the allotment of shares. However, the company may file an appeal before the Securities and Exchange Board of India under Section 22 of the Securities Contracts (Regulation) Act, 1956.

◈ 1 Per Cent Security Deposit

The companies making public/rights issues are required to deposit 1 per cent of issue amount with the Regional Stock Exchange before the issue opens.

This amount is liable to be forfeited by the exchange in the event a company fails to resolve the complaints of investors regarding delay in sending refund orders/share certificates, non-payment of commission to underwriters, brokers, etc.

◈ Listing Fees

All companies listed on the exchange have to pay annual listing fees by the 30th April of every financial year to the exchange as per the rules.

◈ Compliance with Listing Agreement

The companies desirous of getting their securities listed are required to enter into an agreement with the exchange called the Listing Agreement and they are required to make certain disclosures and perform certain acts. As such, the agreement is of great importance and is executed under the common seal of a company. Under the Listing Agreement, a company undertakes, amongst other things, to provide facilities for prompt transfer, registration, sub-division and consolidation of securities; to give proper notice of closure of transfer books and record dates, to forward copies of unabridged Annual Reports and Balance Sheets to the shareholders, to file Distribution Schedule with the exchange every quarter; to furnish financial results on a quarterly basis; intimate promptly to the exchange the happenings which are likely to materially affect the financial performance of the company and its stock prices; etc.

The Listing Department of the Exchange monitors the compliance of the companies with the provisions of the Listing Agreement, especially with regard to timely payment of annual listing fees, submission of quarterly results, etc., and takes penal action against the defaulting companies.

◈ "Z" Group

The exchange has introduced a new category called "Z Group" from July 1999 for companies which have not complied with and are in breach of provisions of the Listing Agreement and/ or have failed to resolve investor complaints. The Governing Board in its meeting held on January 16, 2002, has approved amendments to guidelines for shifting/retaining companies to/ in 'Z' Group. As per the revised guidelines, the exchange considers any three out of the following seven criteria of non-compliance for shifting a company to the 'Z' Group.

◈ Listing Agreement Clause Description

Clauses 15 and 16	Required notice of Book Closure and Record Dates.
Clause 31(1)(a)	Yearly submission of Annual Reports.
Clause 35	Quarterly submission of shareholding pattern.
Clause 38	Payment of Annual Listing Fees.
Clause 41	Publication of Audited/Unaudited results on a quarterly basis.
Clauses 3, 12, 21	Redressal of Investors' Complaints (regarding share transfers, etc.)
Clause 49	Implementation of corporate governance, if applicable.

It has also been decided that:

The Governing Board/Listing Committee has the discretion to shift any company to and from the 'Z' Group.

The Surveillance Department has the discretionary powers to add or remove companies from this group based on their investigation/complaint/trading behaviour, etc.

The Investors' Service Cell has the discretion to add or remove companies from "Z" Group.

Companies, who fail to make de-mat arrangement with both the depositories, would be in 'Z' Group.

The exchange would also take into account punitive action, if any, taken by any regulatory authority against a company for shifting to "Z" Group.

Notwithstanding what is stated above, the exchange may suspend trading in any security of a company for non-compliance of any one or more clauses as it may consider necessary.

Once a company is shifted to 'Z' Group, its compliance with aforesaid clauses of the Listing Agreement would be monitored by the exchange on a quarterly basis and only upon satisfactory compliance record for one quarter, the company would be shifted back to its erstwhile group. This would be applicable even for companies trading in whose scrips have been suspended by the exchange. The quarterly review would be done in the month of February, May, August and November.

The number of companies placed under 'Z' group as on June 30, 2002 was 3,000.

The number of companies listed at the exchange as at the end of June 30, 2002 was 5,786. This is the highest number of companies listed on a exchange among the stock exchanges in the country and perhaps in the world.

◈ Stock Holding Corporation of India Ltd., (SHCIL)

SHCIL's primary aim is to simplify and expedite the transactions involving the transfer of securities, thereby reducing the periodic increase in paperwork of brokers, clearing house and the registrars.

◈ The Objectives of SHCIL

- Make it easy for investors to buy and sell securities in the secondary markets.
- Freeze active share and debentures certificates in the safe custody.
- Introduce scripless trading.
- Computerise trading
- Credit dividend payment directly to the account of the shareholders in the bank through electronic clearing mechanism.
- To act as a bank for shares.

◈ Advantages of SHCIL

- Transfer of shares will be fast and simple.
- Dividends and interest can be electronically transferred to the investors' account.
- Protection against loss and theft of securities.
- Easier to maintain multicompany portfolio for the investors.
- There will be nothing like lot trading and the investors holding odd lot in physical form and unable to trade in them, can now be free to trade in those shares.
- Brokers will be relieved of a lot of paperwork.
- The settlement of transactions would be greatly simplified.

The Bull Run in the markets that has been witnessed in 2003 has had its fallout on the stock markets. The turnover of both BSE and NSE has increased tremendously both in the cash as well as Futures and Options segment.

Another fallout has been that the membership card of BSE has been once again sought after. This stock exchange has inducted 127 new members in three months. Most of these new members are leading foreign and domestic broking houses. Under a scheme that was announced in November 2003 BSE offered trading rights against the traditional BSE card, which came with ownership rights.

8 VENTURE CAPITAL

◈ Introduction and Definition

Definition: Venture capital means, providing seed, start up and first stage financing and funding the expansion of companies that have already demonstrated their business potential but do not have access to the public securities markets or to credit-oriented institutional funding sources.

Venture capitalists also provide management/leveraged buyout financing. The process is of investing of risk capital in an enterprise in which the venture investor shares ownership as well as Board of Directors level management responsibilities with the funding management team.

It is risk finance for entrepreneurial growth-oriented companies. It is investment for the medium- or long-term, seeking to maximize medium- or long-term return for both the parties. The investor can add value to the company because of his knowledge, experience and contact base.

It is an actual or potential equity investment in companies through the purchase of stock, warrants, options or convertible securities.

Venture capital is equity, equity featured capital seeking investment in new ideas, new companies, new products, new processes or new services that offer the potential of high returns on investment. It may also include investment in turnaround situations.

◈ Characteristics of VC

1. Investments are made in equity or equity featured instruments of investment.
2. Young companies that do not have access to public sources of equity or other forms of capital.
3. Industry, products or services that hold potential of better than normal or average revenue growth.
4. Companies with better than normal or average profitability.

5. Products/services in the early stages of their life cycle.
6. Higher than average risk levels that do not lend themselves to systematic quantification through conventional techniques and tools.
7. Turnaround companies.
8. Long-term and active involvement with investee.

The importance of venture capitalists is not on account of the volume of capital it provides; it is more on account of its indirect benefits. These investments enable the development of entirely new lines of business. They typically prefer to invest in knowledge based industries such as Information Technology and Biotech. This has in turn catalyzed entrepreneurship amongst professional managers and technologists to a considerable degree.

Venture capital has played an unparalleled role in bringing technologies to the market-place.

There has to be enabling environment for the venture capital activities to flourish.

Firstly there must exist the culture of entrepreneurship. One of the reasons why venture capital culture has not caught up in India could be this and also the absence of new ideas in the form of new product development.

The next thing is the tax policy. In India income from dividends and long-term capital gains from equity investments made by the approved VC funds or VC companies is exempted from tax. Such companies will be required to invest only in unlisted companies engaged in manufacturing.

Thé VCs to flourish require a well-developed capital market. VCs require an exit route, to make profits. The most preferred exit route for these companies is public offering of the portfolio companies stock. Therefore a vibrant capital market is an important pre-requisite for them.

Innovation is the mother of VC investments. In a protected economy, with no compulsion or incentive to compete through innovation, VC may not find many opportunities to invest. This is true of Indian scenario as well.

The VCs normally does not finance the working capital requirements of the companies in whose capital they invest. It is therefore essential that complementary financial institutions exist to take up these responsibilities.

The ethos of building business for financial gains and the preparedness to sell them off to an acquirer provides an important exit route to the VC investor.

◆ Stages of Venture Capital Financing

Seed Financing: Relatively small amount of capital is provided to an entrepreneur to prove his concept.

Start-up Financing: This is provided to companies completing product development and initial marketing. Usually such firms will have made market studies and assembled the key management, developed a business plan and are ready to do business.

First Stage Financing: This is provided to companies that have expanded their initial capital and require funds to initiate full-scale manufacturing and sales.

◆ Expansion Financing

Second Stage Financing: This is the working capital for the initial expansion of a company that is producing and shipping and has growing accounts receivables and inventories.

Third Stage or Mezzanine Financing: This is provided for major expansion of a company when sales volume is increasing and that is breaking even or profitable. These funds are used for further plant expansion, marketing, working capital or development of an improved product.

Bridge Financing: This type of financing is required at times when a company plans to go public within six months to a year. Often it is structured so that it can be repaid from the proceeds of a public underwriting.

Acquisition (Buyout) Finance: This kind of funding provides funds to finance an acquisition of another company. Management/Leveraged buyout funds enable an operating management group to acquire a product-line or business (which may be at any stage of development) from either a public or private company. Often these companies are closely held or family owned.

◈ The Venture Investment Process

Generating a Deal Flow: The VC investor creates a pipeline of deals or investment opportunities that he would consider for investing in.

It is common for VC funds/investors to develop working relationship with R&D institutions academicians, etc.

Due Diligence: All activities those are associated with evaluating an investment proposal. It includes carrying out reference checks on the proposal related aspects such as management team, products, technology, and market. VC due diligence focuses on the qualitative aspects of an investment opportunity.

◈ Investment Valuation

1. Evaluate future revenue and profitability.
2. Forecast likely future value of the firm based on expected market capitalisation, or expected acquisition proceeds depending upon the anticipated exit from the investments.
3. Target on ownership position in the investee firm so as to achieve trained appreciation on the proposed investment.

The value of a firm is driven by a number of factors like:

(*a*) Overall economic conditions.

(*b*) Demand and supply of capital

(*c*) Specifics of the deal

(*d*) The degree of popularity of the industry/technology in question.

(*e*) The standing of the individual VC

(*f*) Investor's consideration.

◈ Structuring the Deal

The investor tries to ensure the following:

(*a*) Reasonable reward for the given level of risks.

(*b*) Sufficient influence on the management of the company through board representation.

(*c*) Minimisation of taxes.

(*d*) Ease in achieving future liquidity on the investment.

◆ The Entrepreneur Seeks

(*a*) The creation of the business that he has conceptualsied. (Operating/strategic control).

(*b*) Financial rewards for creating the business.

(*c*) Adequate resources needed to achieve their goal.

(*d*) Voting control.

◆ Common Consideration

(a) Flexibility of structure that will allow room to enable additional investments later, incentives for future management and retention of stock if management leaves.

(b) Balance sheet attractiveness to suppliers and debt financiers.

(c) Retention of key employees through adequate equity participation.

SEBI Venture Capital Funds Regulation

REGISTRATION OF VENTURE CAPITAL FUNDS

◆ Application for Grant of Certificate

Any company or trust 1[or a body corporate] proposing to carry on any activity as a venture capital fund on or after the commencement of these regulations shall make an application to the Board for grant of a certificate.

Any company or trust 2[or a body corporate], who on the date of commencement of these regulations is carrying any activity as a venture capital fund without a certificate shall make an application to the Board for grant of a certificate within a period of three months from the date of such commencement:

Provided that the Board, in special cases, may extend the said period up to a maximum of six months from the date of such commencement.

INVESTMENT CONDITIONS AND RESTRICTIONS

◆ Minimum Investment in a Venture Capital Fund

A venture capital fund may raise monies from any investor whether Indian, foreign or non-resident Indian 2[by way of issue of units].

No venture capital fund set up as a company or any scheme of a venture capital fund set up as a trust shall accept any investment from any investor which is less than five lakh rupees:

Provided that nothing contained in sub-regulation (2) shall apply to investors who are:

(*a*) employees or the principal officer or directors of the venture capital fund, or directors of the trustee company or trustees where the venture capital fund has been established as a trust;

Each scheme launched or fund set up by a venture capital fund shall have firm commitment from the investors for contribution of an amount of at least rupees five crore before the start of operations by the venture capital fund.

Restrictions on investment by a venture capital fund — All investments made or to be made by a venture capital fund shall be subject to the following restrictions:

(*a*) The venture capital fund shall not invest in the equity shares of any company or institution providing financial services;

(*b*) At least 80 per cent of funds raised by a venture capital fund shall be invested in:

(*i*) The equity shares or equity related securities issued by a company whose securities are not listed on any recognised stock exchange:

Provided that a venture capital fund may invest in equity shares or equity related securities of a company whose securities are to be listed or are listed where the venture capital fund has made these investments through private placements prior to the listing of the securities.

(*ii*) The equity shares or equity related securities of a financially weak company or a sick industrial company, whose securities may or may not be listed on any recognised stock-exchange.

Explanation: For the purposes of this regulation, a "financially weak company" means a company, which has at the end of the previous financial year accumulated losses, which has resulted in erosion of more than 50 per cent but less than 100 per cent of its net worth as at the beginning of the previous financial year.

(*iii*) Providing financial assistance in any other manner to companies in whose equity shares the venture capital fund has invested under sub-clause (*i*) or sub-clause (*ii*) as the case may be.

All investment made or to be made by a venture capital fund shall be subject to the following conditions, namely:

(*a*) Venture capital fund shall disclose the investment strategy at the time of application for registration;

(*b*) Venture capital fund shall not invest more than 25 per cent corpus of the fund in one venture capital undertaking;

1[(*ba*) Venture capital fund may invest in securities of foreign companies subject to such conditions or guidelines that may be stipulated or issued by the Reserve Bank of India and the Board from time-to-time.]

(*c*) Shall not invest in the associated companies; and

(*d*) Venture capital fund shall make investment 2[***] as enumerated below:

(*i*) At least 3[66.67 per cent] of the investible funds shall be invested in unlisted equity shares or equity linked instruments.

(*ii*) Not more than 6[33.33 per cent] of the investible funds may be invested by way of equity.

(*a*) subscription to initial public offer of a venture capital undertaking whose shares are proposed to be listed to lock-in period of one year;

Debt or debt instrument of a venture capital undertaking in which the venture capital fund has already made an investment by way of equity.]

Preferential allotment of equity shares of a listed company subject to lock-in period of one year;

The equity shares or equity linked instruments of a financially weak company or a sick industrial company whose shares are listed.

Explanation 1: For the purpose of these regulations, a "financially weak company" means a company, which has at the end of the previous financial year accumulated losses, which has resulted in erosion of more than 50 per cent but less than 100 per cent of its net worth as at the beginning of the previous financial year;

Special Purpose Vehicles which are created by a venture capital fund for the purpose of facilitating or promoting investment in accordance with these Regulations.

Explanation: The investment conditions and restrictions stipulated in clause (d) of regulation 12 shall be achieved by the venture capital fund by the end of its life cycle; [venture capital fund shall disclose the duration of life cycle of the fund.]

◆ Investment in Securities Listed on SME Exchange

The venture capital fund may enter into an agreement with merchant banker to subscribe to the unsubscribed portion of the issue or to receive or deliver securities in the process of market making under Chapter XA of the Securities and Exchange Board of India (Issue of Capital and Disclosure Requirements) Regulations, 2009 and the provisions of Regulation 12 shall not apply in case of acquisition or sale of securities pursuant to such subscription or market making.

(*a*) VCFs must be registered with SEBI and pay ₹ 25,000 as application fee and ₹ 5 lakh as registration fee.

(*b*) VCF cannot carry on any other activity.

(*c*) VCFs are authorised to raise funds from 1) Indian, 2) Foreign and 3) NRIs, by issue of units or shares.

(*d*) VCFs must disclose the investment strategy at the time of their registration.

(*e*) They cannot invest more than 25 per cent of their corpus in one company.

(*f*) They are prohibited from investing in associate companies.

(*g*) At least 74 per cent of the investible funds must be invested in unlisted companies.

(*h*) Not more than 25 per cent of the funds may be invested by way of:

(*i*) (1) subscription to IPO of the company whose shares are proposed to be listed subject to a lock-in of one year, and

(2) Debt/debt instruments of a company in which the VCF has already made an investment by way of equity.

(*j*) No VCF would be entitled to get its units listed on any recognized stock exchange, till expiration of three years from the date of issuance of units by it.

(*k*) It may receive money for investment in the VCF through only private placement of its units.

The scene in India on investments by venture capitalists seems to be hotting up. With the investments rising in BPO, this sector seems to have become a favourite destination for these funds.

With the WTO regulations on patents and copyrights becoming effective from Jan 2005, it is said that the Pharma sector is also likely to see a lot of action in India. Many funds are looking at opportunities to invest in this sector as well.

The old favourite ITes continues to attract investments.

In early 2004 thirty-three venture capitalists from US came to India to look for investment opportunities. These funds together have access to $ 10 billion. They have been very keen to invest in India and have seen a lot of potential investment opportunities.

INDIAN VENTURE CAPITAL INDUSTRY

◈ Problems with VCs in the Indian Context

There are mainly three categories of venture capital funds.

1. Funds promoted by All India Development Financial Institutions and State level Development Financial Institutions.
2. Funds promoted by commercial banks.
3. Funds promoted by private sector financial services companies.

Most VC investors in India do not seem to have any stated sectoral preferences.

One can ask why venture funding is so successful in USA and faced a number of problems in India. The biggest problem was a mindset change from "collateral funding" to high risk high return funding. Most of the pioneers in the industry were people with credit background and exposure to manufacturing industries. Exposure to fast growing intellectual property business and services sector was almost zero. All these combined to a slow start to the industry. The other issues that led to such a situation include:

◈ License Raj and the IPO Boom

Till early 90s, under the license raj regime, only commodity centric businesses thrived in a deficit situation. To fund a cement plant, venture capital is not needed. What was needed was ability to get a license and then get the project funded by the banks and DFIs. In most cases, the promoters were well-established industrial houses, with no apparent need for funds. Most of these entities were capable of raising funds from conventional sources, including term loans from institutions and equity markets.

◈ Scalability

The Indian software segment has recorded an impressive growth over the last few years and earns large revenues from its export earnings, yet our share in the global market is less than one per cent. Within the software industry, the value chain ranges from body shopping at the bottom to strategic consulting at the top. Higher value addition and profitability as well as significant market presence take place at the higher end of the value chain. If the industry has to grow further and survive the flux it would only be through innovation. For any venture idea to succeed there should be a product that has a growing market with a scalable business model. The IT industry (which is most suited for venture funding because of its "ideas" nature) in India till recently had a service centric business model. Products developed for Indian markets lack scale.

◈ Mindsets

Venture capital as an activity was virtually non-existent in India. Most venture capital companies want to provide capital on a secured debt basis, to established businesses with profitable operating histories. Most of the venture capital units were offshoots of financial institutions and banks and the lending mindset continued. True venture capital is capital that is used to help launch products and ideas of tomorrow. Abroad, this problem is solved by the presence of 'angel investors'. They are typically wealthy individuals who not only provide venture finance but also help entrepreneurs to shape their business and make their venture successful.

Returns, Taxes and Regulations

There is a multiplicity of regulators like SEBI and RBI. Domestic venture funds are set up under the Indian Trusts Act of 1882 as per SEBI guidelines, while offshore funds routed through Mauritius follow RBI guidelines. Abroad, such funds are made under the Limited Partnership Act, which brings advantages in terms of taxation. The government must allow pension funds and insurance companies to invest in venture capitals as in USA where corporate contributions to venture funds are large.

Exit

The exit routes available to the venture capitalists were restricted to the IPO route. Before deregulation, pricing was dependent on the erstwhile CCI regulations. In general, all issues were underpriced. Even now SEBI guidelines make it difficult for pricing issues for an easy exit. Given the failure of the OTCEI and the revised guidelines, small companies could not hope for a BSE/NSE listing. Given the dull market for mergers and acquisitions, strategic sale was also not available.

Valuation

The recent phenomenon is valuation mismatches. Thanks to the software boom, most promoters have sky high valuation expectations. Given this, it is difficult for deals to reach financial closure as promoters do not agree to a valuation. This coupled with the fancy for software stocks in the bourses means that most companies are preponing their IPOs. Consequently, the number and quality of deals available to the venture funds gets reduced.

Angels

Angels are important links in the entire process of venture capital funding. This is because they support a fledging enterprise at a very early stage – sometime even before commercialization of the product or service offering. Typically, an angel is an experienced industry-bred individual with high net worth.

Angels provide funding by "first round" financing for risky investments – risky because they are a young/start-up company or because their financial track record is unstable. This venture capital financing is typically used to prepare the company for "second round" financing in the form of an initial public offering (IPO). *Example:* A company may need "first round" financing to develop a new product-line, (*viz.*, a new drug which would require significant research and development funding) or make a strategic acquisition to achieve certain levels of growth and stability.

It is important to choose the right angel because they will sit on your Board of Directors, often for the duration of their investment and will assist in getting "second round" financing. When choosing an 'Angel', it is imperative to consider their experience in a relevant industry, reputation, qualifications and track record.

Angels are people with less money orientation, but who play an active role in making an early-stage company work. They are people with enough hands-on experience and are experts in their fields. They understand the field from an operational perspective. An entrepreneur needs this kind of expertise. He also needs money to make things happen. Angels bring both to the table of an entrepreneur.

There are a number of professionally qualified people, especially from IITs who had migrated to USA. Some of them have made their millions riding the IT boom in Silicon Valley. Having witnessed the maturity of the Silicon Valley into the global tech hotspot and thrived in the environment there, these individuals are rich in terms of financial resources and experience. They are the latest angels in the Indian industry.

The Indo-US Entrepreneurs (TiE), a networking society that brings together highly influential Indians across the US was set up in 1992. The aim of the organization is to get the community together and to foster entrepreneurs and wealth creation. The idea was sparked off in 1992, when a group of Silicon Valley entrepreneurs with roots in the Indian subcontinent met by chance for a meeting with a visiting dignitary from India. A delayed flight kept the group waiting, and provided an opportunity for people to get to know one another. It turned out that most of the assembled invitees to the meeting had achieved varying degrees of entrepreneurial success. The group saw value in getting together on a regular basis to network with one another. Thus, the idea of TiE was born as a mechanism for high achievement-oriented Indo-US entrepreneurs to network.

Over the years, a core group of about 10-15 individuals worked hard to establish the organization. Meeting at least once a month, successful veteran entrepreneurs, contributed as speakers, participants and mentors. Gradually, the group started attracting greater participation, and the TiE concept started gaining momentum. TiE membership has now grown to over 600 members, and chapters in Boston, Austin and Los Angeles. TiE is also supported by over 20 institutions that include leading Silicon Valley venture capital investors, law firms, accounting firms and banks.

Fifty per cent of business plans submitted to venture capitalists in the Valley and outside is now from Indians and TiE can take the lion's share of the credit for this. What's more? About 30 per cent of the projects that are funded, are headed by Indians.

TiE isn't about venture capitalist funding. It's about angel investing. The issue here is to identify a good idea that hasn't attracted any money, and then fund it the money coming from the member's own pockets. The environment is traditional in the sense of it following a gurukul environment of sorts, where the gurus transfer knowledge on business plans, management strategies and survival kits to new TiE members.

Some of the famous names include:

- **Vinod Dham**, father of the Pentium chip and now the CEO of the Silicon Spice, one of the most closely watched start-ups in the Silicon Valley today.
- **Sailesh Mehta**, CEO and President of the US$15bn Providian Financial and the man who is using technology to re-order consumer finance.
- **Kanwal Rekhi**, one of the first Indians to become a big name in the valley; founder of Excelan, past CTO and member of Novell's board, now invests in a number of new ventures. He is the current chairman of the TiE.
- **Prabhu Goel**, 'serial entrepreneur', who has started three hi-tech companies so far and is on the board of five other companies as a private investor.
- **Suhas Patil**, who founded the semiconductor company Cirrus Logic in 1984.
- **Prakash Agarwal**, whose NeoMagic integrates memory and logic on a single chip. The six-year-old company already has a market share of 50 per cent.
- **K.B. Chandrashekhar**, heads the US $ 200 mn Exodus Communications, whose fibre optic network carries 30 per cent of all Internet content traffic and whose servers host such popular websites such as Yahoo, Hotmail and Amazon.

But Indian VC investment, for all its brouhaha, is essentially small, far less than China and Japan, and far less exciting. In fact, India has now slipped to the 5th position (from 3rd place in 2002) in Asia. More than the dotcom bust, this is perhaps due to the belated realisation that India remains an untested if not shaky market, and that success is often shaped by a combination of social circumstance and government role.

Take vaccines for instance, where a number of firms are in the race. On surface, the market opportunity looks huge; after all, infant mortality is high in India, over 3 million children under the age of five die each year and one in every 15 persons is a carrier of some immunisable disease. But while vaccine sales are robust and growing, around 20 per cent annually, they have hardly shown the dramatic growth that was projected by many venture capitalists.

Why? Because government is still the largest buyer. Official procurement remains mired in bureaucracy and corruption, while refrigeration and medical infrastructure needed for an effective immunization programme simply does not exist in the far reaches of the country. The bottom line is that no matter how fantastic a discovery, a new vaccine will enjoy only limited market penetration due to the meagre resources of the public health system.

◈ Corporate Venturing

Even though corporate venturing is an attractive alternative, most companies find it difficult to establish systems, capabilities and cultures that make good venture capital firms. Corporate managers seldom have the same freedom to fund innovative projects or to cancel them midstream. Their skills are honed for managing mature businesses and not nurturing start-up companies. If a firm is to apply the venture capital model, it must understand the characteristics of the model and tailor its venture capital programme to its own circumstances without losing sight of these essentials.

Success of venture capital firms rest on the following characteristics:

Focus on specific industry niches and look for business concepts that will

- Although corporate managers have a clear focus in their business, they run into ambiguity with venture programmes. Their biggest challenge is to establish clear, prioritized objectives. Simply making a good financial return is not sufficient.
- Manage portfolios ruthlessly; abandon losers, whereas abandoning ventures has never been easy for large corporations, whose projects are underpinned by personal relationships, political concerns.
- Venture capital firms share several attributes with start-up they fund. They tend to be small, flexible and quick to make decisions. They have flat hierarchies and rely heavily on equity and incentive pay.

Apple Computers established a venture fund in 1986 with the dual objectives of earning high financial return and supporting development of Macintosh software. They structured compensation mechanisms, decision criteria and operating procedures on those of top venture capital firms. While they considered Macintosh as an initial screening factor, its funding decisions were aimed at optimizing financial returns. The result was an IRR of 90 per cent but little success in improving the position of Macintosh.

New ventures can be powerful source of revenues, diversification and flexibility in rapidly changing environments. The company should create an environment that encourages venturing. An innovative culture cannot be transplanted but must evolve within the company. Venture investing requires different mindset from typical corporate investors.

How relevant is corporate venturing in the Indian scenario? The firms, which launched the successful corporate ventures had created new products in the market operating at the higher end of the value chain and had attained a certain size in the market. Most Indian companies are yet to move up the value chain and consolidate their position as players in the global market. Corporate venturing models would probably benefit Indian companies who are large players in the Indian market in another five to ten years by enabling them to diversify and at the same time help start-up companies. Multinationals led by Intel are the best examples of corporate venturing in an Indian context.

Here are the five top deals in India in the year 2011:

Happiest Minds, an IT solutions and service firm had raised $ 45 million in its series A round of investments, the funds who participated included Canaan Partners, Intel Capital, and Ashok Soota himself, in November 2011. Happiest Minds was founded in 2011 by Ashok Soota, who is also the co-founder of MindTree, a former President of Wipro InfoTech and Confederation of Indian Industry. Happiest Minds raised the funds to deliver most advance technology solution and services, hire talented employees, set up additional infrastructure, and increase sales and marketing efforts globally.

The Online Travel Agent, Yatra.com raised $ 44.4 million from Valiant Capital, Norwest Venture Partners, and Intel Capital in April 2011. The company has previously raised $ 33.3 million from Norwest Venture Partners, Reliance Capital, Network 18, and Intel Capital. The company raised the funds for expanding its holiday and hotel booking segment, and for acquisitions. The company was founded by Dhruv Shringi and Manish Amin in 2006 and is ranked as the leading provider of consumer-direct travel services in India. This company is likely to go public in near future. It has grown substantially over the years.

The online shopping site Fashion and You had raised $ 40 million in its series C round of funding from Norwest Venture Partners and Intel Capital and saw the participation of Nokia Growth Partners and existing investors Sequoia Capital in November 2011. The company had raised the funds to expand into additional categories and make strategic acquisitions to complement the existing business. The company was founded in 2010 by Pearl Uppal and backed by Harish Bahl, the Founder of Smile Group. Previously the company had raised funds from European and Indian private investors in series A; and had raised $ 8 million from Sequoia Capital in Series B round of funding. However we will have to wait and see if such ventures will become successful in India. Though the online shopping is catching on fast among the young Indians we have to wait and see what happens in future.

The online shopping site Naaptol.com had raised $ 25 million in VC investment from New Enterprise Associates, and saw the participation of existing investors Canaan Partners and Silicon Valley Bank in August 2011. The funds were raised to fuel Naaptol's massive hiring plans and to invest in its internet business, supply chain and inventory. Founded in 2008 by Manu Aggarwal, the company had previously raised $ 7 million from Canaan Advisors, including a fresh issue of shares and acquisition of shared by Bennett Coleman & Co. Naaptol had also raised ₹ 7 crore from the Silicon Valley Bank in 2010. This again is online shopping platform. It is interesting that Bennett Coleman & Co. which is essentially a newspaper publishing house has made big investments in recent years in many companies.

The e-commerce portal Flipkart had raised $ 40 million in its series C round of funding from its existing investors Tiger Global Management in June 2011. The funds were raised to build capacity in supply chain, to upgrade technology and expand its market. Previously the company had raised $ 10 million from Tiger Global Management; and another investment from Accel Partners in late 2009; to take the total funds to $ 31 million. The company was founded in 2007 by Sachin Bansal and Binny Bansal, and has grown to become India's largest online bookseller. Flipkart has now ventures into mobile phones, gaming consoles, music and movies as well. This is one company that has been declared successful by the market watchers.

It has become popular and seems to be doing pretty well these last few years. The company seems to be firmly on the growth path as of now.

It is interesting to note that Narayana Murthy has started a VC fund. But one big investment that he made was in SKS Microfinance has proved to be a disaster for many reasons. The company was a pioneer in microfinancing and made a very successful public issue at very high valuation. Things have since become very bad with promoter getting into trouble big time and the general anti-microfinance sector sentiments fuelled by the controversy related to very high rates of interest charged to the beneficiaries by these companies. The market price has nosedived making several investors poorer.

Azim Premji on the other hand made a handsome investment in Chennai based fast growing retail chain "Subhiksha". The company has since got into serious financial trouble and has folded up leaving all creditors high and dry including banks that had lent heavily. Premji is now fighting a legal battle to recover his money.

Just goes to show that successful entrepreneurs need not necessarily become successful VC investors!

CURRENT TRENDS

◆ Capital is Pouring into Private Equity Funds

The IPO boom and its exceptional returns to venture and other kinds of private equity investments have led institutional investors, pension funds and endowments to park their money in these investments.

◆ Bigger is Better

The most established venture funds now have more partners and therefore are able to put more money to work effectively. *Also*, venture firms are doing less deal syndication, which enables them to put more money to work in a single deal. *Thirdly*, many traditional early-stage venture firms have shifted to a multistage investment approach. They will back companies in technologies and industries they know intimately, almost *regardless* of the stage.

◆ First-time Firms Never had it so Good

During the 1989-91 downturns, new venture capital firms faced a problem in raising partnership capital, as there was a 'flight to quality' among investors who backed established funds in the private equity market. However, developments over the past few years have demonstrated that investing with an established firm is no more a sure-bet than an investment in a 'first-time fund'.

◆ The State wants its Share of the Pie too

The Department of Electronics of the Government of India announced the creation of a ₹ 1bn IT fund. Many state governments are sponsoring the formation of new venture capital firms to spur the creation and growth of new business quickly followed this move. Andhra Pradesh, Karnataka, Kerala, Gujarat and West Bengal are among the states creating such programmes. They are fairly controversial efforts, because they run the risk of sacrificing return for economic stimulus. Many would believe that they are not a good idea. However, some of them are better designed than others and few might actually work.

◈ Venture Firms are being run more like Businesses

One of the healthiest consequences of the growth in institutional funding has been increased scrutiny that venture firms have come under. Feedback from previous investments and suggestions from the investors in these funds are helping to increase the sense of professionalism in the industry.

◈ No more men in Gray Suits

Another trend that is emerging slowly is the change in the profile of a fund manager. The venture capitalist is no longer a hybrid investment banker trying to cash in on another market boom while still keeping his cards close to his chest. The new-age venture capitalist is industry-bred and highly regarded in the business and is fairly at ease with the technologies and processes in the market.

◈ Tomorrow is coming Faster

Rapid changes in technology have accelerated the pace and raised the efficiencies for getting from idea to market. *Investors are* specializing. Financing sources are becoming much more focused on their way to investment in today's competitive environment. Today, from venture capital firms to leveraged buyout (LBO) houses and corporations, investors are devising specific plans for industries and technologies they want to be in.

◈ More Venture Funds are Seeking Traditional Businesses

More venture capital funds are going after low-tech or no-tech companies. For example, Draper International has picked up a stake in Shoppers' Stop and Indus League Clothing.

◈ Financing Sources are more Flexible

More companies are acquiring new ideas, products and complementary operations to capture growth and gain market share. This means financing must allow for covenants that permit mergers, acquisitions and continued investments.

◈ Financing Sources and Companies are Building Partnering Relationships

Companies need financing sources that allow them to move quickly and will tolerate risk, including acquisitions. Although financing sources are risking more, the rewards of such a partnering relationship can grow and be profitable for all concerned.

◈ Competition is affecting Buyer Prices

Historically, there has been a big difference between strategic buyers who paid a premium for the potential of synergy and financial buyers and LBO houses. Today, the two factions are more directly competitive.

All businesses are not evaluated equally. Venture houses today are looking at what enhances the value of a company, with different 'value drivers' affecting various industry segments. For example, when evaluating a technology company, investors may care about a unique technology or process with great potential. They won't necessarily worry whether the company lacks audited financial statements or an organizational structure. In a non-technology area, however, there must be more than a new idea; 'value drivers' might include historical performance, gross margins and return on investment.

◈ Private Equity

Private equity is a source of investment capital from high net worth individuals and institutions for the purpose of investing and acquiring equity ownership in companies. Partners at private equity firms raise funds and manage these monies for the purpose of yielding favourable returns for their shareholder clients, typically with an investment horizon between four and seven years.

These funds can be used in the purchase of shares of private companies or in uublic companies that eventually get delisted from the stock exchanges under go-private deals. The minimum amount of capital required for investors can vary depending on the firm and fund raised. Some funds have a $ 250,000 minimum investment requirement; others can require millions of dollars. This is the way it operates in US markets. Conditions in India are different. Many international PE funds make investment in India though the money is raised abroad.

◈ Introduction to Private Equity

Private equity has successfully attracted the best and brightest in corporate America, including top performers from *Fortune 500* companies and elite strategy and management consulting firms. Top performers at accounting and law firms can also be recruiting grounds, as accounting and legal skills relate to transaction support work required to complete a deal and translate to advisory work for a portfolio company's management.

The fee structure for private equity firms varies, but it typically consists of a management fee and a performance fee (in some cases, a yearly *management fee* of 2 per cent of assets managed and 20 per cent of gross profits upon sale of the company). How firms are incentivized can vary considerably. The deal fee is negotiable.

◈ Transaction Support and Portfolio Oversight

There are two critical functions within private equity firms:

- Deal origination/transaction execution
- Portfolio oversight

A lot of PE investment is used during mergers and acquisitions. Many also invest in growing companies who need more capital to sustain the high growth rates.

Transaction execution involves assessing management, the industry, historical financials and forecasts, and conducting *valuation analyses.* After the investment committee signs off to pursue a target acquisition candidate, the deal professionals submit an offer to the seller. If both parties decide to move forward, the deal professionals work with various transaction advisors to include investment bankers, accountants, lawyers and consultants to execute the *due diligence* phase. Due diligence includes validating management's stated operational and financial figures. This part of the process is critical, as consultants can uncover deal killers, such as significant and previously undisclosed liabilities and risks.

The second important function of private equity professionals involves oversight and support of the firm's various portfolio companies and their management team. Among other support work, they can walk management through *best practices* in strategic planning and financial management. Additionally, they can help institutionalize new accounting, *procurement* and IT systems in order to increase the value of their investment.

◈ Types of Private Equity Firms

There is a spectrum of investing preferences across the thousands of private equity firms in existence. Some are strict financiers — passive investors — who are wholly dependent on management to grow the company (and its profitability) and supply their owners with appropriate returns. Because sellers typically see this method as a *commoditized* approach, other private equity firms consider themselves active investors. That is, they provide operational support to management in order to help them build and grow a better company.

These types of firms may have an extensive contact list and "C-level" relationships, such as CEOs and CFOs within a given industry, which can help increase revenue, or they may be experts in realizing operational efficiencies and synergies. If an investor can bring in something special to a deal that will enhance the value of the company over time, such an investor is more likely to be viewed favourably by sellers. It is the seller who ultimately makes the choice of whom they want to sell to, or partner with.

It is no surprise that the largest investment-banking entities, such as Goldman Sachs, J P Morgan Chase and Citigroup facilitate the largest deals. These banks typically focus their efforts on deals with enterprise values worth billions of dollars. However, the vast majority of transactions reside in the middle market ($ 50 million - $ 500 million deals) and lower-middle market ($ 10 million - $ 50 million deals).

Because the best investment banking professionals gravitate toward the larger deals, the middle market is a significantly underserved market. That is, there are significantly more sellers than there are highly seasoned and positioned finance professionals that have the extensive buyer networks and resources to manage a deal (for middle-market company owners).

◈ Investing in Upside

Middle-market companies can offer significant financial upside to their private equity owners. Many of these small companies fly below the radar of large multinational corporations and often provide higher quality customer service. These companies provide niche products and services that are not being offered by the large *conglomerates*.

Such upsides attract the interest of private equity firms as they possess the insights and savvy to exploit such opportunities and take the company to the next level. For instance, a small company selling niche products within a particular region might significantly grow by cultivating international sales channels. Or a highly fragmented industry can undergo consolidation (with the private equity firm buying up and combining these entities) to create fewer, larger players. Larger companies typically command higher valuations than smaller companies.

An important company metric for these investors is *earnings before interest, taxes, depreciation and amortization* (EBITDA). When a private equity firm acquires a company, they work together with management in order to significantly increase EBITDA during its investment horizon (typically between four and seven years). A good portfolio company can typically increase its EBITDA both organically (internal growth) and by acquisitions.

A popular exit strategy for private equity involves growing and improving a middle-market company and selling it to a large corporation (within a related industry) for a hefty profit. It is critical for private equity investors to have reliable, capable and dependable management in place. Most managers at portfolio companies are given equity and bonus compensation structures that reward them for hitting their financial targets. Such alignment of goals (and appropriate compensation structuring) is typically a requirement prior to a deal getting done.

Private equity firms have become attractive investment vehicles for wealthy individuals and institutions. As the industry attracts the best and brightest in corporate America, the professionals at these firms are usually successful in deploying investment capital and in increasing the values of their portfolio companies. However, there is also fierce competition in the M&A marketplace for good companies to buy. As such, it is imperative that these firms develop strong relationships with transaction and services professionals in order to secure strong deal flow.

In India we had seen huge flows of PE money in the heady days of 2006-08 in many sectors especially in real estate and even in financial services. These deals were done at very high prices as the markets were booming. One reason for the markets to boom beyond the economic logic was the huge fund flow from PE and FIIs. Some deals were struck at a premium to market prices.

Many promoters were lucky to get high but unsustainable valuations. They brought in PE investments just before they went public. The price paid for such private placement was they touted by them and their merchant bankers to get a very high valuation and consequently priced their issues at astronomical premiums. As the market was firmly in the bull grip their issues sailed through without any problem. Investors thought that markets will continue to go up and had therefore not looked at the fundamentals while buying shares of such companies. One has to also question the so-called expertise of experts who do valuation for these funds. It is difficult to fathom the prices that they shelled out for deals. One gets the feeling that cheap money available and the greed of all concerned made this possible.

Things went horribly wrong after the sub-prime crisis exploded in 2008. The world markets tumbled and Indian markets lost almost two-thirds of its value at the peak of the crisis and even though the markets recovered and touched highs again in the next couple of years, many stocks continued to languish below their issue price! One hope that PEs have learnt their lessons and will be more sober and circumspect in choosing companies to invest in. However, all this will be forgotten once the markets return to the bull phase!

Introduction and Need of Credit Rating

The system of rating got institutionalised following the Great Depression in 1933, when the US Controller of Currency enacted a rule that banks could only purchase securities, which have minimum investment rating.

The need for credit rating is different for different parties depending on the benefits it offers to the various parties utilizing these services, *viz.*, Investors, issuers, intermediaries and the regulatory authority.

In India we have four major rating agencies CRISIL — where majority stakeholder in Standard and Poor, ICRA which has majority stake by Moody's, Fitch which is a foreign agency and CARE which is owned by financial institutions and is least active.

Investors

Rating will supplement the investors' credit evaluation process.

It facilitates comparison of relative value between competing securities.

It helps in recognizing the risk involved in the investment.

Issuers

A company with highly rated instrument has the opportunity to reduce the cost of borrowing by quoting less interest rate.

A company with rating can approach a wider section of investors for resource mobilization.

Companies with rated instruments can avail of the rating as a marketing tool to create better image in dealing with its customers, lenders and creditors.

Rating encourages the companies to come out with more disclosures about their accounting system, financial reporting and management pattern.

Smaller and not so well known companies can access markets.

Encourages financial discipline as borrowers attempt to obtain ratings by improving financial structured reducing operating risks.

◈ Financial Intermediaries

The ratings help them in pricing the debt.

It shifts the burden of establishing credit quality from intermediary to a rating agency thereby easing the due diligence requirement.

With high credit rated instruments, the brokers can convince their clients to select a particular investment proposal. This saves their time, cost and manpower in convincing their clients.

◈ Regulatory Authority

By identifying the risks, rating helps in channelling savings into productive investments.

Credit rating serves the objective of protecting the investors.

What is credit rating and what credit rating is not!

Rating reflects the borrower's accountability, expected capability and inclination to pay interest and principal in a timely manner.

Rating is an isolated function of a credit risk evaluation.

Rating is useful in differentiating credit quality.

Rating will involve issue-specific evaluation.

What credit rating is not?

Rating is not a general purpose evaluation of the issuer.

It is not a recommendation to buy/sell/hold a security.

Rating is not an extensive audit of the issuing company.

Rating is not a one-time assessment of creditworthiness valid over the future life of the security.

Factors that contributed to the growth of credit rating:

High level of defaults in US capital markets in 1970.

Regulators stipulation for mandatory ratings.

Investor's awareness of ratings for risk assessment and risk management.

It helps intermediaries for pricing and placement of financial instruments.

The increasing role of capital and money markets.

Globalisation of credit markets.

The continuing growth of information technology.

The growth of confidence in the efficiency of the market mechanism.

The withdrawal of government safety nets and the trend towards privatisation.

Factors considered by credit rating agencies while rating an instrument.

Rating is search for long-term fundamentals and the probabilities for changes in the fundamentals.

The analytical framework for rating methodology is divided into two independent segments. The first deals with operational characteristics and the second with financial characteristics. Besides quantitative and objective factors, qualitative aspects like assessment of management capabilities play a very important role in arriving at the rating for an instrument. The relative importance of qualitative and quantitative components of analysis varies with the type of issuer.

Credit rating is an opinion on the relative ability and willingness of an issuer to make timely payments on specific debt or related obligations over the life of the instrument. Credit rating thus provides a relative ranking of the instrument of the credit quality of debt instruments.

Credit rating is expressed in terms of rating symbols. This is required for following reasons:

(A) They are easily comprehensible to lay investors.

(B) There are distinct symbols for different instruments.

(C) This differentiation is based on degree of safety which shows investment grade and non-investment grades.

(D) Securities with same rating are of similar but NOT identical investment quality.

Following are some of the key factors generally considered by the rating agencies for the purpose of ratings:

(A) Business analysis:

- Industry risk
- Industry structure:
- Industry size and importance to economy.
- Determinates of revenue growth.
- Entry barriers.

(B) Market position of the company:

- Nature and basis of competition.
- Threat form imports and substitutes.
- Presence of unorganized sector.
- Market share.
- Competitive advantages like brand equity and pricing flexibility.
- Product and customer diversity like proportion of exports and nature and type of customer diversity.

(C) Operating advantages of the company:

- Cost structure.
- Manufacturing efficiency.
- Production flexibility.
- Technology risk.
- Raw material sourcing.
- Location factors.

(D) Financial risk analysis:

- Income recognition.
- Expense capitalisation.
- Depreciation and inventory valuation policies.
- Off-balance sheet and contingent liabilities.
- Non-operating income.

- Profitability measures.
- Interest coverage.
- Capital structure.
- Debt service coverage.
- Working capital indicators.
- Return on capital employed.
- Adequacy of cash flows.
- Debt servicing requirements.
- Sustainability of funds from operations.
- Ability to raise equity and debt funds.
- Alternatives available in times of stress.
- Liquid assets available.

(D) Project risk:

- Project size in relation to existing operations.
- Means of financing.
- Funding tie-up.
- Extent of completion.
- Adherence to implementation schedules.

(E) Management evaluation:

- Strength of linkage to parent/group — operational, financial, managerial support.
- Systems and track record
- Project implementation record
- Management talent and succession.

Legal position: Whether the company has complied with all the legal requirements that they need to follow. This is very important as if the company fails to follow the legal requirements, then it can get into trouble in the future and thus the credit rating assigned could prove to be incorrect.

◈ Financial Analysis

- Accounting quality.
- Financial ratios.
- Adequacy of cash flows.
- Financial flexibility.
- Management evaluation:
- Track record of management.
- Crisis management.
- Goal, philosophy and strategic.

◈ Regulatory and Competitive Environment

- Structure and regulatory framework of the financial system.
- Trends in regulation/deregulation and their impact on company.
- Fundamental analysis:
- Capital adequacy.
- Liquidity management.
- Financial position.
- Interest and tax sensitivity.

From the above points it is very clear that the rating agencies go into the minutest details of the companies working before assigning any credit rating to its instruments.

One of the most important aspects that need to be given a great deal of importance is the track record of the issuer. Many a times we see that even a relatively new company's instruments also gets a very high rating simply because the company is promoted by an established business house with a solid track record.

FLOW CHART OF RATING PROCESS

1. Mandate Activity 1 and 2	Initial stage
2. Assign rating team	
3. Receive initial information conduct basic research	Activity 1 to 5 fact finding and analysis
4. Meeting and visits.	
5. Analysis and preparation of report.	
6. Preview meeting.	Rating finalization.
7. Rating meeting.	Fresh inputs
8. Assign rating.	
9. Communicate rating and the rationale.	Request for review.
10. Acceptance.	Non-acceptance.
11. Surveillance.	

In today's market driven economy, there is a genuine need for authentic investment information characterized by authenticity, quality analysis and good presentation, and specifically designed to facilitate the decision making process of investors and other participants in the financial services world.

◈ Types of Instruments Rated

Credit rating is used extensively for evaluating debt instruments. These include long-term instruments like bonds and debentures as well as short-term instruments like commercial paper. In addition fixed deposits, certificates of deposits, structured obligations including the non-convertible portion of PCDs and preference shares are rated. Equity shares are not rated.

◈ CRISIL's Long-term Rating Symbols

AAA : Highest safety.

AA : High safety.

A : Adequate safety. (Change in circumstances can adversely affect such issues.)

BBB : Moderate safety. (Change in circumstances is more likely to lead to weakened capacity.)

BB : Inadequate safety. (Uncertainty could lead to inadequate capacity)

B : High risk. (Currently obligations being met but adverse conditions could lead to lack of ability.)

C : Substantial risk. (Payment possible only if favourable circumstances continue.)

D : Default.

It should be noted that each credit rating company has its own symbols and they may use different symbols for rating different instruments. For example the symbols used for Commercial paper and Fixed deposits will be different. In India there are presently four companies, in the business of Credit Rating, they are CRISIL, ICRA, CARE and Fitsch. The last named company is an international credit rating company.

It is important to emphasise the limitations of credit ratings. They are not recommendations to invest. They do not take into account many aspects, which influence an investment decision. They do not, for example evaluate the reasonableness of the issue price, possibilities for capital gains or tale into account the risk of prepayment by issuer, or interest or exchange risks. Although these are often related to credit risk, the rating essentially is an opinion on the relative quality of the credit risk.

◈ Following is the CRISIL's Methodology of Rating

CRISIL's rating process and rating committee are designed to ensure that all assigned ratings are based on the highest standards of independence and analytical rigour.

The rating committee comprises members who have the professional competence to meaningfully assess the credit analysis that underlies the rating, and have no interest in the entity being rated. A team of analysts carries out the credit analysis. Each team has at least two members. CRISIL's analysis is based on issuer meetings and an understanding of the business environment. The analysis is carried out within the framework of clearly spelt-out rating criteria.

- Rating process
- Management meeting
- Rating committee and assignment of rating
- Confidentiality
- Advice to issuer
- Publication
- Surveillance and annual review
- Limitations of CRISIL's credit ratings

Specific process safeguards that ensure independence from individual or organisational bias include:

1. Multi-member rating teams
2. Multi-tier rating process
3. Rating committee comprising experienced, competent and reputed professionals to assign all ratings
4. Organisation-wide internal transparency. Each stage of the rating process for all ratings, including the final rating committee discussions, is open to all analytical staff in CRISIL's rating division

5. Rating methodologies and criteria are clearly spelt out, published and consistently applied

CRISIL ensures confidentiality of the information obtained for the rating exercise by putting in place appropriate process safeguards. All CRISIL employees are required to sign a confidentiality agreement. CRISIL does not disclose confidential information that it has obtained for the purpose of credit rating to anyone (other than market regulators or law enforcement authorities, if required).The process of rating starts with the issue of the rating request by the issuer and signing of the Rating agreement. CRISIL employs a multilayered decision making process in assigning a rating. It assigns a team of at least two analysts who interact with the company's management.

A detailed flow chart of CRISIL's rating process is as under:

CRISIL's RATING PROCESS

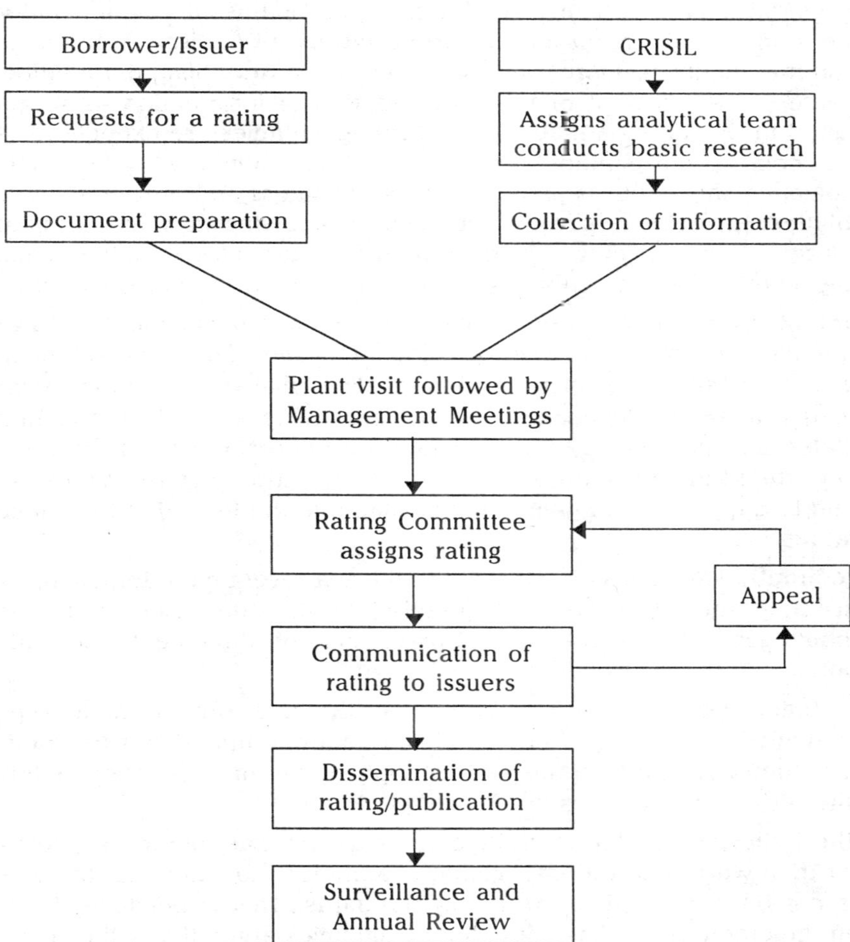

A credit rating is an opinion on the relative degree of risk associated with timely payment of interest and principal on a debt instrument. A simple alphanumeric symbol is normally used to convey a credit rating.

A credit rating agency provides an opinion relating to future debt repayments by borrowers. It has to be remembered that it is only an opinion and the final decision to invest or not must be taken by the investor himself. The rating will only indicate the level of risk as perceived by the rating agency.

A credit rating is not a recommendation to buy, hold or sell a debt instrument. A rating is one of the inputs that is used by investors to make an investment decision. Investors also look at the returns being offered on the debt instrument. Normally investors expect higher returns for lower rated instruments to compensate for the increased risk profile. Rating agencies do not comment on the return being offered on a debt instrument. Also, investors use several other factors like level of portfolio diversification and liquidity levels of the instrument, etc., in making investment decisions.

A credit rating agency relies on a variety of information sources including published annual reports, meetings with the issuer's management, industry data and discussions with bankers. Though rating agencies carry-out due diligence on this information, it does not always amount to the kind of verification that is carried out by an auditor. A credit rating depends significantly on the quality of information on which it is based. Also, the credit rating process may not be able to detect fraud or misrepresentation of information — something that an audit is designed to detect. As a matter of fact rating agencies are expected to look at many perspectives as compared to auditors. Audit is essentially about the books of accounts. Rating is not about balance sheets but is about the entire business and more importantly about the future possibilities. Investors are really interested in knowing how the company is likely to perform in future as they are going to invest money for future growth of the company. It is only if the company does well in future they will get interest and also get back their principal back.

Standards of transparency in emerging markets have been improving in recent years. Moreover, during a rating exercise, issuers provide rating agencies with confidential information and insights into business strategy that are not normally available in the public domain, However, an experienced rating agency can arrive at a reasonably accurate credit rating based on publicly available information, peer analysis and an understanding of the industry. It is the responsibility of the rating agencies to get all the information they must have to give a rating that is true and fair. If the information is not available to the level that they need they should not do the rating.

Most credit rating agencies across the world use a revenue model where the issuer pays for the credit rating. Alternative revenue models (like the one based on investor fees) pose numerous challenges in terms of ease and practicality of implementation that have not yet been overcome.

I believe that a way needs to be found where the investors are made to pay part of the fees of rating agencies as they are beneficiaries of rating. I think they should be asked to pay one per cent of their application money while applying for an issue. May be SEBI should also pay part of the fees from the Investors Protection Fund.

While the issuer-fee model naturally creates a potential conflict of interest (that could lead to higher than warranted ratings), global experience indicates that the existence of this conflict does not by itself lead to lax rating standards. This is because reputation plays a crucial role in the credit rating discipline. Rating agencies argue that if they give higher rating than warranted then the investors at higher risk and may lose money if the company defaults. So they argue if such a thing were to happen they themselves will lose credibility in the eyes of the investors and that will affect their future business as investors may not believe their ratings. However, it must be remembered that there are only three rating agencies that do most of the business in India!.

The capital market regulator regulates rating agencies in most regions. In India, the capital markets regulator, the Securities and Exchange Board of India (SEBI), regulates the rating agencies in the country. SEBI laid down an extensive set of regulations for rating agencies in 1999.

Moreover, the credit rating industry has many structural features, which ensure that any rating agency aspiring for long-term success acts responsibly, failing which its credibility and consequently its business would be eroded.

Regulation of rating agencies is typically concerned with ensuring that only reputable entities are allowed to set up rating agencies and that adequate safeguards are in place to manage the conflicts of interest that arise with respect to both the rating agency and its employees. Regulation that is more intensive or intrusive than this has not resulted in any incremental benefits.

Competition in the rating industry is desirable to meet the 'better quality service at a cheaper price' objective on an ongoing basis. But in view of the industry's rather unique nature, where the buyer and user of the rating service are different entities, it is essential to guard against some undesirable effects of competition. For instance, survival pressures can make some rating agencies vulnerable to the temptation of assigning higher-than-warranted ratings to attract issuers; or they may be pressured into offering the service at a price that may not support an adequate level of research and analysis.

An independent and professional rating agency provides credible and continuing information on credit risk, a crucial component of all debt investment decisions. This service is particularly useful to investors when they are faced with an array of debt investment options that is much larger than what their own credit assessment resources can reliably support. Moreover, published ratings enhance the efficiency of the financial system by reducing the cost of obtaining quality credit information on debt instruments for all players in the system.

◈ What is the Meaning of Various Symbols?

Each rating is an alphanumeric representation of the relative degree of risk associated with debt instruments based on the expected likelihood of their timely payment. Each rating agency uses different rating scales for different kinds of ratings. CRISIL assigns ratings to debt instrument on three basic scales — the long-term scale, the short-term scale and the fixed deposit scale. To illustrate, CRISIL's long-term rating scale and the description associated with each category on the rating scale is given below:

Symbol(Rating category)	*Description (with regard to the likelihood of meeting the debt obligations on time)*
AAA	Highest Safety
AA	High Safety
A	Adequate Safety
BBB	Moderate Safety
BB	Inadequate Safety
B	High Risk
C	Substantial Risk
D	Default

Plus and minus symbols are used to indicate finer distinctions within a rating category. The minus symbol associated with ratings has no negative connotations whatsoever. In fact, ratings in a higher rating category such as 'AA–' are stronger than ratings in a lower rating category such as 'A+'.

Debt instruments rated 'BBB-' and above are classified as investment grade ratings. Instruments that are rated 'BB+' and below are classified as speculative grade category ratings. Instruments rated in the speculative grade carry materially higher risk compared to instruments rated in the investment grade.

A speculative grade rating on a debt instrument does not mean that it is certainly going to default. All it indicates is that the instrument has risks associated with it that make it significantly more vulnerable to default than instruments in the investment grade.

Ratings are assigned either to specific instruments or to the general debt obligations of issuers. CRISIL assigns ratings to debt instruments. Once a rating is assigned and published, CRISIL keeps the rating under surveillance until the instrument is fully repaid. The surveillance process may result in rating changes from time-to-time. Every rating assigned by CRISIL is current at all times and reflects all the available information that may impact the credit quality of the rated instrument. This is what was not really happening in India. However, post-2008 things have changed and reviews of ratings seem to be happening at regular intervals. However, it is the duty of the investor to follow these revisions of rating which most do not.

Ratings are assigned based on certain expectations and assumptions about variables that impact the issuer's performance. These variables are either company-specific factors or factors relating to the business environment. Rating agencies use their best professional judgement on these factors while assigning the rating. However, these variables can change significantly over a relatively short timeframe, especially in emerging markets, causing the rated entities' performance to deviate materially from expectations. This changes their future debt repayment capabilities and is reflected in their changed ratings.

Down grading does not automatically indicate a possible default. In most cases, unless the rating is deep into the speculative category, a downgrade does not mean that a default is anticipated. All it indicates is that the risk associated with the instrument is relatively higher than what it was before the downgrade.

Any debt instrument is rated in the context of its issuer's business and financial plans. Such business plans incorporate debt levels, all of which (whether rated or not) must be serviced by the issuer's operational cash flows. The size and quality of these operational cash flows in relation to the total debt-servicing obligation crucially determine credit quality. Therefore, it is the size of the total debt in the company and not the amount that is sought to be rated that determines the credit rating.

There has been a strong demand for IPO ratings. Some people are against it. However we have already seen that SEBI had experimented with these ratings and had some issues rated. It is quite likely that these ratings may become mandatory in future. Following are the FAQs on these ratings as published by ICRA:

◈ FAQ on IPO Grading

1. What is 'IPO grading'?

IPO grading (initial public offers grading) is a service aimed at facilitating the assessment of equity issues offered to public. The grade assigned to any individual issue represents a relative assessment of the 'fundamentals' of that issue in relation to the universe of other listed equity securities in India. Such grading is assigned on a five-point scale with a higher score indicating stronger fundamentals.

2. How is IPO grading different from an investment recommendation?

Investment recommendations are expressed as 'buy', 'hold' or 'sell' and are based on a security specific comparison of its assessed 'fundamentals factors' (business prospects, financial position, etc.), and 'market factors' (liquidity, demand supply, etc.), to its price.

On the other hand, IPO grading is expressed on a five-point scale and is a relative comparison of the assessed fundamentals of the graded issue to other listed equity securities in India.

As the IPO grading does not take cognizance of the price of the security, it is not an investment recommendation. Rather, it is one of the inputs to the investor to aiding in the decision making process.

All other things remaining equal, a security with stronger fundamentals would command a higher market price.

3. What is the requirement for IPO grading?

SEBI has been taking a pioneering role in investor protection by increasing disclosure levels by entities seeking to access equity markets for funding. This has caused India to be amongst one of the more transparent and efficient capital markets in the world. However, these disclosures demand fairly high levels of analytical sophistication of the reader in order to effectively achieve the goal of information dissemination.

IPO grading is positioned as a service that provides 'an independent assessment of fundamentals' to aid comparative assessment that would prove useful as an information and investment tool for investors. Moreover, such a service would be particularly useful for assessing the offerings of companies accessing the equity markets for the first time where there is no track record of their market performance.

4. How will IPO grading meet this requirement?

As mentioned above, the IPO grade assigned to any issue represents a relative assessment of the 'fundamentals' of that issue in relation to the universe of other listed equity securities in India. This grading can be used by the investor as tool to make investment decision. The IPO grading will help the investor better appreciate the meaning of the disclosures in the issue documents to the extent that they affect the issue's fundamentals. Thus, IPO grading is an additional investor information and investment guidance tool.

5. Who will carry-out the IPO grading?

This can be done by rating agencies registered with SEBI.

6. Does SEBI have a role in the grading exercise?

No. SEBI does not play any role in the assessment made by ICRA. The grading is intended to be an independent and unbiased opinion of ICRA.

7. Is this IPO grading mandatory?

IPO grading is made mandatory.

8. How would the grading be indicated?

It is intended that IPO fundamentals would be graded on a five-point scale which is as follows:

ICRA IPO Grade 5: Strong fundamentals

ICRA IPO Grade 4: Above average fundamentals

ICRA IPO Grade 3: Average fundamentals

ICRA IPO Grade 2: Below average fundamentals

ICRA IPO Grade 1: Poor fundamentals

9. For how long would the assigned grade be valid?

The assigned grade would be a one time assessment done at the time of the IPO and meant to aid investors who are interested in investing in the IPO. The grade will not have any ongoing validity.

10. How can a company get its IPO graded?

The company needs to first contact a CRA and mandate it for the grading exercise. The CRA would then follow the process outlined below.

Seek information required for the grading from the company.

On receipt of required information, have discussions with the company's management and visit the company's operating locations, if required.

Prepare an analytical assessment report.

Present the analysis to CRA's grading committee. The committee would discuss all relevant issues and assign a grade. Communicate the grade to the company along with an assessment report outlining the rationale for the grade assigned. as per a pre-specified format.

CRA's grading committee may review the case, if the company presents any critical additional information after the assignation of the grade.

Though this process will ideally require 2-3 weeks for completion, it may be a good idea for companies to initiate the grading process about 6-8 weeks before the targeted IPO date to provide sufficient time for any contingencies.

Investors need to be cautioned about these grading. A high normally means good for investment. This need not prove to be so. One instance should suffice to convince everyone about this. Reliance Power IPO was graded 5 by both the leading CRAs. It received tremendous response. But on listing the prices crashed big time and the retail investors found that instead of tidy profits they are holding sizeable loss. It was very clear to anyone who had bothered to study the prospectus that the meaningful cash flows will start only after the completion of big projects that the company was undertaking. There were problems of land acquisition and delays were imminent. Only the investors who had the stomach to hold on till then should have applied. However majority of investors had applied hoping that they would be able to sell on listing at a profit. This did not happen.

Another question that arises out of this episode is why the CRAs not took into account the lag in cash flow generation from the time of the issue till the commissioning of plants while offering the grading that they offered. It has to be kept in mind that this was not pre-split Reliance. Yes the company had three major projects in hand, but it was a new entity and had to prove itself on project execution. It seems that CRAs did not consider this at all.

Recent Developments

There has been discussion for a long time now as to whether the IPOs should be brought under compulsory rating process. In the past we have seen that especially during the Bull Run in the stock markets many dubious companies came out with IPOs and the gullible investors fall pray for such issues as they believe that all IPOs will give them a profit after listing. It has been argued that all issues are either appraised by the merchant bankers to the issue or by the lead bankers who are taking exposure by way of funding to the project for which the issue has been brought out. However the counter argument is that the retail investors are not in a position to understand all this. It may be useful therefore that the IPO is assigned credit rating related to the risk profile of the project on the whole.

Some new and the existing credit rating agencies have approached SEBI for allowing them to rate the IPOs. We are likely to see some developments in this direction shortly.

Some rating agencies have also started rating the companies as a whole on its overall performance. This rating obviously is much wider in nature than the issue related rating.

We have also seen that some rating agencies have started rating the corporate governance practices. This is a welcomes development as investors will come to know as to which companies are practising corporate governance in the way it needs to be done. We have also seen some innovation in the ratings for the different schemes of various mutual fund schemes. This is also a good development. The experts have always maintained that before making any investments in a mutual fund scheme, its past performance needs to be evaluated. The credit rating may make this decision making easier for the investors.

We have seen the emergence of securatisation as a financial instrument in the market. This is gaining popularity and many players have started using this instrument very effectively. The pay-through, and pass-through instruments that are issued in this process are presently being rated by the rating agencies. In future the retail investors will be able to invest money in these instruments. The credit rating for these will greatly help the retail investors to make the investment decision in these instruments.

◈ CIBIL

In the recent years we have witnessed a great deal of growth in the retail finance. This has happened due to several factors. The economy has grown very rapidly and consequently this has created a new class of borrowers who are borrowing for housing, vehicles and credit cards, etc. This market has also become very competitive with private and foreign banks leading the way along with some NBFCs, and now the public sector banks have also joined the race. The need is therefore felt to rate the individual borrowers also. It has been seen that a defaulter may be able to get loan from another lender as this lender does not have access to the borrowers past history.

The establishment of CIBIL is an effort made by the Government of India and the Reserve Bank of India to improve the functionality and stability of the Indian financial system by containing NPAs while improving credit lenders' portfolio quality. CIBIL provides a vital service, which allows its members to make informed, objective and faster credit decisions.

At a time when the economy is growing more resilient and self-sufficient, the demand for credit is on the rise. Borrowers are sometimes predisposed towards taking advantage of the system by moving from one institution to another, despite being defaulters in their earlier banking relationships. The aim of CIBIL's Commercial Credit Bureau is to minimise instances of concurrent and serial defaults by providing credit information pertaining to non-individual borrowers such as public limited companies, private limited companies, partnership firms proprietorships, etc. CIBIL maintains a central database of information as received from its members. CIBIL collates and disseminates this information on demand to members, in the form of Commercial Credit Information Reports (CIR) to assist them in their loan appraisal process.

The software for the Commercial Credit Bureau is developed and licensed by Dun & Bradstreet, one of our equity and technical partners, which is a world leader in commercial credit information. The Commercial Bureau was launched on May 8, 2006. All the members who have provided their data to CIBIL are permitted to access Commercial CIRs on the principle of reciprocity. The basic Commercial CIR will broadly contain:

◈ Borrower Information

(*i*) Name and Address
(*ii*) D-U-N-S® Number
(*iii*) Other Identification numbers; e.g., PAN, Registration No.
(*iv*) Legal constitution
(*v*) Relationship details; e.g., major shareholders, directors and their addresses and D-U-N-S® Number
(*vi*) Number of inquiries made on the borrower

◈ Account Details

(*i*) Number of credit facilities
(*ii*) Credit type
(*iii*) Loan amount
(*iv*) Outstanding amount
(*v*) Asset classification
(*vi*) Wilful defaulter and suit-filed status
(*vii*) Guarantor details

◈ Introduction To CIBIL

1. What is CIBIL?

CIBIL — India's first credit information bureau — is a repository of information, which contains the credit history of commercial and consumer borrowers. CIBIL provides this information to its members in the form of credit information reports.

2. Who owns CIBIL?

CIBIL's equity was held by State Bank of India, Housing Development Finance Corporation Limited, Dun & Bradstreet Information Services India Private Limited and Trans Union International Inc. The shareholding pattern was in the proportion of 40:40:10:10 respectively.

◈ Current Shareholding

The shareholding pattern has now been diversified to include the following entities representing varied categories of credit grantors:

3. On which segments does CIBIL provide credit reports?

CIBIL is a composite Credit Bureau, which caters to both commercial and consumer segments. The Consumer Credit Bureau covers credit availed by individuals while the Commercial Credit Bureau covers credit availed by non-individuals such as partnership firms, proprietary concerns, private and public limited companies, etc.

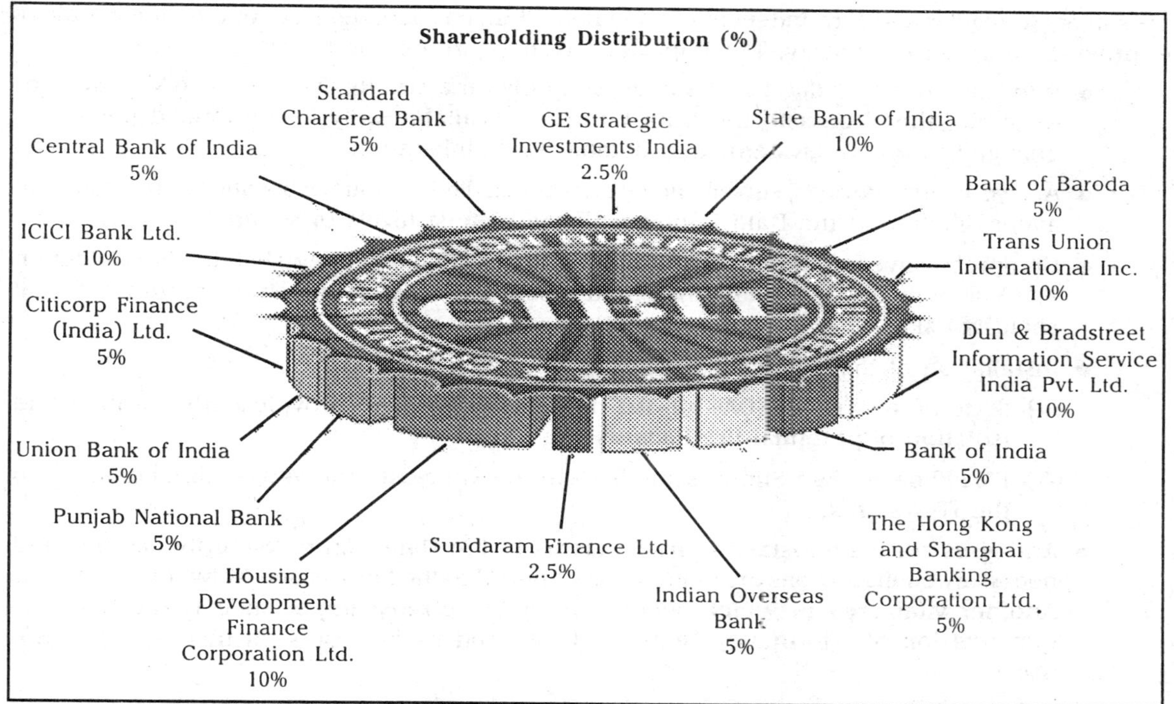

4. Who are members of CIBIL?

Banks, Financial Institutions, State Financial Corporations, Non-banking Financial Companies, Housing Finance Companies and Credit Card Companies are members of CIBIL.

5. How does CIBIL function?

For credit grantors to gain a complete picture of the payment history of a credit applicant, they must be able to gain access to the applicant's complete credit record that may be spread over different institutions. CIBIL collects commercial and consumer credit-related data and collates such data to create and distribute credit reports to members.

6. Where does CIBIL get the information from?

CIBIL primarily gets information from its members only and at a subsequent stage will supplement it with public domain information in order to create a truly comprehensive snapshot of an entity's financial track record.

7. What is a credit information report?

A Credit Information Report (CIR) is a factual record of a borrower's credit payment history compiled from information received from different credit grantors. Its purpose is to help credit grantors make informed lending decisions — quickly and objectively.

◈ Information Security at CIBIL

8. What are the measures taken by CIBIL to ensure the security of member's data?

The security of the members' data is of paramount importance to CIBIL. CIBIL's security measures are aligned with global 'best practices', stringent risk management standards and are subject to regular audits by independent auditors. CIBIL has adopted state-of-the-art technology to provide information security. The important aspects are detailed below:

- Information in our database is accessed only on a strictly 'Need to Know' basis. For example, the access to the Data Centre is available only to authorized personnel engaged in regular systems and database administration.
- Access control devices, surveillance cameras installed at strategic locations and biometric access system at the Data Centre with the highest levels of security.
- Comprehensive perimeter security solution consisting of a Firewall, Intrusion Detection and Vulnerability Assessment System to secure the network infrastructure from external security risk.
- Installation of the following devices to deal with fire hazards:
  (*a*) State-of-the-art (VESDA) smoke detection system to provide early warning and isolation of potential fire hazards.
  (*b*) FM200 based Fire Suppression System to extinguish fire with minimal damage to the IT systems.
- Anti-virus software installed on all servers in the Data Centre. Security patches and necessary configurations are continuously applied to the Servers and Network appliances. Another vital area in which security is of the utmost importance is the two-way transmission of information between CIBIL and its members. In this regard, CIBIL uses:
- 128-bit SSL encryption for all Web-based transactions including FTP.
- Cryptographic solutions for all information sent or received through any physica media, *i.e.*, CD, DAT and DLT.

9. What is encryption?

Encryption is a technique used to mask proprietary information in order to prevent from being accessed by unauthorized individuals. Only authorized individuals who have bee provided with the appropriate decoding software can unscramble the information. Thus, encrypte information that our members provide us with is extremely secure.

◈ Type of Information Held by CIBIL

10. What type of information on a borrower is available in the CIR?

The CIR includes the following information:

- Basic borrower information like:
  (*i*) Name
  (*ii*) Address in case of individuals:
  (*iii*) Identification numbers
  (*iv*) Passport ID
  (*v*) Voters ID
  (*vi*) Date of birth in case of non-individuals
  (*vii*) D-U-N-S® Number

(*viii*) Registration Number

(*ix*) Legal Constitution

- Records of all the credit facilities availed by the borrower
- Past payment history
- Amount overdue
- Number of inquiries made on that borrower, by different members
- Suit-filed status.

11. What type of information is not included in the CIR?

The CIR does not contain:

- Income/Revenue details
- Amount(s) deposited with the bank
- Details of borrowers' assets
- Value of asset(s) mortgaged
- Details of investment(s)

12. When is a credit facility classified as 'default'?

CIBIL does not classify any accounts as default accounts. It merely reflects this information after the member has classified it as such. The Number of Days Past Due and/or Asset Classification as per RBI definition as submitted by members is reflected in the CIR.

13. How do I ensure that a CIR drawn on me as an individual/organisation does not contain negative information?

The best preventive measure is to exercise good money management practices and make repayments on time. Please see 'How to improve your credit' section for more details.

14. If I am a first-time borrower, will I be at a disadvantage as there will be no information on me?

As a new borrower, there will be a new file created for you. It will then be in your interest to build up a favourable repayment track record for future credit applications. Access to CIBIL information.

15. Who can access CIRs?

Reports can be accessed by members on the principle of reciprocity, *i.e.*, only those members who have provided all their data to CIBIL are permitted to access CIRs. Members can do so only to take valid credit decisions. Disclosure to any other person or entity is prohibited.

16. Can the borrower obtain his own CIR from CIBIL?

No. However, if a member has drawn a report on that borrower, a copy of the same can be obtained from the member.

17. Can CIBIL provide CIRs to credit providers in other countries?

No. CIBIL will provide credit information reports only to its members in India.

◈ Lending Decisions

18. Does the CIR indicate if credit should or should not be given?

The CIR only provides available factual credit information and does not provide any opinion, indication or comment pertaining to whether credit should or should not be granted. The credit grantors who have received an application for credit will make the credit decision. CIBIL does not grant or deny credit.

19. If my credit application has been rejected, will this fact appear in my credit record?

The members do not provide this information to CIBIL and hence it will not be in the CIR.

20. If a credit grantor has denied me credit, could others reject my application?

Not necessarily. Different credit grantors may use a CIR differently, or take into account other factors when they assess your application. Although one bank may deny you credit, another bank could take a different view and accept your application.

21. What benefits does a borrower get from CIBIL?

CIBIL's CIRs are aimed at helping credit grantors make fast and objective lending decisions. This will contribute to a more competitive credit marketplace among credit grantors. With a bureau in place, responsible customers can expect faster and more competitive services at better terms from the credit grantors. Rectifying inaccurate information in your credit report.

22. How do I rectify information in a credit report drawn on me?

Please contact the credit grantor from whom you have availed the loan and request the necessary changes. The credit grantor will then report the change to CIBIL and we will subsequently make the necessary updates in our records.

◈ How to Improve Your Credit

◈ The Benefits of a Credit Bureau

Increased Credit Volumes

Credit bureaus facilitate **increased lending opportunities for credit grantors while allowing easier access to credit for borrowers**. The existence of credit bureaus in developed countries has facilitated increased market penetration of credit (to more than 66 per cent as a percentage of GDP as compared to 3 per cent for India) while keeping non-performing loans in check (approximately 1 per cent of outstanding credit).

Operating Efficiencies

Credit Portfolio Quality

The use of CIRs accessed from a credit bureau will enable credit grantors' loan officers to accurately evaluate borrower risk by making comprehensive credit histories available to decision makers. The CIRs will facilitate an objective and transparent assessment of credit applications. Concurrent borrowers and serial defaulters will be identified and minimized early in the approval process - consequently reducing associated recovery and write-off costs. Similarly, premium borrowers will be identified and serviced faster. **Ultimately, CIRs will enable members to judiciously mix relationship-based lending and information-based lending**. CIRs will serve as the first level of due diligence in the appraisal of a credit application.

Speed and Cost

The use of CIRs will make processing loan applications easier, faster and cheaper by sometimes eliminating the need to additionally research and verify borrower details. The average loan in India is sanctioned in 2-3 days. A credit grantor using CIRs will be able to significantly reduce this turnaround time and thus have a competitive edge in the marketplace.

◈ Differential Pricing

Owing to the lack of comprehensive credit information, all borrowers are charged an interest rate with an assumed level of default risk. This means that all borrowers are charged identical risk premiums regardless of their payment history and thus pay a premium that in developed countries is only applied to previously defaulting borrowers. As credit grantors begin to use comprehensive credit information they will be able to differentiate between good borrowers and defaulters. In an increasingly commoditized credit market, **credit grantors will be able to use price in order to differentiate their loan products.**

In addition, borrowers who have diligently serviced their loans in the past will be able to demand cheaper loans in the future. Past defaulters will also have an opportunity to improve their credit histories by servicing their debt obligations in a timely fashion and thus earn access to lower interest rates.

The Indian credit industry has only recently begun to offer differential pricing to their customers. As the credit environment becomes increasingly competitive, CIRs will play a pivotal role in the speed and confidence with which credit grantors will be able to increase their business volume.

Hence, the use of CIRs will prove beneficial to both credit grantors and borrowers.

◈ Credit Grantors

The use of CIRs will enable loan officers to make objective and informed credit decisions quickly, competitively and cost-effectively. The use of CIRs will enable them to increase their lending volumes and improve the quality of their credit portfolios while reducing their delinquencies and loan processing costs. This will translate into improved profit margins.

◈ Borrowers

The widespread use of credit data will provide consumers with fast and easy access to the lending resources they need while reducing operating and risk costs for credit grantors. These reduce costs will be passed on to an extent to consumers with demonstrated credit performance in the form of lower interest rates. This easy availability of reasonably price credit will provide borrowers with the means to a higher standard of living.

◈ The Benefits of a Credit Bureau

More credit. Better pricing. Objective assessment. These are just few of the benefits of your credit information report (CIR), reflecting debt obligations serviced regularly and in a timely fashion. For the first time in India, CIRs containing factual records, credit histories of borrowers are available. Credit grantors across the country can now access reports from CIBIL in order to make quick, objective credit decisions.

When you approach a credit grantor for credit, your application will be evaluated on the basis of your past payment history, existing credit lines and other factors such as income and security. In this case, a good CIR is one of the best indicators of the level of risk you present to the credit grantor. A CIR that reflects a good past payment history may lead to credit being granted on better terms. On the other hand, a CIR, which indicates that a borrower has been delinquent on several occasions, could lead to denial of or extremely expensive credit.

In order to ensure a high-quality CIR, it is important to repay your loans on time. However, as you accrue more debt, special efforts are required to ensure this. The 'buy now, pay later' mindset has left borrowers struggling to strike an adequate cash flow balance. In this scenario, it is extremely important for you to maintain appropriate, reasonable and affordable levels of credit and ensure regular and timely repayment of loans.

◈ Ways to Improve Your Credit

- Immediately establish a budget in order to control your cash outflows.
- Ensure that your income level permits an additional monthly outflow if you plan to take a loan.
- Investigate your options in order to reduce your interest and other credit related costs, e.g., refinance an outstanding loan at fixed interest rates if there is a significant drop in interest rates or you discover a significantly cheaper option, etc. This will make your debt burden easier to manage.
- Use some of your savings to repay some of your debt.
- Always pay on time.

◈ SMERA

Till the recent times the credit rating agencies were only giving their services to the large corporates. However, we have seen the growth of small and medium sector in the last 10-15 years. A need was felt to have a credit rating for these companies. A good rating will mean that their cost of borrowing can decline. Also companies with a good rating will require lesser collateral for borrowing. The managements of these companies will get an incentive to be transparent in their business dealings. This need is being addressed by SMERA.

Let us now see how SMERA works:

1. Wide Recognition and Acceptance
2. MOU with Banks
3. Favourable borrowing terms
4. Faster Access to Credit
5. Lower Rating Fees
6. D-U-N-S NO.
7. SMERA : An initiative of leaders
8. Fair evaluation amongst peers
9. Benefit to SME and SSI Units
10. Benefit to Banks
11. Industry-benchmarked ratings

1. Wide Recognition and Acceptance

With each bank having separate rating processes and disclosure requirements for the purpose of disbursing loans, SMEs find themselves spending significant time, effort and money while approaching different banks for credit. As SMERA has adopted a comprehensive, transparent and reliable rating process, it would have a wider acceptance within the banking system of the country. In addition to this, SMERA would be supported by SIDBI and a large number of public and private sector banks in the country. Such wide acceptance would result in, SMERA ratings becoming a key requirement in the loan application process. It will also simplify the process of credit requests and make the process more cost-effective.

2. MOU with Banks

SMERA has taken the initiative of entering into MOUs with 14 Banks, *viz.*, State Bank of India, Punjab National Bank, Syndicate Bank, Canara Bank, State Bank of Bikaner and Jaipur, Dena Bank, Corporation Bank, Union Bank of India, UCO Bank, CitiGroup, Bank of India, Vijaya Bank, Allahabad Bank and Bank of Baroda. Further a number of banks have announced favourable credit terms including reduction in interest rates to units rated by SMERA. Andhra Bank, Bank of India and SIDBI has already announced reduction in interest rates for units rated by SMERA.

3. Favourable Borrowing Terms

Better ratings from SMERA has already started benefiting units by way of more favourable credit terms in terms of interest rebates.

- Lower collateral requirements
- Reduced interest rates
- Simplified lending norms

4. Faster Access to Credit

SMERA Ratings facilitate banks/lending institutions in reducing the turnaround time in processing credit applications, thereby providing SMEs access to timely and adequate credit.

5. Lower Rating Fees

The rating fees charged by SMERA are very competitive, and the rating fee is subsidised up to 75 per cent for eligible SSI units, *i.e.*, units having a valid Small-scale Industries Registration Certificate (Permanent/Provisional). Units can get at prices as low as rated as low as ₹ 4,209 all taxes included.

6. D-U-N-S NO.

Each unit availing of SMERA ratings is assigned a unique 9-digit number DUNS NO. The Number is a unique nine-digit identification sequence, which provides unique identifiers of single business entities, while used by the world's most influential standards-setting organizations, it is recognized, recommended and/or required by more than 50 global, industry and trade associations.

7. SMERA

An initiative of leaders: SME Rating Agency of India Limited (SMERA) is a joint initiative by Small Industries Development Bank of India (SIDBI), Dun & Bradstreet Information Services India Private Limited (D&B), Credit Information Bureau (India) Limited (CIBIL) and several leading banks in the country. SMERA is the country's first and only dedicated rating agency that focuses primarily on the SME segment. SMERA's primary objective is to provide ratings that are comprehensive, transparent and reliable. This would facilitate greater and easier flow of credit from the banking sector to SMEs.

8. Fair Evaluation Amongst Peers

SMERA ratings categorise SMEs based on size, so that each SME is evaluated amongst its peers. This enables rational comparison of companies of the same size, thus ensuring that the smaller companies are not at a disadvantage while applying for credit.

9. Benefit to SME and SSI Units

- SMERA rating adds credibility to the status of the SME unit
- It also helps open doors to deal with large companies, for example, can lead to reduction of interest rate by 0.25 per cent on receiving rating from SMERA especially those who deal with a big number of vendors
- SMERA ratings serve as motivation to adopt good governance practices which are beneficial in the long run
- SMERA ratings also help in international trade and commerce and serve as first point to generate interest among potential trading partners
- Ratings also acts as a tool for self-correction and self-improvement in event of a 0.25 per cent interest reduction to a unit getting rated by SMERA. The reduction in interest cost comes to ₹ 25,000 on a loan of ₹ 1 crore for one year, thereby outweighing the cost of rating from SMERA.

10. Benefit to Banks

- SMERA ratings facilitates pricing of loan products/attractive terms
- It is also useful in compliance with regulatory and capital adequacy norms
- Helping the banker through early warning signals through review ratings as mandated by it.

11. Industry-benchmarked Ratings

SMERA ratings take into account industry dynamics by factoring in a system through which an SME could compare its strengths and weaknesses with those of other companies in the same line of business. This is done through statistically derived industry benchmarks for various ratios. Post-2008 crisis the rating agencies have come under scanner of the regulators and have also lost much of their credibility. This has been a severe setback for them. They were rightly blamed for not doing their due diligence properly while giving high rating to what turned out to be junk bonds. The US economy collapsed and institutions like Lehman Bros. no more exist. All the blame for this of course cannot be put at the doors of the CRAs, the investors also need to be blamed. It is always difficult for the investors to accept their own mistakes and they can easily pass on the blame on CRAs. Rating agencies also came under fire in euro crisis. Here again the so-called PIIGS countries' sovereign bonds were rated highly and when the countries like Greece started defaulting or were on the verge of it. CRAs methodology was questioned worldwide. They came in for sharp criticism for the second time in two years. One of course hopes that they have learnt their lessons and will be more through in their processes in future. One also hopes that investors especially Banks, PE funds, Hedge Funds have learnt from their mistakes!

❊ ❊ ❊

SHARE BUYBACK AND DELISTING OF SHARES

◈ Introduction and Process of Share Buyback

Since October 1998 the public limited companies in India are allowed to buyback their shares from the shareholders. A company can buyback their own shares or other specified securities including employees' stock option from out of:

1. Its free reserves;
2. The securities premium account; and
3. The proceeds of an earlier issue other than fresh issue of shares made specifically for buyback purpose. The share buyback falls under Section 77 of Companies' Act.

However, a company can purchase its own shares only if following conditions are fulfilled:

1. The articles of the permit such as buyback.
2. A special resolution in general meeting authorising buyback. The company in the notice to shareholders must give an explanatory statement about the need for buy-back, the amount required for it, the time limit and completion of the process.

Following conditions have to be met in the process of buyback:

1. The buyback has to be completed within 12 months of passing the special resolution.
2. Buyback cannot exceed 25 per cent of the total paid capital plus free reserves of the company.
3. Post-buyback the debt equity ratio shall not exceed 2:1.
4. Shares that are eligible for buyback have to be fully paid.
5. Before making purchases under this scheme companies have to file with the Registrar of Companies and SEBI a declaration of solvency.
6. The securities purchased under the buyback arrangement should be extinguished and physically destroyed within seven days of the last date of the completion of the buyback.

7. A company which buysback its securities is prohibited from further issue of securities within a period of two years, expect bonus issues or issues in the discharge of subsisting obligations such as conversion of warrants, stock option schemes, sweat equity or conversion of preference shares/debentures into equity shares.
8. Companies are not allowed to buyback securities
   (*a*) Through any/own subsidiary company.
   (*b*) Through any/group of investment company.
   (*c*) If default subsists in respect of repayment of deposits, term loans to any financial institutions and redemption of debentures or preference shares.
9. The explanatory statement annexed to the notice should contain following additional disclosures: (*a*) The minimum prices at which the buyback of securities would be made. If the promoter intends to offer their securities; the quantum of securities proposed to be tendered and the details of their transactions and their holdings for the last six months prior to the passing of the special resolution for the buyback including the information of the number of shares acquired, the price and the date of acquisition.
10. The company must open an escrow account and deposit the amount as required by the SEBI regulations. The company on or before the opening the offer, deposit in an escrow amount 25 per cent of the consideration payable up to ₹ 100 crore and 10 per cent thereafter.
11. The company has to appoint a merchant banker for the purpose of the buyback.
12. The offer should remain open to the members for period not less then fifteen days and not exceeding thirty days. The company should complete the verification of the offers, received within fifteen days of the closure of the offer and the securities lodged should be deemed to be accepted unless a communication of rejection is made within fifteen days from the closure of the offer.
13. SEBI has now made it mandatory for the company seeking to buyback shares to reserve 15 per cent amount exclusively for retail investors. The amount of up to ₹ 2 lakh worth of surrendered shares will be eligible for this provision. This has been done to give a fair deal to retail investors in a buyback deal.

◆ Obligations of the Company in Share Buyback

The company has to ensure:

1. The letter of offer, the public announcement should contain true, factual and material information and not contain any misleading information and must state that the directors of the company accept the responsibility of all this information.
2. The company should not issue any securities including by way of bonus till the date of closure of the offer made under these regulations.
3. The company must pay the consideration only by way of cash.
4. The company should not withdraw the offer after the draft letter of offer is filed with SEBI or the public announcement in this regard is made.
5. The promoter or the person in control should not deal in the securities of the company in the stock exchange during the period when the buyback offer is open.

◆ The Methods of Buyback

1. From existing shareholders on a proportionate basis.
2. From the open market.
3. Through the purchase of odd lot shares held by the shareholders. (Under the de-mat format there is no concept of odd lot.)
4. By purchasing the securities issued to employees of the company under the Stock options scheme or Sweat Equity scheme.

◆ The Effects of the Buyback

1. It is a way of returning surplus cash to shareholders.
2. To increase the underlying shares value. The decrease in share capital will increase the earnings per share.
3. It helps to support the prices during a period of temporary weakness in the stock markets.
4. It helps the company to maintain target capital structure.
5. It can also be used as the mechanism against a possible hostile takeover bid. By buying back the shares the company reduces the floating stock in the market, thereby reducing the scope of the raider to acquire enough shares to gain the management control.
6. This is a method used for downsizing, especially during declining sales.
7. Share buyback leads to erosion of the net worth of the company. This has negative effect on the creditors and lenders.
8. If the shares are not extinguished then the company becomes its own shareholder. In USA companies who buyback shares are not required to extinguish them and can reissue them.
9. It is argued that unscrupulous promoters may deliberately keep markets subdued with a view to back shares at lower prices.

◆ Types of Share Buybacks

1. **Open market purchases:** This is done by giving notice to the shareholders at least seven days prior to buyback. The company has to disclose the total number of shares it intends to buyback. Since the process is carried out in the open market no minimum price is mentioned for the buyback. This is an easy, quick and simple process.
2. **Tender offer:** The buying company has to disclose the total number of shares and the price at which it wishes to buyback. The maximum price offered is 20 per cent above the average price. The offer period could be between 15/30 days. If shares tendered are more than the total number to be bought back, then buyback is done on the proportionate basis.
3. **Dutch auction:** In this method the price of buyback is done by the shareholders themselves. This is like the process of book-building.

In effect most companies are buying back shares from the open market. In this method the company will obtain the approval of shareholders to buyback shares at a price not exceeding a particular amount per share. The offer will be communicated to all the shareholders. The actual buyback will be conducted through the open market. The shareholders who wish to participate in buyback offer will have to sell their shares in the open market. If the market price goes above the maximum price then the company will stop buying shares from the open markets.

SEBI has allowed buyback of shares up to 10 per cent of total shares, without the requirement of the special resolution. The only requirement is the board resolution passed to this effect. The company cannot issue fresh equity for 12 months after such a buyback. This amendment was made to enable companies to buyback shares at the time when share markets are depressed.

The Indian experience of buyback has displayed some curious results so far. The companies, who went for buyback immediately after it was allowed, seem to have paid a very high price for the buyback. Due to this the market prices post-buyback did not rise. This trend has been visible even today.

One major criticism against buyback is that though the buyback is done with companies' funds, the actual beneficiaries of this are the promoters of the company. This is so because without actually investing any money directly in the companies, the promoters' stake in the company goes up because of the buyback. This according to some critics gives undue advantage to the promoters. The counter argument is that shareholders who give their shares for buyback are adequately compensated as they normally get a price which is at a premium to the existing market price. It is also argued that if shareholders believe that the company's performance and therefore its market price are likely to better, then they should not participate in the buyback offer.

It must be understood that all buyback offers do not receive good response from the shareholders. Reliance Industries had offered buyback of shares on three different occasions but the response was luke warm all the three times. Even now offer is open but the company is nowhere near its target. Same fate was witnessed a few years back during the buyback offer of Hindustan Unilever.

This just goes to show that whatever may be the intention of the management to offer buyback, the investors take their own call. If the investors believe that in future the company is likely to do well and hence expect the market price of the shares going higher than the buyback price offered, then they will not sell their shares during the buyback.

Company Name	*No. of Shares Bought*	*Avg. Price (₹)*	*Amount Used (₹ Cr.)*
Reliance Infra.	4430262	528.91	234.32
Zee Entertainment	19372853	119.72	231.92
SRF	3083080	291.89	89.99
Praj Inds.	7313644	76.38	55.86
Bhagyanagar Ind.	4410000	18.61	8.20
Allied Digital	597075	54.21	3.24
Avantel	223473	64.08	1.43

Another trend that is visible these days is that many MNCs are buying back their shares from the domestic market with the express purpose of delisting, these shares form the Indian stock markets. As per the company law if promoters hold more than 90 per cent equity, then the company can be delisted. Many MNCs like Phillips, Atlas CAPCO, Cadbury, Castrol are some companies who have done this.

When this happens these companies are not required to publish their financial results as many of them become 100 per cent subsidiaries of their parent companies. There are investors who do not give their shares in such buyback offer as they believe that post-delisting these companies will naturally give more dividends as the dividend will accrue to the promoters only. However the down side of this is that the investment in this scrip will become completely illiquid as there will be no market price and thus the investors will have no exit route available to him in case he wishes to sell his investments.

In the present Bull Run on the markets very few companies are going for buying back of shares. It must be remembered that buyback will make sense in the bear market and not in the bull market as the cost of buyback will be least in the bear markets.

In the past two years we have also witnessed another type of buyback which may not qualify to be strictly called as buyback in the traditional way. Infosys bought back shares from its Indian shareholders at a premium to their market prices and then issued these shares in the American markets as ADS at a premium. The company thus increased the liquidity of their shares in the US markets. Last Infosys also issued such shares in the Japanese markets.

Securities market regulator SEBI has decided to tighten corporate share buyback norms and increase disclosure norms for preferential issues, and came up with guidelines for angel funds as part of forming alternative investment fund regulations.

It also approved the recommendations of the KM Chandrasekhar-chaired Committee on Rationalisation of Investment Routes and Monitoring of Foreign Portfolio Investments, which submitted its report on June 12. The report suggested formation of a new category to club foreign portfolio investors and risk-based KYC norms.

◈ Buybacks

News norms would make share buybacks a serious exercise for companies, as against being a share price propping activity.

SEBI has increased the mandatory minimum buyback limit from 25 per cent to 50 per cent of the amount earmarked for the buyback. If a firm fails to meet this requirement, the amount in the escrow account would be forfeited subject to a maximum of 2.5 per cent of the total amount earmarked.

The guidelines require companies to create escrow accounts towards security for performance with an amount equivalent to at least a quarter of the amount earmarked for the buyback.

SEBI has reduced the maximum buyback period to six months from 12 months.

SEBI has stipulated that a company shall not raise further capital for a year from the closure of the buyback except in discharge of subsisting obligations as against the existing six months; it shall not make another buyback offer within a year from the date of closure of the preceding offer.

The market regulator has said companies can buyback 15 per cent or more of capital (paid-up capital and free reserves) only by way of tender offers. It modified the procedure for buyback of physical shares (odd-lot) with the creation of a separate window in the trading system, requirement of PAN/Aadhaar for verification, etc.

SEBI has mandated that the promoters of the company shall not execute any transaction, either on-market or off-market, during the buyback period.

In another move, it rationalised norms requiring disclosure of the shares bought back on a cumulative basis on the website of the company and the stock exchange; now the disclosure needs to be made only on a daily basis instead of the current requirement of disclosure on daily, fortnightly and monthly basis.

◈ Delisting of Securities

The Securities and Exchange Board of India (the "SEBI") in the year 2002 constituted a committee on delisting of shares and to examine and review the conditions for delisting of securities of companies listed on recognized stock exchanges and suggest norms and procedures in connection therewith. The report of the committee was considered and accepted by SEBI Board. And on the basics of the Report SEBI issued the SEBI (Delisting of Securities) Guidelines, 2003; these have since been amended in 2006.

SEBI again proposed amendments to its current guidelines relating to delisting of a company in India, which were issued in 2003. SEBI has issued the draft SEBI (Delisting of Securities) Regulations, 2006 (the "Revised Guidelines") on November 23, 2006. The Revised Guidelines are in the draft form and will be adopted by SEBI in the first week of January 2007.

Under the Revised Guidelines, SEBI has proposed an alternative pricing mechanism for determining the price to be offered by promoters to shareholders for tendering their shares. Under the Revised Guidelines, SEBI has put an end to the current reverse book-building method for determining the price because it has lead to cartelization and gave disproportionate power to the largest shareholders for determining the price, which has resulted in failure of delisting offers in India.

The amendments recommend a minimum listing period of three years and approval from three-fourths of the shareholders as two of the three criterions for voluntary delisting; the draft rules also suggest that the promoters and directors have to commit to purchase the outstanding shares from minority and non-promoter shareholders.

There are some different views about the amendments. Some people are of the opinion that the government seems to have created conditions for companies to raise public money, siphon it off to their private coffers and get a smooth and automatic exit after three years of losses. This might be a loophole in the Act. Companies can also take advantage of few years of Bull Run to pick-up public funds through an over-priced and much hyped public offering and walk away with it in three years.

The new delisting norms may prompt investors to exit investments in many such companies which have been making losses for the past several years. According to delisting norms, stock exchanges can delist a company if it posts losses during the previous three years and its net worth has turned negative. Delisting might not be in the interests of investors even if companies are loss making as the past performance cannot be indicative of future performance. A loss making company can be a good investment bet if it has potential to grow and make profit in future.

On the brighter side, this move might be a help to the small and mid-sized companies to delist with ease, as the cost of compliance to the normal delisting process was very expensive for them. And this will also decrease the burden on the big stock exchanges who have to deal with many small and mid-sized companies who have less market capitalisation and also have less amount of transactions.

In the recent past promoters of many companies particularly multinationals have bought out the entire public holdings at the market related prices which were much lower than their book value, this had left common shareholders at disadvantageous position. This has made SEBI issue some guidelines regarding this matter.

SEBI guidelines are applicable to delisting of securities of companies and specifically apply to:

(*a*) Voluntary delisting being sought by the promoters of a company.

(*b*) Any acquisition of shares of the company (either by a promoter or by any other person) or scheme or arrangement, by whatever name referred to, consequently to which the public shareholding falls below the minimum limit specified in the listing conditions or listing agreement that may result in delisting of securities.

(*c*) Promoters of the companies who voluntarily seek to delist their securities from all or some of the stock exchanges.

Cases where a person in control of the management is seeing to consolidate his holding in a company, in a manner which would result in the public shareholding in the company falling below the limit specified in the listing conditions or in the listing agreement that may have the effect of company being delisted.

◈ Voluntary Delisting

- Any promoter or acquirer desirous of delisting securities of the company under the provisions of these guidelines should obtain the prior approval of shareholders of the company by a special resolution passed at its general meeting, make a public announcement in the manner provided in these guidelines, make an application to the delisting exchange from specified by the exchange, and comply with such other additional condition as may be specified by the concerned stock exchange from where securities are to be delisted.
- Any promoter of a company which desires to delist from the stock exchange should determine an exit price for delisting of securities in accordance with the book-building process as stated in the guidelines.
- The stock exchange shall provide the infrastructure facility for display of the price at the terminal of the trading members to enable the investors to access the price on the screen to bring transparency to the delisting process. The stock exchange shall also monitor the possibility of price manipulation and keep under special watch the securities for which announcement for delisting has been made.

◈ Compulsory Delisting of Companies

- The stock exchange may delist companies which have been suspended for a minimum period of six months for non-compliance with the listing agreement.
- The stock exchanges have to give adequate and wide public notice through newspapers and also give a show cause notice to a company. The exchange shall provide a time period of 15 days within which representation may be made to the exchange by any person who may be aggrieved by the proposed delisting.
- Where the securities of the company are delisted by an exchange, the promoter of the company should be liable to compensate the security holders of the company by paying them the fair value of the securities held by them and acquiring their securities, subject to their option to remain securityholder with the company.

◈ Reinstatement of Delisting Securities

Reinstatement of delisted securities should be permitted by the stock exchange with a cooling period of two years. It should be based on the respective norms/criteria for listing at the time of making the application for listing and the application should be initially scrutinized by the CLA.

DELISTING OF SECURITIES (2006)

◈ Applicability

These regulations shall apply to delisting of securities of a company from the stock exchange or stock exchanges where such securities are listed. The delisting of securities can be done under following two manners.

(1) Stock Exchange

A recognized stock exchange may delist any securities listed thereon on any of the following grounds in accordance with the regulations made under the Act by the Securities and Exchange Board of India, namely:

(a) The company has incurred losses during the preceding three consecutive years and its net worth has reduced to less than its paid-up capital;

(b) Trading in the securities of the company has remained suspended for a period of more than six months;

(c) The securities of the company have remained infrequently traded during the preceding three years;

(d) The company or any of its promoters or any of its directors has failed to comply with any of the provisions of the Act or the Securities and Exchange Board of India Act, 1992 or the Depositories Act, 1996 or rules, regulations, agreements made there under as the case may be, which warrants a penalty of not less than rupees one crore or imprisonment of not less than three years;

(e) The addresses of the company or any of its promoters or any of its directors are not known or false addresses have been furnished or the company has changed its registered office in contravention of the provisions of the Companies Act, 1956 (1 of 1956);

(f) Shareholding of the company held by the public has come below the minimum level applicable to the company as per the listing agreement under the Act: Provided that the securities of a company shall not be delisted unless the company concerned has been given a reasonable opportunity of being heard.

(2) Voluntary Delisting

A recognized stock exchange may, on a request by the company, delist any securities listed thereon in accordance with the regulations made under the Act by Securities Exchange Board of India, subject to the following conditions, namely:

(*a*) The securities of the company have been listed for a minimum period of three years on the recognized stock exchange;

(*b*) The delisting of such securities has been approved by the three-fourths of the shareholders in a general body meeting and;

(*c*) The promoters or the directors of the company commit to purchase the outstanding securities of the minority and non-promoter holders.

Delisting not permissible in certain circumstances and conditions for delisting.

1. No company shall apply for and no stock exchange shall grant delisting of securities of a company, pursuant to a buyback of securities by the company or pursuant to a preferential allotment made by the company.
2. No company shall apply for and no stock exchange shall grant delisting of any class of securities of a company unless a period of three years has elapsed since the listing of that class of securities on any stock exchange.
3. No company shall apply for and no stock exchange shall grant delisting of securities where any instruments issued by the company, which are convertible into the same class of securities that are sought to be delisted, are outstanding.
4. Nothing contained in Sub-regulations (2) and (3) shall apply to delisting of securities falling under clause (a) of Regulation 6.
5. No company shall apply for and no stock exchange shall grant delisting of convertible securities.
6. Notwithstanding delisting of any class of securities of a company, any other class of its securities may continue to be listed on the stock exchange.
7. Delisting of securities shall also be subject to the Securities Contracts (Regulation) Rules, 1957.

VOLUNTARY DELISTING

◈ Delisting from all Stock Exchanges

Subject to the provisions of these regulations the securities of a company may be delisted from all the stock exchanges where they are listed or from the stock exchange where they are listed: *Provided that* all public holders of the securities which are sought to be delisted are given an exit opportunity.

◈ Delisting from only Some of the Stock Exchanges

The securities of a company may be delisted from one or more stock exchanges where those are listed and continue to remain listed on one or more other stock exchanges subject to the provisions of these regulations and subject to the following —

(a) If after the proposed delisting from any one or more stock exchanges, the securities of a company would remain listed on any stock exchange which has nationwide trading terminals, no exit opportunity needs to be given to the shareholders; and,

(b) If after the proposed delisting, the securities of a company would not remain listed on any stock exchange having nationwide trading terminals, exit opportunity shall be given to all the public holders of the securities sought to be delisted in accordance with exit opportunity.

◈ Procedure for Delisting Where no Exit Opportunity is Required

1. In a case falling under clause (a) of Regulation 6 —

   (*a*) the proposed delisting shall be approved by a resolution of the Board of Directors of the company in its meeting;

   (*b*) the company shall give a public notice of the proposed delisting in at least one English national daily with wide circulation, one Hindi national daily with wide circulation and one regional language newspaper of the region where the concerned stock exchanges are located;

(*c*) the company shall make an application to the concerned stock exchange for delisting its securities; and,

(*d*) the fact of delisting shall be disclosed in the first annual report prepared after the delisting.

2. The public notice made under clause (b) of Sub-regulation (1) shall mention the names of the stock exchange from which the securities of the company are intended to be delisted, the reasons for such delisting and the fact of continuation of listing of securities on stock exchange having nationwide trading terminals.
3. Every application for delisting made under clause (c) of Sub-regulation (1) shall be accompanied by an audit report as required under Regulation 55A of the Securities and Exchange Board of India (Depositories and Participants) Regulations, 1996 covering a period of six months prior to the date of the application.
4. An application for delisting made under clause (c) of Sub-regulation (1) shall be disposed of by the stock exchange within a period not exceeding thirty days from the receipt by it of such application complete in all respects.
5. If any application for delisting is not disposed of within the period stipulated under Sub-regulation (4) the concerned stock exchange shall report it to the Board with reasons for such delay.

◈ Conditions and Procedure for Delisting Where Exit Opportunity is Required

1. Any company desirous of delisting its securities under the provisions of Chapter III shall, except in a case falling under clause (a) of Regulation 6:

   (*a*) obtain the prior approval of the Board of Directors of the company in its meeting;

   (*b*) obtain the prior approval of shareholders or securityholders of the company by special resolution passed through postal ballot;

   (*c*) make an application to the concerned stock exchange for in-principle approval of the proposed delisting in the form specified by the stock exchange; and

   (*d*) within one year of passing the special resolution, make the final application to the concerned stock exchange in the form specified by the stock exchange:

2. No delisting shall, except in a case falling under clause (a) of Regulation 6, be made —

   (*a*) unless the company whose securities are sought to be delisted complies with the minimum public shareholding requirements of twenty-five per cent or ten per cent, as the case may be, applicable to it under the listing agreement; or

   (b) if successful completion of the exit opportunity may result in change in control over the company whose securities are sought to be delisted.

3. Nothing contained in clause (a) of Sub-regulation (2) shall apply to a case where the company was not in compliance with the minimum shareholding requirements as specified in the listing agreement as on the first day of May 2006 and either —

   (*a*) Its paid-up capital was less than one crore rupees as on that date; or

   (*b*) Its paid-up capital was more than one crore rupees but less than three crore rupees as on that date and the number of its shareholders was three hundred or less as on that date.

4. An application seeking in-principle approval for delisting under clause (c) of Sub-regulation (1) shall be accompanied by an audit report as required under Regulation 55A of the Securities and Exchange Board of India (Depositories and Participants) Regulations, 1996 in respect of the securities sought to be delisted covering a period of six months prior to the date of the application.
5. An application seeking in-principle approval for delisting shall be disposed of by the stock exchange within a period not exceeding thirty days from the receipt by it of such application complete in all respects.
6. While considering an application seeking in-principle approval for delisting, the stock exchange shall not unfairly withhold such application, but may require the company to satisfy it as to:

   (*a*) the resolution of investor grievances by the company;

   (*b*) payment of listing fees to that stock exchange;

   (*c*) the compliance with any condition of the listing agreement with that stock exchange having a material bearing on the interests of its security holders;

   (*d*) any litigation or action pending against the company pertaining to its activities in the securities market or any other matter having a material bearing on the interests of its securityholders.
7. If any application seeking in-principle approval for delisting is not disposed of within the period stipulated under Sub-regulation (5), the concerned stock exchange shall report it to the Board with reasons for such delay.
8. A final application for delisting made under clause (d) of Sub-regulation (1) shall be accompanied with a true copy of the special resolution passed under clause (a) of Sub-regulation (1) and with such proof of having given the exit opportunity in accordance with the provisions of exit opportunity, as the stock exchange may require.

Exit Opportunity

The provisions of this part shall apply to any delisting sought to be made under Regulation 5 or under clause (b) of Regulation 6.

◆ Public Announcement

1. The promoters of the company shall upon receipt of in-principle approval for delisting, make a public announcement in at least one English national daily with wide circulation, one Hindi national daily with wide circulation and one regional language newspaper of the region where the concerned stock exchanges are located.
2. The public announcement shall contain all material information including the information specified in the Schedule and shall not contain any false or misleading statement.
3. The public announcement shall also specify a date, being a day not later than thirty days from the date of the public announcement, which shall be the 'specified date' for determining the names of shareholders to whom the letter of offer shall be sent.
4. Before making the public announcement, the promoter shall appoint a merchant banker registered with the Board and such other intermediaries as are considered necessary.
5. It shall be the responsibility of the promoter and the merchant banker to ensure compliance with the provisions of this part.

6. No promoter shall appoint any person as a merchant banker under Sub-regulation (4) if such a person is an associate of the promoter.

◆ Escrow Account

1. The promoter shall open an escrow account before making the public announcement under Regulation 10 and deposit therein the total offer price payable, assuming full acceptance of the offer by publicholders.
2. The escrow account shall consist of either cash deposited with a scheduled commercial bank, or a bank guarantee in favour of the merchant banker, or a combination of both.
3. Where the escrow account consists of deposit with a scheduled commercial bank, the promoter shall, while opening the account, empower the merchant banker to instruct the bank to issue a banker's cheque or demand draft for the amount lying to the credit of the escrow account, for the purposes mentioned in these regulations and the amount in such deposit, if any, remaining after full payment of consideration for securities tendered in the offer and those tendered under Sub-regulation (1) of Regulation 19 shall be released to the company after expiry of the period referred to in that Sub-regulation.
4. Where the escrow account consists of a bank guarantee, such bank guarantee shall be valid till expiry of the period referred to in Sub-regulation (1) of Regulation 19.

◆ Letter of Offer

1. The promoter shall dispatch the letter of offer to the publicholders of securities, not later than forty-five days from the date of the public announcement, so as to reach them at least five days before the opening of the offer period.
2. The letter of offer shall be sent under Sub-regulation (1) to all publicholders of securities of the company whose names appear on the register of the company or depository as on the specified date fixed under Sub-regulation (3) of Regulation 10.
3. The letter of offer shall contain all the disclosures made in the public announcement and such other disclosures as may be necessary for the securityholders to take an informed decision.

◆ Offer Period

1. The date of opening of the offer shall not be later than the fifty-five days from the date of the public announcement.
2. The offer shall remain open for a period of twenty days, during which the publicholders of securities may tender their securities.

◆ Offer Price

1. The floor price shall not be less than:
   (*a*) where the securities are frequently traded in all the stock exchanges where they are listed, the average of the weekly high and low of the closing prices of the securities of the company as quoted on the stock exchange, where the securities of the company are most frequently traded, during the twenty-six weeks or two weeks preceding the date on which the stock exchanges were notified of the

Board meeting in which the delisting proposal was considered, whichever is higher;

(*b*) where the securities of the company are infrequently traded in all the stock exchanges where they are listed, the floor price determined in accordance with the provisions of Sub-regulation (2); or,

(*c*) where the securities are frequently traded in some stock exchanges and infrequently traded in some other stock exchanges where they are listed, the highest of the prices arrived at in accordance with clauses (a) and (b) above.

2. For the purposes of clause (b) of Sub-regulation (1), the floor price shall be determined by the promoter and the merchant banker taking into account the following factors:

   (*a*) the highest price paid by the promoter for acquisitions including by way of allotment in a public or rights issue or preferential allotment, if any, during the twenty-six weeks period prior to the date on which the stock exchanges were notified of the Board meeting in which the delisting proposal was considered and up to the date of the public announcement; and,

   (*b*) other parameters including return on net worth, book value of the shares of the company, earnings per share, price earning multiple *vis-à-vis* the industry average.

3. Notwithstanding anything contained in Sub-regulations (1) and (2), where the securities proposed to be delisted are debt instruments, the floor price shall not be less than the aggregate of the face value and interest accrued thereon.

4. The offer price shall not be less than the higher of the following —

   (*a*) The floor price determined under Sub-regulation (1), as increased by a premium of twenty-five per cent thereof;

   (*b*) The fair value of the securities determined by a registered credit rating agency, as increased by a premium of twenty-five per cent thereof.

◈ Special Depositories Account and Handling of Securities Tendered

1. Before opening of the offer, the merchant banker shall open a special depositories account with a depository.

2. Where securities tendered by a publicholder are in dematerialized form —

   (*a*) they shall be deposited by the merchant banker in the special depositories account; and

   (*b*) they shall not be transferred to the promoter unless the offer is found to be successful in terms of Regulation 16 and the full consideration in respect thereof is paid to the public holders in compliance with Regulation 18.

3. Where securities tendered by a public holder are in physical form —

   (*a*) they shall be forwarded to the share transfer agents of the company to verify the genuineness of the security certificate and transfer deed and where they are found to be not genuine, a communication of rejection shall be sent to the publicholder within ten working days of closure of the offer; and

   (*b*) the securities which are verified to be genuine shall be in the custody of the merchant banker and shall not be registered in the name of the promoter, unless the offer is found to be successful in terms of Regulation 16 and the full consideration in respect thereof is paid to the publicholders in compliance with Regulation 18.

◈ Minimum Number of Securities to be Acquired

(1) Where the offer results in acceptance of a fewer number of securities than the total securities for which the offer was made and the promoters shareholding (together with holdings of persons acting in concert with him) is not likely to exceed ninety per cent of the total outstanding shares of that class, the offer shall fail and no securities shall be acquired pursuant to such offer: *Provided that* in a case where the company whose shares are proposed to be delisted has an applicable minimum public shareholding level of ten per cent under the listing agreement, Sub-regulation (1) shall apply as if for the words "ninety per cent" the words "ninety-six per cent" were substituted.

(2) Where the offer fails —

(*a*) the securities tendered by a holder shall be returned to the holder within seven days of closure of the offer period;

(*b*) no final application shall be made to the exchange for delisting of the securities; and

(*c*) the escrow account opened under Regulation 11 shall be closed.

◈ Procedure after Closure of Offer

1. Within seven days of closure of the offer, the promoter and the merchant banker shall make a public announcement in the same newspapers in which the public announcement under Sub-regulation (1) of Regulation 10 was made, as to whether the minimum number of securities required for success of the offer under Regulation 16 were tendered.
2. Where the offer succeeds in terms of Regulation 16, the securities tendered shall be deemed to be acquired by the promoter unless a communication of rejection, upon verification of the securities tendered (in respect of securities in the physical form), is made within ten working days of closure of the offer and the promoter shall be liable to pay the consideration for such securities.

◈ Payment of Consideration

1. The promoter shall immediately on ascertaining success of the offer, open a special account with a banker to an issue registered with the Board and transfer thereto, the entire amount due and payable as consideration in respect of securities tendered in the offer, from the escrow account.
2. All the securityholders whose securities are verified to be genuine shall be paid the final price stated in the public announcement within ten working days from the closure of the offer.

◈ Right of Remaining Securityholders to Tender Securities

1. Where, pursuant to acceptance of securities tendered in terms of these regulations, the securities are delisted, any remaining publicholder of such securities may tender his securities to the promoter up to a period of six months from the date of delisting and, in such a case, the promoter shall accept the securities tendered at the same final price at which the earlier acceptance of securities was made.
2. The payment of consideration for securities accepted under Sub-regulation (1) shall be made out of the balance amount lying in the escrow account.

3. The amount in the escrow account or the bank guarantee shall not be released to the promoter unless all payments are made in respect of securities tendered under Sub-regulation (1).

COMPULSORY DELISTING

◈ Compulsory Delisting by a Stock Exchange

1. A stock exchange may, by order, delist any securities of a company on any ground prescribed in the rules made under Section 21A of the Securities Contracts (Regulation) Act, 1956 (42 of 1956): *Provided that* no order shall be made under this Sub-regulation unless the company concerned has been given a reasonable opportunity of being heard.
2. The decision regarding compulsory delisting shall be taken by a panel to be constituted by the stock exchange consisting of —
   (*a*) two directors of the stock exchange (one of whom shall be a public representative);
   (*b*) one director nominated by the Board; and
   (*c*) the Executive Director or Secretary of the stock exchange.
3. Before making an order under Sub-regulation (1), the stock exchange shall give a notice in one English national daily with wide circulation and one regional language newspaper of the region where the concerned stock exchange is located, of the proposed delisting, giving a time period of not less than fifteen days from the notice, within which representations may be made to the stock exchange by any person who may be aggrieved by the proposed delisting and shall also display such notice on its trading systems and website.
4. The stock exchange shall while passing any order under Sub-regulation (1), consider the representations, if any, made by the company as also any representations received in response to the notice given under Sub-regulation (3).
5. The provisions of Chapter IV shall not be applicable to a compulsory delisting made by a stock exchange under this Chapter.
6. Where the stock exchange passes an order under Sub-regulation (1), it shall forthwith publish a notice in one English national daily with wide circulation and one regional language newspaper of the region where the concerned stock exchange is located, of the fact of such delisting, disclosing therein the name and address of the company, the fair value of the delisted securities determined under Sub-regulation (1) of Regulation 21 and names and addresses of the promoters of the company who would be liable under Sub-regulation (3) of Regulation 21.
7. A listed company or any investor aggrieved by an order passed under Sub-regulation (1), may file an appeal against the order before the Securities Appellate Tribunal under Sub-section (2) of Section 21A of the Securities Contracts (Regulation) Act, 1956 (42 of 1956), in accordance with that Act and the rules made thereunder.

◈ Rights of Publicholders of Securities in Case of a Compulsory Delisting

1. Where securities of a company are delisted by a stock exchange under this Chapter, the stock exchange shall appoint an independent valuer or valuers who shall determine the fair value of the delisted securities.

2. The stock exchange shall form a panel of expert valuers from whom the valuer or valuers shall be appointed for purposes of Sub-regulation (1).
3. The promoter of the company shall acquire delisted securities of the publicholders by paying them the value determined by the valuer, subject to the option of the publicholders of the securities to retain the securities.

Explanation: For the purposes of Sub-regulation (1),

(*a*) 'valuer' means a Chartered Accountant or merchant banker appointed to determine the value of the delisted securities;

(*b*) value of the delisted securities shall be determined by the valuer having regard to the factors mentioned in Regulation 14.

◆ Directions by the Board

Without prejudice to provisions of the Act and those of the Securities Contracts (Regulation) Act, 1956 (42 of 1956), the Board may in case of any violation of these regulations and in the interests of the investors and the securities market give such directions as it deems fit including:

(*a*) suspending the trading of any security in an exchange;

(*b*) restraining persons from accessing the securities market and prohibiting any person associated with securities market from buying, selling or dealing in securities;

(*c*) directing the Board of Directors or promoters of a company whose securities are delisted consequent upon withdrawal of recognition or non-renewal of recognition granted to a stock exchange, for getting its securities listed on any such stock exchange as may be specified by the Board; or

(*d*) directing a stock exchange to delist any securities of any company: *Provided that* the Board shall, either before or after passing such orders, give an opportunity of hearing to the company or other concerned person.

◆ Listing of Delisted Securities

1. No application for listing shall be made in respect of any securities which have been delisted under these regulations or under any other law for the time-being in force for a period of seven years from the delisting.
2. While considering an application for listing of any securities which had been delisted, the stock exchange shall have due regard to facts and circumstances under which delisting was made.
3. Except to the extent provided in Sub-regulation (2), an application for listing made under Sub-regulation (1) shall be deemed to be an application for fresh listing of such securities.
4. Nothing in this regulation shall apply to a listing of delisted securities pursuant to orders of a court or tribunal.

◆ The Old Guidelines

The old guidelines came into force on February 17, 2003. The salient features of these guidelines are brought out below:

1. An exit option to the public shareholders is mandated if the company or its promoters wish to delist its securities from all the stock exchanges in which they are listed.

2. No exit opportunity to be given in case of securities to be delisted from exchanges other than exchanges having nationwide trading terminal (BSE/NSE) if these securities continue to be listed on stock exchanges having nationwide trading terminals.
3. Price discovery by a method of book-building in which the price is determined at the rate at which maximum number of shares are tendered.
4. Eligibility to participate in the book-building process extended only to de-mat shareholders.
5. Option available to the promoters to accept or reject the price determined by the book-building process.
6. Settlement of shares after the offer through the stock exchange clearing mechanism.
7. The exit option to be open for a period of six months after the closure and acceptance of the offer.

◈ New Guidelines (Changes)

In order to provide protection for the investor's interest, certain changes has been made to the existing guidelines. The following points highlight the nature of changes proposed and the rationale behind the proposed changes:

1. Conversion of Guidelines into Regulations

The provisions governing delisting of securities were initially envisaged only as a guiding framework to provide for an exit option at a determined price with the stock exchange overseeing the compliance. Consistent with the need to have appropriate instrumentalities, it has been decided to convert the Guidelines into Regulations.

2. Book-building Process

The following was noticed in the scrutiny of the current process of price discovery through book-building:

(*a*) Disproportionate powers with public shareholders holding major chunk

(*b*) Possibility of frivolous bids to destabilize the delisting offer

(*c*) Freedom to promoters to reject the price discovered.

(*d*) Revision of bids leading to cartelization in the discovery of price. It was increasingly felt that the book-building process, which was to aid in the determination of a fair exit value for the shareholders, was not fully achieving the said objective and the perceived investor friendliness of the price discovery mechanism was not necessarily translating into genuine discovery of price.

Thus it was necessary to look for an alternate pricing mechanism and hence the new proposal is as under:

It is proposed that the price would be the higher of —

(*a*) The fixed price which would be the floor price plus a premium of 25 per cent. The floor price would be determined in terms of Regulation 20 of SEBI (Substantial Acquisition of Shares and Takeover) Regulations.

(*b*) Fair value determined by an accredited rating agency plus a premium of 25 per cent. The relevant provision is annexed at Regulation 14(4) of the proposed draft Regulations.

Further, it was proposed that the reference date for calculation of floor price would be the date on which the stock exchanges are notified of the Board Meeting in which the delisting proposal was considered. This is in line with the provisions of the Takeover Regulations.

3. Absence of Minimum Subscription

The success of the exit offer under the current provisions of the guidelines is linked to the crossing of the continuous listing requirement. This gave rise to a situation that securities were bound to get delisted if the public shareholding reduced from the levels required to be maintained for the purpose of continuous listing.

While the rationale of mandating levels for continuous listing is based on good corporate governance, providing the same levels as eligibility for delisting was resulting in delisting of securities even while a huge residue of public shareholding remains, which is primarily against investor interest.

World over, in matters of delisting, it is a known fact that a 10 per cent level of public shareholding was considered as a prudent level for squeeze out option to the promoters whenever companies wanted to delist. Thus as a measure to arrive at plausible levels of public shareholding, below which companies wishing to delist their securities could do so, it is proposed to introduce a level of 10 per cent of public shareholding (in consonance with international practices) as the breach percentage level for eligibility for delisting. The relevant proposal is as under: Minimum subscription to be introduced: Success of the offer depends on a minimum subscription resulting in the public shareholding reducing below 10 per cent or 4 per cent. Thus, the promoter holding should breach the 90 per cent level or 96 per cent level as the case may be depending on the categorization of the company under clause 40A.

4. The Exit Offer to be Available for all Shares

With the dispensing of the book-building mechanism which was available only for shares in de-mat mode, the anomaly arising therein has been addressed. Now shareholders holding shares in both physical and de-mat mode can participate in the offer.

5. Settlement Procedure

In order to simplify the settlement system, it is now proposed that the settlement would be made separately through the Merchant Bankers and Registrars as is being currently done in open offers under SEBI (SAST) Regulations.

6. Timelines for Various Activities

Current guidelines give only the skeletal framework for delisting the securities. It was felt that many procedural aspects needed clarification. Hence, in order to bring about clarity and provide for a structured framework, certain timelines have been proposed in the Regulations.

7. Reporting Requirements

The earlier guidelines do not prescribe any kind of reporting by the stock exchanges. Though it is intended to keep the monitoring aspect purely with the stock exchange, certain overall reporting requirements are being prescribed which were felt necessary for the smooth working of these Regulations.

◈ Some Data on Buyback

COMPANIES OFFERING BUYBACK

Scrip Code	*Name of the Company*	*Offer Type*	*Maximum Buyback Price(A)*	*Total Aggregate Amount (₹ crore)*	*Start + Date*	*End ++ Date*
520077	Amtek Auto-$	Open Market Purchase	200.00	219.00	16 Jan 2012	24 Aug 2012
507828	Ansal Housing-$	Open Market Purchase	45.00	11.00	23 Jan 2012	30 Nov 2012
502219	Borosil Glass	Open Market Purchase	850.00	82.00	19 Dec 2011	10 Nov 2012
500092	CRISIL	Open Market Purchase	1,000.00	30.00	26 Dec 2011	6 Dec 2012
532491	ECE Inds-$	Open Market Purchase	125.00	9.00	18 Apr 2012	27 Mar 2013
532764	GEECEE*	Open Market Purchase	65.00	10.00	9 Feb 2012	8 Jan 2013
532832	Indiabulls Real Est	Open Market Purchase	75.00	450.00	30 Apr 2012	14 Dec 2012
500380	JK Lakshmi Cem	Open Market Purchase	70.00	98.00	26 Mar 2012	6 Feb 2013
533293	Kirloskar Oil Engines	Open Market Purchase	170.00	74.00	5 Mar 20122	4 Jan 2013
513446	Monnet Ispat Energy	Open Market Purchase	500.00	100.00	21 Mar 2012	21 Dec 2012
532944	Onmobile Global	Open Market Purchase	85.00	25.00	30 Sep 2011	31 Aug 2012
500325	RIL	Open Market Purchase	870.00	10,440.00	7 Feb 2012	19 Jan 2013
532663	Sasken Comm	Open Market Purchase	180.00	86.00	21 May 2012	22 Apr 2013
532344	Softsol India	Open Market Purchase	65.00	7.00	24 Nov 2011	30 Sep 2012
512070	United Phos	Open Market Purchase	150.00	288.00	4 Jun 2012	6 May 2013
526775	Valiant Comm-$	Open Market Purchase	18.00	2.00	25 Jan 2012	20 Dec 2012
505537	Zee Entert	Open Market Purchase	140.00	280.00	23 Apr 2012	3 Apr 2013

11 PORTFOLIO MANAGEMENT

A portfolio is collection of assets. In portfolio management these assets are financial in nature. The portfolio manager invests the money in diverse assets with the aim of maximizing return and minimizing the risk.

All individuals who save money tend to invest their savings in various asset classes. In India almost 65 per cent of savings are said to be invested bank Fixed Deposits. Many believe that this is an inefficient way of investing money and the post-tax returns do not cover the rate of inflation and as such destroys the capital over the years. The bank interest rates vary as per the monetary policy of RBI. Today the rates are probably at their highest levels. This will naturally prompt many to park their funds in banks for a longer period of time, because even if the rates were to start declining they would still get the higher contracted rate till the maturity of their deposits. However, it must be noted that the interest earned on these deposits is taxable and hence for the taxpaying investor the return will be less than the interest that he earns. This is a good product for retired persons many of whom do not have to pay income tax. This product is also good for all those who have no risk appetite. Most people in India are risk averse and hence the popularity of this product. However as is well known lower risk appetite would automatically lean lower return expectation. If one wishes higher return then he has to take larger risk!

Indians also seem to invest money mainly in tax saving instruments like, PF,PPF, NSC, ELSS,ULIPs and insurance premium. Out of these PPF seems to be the best product as it earns these days interest @8.6 per cent p.a. and this interest is tax-free on maturity. However one disadvantage of PPF is that the money deposited has a long lock-in period. For employed persons PF is mandatory. ELSS seems to be the most efficient product in this asset class as the money gets invested in equities and many ELSS schemes have delivered better returns than all other products mentioned. However many ELSS scheme have not done well is also a fact. ULIPs in general do not seem to have done very well. Insurance is not and never will be a saving product, though many look at it as one. Insurance essentially is a risk mitigation product and as such it cannot be a saving product. Yes all of us need to have the protection of insurance.

Many look to invest money in real estate. Buying a house is a necessity. If one buys a house and stays in that, then it does not generate any return, but it does save on the rent that one would have to pay otherwise. Investing in real estate require a lot of funds. Most people will find it difficult to raise such funds. Real estate prices have sky rocketed in the past decade and show no signs of moderating, making it extremely difficult for middle-class Indians to even buy a house for their own use. So this investment option is really only for people who have a lot of spare money.

Another asset class that is the flavour for the past 5-6 years has been gold. Indians have always bought gold crazily without any consideration for returns on the money that they invest in it. Most buy gold for cultural reasons rather than as an asset in portfolio. Gold prices have tripled in the last six years are so and still the demand for the yellow metal is rising. Historically there is a relationship between gold prices and $. Historically gold prices have declined by as much as 80 per cent from their peak levels. One does not know if this will happen again but it would be better for middle-class investors to be careful about this. This has already happened to silver which rose to ₹ 75,000 and is now around ₹ 55,000.

It said that for young people the best asset class is equities directly or through the mutual fund route. In India the population of investors in equities has declined alarmingly over the past twenty years, even as Indian markets have given an annualised return of about 15 per cent over the past two decades!

Most people in our country as financially illiterate without realizing this and hence end up making wrong investment decisions. Thus at the end of their working life and even during it many find that they do not enough to live a comfortable life. Many times it happens due to the sheer neglect towards investments.

This is where a portfolio manager comes into picture. He is one who can advise us as to how build our corpus from our current earnings. We also know certain expenses that we will have to incur at different stages like the children's education, marriage, our requirement post-retirement, etc. A portfolio manager can advise us as to how to invest our funds for meeting all these requirements. However they would charge fees for doing this and many of us are most reluctant to pay these fees.

SEBI has made it mandatory for investment advisors to be qualified for offering such services. They have to acquire the certification called 'Certified Financial Planner". This is to make sure that the advisors themselves know the products well and also to protect the interests of investors. We keep reading many reports of investors being taken for a ride. This is because many conmen dupe investors of their hard earned money by promising astronomical returns and then run away with all the money. A very few if any are ever caught and the money is almost never recovered. The tragedy is that people never learn and new *"Bakaras"* get trapped in the new scam!

According to SEBI, portfolio means the total holdings of securities belonging to one person.

Portfolio manager means any person who pursuant to a contract with a client undertakes the management of a portfolio of securities or the funds of the client.

1. To frame investment strategy and select an investment mix.
2. To provide a balanced portfolio, this will hedge against inflation and also optimise returns.
3. To make timely decisions regarding sale and purchase of securities.
4. To maximize after tax return by investing part of the portfolio in tax savings investments.

Portfolio management can be institutional in nature. The mutual funds are a kind of portfolio schemes. Recently many new pension funds have been launched. These funds also have to build a portfolio so that a return can be generated for the participants.

◈ Advantages of Portfolio Management for Individuals

1. Capital markets over a long period have always given a better return than any other investment.
2. The investment in stock markets by individuals is a complicated business. It is better that a professional handles this.

◈ Can You Create an Ideal Portfolio for Yourself?

◈ Types of Portfolio Management:

1. The discretionary portfolio management service (DPMS)

In this type, the clients gives his money for investment to the manager, who handles the paperwork, makes all investment decisions and gives a good return to the investors and charges a fee for the service rendered.

2. The non-discretionary portfolio management service

In this scheme the manager functions as a counsellor, but the investor is free to accept or reject the manager's advice; the paperwork is also undertaken by the manager for a service charge. The manager concentrates on stock market instruments with a portfolio tailor-made to the risk taking ability of the investor.

◈ Qualities of Portfolio Manager

1. Sound general knowledge

This is an exciting and challenging job. The atmosphere is uncertain and ever-changing. Any news can affect the stock markets. He therefore must be aware and well informed and must be able to use the information that he gets.

2. Analytical ability

He has to be good at analysing the information so that he can make a good prediction about the behaviour of the markets. His ability to analyse the economy and the industry is very important.

3. Marketing skills

He has to be a good salesman. He has to convince the clients about the securities he is buying for the client or is recommending to the client.

4. Experience

It is said that stock markets are cyclical in nature. He therefore must be aware of these cycles. Such experience can help him in taking proper decisions.

◈ Steps in Portfolio Management

This is an ongoing process and following steps are taken:

1. Specification and quantification of investor objectives, constraints and preferences in the form of policy statement.

2. Determination and quantification of capital market expectations for the economy, market sectors, industries and individual securities.
3. Allocation of assets and selection of individual securities.
4. Performance measurement and evaluation of the portfolio to ensure that investor's objectives are attained.
5. Monitoring the performance and responding to changes in investor objective constraints and capital market expectations.
6. Rebalancing the portfolio whenever necessary.

◈ Criteria for Portfolio Decisions and Factors that Influence Portfolio Decisions

Emphasis is on identifying the collective importance of all investor's holdings. Each portfolio has to be tailored to the particular needs of its owners. The strategies are required to be moulded to the unique needs and characteristics of the portfolio owner. The risk can be reduced by diversifying the portfolio. Since risk and returns are related, the important decision to make is the amount of risk, which is acceptable.

◈ Investor's Characteristics

A study of investor's characteristics such as age, health condition, personal habits, business or professional situation and tax status affect the risk taking ability of an investor, and therefore his requirement of different securities. A young person for example may put more emphasis on growth and lesser on liquidity. The investor's responsibilities towards his family and the number of dependents on him will have an impact on his investment needs and goals.

◈ Liquidity Needs

Liquidity needs vary considerably among investors. For this the portfolio should be built on the securities which are highly liquid in nature, if liquidity is the main criteria.

◈ Tax Considerations

Different individuals have different incomes and hence different tax liabilities. Tax treatment form income form investment can be different for different securities. Investors in high marginal tax brackets are faced with complex portfolio decisions. High tax bracket investors are interested in investments that are designed to postpone a tax, or to reduce tax or to avoid paying taxes. They also will be interested in investing in tax-free instruments. They may be also interested in getting their income through capital gains, as tax on capital gains is lower than the income tax.

◈ Safety of Principal

The protection of the value of the investment is the most important objective of an investor. The investor is expected to invest in such securities, which would increase in value proportionate to the inflation to protect from the purchasing power loss of the money. The relative importance of safety of principal has bearing on the degree of the risk an investor is willing to take.

◈ Assurance of Income

Investors have different current income needs. If an investment income needed for current consumption, then this will become the prime objective. If current needs are fulfilled through other means then the investors will look for capital appreciation.

◆ Investment Risk

All investment decisions revolve around the trade-off between risk and return. All investors want maximum possible return from their investments, but are not always willing to take the necessary risk for such returns.

◆ Interest Rate Risk

Interest rate risk is the risk of loss of principal brought about by changes in the interest rate paid on new securities currently being issued. Increase or decrease in interest rate will have an effect on the market prices of such securities. The investor therefore should be aware of this risk while making the investments in the fixed-income securities.

◆ Business and Market Risk

Changes in a company's business fortunes would have an impact on the market prices of the company's share prices. When stock markets are going up, then most stocks will also rise; on the other hand when the stock prices are falling then most stocks will fall. This behaviour may not be in line with the company's financial and other fundamentals.

◆ SEBI Regulations Governing Portfolio Management Activities

1. A portfolio manager must register himself with the SEBI.
2. The applicant needs to have necessary infrastructure.
3. He must have in his employment at least two persons who are experienced in the business of portfolio management.
4. The applicant must fulfil the capital adequacy norms laid down from time-to-time.
5. The applicant must not be involved in any litigation connected with the securities market.
6. He must have the professional qualifications from a recognized institution in finance, law, and accountancy or business management.
7. The applicant has to pay registration fees as are in force.
8. Portfolio manager must enter into an agreement clearly defining the *inter-se* relationship, and setting out their mutual rights, liabilities and obligations relating to management of the portfolio of the client.
9. The funds of all clients shall be placed by the portfolio manager in a separate account to be maintained by his in a scheduled commercial bank.
10. The portfolio manager shall charge an agreed fee from the client for rendering portfolio management services without guaranteeing or assuring, either directly or indirectly any return and such fee shall be independent of the return to the client and shall not be on a return sharing basis.
11. The portfolio manager shall not accept money or securities from his client for a period of less than one year.
12. Any renewal of portfolio fund on maturity of the initial period shall be deemed as a fresh placement and shall be for minimum period of one year.
13. The portfolio manager shall purchase or sell securities separately for each client.

◈ Code of Conduct — Portfolio Manager

1. In conduct of his business he shall observe high standards of integrity and fairness in all dealings.
2. The client's money should be deployed as soon as possible and money due and payable to a client should be paid forthwith.
3. He shall render at all time high standards of services, exercise due diligence, ensure proper care and exercise independent professional judgement.
4. He shall not get involved in unfair competition.
3. He should not disclose any confidential information about his client.
5. A portfolio manager shall not be a party to:
   (a) Creation of false market in securities.
   (b) Price rigging or manipulation of securities.
   (c) Passing of price sensitive information to any participants in the market.

12 CORPORATE GOVERNANCE

How does one define Corporate Governance? Essentially it covers the gamut of activities having a direct or indirect effect on the health of the entity. Nobel Laureate Milton Friedman stated; "Corporate Governance is to conduct business in accordance with shareholders' desire while confirming to local laws and customs". More recently the President, World Bank – J.Wolfensohn made a more contemporary definition of the same. "Corporate Governance is all about promoting Corporate Fairness, Transparency and Accountability." How much of this is a pertinent and really followed today remains to be seen.

◈ Historical Perspective

The concept of Corporate Governance in its present form is rather new. The seeds of Corporate Governance were laid during the Watergate scandal that shook the Presidential House in the United States. Also, 1980s were characterised by a string of high profile business failures. An investigation into these pinpointed the fault to; lack of proper internal controls. And also the absence of independent audits (internal as well as external).

The failure of Enron and World Com accelerated the process and the US government responded with Sarbanes-Oxley Act. The top conspirators were tried swiftly and jailed unlike in India where the legal process takes inordinately long time and the guilty hardly get punished. . However in 2008 meltdown of financial sector showed that in spite of the act companies flouted norms and CEOs were rewarded for their wrong doings and reporting.

◈ Background for Formation of Birla Committee

The first real work in this field was done by Cadbury Committee was set up in UK. The report submitted by Sir Cadbury proved to be a landmark in the field of Corporate Governance. Concurrently, India could not stand isolated in this fast changing scenario. A number of financial scams back home prompted the government to set up a committee under the chairmanship of Kumaramangalam Birla.

The objective of the committee was "enhancement of the long-term shareholders' value. While at the same time protecting the interests of other stakeholders."

The key recommendations of the report were;

(i) Board of Directors

It provides leadership, strategic guidance and objective judgement independent of management to the company and exercises control over the company, while remaining at all times accountable to the shareholders.

◈ The Board has 5 Basic Responsibilities:

- Overseeing Strategic Development and Planning.
- Management Selection, Supervision and Upgrading.
- Maintenance of Good Member Relations
- Protecting and optimising the Organizations' Assets.
- Fulfilling Legal Requirements.

(ii) Composition of the Board of Directors

- Lays emphasis on the calibre of the non-executive directors.
- Independent directors have a key role.

This is an important issue in the Indian context. A major chunk of shares were held by financial institutions like UTI, IFCI, etc., which could be termed as quasi-government institutions. They would appoint a director, who would generally not have any sector specific knowledge. In the process however it is the company that suffers.

(*i*) Audit Committee

◈ Key Components

The board, the internal auditor and the outside auditors —

(*iii*) Disclosures of Remuneration Package

(*iv*) Board meetings

Should be held at least four times in a year

The report stressed the importance of the proxy voting/ballot system.

A few years back, companies would hold their AGM in the most remote location possible. It would be guaranteed to be the most inaccessible place. The reason for this obviously is to avoid facing shareholder's wrath or get some crucial resolutions passed.

(*vi*) Functions of the Management

Chief Executive, Executive-directors and the key managers

- Assisting the board in its decision making process
- Implementing the policies and code of conduct of the board
- Ensuring compliance of all regulations and laws
- Providing timely, accurate, substantive and material *information*

(*vii*) Shareholders

Have certain rights and responsibilities

Effectively participate in general body meetings

Should demand complete information

(Annual General Meetings in obscure places)

However the report ended with a note of **Caution**

It stated that no "one size fits all" structure possible ethics should play an important role.

It is a continuously evolving system.

Reasons for failure in spite of these norms

Ineffective leadership

Incompetence of the board members

Lack of mutual trust

Time deficit

Constant change —

Less predictability in decision making;

Need for quicker decisions.

Superficial commitment to vision, mission and values

◆ Mandatory Recommendations of Birla Committee

1. Board of Directors

(*a*) There should be a combination of executive and Non-executive directors. The board should consist of not less than 50 per cent of Non-executive directors in case of an executive chairman and not less than 1/3rd of Non-executive directors in case of a non-executive chairman.

2. Audit Committee

(*a*) The board should appoint a qualified and independent audit committee. The committee should have minimum three members, all being non-executive directors, with majority being independent, and at least one director having financial and accounting knowledge.

(*b*) The chairman of committee should be independent director and should be present at company AGM.

(*c*) The chairman should invite Finance Director, Head of internal audit and representative of External auditor for committee meetings. Company secretary should act as secretary of the committee.

3. Powers of the Audit Committee

(*a*) The audit committee should look into the reasons for substantial default to depositors, creditors, debentureholders and shareholders.

4. Frequency of Meetings and Quorum

(*a*) The committee should meet at least thrice a year, once before finalization of annual accounts and once compulsorily every six months. Quorum should be either two members or 1/3rd of audit committee, whichever is higher, and there should be minimum two independent directors.

5. Remuneration

(*a*) The board of directors should decide remuneration of non-executive directors.

(*b*) All elements of the package inclusive of salary benefits, bonuses, stock options, etc., should be disclosed.

6. Committee Membership of Directors

(*a*) Directors should not be members of more than ten committees and Chairman of not more than five committees. Directors need to disclose about their membership with other committees to the company.

7. Shareholder's Committee

(*a*) This committee would be framed to attend to shareholder's grievances and board of the company should delegate power of checking share transfer to either officer or committee or to registrar and share transfer agents.

Information to be Placed Before Board of Directors

1. Annual operating plans, budgets and an updates.
2. Capital budgets and any updates.
3. Quarterly results for the company and its operating divisions or business segments.
4. Minutes of meetings of audit committee and other committees of the board.
5. The information on recruitment and remuneration of senior officers just below the board level, including appointment or removal of Chief Financial Officer and the Company Secretary.
6. Fatal or serious accidents, dangerous occurrences, any material effluent or pollution problems.
7. Any material default in financial obligations to and by the company, or substantial non-payment for goods sold by the company.
8. Any issue, which involves possible public or product liability claims of substantial nature, including any judgement or order which, may have passed strictures on the conduct of the company or taken an adverse view regarding another enterprise that can have negative implications on the company.
9. Details of any joint venture or collaboration agreement.
10. Transactions that involve substantial payment towards goodwill, brand equity, or intellectual property.
11. Significant labour problems and their proposed solutions. Any significant development in Human Resources/Industrial Relations front like signing of wage agreement, implementation of Voluntary Retirement Scheme, etc.
12. Sale of material nature, of investments, subsidiaries, assets, which is not in normal course of business.
13. Quarterly details of foreign exchange exposures and the steps taken by management to limit the risks of adverse exchange rate movement, if material.
14. Non-compliance of any regulatory, statutory nature or listing requirements and shareholders service such as non-payment of dividend, delay in share transfer, etc.

Infosys was the first company that decided to use postal ballots for voting on resolutions at the AGM. This practice has now been accepted by most companies and the shareholders are now able to vote on proposed resolutions through this method without attending the meetings.

Infosys made use of the Department of Company Affairs (DCA) recent rules for the postal ballot, which requires that certain items of the business needing shareholders consent necessarily need to be voted on through a postal ballot. Besides this Section 192 A of the Companies Act allows the companies to present other items of business not covered in the rules to be voted on through a postal ballot.

To attract top quality professionals to join the boards of companies as independent directors the DCA is planning to substantially raise the ceiling on the sitting fees of the directors. There are reports that these fees may be raised to ₹ 20 to 25,000 per meeting. The prevailing ceiling is ₹ 5,000 per meeting.

Various industry groups have sent representations to the government for relaxation of the remuneration ceiling, citing difficulty in attracting top professionals to join the boards of companies as independent directors.

The responsibilities of non-executives directors have increased manifold in recent years but their compensation has not kept pace with this. The government has now raised the maximum sitting fees of these directors to ₹ 20, 000. Many companies like Reliance, HLL, Tata Motors, HDFC, ICICI Bank and L&T have increased the sitting fees of their directors to this level. Many more companies are likely to follow in the months to come. This is a good development. The companies will now be in a position to attract the required talent on their boards.

The DCA is also considering a proposal that will allow ex-employees of the company to join the boards of the companies as independent directors after a three years cooling period. Appropriate changes are likely to be incorporated in the Companies' Amendment Bill, 2003.

◈ Clause 49 of the Listing Agreement

There has been a lot of discussion these days about this clause, which has been amended recently by SEBI. Let us now understand what this clause means.

Clause 49 lays down tighter qualification criterion for independent directors to be appointed to the Board of the companies. It disqualifies material suppliers and customers, a shareholder with more than 2 per cent stake in the company, a former executive of the company who left the company less than three years earlier from being appointed as independent director. Partners of current legal, audit and consulting firms as well as partners of such firms that had worked in the company in the preceding three years are also not eligible to be appointed as independent directors. A relative of a promoter, or an executive director or a senior executive one level below an executive director, too cannot be an independent director.

The minimum gap between two board meetings has been reduced form four to three months. The original clause 49 had given freedom to the board to decide whether a materially significant relationship between a director and the company affected his independence, the new clause has taken away this discretionary power from the board.

The new clause also makes it mandatory for the audit committee a minimum of four times in a year with a maximum gap of four months. It also states that all members of this committee have to be financially literate and at least one should have financial or accounting management expertise. It has defined the terms 'financial literacy' and 'accounting and related financial management expertise'. It has also strengthened and widened the role of and responsibility of the audit committee.

The clause recognizes nominee directors of financial institutions as independent directors.

This clause requires the board to lay down a code of conduct for all board members and the senior management of the company that they have to compulsorily follow.

The CEO and the CFO will have to certify the financial statements and the cash flow statements of the company.

At least one independent director of the holding company will be member of the board of a material non-listed subsidiary.

The audit committee of the listed company shall review the financial statements of the unlisted subsidiary, in particular its investments.

If while preparing financial statements, the company follows a treatment that is different from that prescribed in the accounting standards, it must disclose this in the financial statements and the management should also provide an explanation for doing so in the corporate governance report of the annual report.

The company will have to lay down procedures for informing the board members about the risk management and minimization procedures.

Where money is raised through public issues, right issues, etc., the company will have to disclose the uses/applications of the funds according to major categories (Capital expenditure, working capital, marketing costs, etc.), as a part of quarterly disclosure of financial statements. Further on an annual basis, the company will prepare a statement of funds utilized for the purpose other than those specified in the offer documents/prospectus and place it before the audit committee.

The company will have to publish its criterion for making its payments to non-executive directors in its annual report.

It has been reported that many Indian companies are on the look out for good quality persons for appointing them as independent directors on their boards. Some companies have already moved forward in this direction.

One company that has moved rapidly in this is Godrej. The board meetings of Godrej Consumer Products last at least for half a day. The company also arranges a two days offsite strategic board meeting once a year. Mr. Adi Godrej Chairman of the group is quite clear about what he expects from his board and more specifically independent directors. He says, "Independent Directors" are supposed to provide tremendous value to the company's performance. We pay them well and expect them to spend quality time with the company.

Infosys is of course the leading company to take tremendous initiatives in this field. It pays the highest sitting fees to its directors. According to a report in *Economic Times* of 13.5.05 the fees paid is around $ 45,000 per annum. Infosys also has a peer review system in place, wherein the directors are required to rate each other on seven parameters. Every year the directors are also asked to list their contribution to the board and areas where they think they could have done better.

With the application of clause 49 imminent the back of the envelope calculations suggest that there is a requirement of around 2,500 independent directors for just the top 500 companies listed on the stock exchanges.

Many new clauses may get added to this if and when the long awaited and pending bill to amend the Companies' Act is passed by the Parliament.

◆ Ambani vs. Ambani

One of the most interesting cases in corporate governance that is news practically daily since the end of the 2004 is the case of Reliance Industries. The Ambani brothers have been fighting it out in the full public glare the ownership issues in the flagship company and the status of Reliance Infocom. The late Dhirubhai Ambani it transpires has not left a will. The ownership of shares in Reliance Industries is shroud in mystery as a lot of stock has been controlled by a slew of investment companies, apart from the promoters holding that is of public knowledge. It seems that the voting rights of these shares are conferred on the Chairman of Reliance Industries. Having appointed Mr. Mukesh Ambani as Chairman of the company after the death of Dhirubhai, he has total control on the flagship company, a fact that is resented by Mr. Anil Ambani. The company controls controlling stake in many other group companies including Reliance Energy and Reliance Capital, which are under the management control of Mr. Anil Ambani. The parent company has also got a hugh stake in Reliance Infocom, wherein Mr. Mukesh Ambani has been shown as the promoter, though a lot of the investment has actually come from Reliance Industries.

Mr. Mukesh Ambani has been allocated 12 per cent equity in Reliance Infocom as Sweat Equity for a sum of ₹ 50 crore and a large number of shares were allotted to two companies at face value on preferential basis. These two companies have since surrendered these shares following the uproar caused after that disclosure. It has been argued that Reliance Industries were allotted shares in Infocom at a premium while the others got them at the face value, thus defrauding the shareholders on Reliance Industries.

It can thus be seen that India's largest private sector group with a combined turnover of over ₹ 1,00,000 crore is in turmoil not because the stakeholders or regulators have asked for strict disclosures but because of the infighting between the two brothers. If any proof is required that family run businesses that are supposed to be professional do have a soft under belly and family feuds like this one can cause enormous harm not only to the shareholders but also to the economy at large.

It must however be mentioned that in spite of this public feud the performance of the most of the group companies does not seem to have been affected so far. At least in the operations part the professional managers and the brothers have behaved in responsible manner. However this had an impact on the share prices of the group companies as the prices of the companies' shares have probably not been reflecting their fair value, especially in a bull market.

There have been efforts to resolve the ownership issue by dividing the companies and each brother getting management control over some of the companies and buying the other out from the companies under his control. The valuation and compromise deal is to be worked out by Mr. Kamat, Chairman of ICICI Bank, who is also close to the family. However the final settlement seems to be still elusive.

Recently Mr. Anil Ambani refused to sign the final balance sheet of Reliance Industries. He has accused the board and the management of the company of the violation of corporate governance practices. On the other had Reliance Industries has accused Reliance Energy of not having shared some vital information with them, as they are the largest shareholders of that company.

It must be noted that Reliance is not the only company where the holding of promoters is a matter of concern. It is quite possible that this is the problem with many other private sector companies. It is high time that the regulators got their act together and forced the managements to revel their shareholding through investment companies. One of the most important things that need to be probed is the source of funds for these companies and the identity of the shareholders of these companies.

Mr. Anil Ambani has written many letters to the market regulator SEBI pointing out omissions on the part of Reliance Industries in respect to corporate governance guidelines. He has also accused the board of ignoring the interests of the shareholders. The regulator has announced that it is looking at all matters related to the Reliance.

In the recent past we have witnessed problems in Bajaj family over ownership, but that seems to be on its way to amicable settlement among the family members after a lot of acrimony played publicly, though not in the same manner of Reliance.

The Birla family is embroiled in the controversy of the Will left by Priyamwada Birla that gives all her rights to Mr. Lodha. This will has been challenged by Birla family in the High court. The final decision in this matter is awaited.

It has been argued in some quarters that the funds in these companies are actually brought in by the promoters themselves, by first siphoning the funds off from the parent companies. It is argued that pre-liberalisation this was the most preferred way adopted by various owners and some of the funds may have also come in through the Havala way.

All this suggests that Indian corporate has still a long way to go before best practices of Corporate Governance become apparent. It is also true that SEBI does not seem to be pro-active in this matter to the extent it needs to be. There has been talk suggesting that the Company's Act may be completely overhauled to take into account the developments that have come to the fore post liberalisation and due to the need for integrating Indian practices with the best practices of the world.

The need of the hour is that the government and SEBI need to act together and create an environment to foster the spirit of Corporate Governance.

◆ Satyam Horror

Satyam was an admired company. It all changed the day Satyam board decided to acquire Raju family owned Maytas. The independent directors and they were all respected people; a professor from Harvard, A retired Chief Secretary to government of India and others did not raise any objection to the move and meekly voted with the promoters. The resistance really came from the institutional investors who smelled a rat. The question was why should the then fourth largest Indian IT company spend its money to acquire a company in infrastructure? Raju sensing the mood backtracked quickly. However, the bomb that he exploded immediately by confessing that he had doctored the balance sheet of the company for the past seven years and all the cash shown on the books was actually not there caused a huge furore. Imagine this coming from a company that was honoured with Golden Peacock award for excellent corporate governance twice over!

The regulators were red faced. The auditors PricewaterhouseCoopers who had done something similar in Global Trust Bank were once again found awfully wanting. Questions were raised regarding the nexus between the auditors and management. Auditors' explanation that they had gone by what the company told them did not wash at all.

The government for once did a lot of sensible things. It appointed a board of impeccable people like Deepak Parekh, Tarun Das and Kiran Karnik to look after the company to assess the situation and then take steps to clean up the act and finally sell-off the company through an open auction. Fortunately it itself did not get involved in the company at any stage.

Soon it was established that the company had forged bank FD receipts and shown them to the auditors who accepted them without any verification for years. It was also found that the company's workforce was much lesser by as much as 10,000 people than what was claimed by the company and the salaries of this fake staff were siphoned off systematically.

Eventually the company that was facing litigation in US and black listing by World Bank was rescued. The employees were not responsible for all this and many jobs were saved. The company did undertake herculean efforts to retain most of its clients.

The company has since been acquired by Tech Mahindra. One thing that was in favour of the company was that it was doing good work and many of its clients after initial shock and disbelief decided to stay on with the company.

One really hopes that this is a one off case and we would not have face this kind of ignonimity again. The regulators will have to be more alert and the shareholders will have to subject companies to greater and detailed scrutiny.

13 MERGERS AND TAKEOVERS

In the liberalised economy of our country mergers and takeovers are destined to play a very important role in the coming years. If one looks at the developed economies around the world it will be clear that these countries allow these activities freely.

In India this phenomenon is still new and hence there is need for good regulation to oversee this.

SEBI therefore, had appointed a committee under the Chairmanship of the Retired Chief Justice of the Supreme Court of India, Justice P. N. Bhagwati, to devise a code for mergers and the hostile takeovers. The guidelines issued for this activity are from the recommendations made by this committee. Recently SEBI has taken overview of these recommendations and has incorporated certain changes based on the experience so far.

The takeover of Saurashtra cement by Autorider in March 1998, involving an open offer of ₹ 18 crore, was the first hostile takeover under the new takeover code. This was followed by the takeover of Rassi Cement by India Cement for ₹ 100 crore. The other prominent instances where the takeover of BSES by Reliance, Indal by Hindalco.

Many other managements' were caught unawares by raiders who tried to raid their companies. Bombay Dyeing and Ballarpur Industries Ltd., were sought to be raided by Arun Bajoria. The shares of East India Hotels were picked up by archrivals ITC Hotels.

In the eighties Lord Swaraj Paul mounted a takeover bid on two companies, *viz.*, DCM and Escorts. This bid turned out to be very messy and the incumbent managements were fully supported by the government of the day and the raider had to suffer huge losses. The managements of DCM and Escorts controlled only 7 and 15 per cent of equity and thus were really minority shareholders.

For promoters who have meagre holdings in their company's hostile acquisition by others is a real threat. Many managements have moved quickly to increase their holdings in their companies either through creeping acquisition or through buyback offers. Under the creeping acquisition managements can acquire 5 per cent equity in each financial year, without the requirement of open offer. Mr. Ratan Tata the Chairman of Tata Group has used this route to consolidate the holdings in the group companies.

Promoters are obviously not very pleased with the new regulations as they feel that the companies that they have built for generations can be acquired by others. On the other hand there is a feeling that the promoters of successful companies have not cared for their shareholders, and have been only interested in making money for themselves.

At a time when most corporates are worried about hostile takeovers and mergers, retail investors have gained about ₹ 5,000 crore from the new takeover code.

The financial institutions have a very crucial role to play in takeovers. Many of these institutions control large stakes in many companies. The raiders on such companies can only succeed in getting management control of these companies, if the institutions sell their shares to the raiders. The institutions should be mainly guided by the price offered for their holdings. Recently UTI refused to sell its holdings in ITC to BAT even though BAT was willing to pay a hefty premium to the market price. This at a time when UTI's finances are in bad shape and the government has to support it for redemption of assured return schemes. The decision making of institutions in such cases is subject to political interference and therefore not based on sound financial and economic logic. On the other hand in the Grasim's bid on L&T the institutions were insisting that Grasim must buy them out entirely.

◈ Procedure of Mergers and Takeovers

Substantial acquisition refers to a company buying stakes in another company with the intention of acquiring the management control of the said target company.

When an "acquirer" takes over the control of the "target company", it is termed as takeover. When an acquirer acquires "substantial quantity of shares or voting rights" of the target company, it results into substantial acquisition of shares. The term "Substantial" which is used in this context has been clarified subsequently.

◈ Target Company

A target company is a listed company, *i.e.*, whose shares are listed on any stock exchange and whose shares or voting rights are acquired/being acquired or whose control is taken over/ being taken over by an acquirer.

◈ Acquirer

An acquirer means (includes persons acting in concert (PAC) with him) any individual/ company/any other legal entity which intends to acquire or acquires substantial quantity of shares or voting rights of target company or acquires or agrees to acquire control over the target company.

◈ Persons Acting in Concert (PACs)

PACs are individual(s)/company(ies)/any other legal entity(ies) who are acting together for a common objective or for a purpose of substantial acquisition of shares or voting rights or gaining control over the target company pursuant to an agreement or understanding whether formal or informal. Acting in concert would imply cooperation, coordination for acquisition of voting rights or control. This cooperation/coordinated approach may either be direct or indirect.

The concept of PAC assumes significance in the context of substantial acquisition of shares since it is possible for an acquirer to acquire shares or voting rights in a company "in concert" with any other person in such a manner that the acquisition made by them may remain individually below the threshold limit but may collectively exceed the threshold limit.

Unless the contrary is established certain entities are deemed to be persons acting in concert like companies with its holding company or subsidiary company, mutual funds with its sponsor/trustee/asset management company, etc.

This is something that a target company has to look out for in the case of a hostile acquisition bid being launched against it.

◈ Substantial Voting Rights

The SEBI (Substantial Acquisition of Shares and Takeovers) Regulations, 1997 has defined substantial quantity of shares or voting rights distinctly for two different purposes:

I. Threshold of disclosure to be made by acquirer(s):

1. 5 per cent and more shares or voting rights: A person who, along with PAC, if any, (collectively referred to as "Acquirer" hereinafter) acquires shares or voting rights (which when taken together with his existing holding) would entitle him to more than 5 per cent or 10 per cent or 14 per cent shares or voting rights of target company, is required to disclose at every stage the aggregate of his shareholding to the target company and the stock exchanges within two days of acquisition or receipt of intimation of allotment of shares.
2. Any person who holds more than 15 per cent but less than 55 per cent shares or voting rights of target company, and who purchases or sells shares aggregating to 2 per cent or more shall within 2 days disclose such purchase/sale along with the aggregate of his shareholding to the target company and the stock exchanges.
3. Any person who holds more than 15 per cent shares or voting rights of target company and a promoter and person having control over the target company, shall within 21 days from the financial year ending March 31 as well as the record date fixed for the purpose of dividend declaration, disclose every year his aggregate shareholding to the target company.
4. The target company, in turn, is required to inform all the stock exchanges where the shares of target company are listed, every year within 30 days from the financial year ending March 31 as well as the record date fixed for the purpose of dividend declaration.

(II) Trigger point for making an open offer by an acquirer

1. 15 per cent shares or voting rights:

An acquirer who intends to acquire shares which along with his existing shareholding would entitle him to exercise 15 per cent or more voting rights, can acquire such additional shares only after making a public announcement (PA) to acquire at least additional 20 per cent of the voting capital of target company from the shareholders through an open offer.

2. Creeping acquisition limit:

An acquirer who holds 15 per cent or more but less than 55 per cent of shares or voting rights of a target company, can acquire such additional shares as would entitle him to exercise more than 5 per cent of the voting rights in any financial year ending March 31 only after making a public announcement to acquire at least additional 20 per cent shares of target company from the shareholders through an open offer. This is for the existing promoters who wish to increase their own holdings in the company to make sure that a hostile bid is not made on their company or in case such a bid is made then the promoters can successfully defeat the same.

3. Consolidation of holding:

An acquirer who holds 55 per cent or more but less than 75 per cent shares or voting rights of a target company, can acquire further shares or voting rights only after making a public announcement to acquire at least additional 20 per cent shares of target company from the shareholders through an open offer. As per the new SEBI regulation a listed company has to have at least 25 per cent non-promoter holding to be eligible for being listed.

◆ What is Control?

Control includes the right to appoint directly or indirectly or by virtue of agreements or in any other manner majority of directors on the Board of the target company or to control management or policy decisions affecting the target company. However, in case there are two or more persons in control over the target company the cesser of any one of such persons from such control shall not be deemed to be a change in control of management nor shall any change in the nature and quantum of control amongst them constitute change in control of management provided this transfer is done in terms of Reg. 3(1)(e). Also if consequent upon change in control of the target company in accordance with Regulation 3, the control acquired is equal to or less than the control exercised by person(s) prior to such acquisition of control, such control shall not be deemed to be a change in control.

◆ Public Announcement (PA)

A public announcement is an announcement made in the newspapers by the acquirer primarily disclosing his intention to acquire shares of the target company from existing shareholders by means of an open offer. This is required to have transparency in the process.

◆ Disclosures Required to be Made Under Public Announcement

The disclosures in the announcement include the offer price, number of shares to be acquired from the public, identity of acquirer, purpose of acquisition, future plans of acquirer, if any, regarding the target company, change in control over the target company, if any, the procedure to be followed by acquirer in accepting the shares tendered by the shareholders and the period within which all the formalities pertaining to the offer would be completed.

◆ Objective of Public Announcement

The public announcement is made to ensure that the shareholders of the target company are aware of an exit opportunity available to them. It has been observed that many retail investors do not read these and miss the opportunity of getting out of a company.

◆ Minimum Open Offer

No, the acquirer cannot make an offer for less than 20 per cent of shares. The acquirer has to make an offer for a minimum of 20 per cent (less only in specified cases).

The acquirer is required to appoint a merchant banker (MB) registered with SEBI before making a PA . PA is required to be made through the said MB. The acquirer is required to make the PA within four working days of the entering into an agreement to acquire shares or deciding to acquire shares/voting rights of target company or after any such change or changes as would result in change in control over the target company.

In case of indirect acquisition or change in control, the PA shall be made by the acquirer within three months of consummation of such acquisition or change in control or restructuring of the parent or the company holding shares of or control over the target company in India. The offer price in such cases shall be determined with reference to the date of the public announcement for the parent company and the date of the public announcement for acquisition of shares of the target company, whichever is higher, in accordance with the parameters mentioned in the Takeover Regulations.

It is mandatory for an acquirer to appoint a Merchant Banker for this purpose.

◈ Documents that Need to be Filed with SEBI Regarding the Public Announcement:

A hard and soft copy of the PA are required to be submitted to SEBI simultaneously with the publication of the same in the newspapers.

A draft letter of offer is required to be filed with SEBI within 14 days from the date of Public Announcement along with a filing fee of ₹ 50,000 per letter of offer (payable by banker's cheque/demand draft). A due diligence certificate as well as registration details as per SEBI Circular no. RMB (G-1) series dated June 26, 1997 are also required to be filed along with the draft letter of offer.

Filing of draft letter of offer with SEBI should not in any way be deemed or construed that the same has been cleared, vetted or approved by SEBI. The letter of offer is submitted to SEBI for a limited purpose of overseeing whether the disclosures contained therein are generally adequate and are in conformity with the Takeover Regulations. This requirement is to facilitate the shareholders to take an informed decision with regard to the offer. SEBI does not take any responsibility either for the truthfulness or correctness of for any statement, for financial soundness of acquirer, or of persons acting in concert, or of target company, whose shares are proposed to be acquired or for the correctness of the statements made or opinions expressed in the letter of offer. It should be understood that while acquirer is primarily responsible for the correctness, adequacy and disclosure of all relevant information in this letter of offer, the manager to the offer (a merchant banker) is expected to exercise due diligence to ensure that the acquirer duly discharges its responsibility adequately.

◈ Letter of Offer

A letter of offer is a document addressed to the shareholders of the target company containing disclosures of the acquirer/PACs, target company, their financials, justification of the offer price, the offer price, number of shares to be acquired from the public, purpose of acquisition, future plans of acquirer, if any, regarding the target company, change in control over the target company, if any, the procedure to be followed by acquirer in accepting the shares tendered by the shareholders and the period within which all the formalities pertaining to the offer would be completed.

The MB will incorporate in the letter of offer the comments made by SEBI and then send within 45 days from the date of PA the letter of offer along with the blank acceptance form to all the shareholders whose names appear in the register of the company on the Specified Date. The offer remains open for 20 days. The shareholders are required to send their share certificate(s)/related documents to registrar or merchant banker as specified in PA and letter of offer. The acquirer is required to pay consideration to all those shareholders whose shares are accepted under the offer, within 15 days from the closure of offer.

In their own interest, the shareholders are advised to send such documents under registered post. Further, the shareholders may also note that under no circumstances such documents should be sent to the acquirer.

◈ Determination of Price Under Open Offer

SEBI does not approve the offer price. The acquirer/merchant banker is required to ensure that all the relevant parameters are taken in to consideration while determining the offer price and that justification for the same is disclosed in the letter of offer.

The relevant parameters are:

(*a*) negotiated price under the agreement which triggered the open offer.

(*b*) price paid by the acquirer or persons acting in concert with him for acquisition, if any, including by way of allotment in a public or rights or preferential issue during the twenty-six weeks period prior to the date of public announcement, whichever is higher;

(*c*) the average of the weekly high and low of the closing prices of the shares of the target company as quoted on the stock exchange where the shares of the company are most frequently traded during the twenty-six weeks or the average of the daily high and low prices of the shares as quoted on the stock exchange where the shares of the company are most frequently traded during the two weeks preceding the date of public announcement, whichever is higher.

In case the shares of Target Company are not frequently traded then instead of point (c) above, parameters based on the fundamentals of the company such as return on net worth of the company, book value per share, EPS, etc., are required to be considered and disclosed.

In case of non-complete agreement for payment to any person other than the target company, if the payment is more than 25 per cent of the offer price arrived in terms of the regulations, the same has to be factored into the offer price.

The shares of the target company will be deemed to be infrequently traded if the annualized trading turnover in that share during the preceding six calendar months prior to the month in which the PA is made is less than 5 per cent (by number of shares) of the listed shares. If the said turnover is 5 per cent or more, it will be deemed to be frequently traded.

Any shareholder who holds the shares on or before the date of closure of the offer is eligible to participate in the offer.

◈ What is a Competitive Bid?

Competitive bid is an offer made by a person, other than the acquirer who has made the first public announcement. Since the competitive bid is at a higher price switching of acceptances between different offers is possible. The shareholder has the option to withdraw acceptance tendered by him up to three working days prior to the date of closure of the offer. This enables investors to get a better price for their shares in case of competitive bidding happening between two potential acquirers.

To enable the shareholders to be in a better position to decide as to which of the subsisting offers is better and also not to cause last minute decisions/confusions, the offer price and size are effectively frozen for the last seven working days prior to the closing date of the offers. Shareholders may wait till the commencement of that period to be aware of upward revisions in the offer price and size of the offers, if any.

The offer once made cannot be withdrawn except in the following circumstances:

- Statutory approval(s) required have been refused;
- The sole acquirer being a natural person has died;
- Such circumstances as in the opinion of the Board merits withdrawal.

The public announcement contains procedure for such cases, *i.e.*, where the shareholders do not receive the letter of offer or do not receive the letter of offer in time. The shareholders are usually advised to send their consent to Registrar to Offer, if any or to MB on plain paper stating the name, address, number of shares held, Distinctive Folio No., number of shares offered and bank details along with the documents mentioned in the public announcement, before closure of the offer. The public announcement and the letter of offer along with the form of acceptance is available on the SEBI website at www.sebi.gov.in.

Acquirers are required to complete the payment of consideration to shareholders who have accepted the offer within 15 days from the date of closure of the offer. In case the delay in payment is on account of non-receipt of statutory approvals and if the same is not due to wilful default or neglect on part of the acquirer, the acquirers would be liable to pay interest to the shareholders for the delayed period in accordance with regulations.

If the delay in payment of consideration is not due to the above reasons, it would be treated as a violation of the regulations and therefore, also liable for other action in terms of the regulations.

(Please refer to the case of Sterlite's acquisition bid on Indal)

If the shares received by the acquirer are more than the shares agreed to be acquired by him, the acceptance would be on proportionate basis.

◈ Safeguards for Investors

Before making the public announcement, the acquirer has to open an escrow account in the form of cash deposited with a scheduled commercial bank or bank guarantee in favour of the merchant banker or deposit of acceptable securities with appropriate margin with the merchant banker. The merchant banker is also required to confirm that firm financial arrangements are in place for fulfilling the offer obligations. In case, the acquirer fails to make the payment, MB has a right to forfeit the escrow account and distribute the proceeds in the following way.

(*a*) 1/3 of amount to target company

(*b*) 1/3 to regional SEs, for credit to investor protection fund, etc.

(*c*) 1/3 to be distributed on *pro rata* basis among the shareholders who have accepted the offer.

The merchant banker is required to ensure that the rejected documents which are kept in the custody of the registrar/merchant banker are sent back to the shareholder through registered post.

Besides forfeiture of escrow account, SEBI can initiate separate action against the acquirer which may include prosecution/barring the acquirer from entering the capital market for a specified period, etc.

◆ Exemptions

Certain type of acquisitions as stipulated under Regulation 3 of Chapter I of the regulations, are specifically exempted from the open offer process subject to the acquirer complying with the requirements/conditions, as may be applicable, for such acquisitions. Such exemptions include acquisitions arising out of firm allotment in public issues, rights issues, *inter-se* transfer amongst group companies, relatives, promoters, acquirer and PACs, Indian promoters and foreign collaborators and transfer of shares from state level financial institutions to co-promoters of company pursuant to the agreement, etc.

◆ Mandatory Reporting to SEBI

Reporting is mandatory under Regulation 3(4) in respect of acquisitions arising out of firm allotment in public issues, rights issues, *inter-se* transfer amongst group companies, relatives, promoters, acquirer and PACs, Indian promoters and foreign collaborators and transfer of shares from state level financial institutions to co-promoters of company pursuant to the agreement.

The report is required to be submitted to SEBI within 21 days from the date of acquisition/ allotment along with a fee of ₹ 10,000 per report.

For transactions, which entail reporting requirements, details of the proposed acquisition need to be filed with SEs where shares of target company are listed, at least four working days before the date of actual acquisition/ allotment.

A person who, along with PAC, if any, (collectively referred to as " Acquirer" hereinafter) acquires shares or voting rights (which when taken together with his existing holding) would entitle him to more than 5 per cent or 10 per cent or 14 per cent shares or voting rights of target company, is required to disclose at every stage the aggregate of his shareholding to the target company and the stock exchanges within two days of acquisition or receipt of intimation of allotment of shares.

Any person who holds more than 15 per cent but less than 55 per cent shares or voting rights of target company, and who purchases or sells shares aggregating to 2 per cent or more shall within two days disclose such purchase/sale along with the aggregate of his shareholding to the target company and the stock exchanges.

Further, annual disclosures have to be given regarding holding of promoters, persons in control and persons holding more than 15 per cent shares or voting rights of the target company. Further, a copy of the public announcement to acquire shares from public is to be given to the stock exchanges simultaneously with the publication in the newspapers. Subsequently, upward revisions in offer, withdrawal of offer has also to be intimated to the stock exchanges simultaneously.

◆ Violations of Procedure

The regulations have laid down the general obligations of acquirer, target company and the merchant banker. For failure to carry-out these obligations as well as for failure/non-compliance of other provisions of the regulations, the regulations have laid down the penalties for non-compliance. These penalties include:

(*a*) forfeiture of the escrow account,

(*b*) directing the person concerned to sell the shares acquired in violation of the regulations,

(*c*) directing the person concerned not to further deal in securities,

(*d*) levy monetary penalties,

(e) initiate prosecution proceedings.

(f) directing appointment of a merchant banker for the purpose of causing disinvestment of shares acquired in breach of Regulations 10, 11 or 12.

(g) directing transfer of any proceeds or securities to the Investors Protection Fund of are cognised stock exchange;

(h) directing the target company or depository to cancel the shares where an acquisition of shares pursuant to an allotment is in breach of Regulations 10,11 or 12;

(i) directing the target company or the depository not to give effect to transfer or further freeze the transfer of any such shares and not to permit the acquirer or any nominee or any proxy of the acquirer to exercise any voting or other rights attached to such shares acquired in violation of Regulations 10, 11 or 12;

(j) debarring any person concerned from accessing the capital market or dealing in securities for such period as may be determined by the Board;

(k) directing the person concerned to make public offer to the shareholders of the target company to acquire such number of shares at such offer price as determined by the Board;

(l) directing disinvestment of such shares as are in excess of the percentage of the shareholding or voting rights specified for disclosure requirement under the Regulations 6,7 or 8;

(m) directing the person concerned not to dispose of assets of the target company contrary to the undertaking given in the letter of offer;

(n) directing the person concerned, who has failed to make a public offer or delayed the making of a public offer in terms of these regulations, to the shareholders, whose shares have been accepted in the public offer made after the delay, the consideration amount along with interest at the rate not less than the applicable rate of interest payable by banks on fixed deposits.

Further, the Board of Directors of the target company would also be liable for action in terms of the regulations and the SEBI Act for failure to carry-out their obligations specified in the regulations.

Action can also be initiated for suspension, cancellation of certificate of registration against an intermediary such as the merchant banker to the offer.

Only takeovers and substantial acquisition of shares of a listed company fall within purview of SEBI (Substantial Acquisition of Shares and Takeovers) Regulations, 1997. Mergers and amalgamations are outside the purview of SEBI as they are a subject matter of the Companies Act, 1956.

◈ Takeover Panel of SEBI

An acquirer who proposes to acquire shares through a mode which is not specifically covered under Regulation 3 may seek exemption from the applicability of the provisions of the offer process by making an application. SEBI has constituted a panel consisting of independent persons to examine such applications which is called the Takeover Panel.

◈ Provisions for Disinvestment in PSUs by the Government

To facilitate acquisition of shares or voting rights or control by strategic partner from the Central Government in a listed PSU and to harmonise the process of disinvestment and investor protection.

The said amendments include the following:

Transfer of shares and control to the strategic partner/acquirer even before completing the open offer formalities in terms of the regulations;

The date of entering into the share purchase agreement would be the reference date for making the public announcement.

The date on which the Central Government opens the financial bids would be the reference date for classifying the shares of the company as frequently or infrequently traded and for determination of the offer price. Non-applicability of requirement of second offer for subsequent stage of acquisition subject to certain conditions prohibiting from making a competitive bid. It may be noted that these amendments were made only for the purpose of PSU disinvestment and are not available to other acquisitions.

SEBI has made substantial amendments to the takeover code in 2011 and they have come into effect. Following are the changes made by SEBI.

SEBI has notified the new takeover code and informed that the same would become effective from the 22nd of October 2011.

There are three major changes in the takeover code which are different from the earlier takeover code. These changes are as follows:

1. **The point at which the open offer is triggered has been changed from the earlier 15 per cent to 26 per cent.**
2. **The size of the open offer has been increased from 20 per cent to 25 per cent.**
3. **Non-compete fees which were paid earlier to promoters is now not permitted.**

The offer price shall be the highest of the four prices. The four prices would be the negotiated price, volume weighted average price over the last 52 weeks prior to the public announcement, the highest price payable or paid in the last 26 weeks before the public announcement, or the volume weighted average price of 60 trading days prior to the public announcement.

The takeover code also specifies that companies cannot breach the maximum promoter shareholding limit of 75 per cent. In case it happens, the acquirer has to shed the portion that is above 75 per cent. If one were to take the theoretical example of a company where the promoter holds 51 per cent and sells 25 per cent to another person. The combined holding of the new promoter and the erstwhile promoter would be 51 per cent with an open offer of 26 per cent, which if fully subscribed would make the promoter holding 77 per cent. The excess holding of 2 per cent would have to be divested by the new promoter.

SEBI has also disallowed automatic delisting and acquirers whose stake exceeds 75 per cent are ineligible to voluntarily delist before 12 months of completion of the open offer.

The takeover code has also defined indirect acquisition or control. This is defined as the ability to exercise or direct the exercise of voting rights which would otherwise attract the obligation of making a public announcement of an open offer. The threshold point for this control or ability is 80 per cent of assets or net sales or market capitalization of the target company, it would be deemed to be a direct acquisition.

SEBI has also clarified that any open offer for which a public announcement has already been made would be governed by the old regulations and would be completed under the earlier norms.

There are some experts who believe that hostile takeovers will now become difficult now with the new code in place. They say that since the trigger has been raised to 25 per cent acquirers will find it difficult to quickly gain management control and existing managements will have a better chance to defend their companies. Initially SEBI wanted the open offer to be made for all the balance shares. This was vehemently opposed by the industry as impractical. They argued that they will have to have a large amount to acquire all shares if tendered in an open offer. It has to be noted in this context that RBI does not favour banks funding acquisitions of this kind. Thus the funds required for acquisition have to be sourced from outside the banking industry. Subsequently SEBI relented and gave up this.

◈ Case Studies in Hostile Takeovers

Let us now briefly take a look at some of the takeover attempts:

Bombay Dyeing Ltd. This company was attractive for a takeover bid for various reasons. It was a cash rich company sitting over liquid cash worth ₹ 450 crore, and its market price was below the book value.

Bajoria is a very shrewd businessman who made his fortune in jute industry in Kolkata. Bombay Dyeing was his big corporate raid. One day he claimed that he had acquired 14 per cent equity in the company. This announcement sent shock waves through the corporate world. Thus began the war between Bajoria and Wadia. Bajoria had picked up equity from the price levels of ₹ 40 and stopped once the price reached ₹ 115 per share. It is estimated that he spent nearly ₹ 50 crore for this.

Bombay Dyeing complained that Bajoria had violated the takeover code by not informing the company and the stock market upon acquiring 5 per cent equity as required by the regulations. The legal battle was now joined in earnest. However, during this battle Bajoria liquidated 8.5 per cent of his holding in the company. On the other hand Wadia announced the share buyback scheme to consolidate his holding in the company.

Two important points have emerged from Bajoria's raid — a small mistake in timely disclosing to the company when his stake crossed five per cent limit has cost him lot of embarrassment and avoidable litigation.

◈ Gesco Corporation Ltd.

A.H. Dalmia Group mounted a ₹ 35 crore raid to takeover Gesco Corporation Ltd., controlled by the Seth family. The Dalmia's acquired 10.4 per cent equity and made an open offer for another 45 per cent at the rate of ₹ 27 per share.

Gesco originally was the real estate division of Great Eastern Shipping Company Ltd. In April 1999 it was spun-off into an independent company It had made investments in real estate in Mumbai, Pune, New Delhi and Bangalore.The book value of Gesco was around ₹ 50 and the market value of company's assets was much higher than the book value. However, the share value was only about ₹ 10 resulting in market capitalisation of ₹ 30 crore. The equity capital of the company was ₹ 29 crore and the reserves were to the tune of ₹ 100 crore. The company was debt free. It had fixed assets worth ₹ 90 crore, liquid investments of about ₹ 38 crore and reserves and surplus of ₹ 24 crore. This made the company an attractive target with the promoter's holding just 12 per cent equity. The institutions were holding further 25 per cent equity.

The Dalmia's began negotiations with the institutions for buying the equity held by them. If the open offer had been fully subscribed then Dalmia would gain control over the company. The Seth's now had only two choices — one to make a counter offer, or the other was to sell their holdings to Dalmia.

The Seths appointed Kotak as their advisors for the counter offer. HDFC Chairman Mr. Deepak Parekh suggested to Mahindra's partnering Seths in the counter offer. The counter offer was made for ₹ 36 per share. HDFC extended a one-year credit line to Mahindra Realty and Infrastructure Developers Ltd.

This is the first instance in Indian corporate history that a white Knight had been used to stave off a possible hostile takeover. Seths in the mean time bought out the entire 6.34 per cent stake of IFC Washington @ ₹ 44 per share, in a negotiated deal. In view of this the counter offer price also now became ₹ 44 per share. Dalmia raise his offer to ₹ 45 per share after this. Seths raised their offer price to ₹ 54 per share as their counter offer. Finally Dalmia sold his holding of 10.4 per cent to Seths for ₹ 54 per share.

This is a classic case of takeover, where two companies fought out the battle in the open and in the most transparent manner. This also helped the small shareholders in getting a very good price for their holdings.

Many instances of hostile takeovers successful or unsuccessful can be seen in the recent past. Some of the cases are as follows:

1. Sterlite's unsuccessful bid on Indal.
2. Hindalco's successful takeover of Indal.
3. Abhishek Dalmia's unsuccessful raid on Gesco.
4. ICI's bid to buy equity of Asian Paints.
5. Grasim's takeover of L&T's cement division.

A few years back ITC which has interest in hotel industry started acquiring shares of EIH, Oberoi controlled hotel chain. ITC maintained that it was not interested in acquiring management control of the company and was only making an investment. Oberoi's naturally did not believe this line. The industry is hit by recession and the profitability of the industry is under pressure. ITC has adequate resources to launch a hostile takeover bid on EIH any time it so desires.

The nervous Oberoi family then approached Mukesh Ambani to play the role of "White Knight". Ambani agreed and acquired shares in the company through a preferential allotment. The combined Ambani-Oberoi holding will obviously make it very difficult for ITC to mount a deal to acquire management control. ITC had kept its holding below the 15 per cent threshold level. With the trigger being now shifted to 25 per cent, ITC if it wishes can raise its stake without inviting the provisions of open offer as long as they keep their holding below 25 per cent.

One of the biggest acquisitions that happened in India was when the promoters of Ranbaxy decided to sell their 35 per cent holding to Daichi-Sankyo of Japan in a all cash deal. However, this cannot be called a hostile takeover, since the promoters themselves wanted to sell their stake in their company. Daichi acquired the stake and then made an open offer for 20 per cent additional shares from the other investors in the company, as required by the regulation code. The price offered was same as that was paid to the promoters. Investors who offered their shares have made profits, considering the fact that since then the stock prices of Ranbaxy never reached those levels! It only shows that investors have to make the right call in such situations.

Jindal Steel also acquired a struggling and debt ridden Ispat. Again this was a sell initiated by the incumbent management that was unsuccessful in turning around the company in spite of repeated help extended by the banks to the company.

We also saw the acrimonious acquisitions in Airlines industry when Jet acquired Sahara and King Fisher acquired Air Deccan. Both have put the acquirers in difficult position. This is truer for King Fisher which is now struggling to survive. This is one acquisition that has gone horribly wrong. As has been observed that many times companies acquire other companies for something special that it offers. In this case Deccan was eligible to fly internationally, while KF would have to wait a few more years to have that privilege. So KF went and acquired a loss making company probably at a very high price. One thing is sure Capt. Gopinath got his money and also those investors who sold out have been happy as opposed to the shareholders of KF!

14 LEASE AND HIRE PURCHASE

The activities of leasing and hire purchase are being carried out in India by Non-banking Finance Companies. These companies are involved in many other activities as well. Housing finance, infrastructure finance, stock broking and financing companies are all part of NBFCs.

One area that has exploded in the past five years is companies that are providing financing against gold, Muthut Finance and Manhoot Finance. The tremendous increase in gold prices seems to have helped such companies. People are investing in gold and then taking loans against the security of this gold. One wonders where the borrowed money is used by these borrowers. It is quite possible that some of them are taking loan and investing this money back in gold itself. This can be a dangerous thing. Gold prices are ruling at historical highs. As and when the world economy improves these prices are likely to come down substantially.

Many foreign NBFCs have set up shop in India in past few years. This is inevitable on the back of the WTO agreement which requires India to gradually open up her financial markets.

◈ Lease Finance

An equipment lease can be defined as a contractual arrangement where the lessor of equipment transfers the right to use the equipment to the lessee for an agreed period of time in return for rental. At the end of the period the asset reverts back to the lessor, unless there is a provision for the renewal of the contract or there is a provision for transfer of ownership to the lessee.

At the end of each accounting period, the hire purchase price less the instalments received is shown as a receivable (stock on hire) and the finance income component of these instalments is shown as a current liability.

◈ Advantages of Lease

- Flexibility
- User oriented Variants
- Tax Benefits

- Less paperwork and Expeditious Disbursement.
- Convenience
- 100 per cent financing
- Better utilisation of own funds
- Off-balance sheet financing.

With the recent changes in the accounting standards lease is no more an off-balance sheet finance. The lessee is now expected to capitalise the leased assets in his book and claim depreciation on these assets as far as book profits are concerned. The lessee however is allowed to claim lease rentals as tax deductible expense as far as income tax Act is concerned. It is essential that the liability of the assets on lease be shown in the balance sheet for the knowledge of the lenders as well as the shareholders of the company.

By and large most lease agreements in India are financial leases. The lease agreement does not provide for a transfer of ownership to the lessee either at the end of the lease period or during the period of lease. The lease rentals are so structured as to recover the entire investment cost during the primary period. Typically the lease rentals are payable in equated monthly instalments at the beginning of every month. Leasing companies satisfying certain criterions are permitted to undertake leasing of imported equipment. But the existing regulatory framework imposes certain restrictions on undertaking cross-border lease transactions.

As per the existing provisions of income tax Act, the lease income is taxed in the hands of the lessor as business income, and the lessor claims the tax relevant depreciation on the equipment leased as a tax-deductible expense. The lessee is entitled to claim the lease rentals payable for each period over the lease period as a tax-deductible expense.

The excise duty on the assets on lease has been made modvatable; this means that the lessee can claim refund of the excise duty paid while acquiring the asset. This is of great benefit for the lessee.

There has been a great problem faced by the leasing industry, ever since service tax has been imposed on the interest portion of the lease rental. This has made leasing very expensive. This tax has been increased subsequently from 10 per cent to 12 per cent. Many leasing companies have obtained stay orders from High Courts against the levy of the service tax. The leasing companies argue that assets under lease are capital assets and they suffer the imposition of excise duty as well as sales tax, and hence the levy of service tax is unjustifiable. They also argue that no other lender has to bear this burden and this levy therefore is discriminatory in nature. The legal battle is still on and it will be quite some time before the courts will give their final judgment on this. Leasing companies say that they are willing to pay service tax on the lease management fee that they charge from their clients. However things have changed now. The service tax paid by companies is now refundable from their excise liability. Thus this charge has now become revenue neutral.

Some states also impose sales tax on lease transactions, following the 46th constitutional amendment.

In a financial lease, lessee is under obligation to pay lease rentals regardless of its financial condition. It therefore follows that knowledge of the future financial obligations under the finance lease contracts entered into by the lessee is absolutely essential for a proper assessment of the creditworthiness and the borrowing capacity of the lessee. The lessee is therefore required to disclose the financial commitments outstanding under the finance lease as a part of "Notes on Accounts" in the Annual Report.

◈ Sources of Funds for the Finance Companies

1. Equity and Preference Capital
2. Debentures
3. Term Loans from Financial Institutions and Banks
4. Public Deposits
5. Inter-corporate Deposits.
6. Commercial Paper
7. Securatisation of receivables.

A finance company is required to maintain liquid assets at 15 per cent on deposits. At least two-thirds of these liquid assets, *i.e.*, 10 per cent of the deposits must be maintained in the form of Central or State Government securities or Government guaranteed bonds. The balance can be held either in the form of accounts with commercial banks. This requirement is for leasing companies who are accepting public deposits. The eligibility for accepting public deposits is linked to the credit rating received by a company. This provision is essential for safeguarding the interest of the retail investors. This provision came into effect in the late 90s when a slew of finance companies went under and a lot of retail investors lost large amounts of money.

◈ Contents of Lease Agreement

Description Clause: provides the description of the lessor, the lessee, the equipment and the location.

Period Clause: specifies the period for which the equipment is leased.

Rental Clause: specifies the amount of rentals to be paid the periodicity and the mode of payment.

Exemption Clause: clearly states the lessee has selected the equipment based on his own judgement and has not relied on any statements or representations made by the lessor.

Ownership Clause: unequivocally states that no right, title or interest in the equipment shall pass to the lessee and the lessee shall, at no time contest or challenge the lessor's sole and exclusive right, title and interest in the equipment.

Repairs and Alteration Clause: specifies that the lessee at its own cost and expense will keep the equipment in good repair, condition and working order.

Insurance in favour of the lessor and lessor's lenders.

Surrender clause states that upon expiry of the lease term or earlier termination of the lease the lessee must deliver the equipment to the lessor in good working condition.

◈ Sale and Lease Back Transactions

A lessee and a lessor can enter into an agreement whereby a lessee sells the existing assets to the lessor and take these assets back from him on lease. This arrangement is known as sale and lease back transaction.

The purpose of these transactions used to be that the company which had invested its own funds in purchase of fixed assets in the past now may be facing liquidity crunch. The way to address this problem was to sell these assets to a leasing company and take it back on lease. This serves the dual purpose: (a) the company continues to use the fixed assets, and (b) the company also gets the liquidity that it is looking for.

However, what happened in some cases was that the assets were revalued by the companies at the time of the sale and lease back transactions thereby inflating its price. This allowed them access to large amounts of money. They also got tax shield on their rental payments. At the same time the leasing companies were charging depreciation on this inflated amount. The government's revenues suffered because of this.

This provision was grossly misused in the late 80s and early 90s. The assets which were sold to lessor were revalued at an unrealistic value, before they were taken back on lease. In the aftermath of CRB fiasco, RBI clamped down on such deals. The RBI issued guidelines for such deals by stating that these transactions can be done only at book value and revaluation of assets for this purpose was disallowed.

Leasing industry in India is going through a very bad phase for sometime now. The collapse of several Non-banking Finance Companies, in the wake of CRB scam in the late 90s, saw lots of small investors suffer, as their fixed deposits with these companies were stuck up. They were neither getting interest on their deposits nor were they able to withdraw their monies. This created an atmosphere where everybody looked at all NBFCs very suspiciously.

The policy of the government towards the industry is also not very clear. RBI wants these companies to convert themselves into banks. Two leading NBFCs have adopted this course. They are the Centurion Bank and the recently established Kotak Bank.

Leasing companies collect savings from individuals and use this money to help corporates create productive assets. Today when lots of funds are required for infrastructure development, the leasing companies can play a crucial role in mobolising savings for funding such projects.

◈ Hire Purchase

A hire purchase can be defined as a contractual arrangement under which the owner lets his goods on hire to the hirer and offers an option to the hirer for purchasing the goods in accordance with the terms of contract.

◈ Salient Features

The finance company purchases the equipment from the equipment supplier and lets it on hire to the hirer.

The hirer may be required to make a down payment and the balance can be repaid in maximum 60 months.

The interest is calculated on the basis of flat rate of interest.

During the currency of the contract the hirer can opt for an early repayment and purchase the asset. The hirer, exercising this option, is required to pay the remaining amount of hire purchase instalments less an interest rebate.

◈ Sales Tax Aspects

Hire purchase transactions are liable to sales tax. The 46th amendment clearly states that the tax on the sale or purchase of goods includes the tax on the delivery of goods on hire purchase or any other system of payment by instalments.

The state in which the goods have been delivered is the state entitled to levy and collect sales tax.

◈ Accounting Aspects

The cash purchase price of the asset is capitalised and the capital content of the hire purchase instalments is recorded as a liability.

Depreciation is charged on the cash purchase price of the asset in line, with the depreciation policy of the hirer with regard to other owned assets.

At the inception of the transaction, the finance company records the hire purchase instalments receivable as a current asset and the unearned finance income component of these instalments as current liability under the head "Unmatured finance charges".

At the end of each accounting period, the finance company recognizes an appropriate part of the unmatured finance income as current income of the period. At the end of each accounting period, the hire purchase price less the instalments received is shown as a receivable (stock on hire) and the finance income component of these instalments is shown as a current liability.

◈ Summary Regulations Governing NBFCs Issued by RBI

1. All NBFCs must register themselves with the RBI. No company can undertake NBFC activities without the registration certificate issued by the RBI.
2. NBFCs having net owned funds of less than ₹ 25 lakh cannot accept public deposits.
3. The ceiling on the quantum of public deposits for NBFCs has been linked to its level of credit rating and the type of activity conducted by the company. For leasing companies a triple A rated company can raise deposits worth four times of its net worth, a AA rated company can raise 2.5 times of its net worth and so on. The minimum investment grade is A –.
4. Deposits can be accepted for a maximum period of five years.
5. Maximum rate of interest on deposits 12 per cent
6. The capital adequacy ratio has been fixed at 12 per cent
7. Credit concentration per borrower and a group of borrowers not to exceed 15 per cent and 25 per cent of its net owned funds.
8. They are expected to maintain liquid assets equal to 15 per cent of the outstanding public deposits with them.
9. Bank borrowings not to exceed four times of the net owned funds.
10. They cannot borrow in excess of ten times of their net owned funds. Borrowings include deposits accepted from the public.

The leasing business in our country is probably not growing though hire purchase is doing very well. Most white goods and four-wheelers and two-wheelers are being financed through this mode.

Foreign NBFCs are trying to establish themselves in India right now and it is expected that would introduce newer products in our markets in the coming years.

15 HOUSING FINANCE

◈ Introduction and Background

These days housing finance is in the limelight. Not long ago the housing finance meant HDFC. It is no more so. Virtually all banks led by New Private Sector Banks and even Public Sector Banks have become extremely active in this field. There is no doubt whatsoever that there is tremendous shortage of housing in our country. With the interest on housing loans at historical low, many people are willing to take loans today. The banks on the other hand are flush with funds due to less off take of credit by the corporate sector, due to the recessionary conditions prevailing for the past few years. Secondly, the rate of default in this sector is pretty low, making these loans very attractive for the banks. With the new thrust in the retail segment by the banking community on the whole, this sector has become attractive both for the lenders and the borrowers. What has also helped is that the real estate rates seem to have stabilised.

Another thing that has contributed to this growth is the tax breaks that are available for this sector. Interest up to ₹ 1.5 lakh is tax deductible from the income of the assessee. What is more is that the assessee can claim deduction under Section 80c of Income Tax Act up to ₹ 1 lakh towards the principle payment in every financial year. These tax breaks unfortunately are also available for the purchase of second house as well. This benefits only well to do people in the country. A normal middle-class person barely manages to buy one house in his lifetime and there are scores who cannot even afford to do this. Actually there is no need to extend tax relief to buyers of the second house.

One major cost in real estate deals is that of the stamp duty that has to be paid. Since the duty is pretty steep and can be different in different states, there is tendency to undervalue these transactions. This leads to a loss to the government and gives rise to black money in the economy. The government is in the process of streamlining the stamp duty structure. The central government has indicated to the state governments that it would prefer a uniform duty on real estate transactions in all the states. The second initiative that is being debated seriously is to charge duty on the capital portion of a transaction like value added tax. This would mean that if one buys a flat for ₹ 10 lakh and the cost of the land for this flat is ₹ 2 lakh, then the builder has already paid stamp duty on the land, hence one will now pay the duty only on ₹ 7 lakh. This will eliminate the cascading effect of duty. Further if this flat is sold for ₹ 20 lakh after a few years, then in this transaction the stamp duty will be payable only on the capital appreciation of ₹ 10 lakh. The government rightly believes that if this done then the undervaluing of the properties can be better controlled. Let us hope that this change is brought about without any delay.

With interest rates in the economy having going up the housing finance activity was expected to slow down. It was also thought that the real estate rates would decline. However the rates that declined for sometime in 08-09 have since been on the upward march once again. The rates of loans have also firmed up considerably since the lows of 2007. In spite of this the demand has been constant or even rising. This is obviously due to the fact that the incomes of the middle-class.

One of the biggest push that this sector has received is the development of the IT sector. One can see this as all cities where IT industry is dominant the real estate prices are on the up relentlessly. Gurgaon, Hyderabad, Bangalore, and Pune to name a few are witness to this phenomenon. But this also has a negative side effect. The employees in other sectors are not able to afford houses in these cities. They have been forced to relocate on the fringes of these cities and since public transport is what it is in their lives have become difficult.

◈ National Housing Bank

Housing finance is offered by many specialised housing finance companies approved by the regulator National Housing Bank, a subsidiary of the Reserve Bank of India. It is also offered by public and private sector banks along with many cooperative banks.

The NHB specifies various norms to be followed by the HFCs (Housing Finance Companies) and regulates the industry. It specifies the interest rates to be followed in lending and borrowing, income recognition and prudential norms, borrowing limits and audit to the housing finance companies. It provides refinance facility to the HFCs and facilitates promotion of these companies on the specified lines.

◈ Objectives of NHB

1. To promote, establish, support or aid in the promotion, establishment and support of housing finance institutions.
2. To make loans, advances or render any other form of financial assistance whatsoever to housing finance institutions, scheduled banks, and to any authority established under any Central/State Act engaged in slum clearance.
3. To subscribe to or purchase stocks, shares, bonds, debentures and securities of every other description.
4. To guarantee the financial obligations of these institutions and underwrite their issues of securities.

◈ Norms of Approval of HFCs by NHB

1. Minimum paid-up capital has to be ₹ 1 crore.
2. At least two directors have to be nominated by banks, financial institutions or by NHB.
3. Any appointment of auditors has to be done with the approval of NHB.
4. At least 75 per cent of the loans have to long-term in nature.

5. Promoter's contribution has to be minimum of 30 per cent of the paid-up capital. Of the remaining capital at least 20 per cent should be contributed by one or more banks, financial institutions, and government or approved housing finance companies.
6. The proposed HFC should not promote a real estate or a construction company and should maintain an "arm's length" distance from such companies.

◈ Refinance Facility Offered by NHB

Annual limits are fixed for the HFCs based on various parameters such as average refinance drawn during the previous years, repayment of refinance earlier availed from it and the overall borrowing limit prescribed under the refinance policy. The refinance made available to any HFC is not to be more than 60 per cent of its outstanding housing loans at any point of time. The HFCs whose overdue of over three months exceed five per cent of the aggregate demand for the year, are ineligible to draw further refinance.

◈ The Limits of Refinance

1. Cannot exceed five times of Net Owned Funds of HFC.
2. Not to exceed 50 per cent of total loan funds of HFCs.
3. Not to exceed 15 per cent of Net Owned Funds of NHB, 25 per cent if HFC is sponsored by scheduled bank.
4. Demand overdue for more than three months, not to exceed 5 per cent of aggregate demand.
5. Restricted to 30 per cent of HFCs disbursement on project lending.

◈ Regulatory Guidelines of NHB

1. Capital adequacy norms: By ensuring a minimum capital adequacy ratio, the regulators are assured that sufficient capital is existent so as to withstand the abnormal shocks in the financial system. The total capital includes both Tier I and Tier II capital.
2. NHB has specified that of the total receivables of the housing finance company, at least 95 per cent of the total money should be recovered.
3. NHB does not specify any norms as far as determination of money that is to be lent is concerned. The interest rates charged by HFCs are freely determinable.
4. Reporting norms:

All HFCs are mandatorily required to file annual returns with NHB, with a copy to RBI stating

(*a*) Particulars of deposits.

(*b*) Particulars of exempted borrowings not counted as deposits.

(*c*) Statement showing net owned funds, statements showing outstanding loans and advances.

(*d*) Statement of investments.

(*e*) Statement relating to deposits and maintenance of liquid assets.

HFCs are also required to submit the audited balance sheets of the company along with the certificate from the auditors stating that the full liabilities of the company have been reflected in the balance sheet and the company is in a position to meet the amount of such liabilities.

◈ Procedure for Disbursement of Loans by HFCs

- Any proposal can be considered only if the applicant satisfies all the conditions stipulated by the NHB, as a test of eligibility. Broad criterions for eligibility are as follows:
- The loans should be directly to individuals or group of individuals.
- A co-applicant, if there is any may be a co-owner of the property. Minors cannot be co-applicants.
- Residual active (earning) life of the applicant reckoned at 60 years should cover the repayment period.
- Any other criterion that may be stipulated by NHB from time-to-time.

◈ Appraisal

◈ Credit Appraisal

The main objective of this is to assess the applicants sustained repayment capacity over the period. The main points that are considered are:

- Income
- Age
- Academic background and employment stability
- Family background
- Assets and liabilities
- Servicing record in respect of other institutional borrowings
- Savings history and capacity
- Number of dependents
- Income and expenditure pattern

◈ Documents Required for Scrutiny

◈ Salaried Class

- Salary certificate
- Copy of ration card/electricity bill
- Rent receipt if applicable.

◈ For Self-employed

- A brief introduction to business/profession
- Balance sheet and Profit and Loss account, duly certified by a chartered accountant.
- Income tax/wealth tax return for the past three years.
- Copies of challans of advance tax.
- Assessment orders.
- Shop and Establishment Act certificate of registration.
- Ration card/Electricity bill/Rent receipt (if applicable)

◆ Legal Appraisal

After credit appraisal is done, legal appraisal is done, wherein all other documents like original title deeds, revenue receipts, and encumbrance (search) certificates for the past 30 years are verified by a lawyer to confirm that the withholder can create an equitable mortgage in favour of the HFC by simple deposit of title deeds.

◆ Technical Appraisal

The technical officer will verify the original documents and counter check all the furnished information. Following documents are generally required:

- Layout Plan
- Approved Plan
- No-encumbrance certificate
- Clearance under Urban Land Ceiling Act
- Commencement certificate
- A detail estimate of cost of construction
- NOC for mortgage of the property in case the purchase is from a Development Authority or any Government allotted scheme.

◆ Securatisation and Housing Finance

One way of funding housing Finance companies that is becoming popular in India these days is "Securatisation". This is prevalent in developed countries for quite sometime now. Mortgage backed Securatisation is new in India, but is gaining acceptance very rapidly.

Securatisation refers to conversion of illiquid assets to liquid assets by converting longer duration cash flows into shorter ones. It denotes the process of selling of assets by the person holding it, to an intermediary who in turn breaks such assets in marketable securities. The assets may be anything ranging from future sales of cinema tickets and airline tickets to hire purchase deals to future receivable of EMIs towards housing loans to Non-performing Assets.

◆ The Process of Securatisation

1. Transfer of assets by the Originator (person holding the asset) to a person (company or trust) specially created for the purpose called Special Purpose Vehicle (SPV). SPV is a separate entity formed exclusively for charting this deal and providing funds to the originator. SPV may be formed as a company under the Company's Act, or a Trust formed under the Indian Trusts Act.
2. The assets transferred should preferably be homogeneous in nature in terms of risks attached to them and/or maturity such that the pooling of such assets will be convenient. SPV divides these assets into marketable securities called Pay or Pass Through Certificates and resells it to various investors.
3. Investors may either be a bank, mutual fund or State or Central government. The investors could even be the parent company or the financier of the originator.
4. The issue of securities is managed by a merchant banker who may underwrite the whole issue or it may be a syndicate of merchant bankers. The originator continues to administer the loan portfolio for some fee and he passes the collections to the trust, which services the securities.

5. Apart from the SPV, a Trustee is normally appointed to oversee the process of Securatisation. An escrow account is created for the purpose of distributing the receivables to the investors in the deal. The Trustee maintains such escrow account.

◈ What is Pass Through Certificates?

A PTC is an instrument that signifies transfer of interest in the receivable in favour of the holder of the PTC. The investors in these transactions acquire the receivables subject to all their fluctuations; prepayments, etc., are transferred to the investors.

◈ The Features of PTCs

- Investors get a proportional interest in pool of receivables.
- Collections month-after-month are divided proportionately.
- All investors receive proportional payments.
- No reinvestment of cash collected by the SPV.

◈ What are Pay Through Certificates?

In case of these the SPV instead of transferring undivided interest on the receivables issues debt securities such as bonds, repayable on fixed dates, but such debt securities in turn would be backed by the mortgages transferred by the originator to the SPV. The SPV may make temporary reinvestment of cash flows to the extent required for bridging the gap between the dates of payments on the mortgages along with the income out of reinvestment to retire the bonds. Such bonds were called mortgage-backed bonds.

◈ What are the Demerits of Securatisation for the Originator?

Securatisation is off-balance sheet funding, the true picture of the originators financial position is not clear merely from the balance sheet, The best assets of the company may be transferred to the SPV and the company may be left with sub-standard assets on its books. A company may have taken hugh liabilities but that may not be apparent from the balance sheet or conventional financial statements of the company. This is especially true where the securatisation in with recourse, *i.e.*, if the receivables, which have been securatised to the SPV become bad, the SPV will have the right to recover the dues from the originator. The originator may have a lot of contingent liabilities without anyone being aware of it.

◈ What is the Process of Securatisation of Receivables?

The originator determines which assets he wants to securatise for raising funds.

The SPV is formed.

The SPV is funded by investors and issues securities to the investors.

The SPV acquires the receivables under an agreement at their discounted value.

The servicer for the transaction is appointed, he is normally the originator.

The debtors may or may not be informed as per the legal requirements.

The servicer collects the receivables, usually in an escrow mechanism and pays off to investors at the stated intervals.

In case of default, the servicer takes action against the debtors as the SPV's agent.

When only small amount outstanding receivables are left to be collected, the originator may clean up the transaction by buying back the outstanding receivables.

At the end of the transaction, the originator's profit, if retained and subject to any losses to the extent agreed by the originator, in the transaction is paid-off.

◈ Credit Enhancement

To obtain an investment rating and make the transaction attractive to the investors, some type of credit enhancement procedure is usually necessary. In order to cover the possibility that the loan portfolio will generate insufficient payment to fund payment to fund payment to fund payments of notes interest when due, some form of liquidity support is provided, usually by a credit facility from a third party lender.

Since this process of securatisation often involves dealing with the backing of assets, it is referred to as Asset Backed Securatisation (ABS). There is another kind of securatisation that deals with mortgages instead of assets called as Mortgage Backed Securatisation (MBS).

In MBS, securatisation will be done on a pool of mortgages that are placed with the originator. In case of housing finance company, which finances construction/acquisition of dwelling units in return of mortgaging the same, the HFC may securatise the mortgages thereby seeking the advantages of securatisation.

◈ Mortgage Backed Securatisation

Evolution and development of securatisation is slow due to several legal hassles involving mortgaging.

Is backed by easily traceable immovable property like real estate.

Mortgage has to exist necessarily at the time of securatisation.

Process takes into consideration appreciation in the value of the assets.

Legal hassles in recourse to the originator in case of default in receivables. Also, mortgage property can only be taken control of but not disposed of by the originator, SPV or the Trustee without intervention of court of law.

Stamp duty is levied on the basis of the rates specified in the State where the deal is struck.

Low yield to the investor.

Benefits of securatisation:

The loan originator can raise money as soon as they create loans.

They need not hold their asset portfolios till maturity.

This will help in multiple asset creation thereby helping routing of funds into business thereby increasing the profitability.

The investor benefits in that the security he buys is of a good quality debt (usually rated AAA as it is credit enhanced) at higher yields and good liquidity.

In most of the cases a merchant banker underwrites the deal.

Also, the deal will have a trustee to oversee the operation of transfer of receivables to the investors in due course.

Securatised debt can be cheaper than other forms of funding as the securities enjoy a wider investor base and certain liquidity.

Not only it helps in getting funds at low cost, it also enables the originator to take advantage of more profitable investment opportunities with the revenue generated through securatisation.

Securatised assets give originators the ability to pass on or eliminate credit, interest rate and lending risks associated with balance sheet funding.

The originator can minimise the accounting leverage as measured by the debt ratio and thus enables raising more funds without impairing its borrowing ability.

The originator through securatisation can tremendously increase the capital adequacy of the company.

The whole process of securatisation has come in for sharp criticism as excessive use of this product majorly led to the crash in housing sector of the US economy in 2008. The uncontrolled use of derivative products based on the mortgages and the greed of bankers and other financial institutions was also responsible. The credit rating agencies also played a major role in all this. They gave high rating to the bonds issued and in a way lured more investors in the market.

- With the increased competition in the sector the players have been forced to constantly innovate and create newer products. Let us now see some of these new developments:
- Flexible Loan Instalment Plan.
- In this case the loan product offers a customized solution to suit the needs of the customers whose repayment capacity is likely to alter during the period of the loan. This kind of a loan is structured in such a way that the EMI is higher during the initial years and subsequently the EMI decreases in the later part. This allows borrowers whose income is likely to reduce in the future. For example, if a loan is taken in the joint name of the husband and wife and if one of them is going to retire during the tenor of the loan, then they would like to play a higher EMI when both of them are working and then the EMI reduces after one of them stops working.
- Step-up Repayment Facility.
- Under this scheme the payment of principal amount is differed to later years. The objective is to provide the customer with a repayment schedule linked with a repayment schedule linked to his expected growth in income. Thus the customer can avail of a higher amount of loan and pay lower EMIs in the initial years and the repayment is accelerated proportionately with the assumed increase in his income. This allows the customer to get a higher amount of loan. Considering the tax benefits that are available on housing loan at present this loan will give them better tax cover in the initial years. This is because the EMIs for the first five years constitute a large part of interest and a nominal sum of the principal.
- However, there is a slight disadvantage to someone who would want to pre-pay the loan in the later stages of the loan. This is because one would have already paid-off most of the interest in the initial years itself and the pre-payment would be only towards the principal amount essentially.
- Balloon payment.
- This scheme allows the borrower to increase his loan eligibility without increasing his EMI. In such type of loans a borrower typically assigns securities like insurance policies, government bonds, NSCs, etc., in favour of the lender. The present value of the maturity amount of these securities is added to the amount of loan that the borrower is eligible to borrow, thus increasing the amount of loan that he is eligible for. The EMI is calculated on the loan amount minus the present value of the securities.
- Acceleration of EMIs.

- Under this scheme the borrower has an option to increase the EMIs every year in proportion to the increase in his income. In case a customer avails of a loan with a repayment period of 15 years and increases his EMI by say 10 per cent every year he will end up paying off the loan in much shorter period.

REVERSE MORTGAGE

◈ Why Reverse Mortgage?

My friend had worked in Liberia for a number of years. He had also started a shop there. He was making good money. Then there was civil war in the country and he lost his shop to the looters and his savings got wiped out. He came back to India and tried his hand at various businesses but could not really succeed. His misfortune continues. He was convinced to invest money in two properties in NCR along with some relatives and friends with a carrot of huge capital appreciation. Alas now he is told there is slowdown and there are no buyers! He gets some amount as rent or something but the capital is blocked and he does not know when it will be freed. In the mean time he has to accept a lower than market return on his investment.

Another case is of my brother-in-law. He slogged in Dubai for almost 25 years. He lived alone there for many years. But says he has no real investments! It does not seem so but that is what he maintained. And now for one-and-a-half years he is bed ridden due to a stroke.

Now both these guys will have to depend on their children for financial support. And that is not a very sobering thought! Children these days have their own priorities. We all have to make sure that we are not dependent on our children for money, something that is in our control to a large extent. If one is emotionally or physically dependent that would be different. However, one hears horror stories on this score also. Yes one does hear about good children as well, who take exceptionally good care of their parents. My in-laws are extremely well looked after by their son!

One good thing about the two cases quoted above is both have own houses. Now this house can take care of their financial needs in the old age if they were to get into Reverse Mortgage of their properties.

GENERAL GUIDELINES OF REVERSE MORTGAGE

◈ Guidelines of Reverse Mortgage

The Reserve Bank of India has formulated the following guidelines for a Reverse Mortgage.

- Maximum loan amount would be up to 60 per cent of the value of the residential property.
- Maximum tenure of the mortgage is 15 years and minimum is ten years. Some banks are now also offering a maximum tenure of 20 years.
- Option of monthly, quarterly, annual or lump sum loan payment.
- Property revaluation to be undertaken by the lender once every five years.
- If at such time, the valuation has increased, borrowers have the option of increasing the quantum of the loan. In such a case, they are given the incremental amount in lump sum.
- Amount received through reverse mortgage is a loan and not income. Hence, it will not attract any tax. However, a borrower is liable to capital gains tax, at the point of

alienation of the mortgaged property by the mortgagee for the purposes of recovering the loan.

- **Reverse mortgage** interest rates could be either fixed or floating. The rate would be determined by the prevailing market interest rates.

❖ Eligibility Criteria for Reverse Mortgage

- House owners above the age of 60 years. If spouse is a co-applicant, then she should be above 58 years.
- Owners of a self-acquired, self-occupied residential house or flat, located in India. The titles should be clear, indicating the prospective borrowers ownership of the property.
- Property should be free from any encumbrances.
- The life of the property should be of minimum 20 years.
- Property should be the permanent primary residence of the individuals.

❖ Settlement of a Reverse Mortgage

A reverse mortgage loan becomes due when the last surviving borrower dies, or if the borrower chooses to sell the house. The bank first gives an option to the next of kin to settle the loan along with accumulated interest, without sale of property. If the next of kin is unable to settle the loan, the bank then opts to recover the same from the sale proceeds of the property.

Any extra amount, after settlement of the loan with accrued interest and expenses, through the sale of the property, will be passed on to the legal heirs. If the sale proceeds are lower than the accrued principal plus interest amount, the loss is borne by the bank. This loss could happen in cases where the banks original estimation is not in line with the real estate market movement.

❖ Other Highlights of Reverse Mortgage

- **Prepayment of Loan:** Borrowers could prepay the loan at any time during the tenor of the loan, at no prepayment penalty or charges.
- **Outliving the tenure of the loan:** If the borrower outlives the tenure of the loan, he could continue to stay in the house. The lending institution may however cease the monthly payments. Settlement of the loan is done only after the borrower's death.
- **Death of one of the spouses:** If one of the spouses dies, the other can still continue living in the house. Only on death of both, settlement of the loan takes place.
- **Foreclosure:** The loan could be foreclosed by the lender if:
- The borrower has not stayed in the house for a continuous period of one year.
- The borrower has not paid property taxes and fails to insure the home.
- If the borrower declares himself as bankrupt.
- If the mortgaged property is donated or abandoned by the borrower.
- If the borrower makes changes in the residential property, that could affect the security of the loan for the lender. This could be renting out part or entire house, addition of a new owner to the houses title or creating further encumbrance on the property.

- If the government under statutory provisions, seeks to acquire or condemn the residential property for health or safety reasons.

Drawbacks of Reverse Mortgage

- **Lengthy documentation procedures:** Banks require various documents of the property. For a senior citizen this procedure could be tedious, complicated and difficult to understand.
- **Fixed monthly amounts:** The monthly payouts are fixed. There is no provision to increase this amount in case of an emergency or contingency.

Popularity of the Scheme in India

Though introduced in 2007, reverse mortgage has not gained much popularity in India for the following reasons.

- Inadequate marketing of the product. Recent reports indicate that many of the senior citizens are not aware of the existence of such a product.
- Many banks which offer reverse mortgage have capped the maximum loan amount available for individuals to a maximum amount of ₹ 50 lakh to ₹ 1 crore.
- Children have resentment for a reverse mortgage as they see it as giving away their family home or legacy.

Reverse mortgage is a relatively new concept in India. It would take sometime for a change in mindset of individuals to accept it. As a financial tool, reverse mortgage is ideal to augment a senior citizen's income in his years ahead. Despite all its shortcomings in India, it could make good the shortfall in one's pension or income to live a quality life ahead.

16 FINANCIAL ENGINEERING

◈ Introduction to Financial Engineering

Financial engineering (FE) is a new discipline that has emerged in the late 80s. The bankers of London introduced the term. This innovative technology emerged in response to the rapid changes in corporate finance; bank finance and investment finance to enable managers to deal better with the changes. New problems in the field of finance require new and innovative products. Financial engineering is R&D in the finance field. New products have to be developed to overcome financial obstacles in the path of attaining the goals of the organisation.

American Association of Financial Engineers (AAFE) defines financial engineering as "the development and creative application of financial technology to solve financial problems and exploit financial opportunities".

Financial engineering is very different from financial analysis. Financial engineering starts where financial analysis ends. The analysis establishes the problems and the probable causes of the problem. On the other hand financial engineer puts together the established knowledge for the formulation and implementation of new processes and products that he devises in response to the existing problem, with the intention of solving the problem.

Financial engineering involves the design, development, and implementation of innovative financial instruments and processes. It seeks to formulate creative solutions to manage financial risks or problems such as reduction in costs in the existing system and to develop new products, services and markets.

Following factors are responsible for the growth of FE:

- Price volatility
- Globalisation of financial markets.
- Tax asymmetries
- Technological advances
- Advances in financial theory

- Regulatory changes
- Increased competition
- Cost of information and cost of transaction
- Intra-firm factors such as liquidity needs of the business
- Risk aversion of managers and owners
- Pressure on profitability
- Greater levels of quantitative sophistication among investment managers

◈ Tools of Financial Engineering

There are two types of tools that are used in FE. One is Conceptual and the other Physical.

◈ Conceptual Tools

Ideas and concepts, which underlie finance as a formal discipline. They include Valuation Theory, Portfolio and Hedging Theory, Tax Treatment.

◈ Physical Tools

Instruments and processes which can be pieced together to accomplish some specific purposes, example, fixed income securities, equity/swaps/futures/options, etc.

The process of FE is to identify risks. Once the risks are identified, they need to be measured. This has to be related to the outcomes that are to be achieved through the process of financial engineering.

There are three main categories of financial engineers.

◈ The First are Deal Makers

These are the marketers. They are on the lookout for corporates who are looking for innovative and creative solutions for their financial requirements.

We can take an example here. Some finance companies like housing finance companies lend money for long-term. This entails blocking of money over a long period of time and thus their requirement of funds is ever-increasing. The deal makers realised this. When the idea generators addressed this problem, they came out with a solution of securatisation, wherein illiquid assets can be converted into cash.

◈ The Second Category is that of Idea Generators

They are the innovators. They work on the requirements of corporates as identified by the deal makers. Once they know what the client is looking for they use all tools at their disposal to create a product that will serve the purpose of the client. They have to take care and see that the product that they develop will be attractive for the investors or the lenders. The real financial engineering probably happens here. Therefore this is the crucial area for the success of the product ultimately. These engineers have to be well versed in the theory of finance and mathematics. The idea generators or all financial engineers for that matter view problems as personal challenge.

Reliance Industries was the first company to introduce the concept of convertible debentures in India. This was a completely new product that was developed, keeping in mind the company's requirements.

◆ The Final Category of the Financial Engineers is Known as Loophole Exploiter

They are also interestingly known as outlaws. They do not do or propose to anything illegal. What they actually try and do is to find loopholes in the existing legal system that can be exploited to create an innovative product. They therefore are required to the laws very well and they have to study the law in minute details to try and find the loopholes, which can be exploited by them.

Few years' back the dividend was made tax-free in the hands of the receiver. However the companies were asked to pay dividend distribution tax on the dividends paid by them. At this time the companies were not very happy that they would have to this tax. Enter the Outlaws. They found a way out, which would be available only for one year. The companies were asked to declare interim dividends before the financial year-end of March end. They argued that in this case the dividend tax would not have to be paid by the companies for that year at least. The interim dividend was to be converted into final dividend for that year. This worked out successfully for the companies who accepted this advice. When the government decided to make the dividend taxable in the hands of the receiver again, the outlaws were again at work. This time they also decided to pay interim dividend to protect their shareholders from the tax for one year. But this time the government had learnt the lesson of the last time and they invoked provisions of the Company's Act to stall this move successfully.

◆ Examples of Some Products Developed by Financial Engineers

We shall now take a look at some of the products that are developed by the financial engineers over a period of time.

One of the most effective products that were used in Indian stock markets for a long time was Badla. This product allowed investors who did not have shares in their possession sell them, while it made it possible for investors who had no funds to buy shares through this mechanism. Investors who had no shares were lent shares and investors who were short of funds were lent funds, through the Badla mechanism at a rate of interest rate that was market determined. The Badla system has now been banned by SEBI.

The system of derivatives trading which has replaced the Badla is also a financial engineered product. Today there is more trade done in the form of options and futures not only in stock markets but also in the commodity markets and the forex markets. In India the commodities future market was always operative in commodities like turmeric. Now the scope of these markets has been widened to include many other products. This market is at the take-off stage now.

Another product that came to the market in the recent past was the securatisation of future debts. This product was created for the Reliance Oil and was executed by ICICI. Reliance was given rights for oil exploration in certain blocks by the government. Once it was established that the said block has potential of producing crude oil, the deal was developed. An assumption was made of the likely billing of the company from this oil field. Part of this future sale proceeds were then securatised by ICICI. In short through this deal Reliance got cash up front, thus reducing their funds requirement. What helped in this deal was the credit enhancement provided through a corporate guarantee given Reliance Industries Ltd., in favour of ICICI.

We have already discussed the issue of bonus debentures issued by HLL. This is brilliantly engineered financial instrument that was innovated to take care of the requirement of the company and also keeping mind the interest of the shareholders of the company.

Another financially engineered product that has been recently introduced in the markets by Government of India is the Tax Free Bonds carrying tax-free interest of 6.75 per cent for converting US 64 units into these bonds. This again is a wonderful product. The investors, who were unable to get redemption for their holdings, got a new investment opportunity and also were able to get out of their US-64 investment. This also saved the government from finding ₹ 3,500 crore it was committed to give to UTI towards the redemption of these units.

Another financially engineered product that was used by the government was known as Oil Bonds. This was before the administered price mechanism in oil sector was abolished. When the oil prices went up in the international markets and the government was unable to increase the domestic prices, the oil companies had to be compensated as their selling price was less than their purchase and processing cost. Since government in this situation had to fund this deficit through the budget, the budget deficits would go awry. Since they did not want to do this, a new product was devised. The government floated Oil Bonds. The banks subscribed to these bonds for their investment portfolio. The bonds carried an attractive coupon rate to entice the investors. The amount thus raised was paid to the oil companies. These bonds were redeemed when international oil prices fell, thereby generating surpluses in the oil pool account.

Many mutual funds have developed new products. Some of these products are index-related funds, funds that track the PE of markets and individual companies. The latest development in this market is likely to be mutual fund devoted to real estate market. With securatisation becoming popular in India, there is no doubt that many new products related to this will soon come to the market.

In 2008 US crisis was a wakeup call for financial engineering pioneers. The abuse of derivative products for speculation instead of hedging was the norm adopted for almost ten years before the crisis. Excessive use of securatisation led to sub-prime crisis and since many financial institutions were holding this paper on their books they all had to take big hits on their books as more and more borrowers started defaulting. Products like Credit Swaps also contributed to this. Insurance giants like AIG started offering insurance against credit default! This product almost finished off the company and it had to bailed out by the US government with an infusion of $ 80 billion in capital!

One has to say that in spite of this experience the new risky products are still being developed and sold in the market. The latest is that some banks in Europe have offered a product based on the just listed and hammered stock of Face Book!

ANNEXURES

ANNEXURE-I

1. Warren Buffett on Investments

1. A frugal billionaire Buffett believes in simplicity. He advises investors to take easy decisions. Never buy when you are doubtful. Invest only if you understand the businesses well.
2. Focus on not losing money rather than making it. Don't own any stock for ten minutes that you wouldn't own for ten years.
3. A proponent of value investing, he believes that one must take decisions on his own. He doesn't believe in listening to analysts or brokers. The best investing decisions come from one self. It is not necessary to do extraordinary things to get extraordinary results.
4. Buffett advises to invest in 'old economy' businesses, companies, which have been around for fifty years and will continue to have a long innings.
5. We have often heard of people suffering heart attacks when markets crash. Well, Buffett advocates a sound temperament for stock market success.
6. You don't need to be a genius to succeed in the stock markets. People who can stay cool will succeed in the long run. Always keep in mind the hidden costs, from commissions on active stock trading to high mutual fund fees.
7. Buffett always looks at businesses he can understand, look at the profits in the past, long-term potential of the company, good top level management of the company and companies that have a good value proposition. The strategy is to think about the business in the long-term.

   "You are neither right nor wrong because the crowd disagrees with you. You are right because your data and reasoning are right."

8. Invest in businesses with great management. Always keep a track of the management of the company. The top decision makers have a lot to do with the company's performance.
9. One of Buffett's biggest strengths is independent thinking. Many people go by what the experts says or what others do but belief in one's own judgement is the key to stock market success.
10. Patience pays, says Buffett. He says one must not worry too much about the price of the stocks. What's more important is the nature of business of the company, earnings capability and its future potential.
11. Don't target just stocks, look at businesses. How a company performs is key to its stock market performance. You must know the track record of a company before you invest in it.

    "Price is what you pay. Value is what you get."
12. Prices keep changing. Don't get worried by the ups and downs. Investing is all about creating wealth. It's important to understand the value of a stock than its price.
13. He believes that franchisee businesses are good opportunities to invest in. Avoid hi-tech, complex businesses. Look for businesses that are set to diversify and grow.
14. Never be disappointed when markets fall. Take it as a buying opportunity. Buffett says one must have lesser number of investments with more money in each lot.
15. He advises to avoid diversification. Invest in companies with sound business models. Choose a few good ones and stay invested, it will give you the benefits.

    "I don't look to jump over 7-foot bars; I look around for 1-foot bars that I can step over."
16. Doing nothing pays at times! One must not jump at price fluctuations and take impulsive decisions.
17. Don't get carried away by market forecasts. Ignore market swings and remain an investor with a good business sense.
18. Buffett advises to be fearful when others are greedy and greedy when others are fearful. Buy when people are selling and sell when people are buying.
19. Make a list of companies, sectors that you find safe to invest in and try to stick to the list.
20. A sound business, strong management, good fundamental and low stock price should be a must-buy.

    "Most people get interested in stocks when everyone else is. The time to get interested is when no one else is. You can't buy what is popular and do well."
21. Try to ignore stock charts, says Buffett. They may not give the right indicators. A stock which may have done well earlier may not do so in future.
22. Buffett spends a lot of time on reading and more importantly thinking. Reading helps investors, so spend a lot of time reading about the stocks, companies and markets. A good investor must have a good knowledge base.
23. A good investor also needs to be efficient. Investors may have great capabilities but many do not make use of it. One needs to hone skills to meet the targets.
24. Good investors never rush to make money. They give time, thought and work on investment decisions. The mistakes that others make should be a lesson for you.

2. Common Investor's Dilemma!

I think I am a small investor. I don't understand the difference between a small and big investor. As an investor I should invest what I can. If I invest a large proportion of my income like 50 per cent then I am a large investor. If I need to spend 75 per cent of my income and am able to save only 25 per cent then I am a small investor. By this definition I am not exactly a small investor. I reckon that the dilemma that I am referring to is same for all investors.

I invested ₹ 20,000 in a mutual fund scheme in Sept. 04. The scheme has given me dividend of 20 per cent recently. The NAV of the scheme now is around ₹ 23. This means that my principal has now grown to ₹ 46,000 plus I have received a dividend of ₹ 2,000. My total gain from this investment as on day thus is ₹ 28,000. I must congratulate myself for making an excellent investment. Should I now shout from the roof tops that I am good at spotting winners well in advance and become an Investment Consultant?

Now the real dilemma! Is it time to sell and book my paper profits by converting them in actual cash that I can use to spend or spot another winning opportunity to double my capital again in the next 18 months as I have done with this investment. I am struggling with this for the past two months now.

I have thought that I should sell 50 per cent of my investment and take my capital out. For me this is always the most sensible thing to do. I believe that I must have a portfolio but no investment of capital in it. If I sell 50 per cent units this is what I will be able to achieve.

On the other hand there is the Sensex that keeps rising and with it rises my NAV. Then the old virus of greed takes over and says how you can disinvest when the going is good and you are making money without working for it. There are days when the markets go down and I am compelled to think of divesting. But the markets rise again and I am back to square one.

Finally now I have decided that if markets fall below 12,000 then I will divest come what may. If markets keep going up I shall move my stop loss limit to 12,250 and so on. I only hope that I will actually sell if the markets fall to 12,000 and will not think like a small investor that I should wait because the markets will go up.

A big investor is one who knows when to get out of his profitable investment, because he knows where to take his profit and make more money from the profits. I also want to become a big investor. I can only become one when I will learn to sell and know what to do with the profits.

I think I have solved my dilemma. Big investors always try and get answers to their own dilemmas!

3. Falling Market Represents an Opportunity!

Many of us got caught in the panic of 2008 as the markets plunged from 21,000 to under 8,000. Those who were speculating on markets reaching 25,000 and investing in companies that were not sound suffered huge losses. These companies especially in real estate sector and broking firms did not recover even as the markets recovered and reached a high of 20,000 last November. 2008 actually was an opportunity to buy fundamentally strong company stocks at very attractive valuations. Many missed it only to rue as the markets went up.

The current turmoil in the markets represents another opportunity for those who are very clear about their investment targets. We do not know as of now where the bottom of the markets will be. It is often said rightly that timing the markets is not possible. It is quite possible that markets may breach 15,000 levels due to the current situation. If you have stocks that have done well over a long period of time then you will know how their prices behaved between 2008 and now. If you own stocks that recovered fast after the fall and if these companies are still doing well, one should look at buying these stocks in falling markets. When the markets recover and that could be one year from now the prices of fundamentally strong companies will recover before every other company for sure.

So do not panic. If one has to make profits in bull markets then one has to have courage of buying during the bear phase. If you have bought low only then high will give you money!

If you have stocks whose prices have gone down and those companies have in any case not done well even in good markets, it may be worthwhile to sell those stocks even at a loss and invest that money in good stocks. This will help one to not only recover losses made but will also have an opportunity to make profits. It is time to take a hard look at one's portfolio and clean it. All investors make mistakes; there is no point in brooding over them. Accept the mistakes and minimize the loss and then take that money elsewhere where profits can be made.

Many will be tempted to get into short selling. Avoid this trap. It is not meant for retail investors. Many brokerage firms will try and allure you in this by promising great profits. Ignore such offers.

I would suggest 4-5 very strong companies with assured cash flows and good track record and make your investments only in these stocks. Do not look at fancy stocks. Do not look at companies that are not part of the Sensex. Top ten companies in Sensex account for the maximum weightage. It may be a great idea to stick to some of these companies.

If you are investing in diversified equity schemes through SIP keep doing it. If possible you can increase your SIP amount. With the NAV of these funds plummeting with the falling markets you will get more units now. So do not make the mistake of stopping your investments.

Opportunities like this do not come often and when it comes we are somehow paralysised with fear and do not take advantage of them. We have all made this mistake in the past. The time has come to realise that we now have an opportunity to make sensible investments in stocks that we admired and always wanted them to be in our portfolio but could not buy due to high prices. Now is the time to take the plunge.

Do not buy large quantities at one go. Buy in small lots but keep buying.

This is one of the biggest sales going right now. For this festival season make your buying in this market. Great offers are on and the sale may go on for quite sometime. Do not give yourself the opportunity to shied yourself two years from now saying "Oh, I should have bought in 2011" You have already done it many times earlier!

Happy buying and sensible buying!

4. To Give the Devil its Due

We normally always criticize our government and hold it responsible for most of our problems. We do this either out of frustration or because we ourselves are completely insensitive to contribute anything. But there are times when the government actually does things in the best possible way but we are loath to acknowledge this. This attitude is absolutely ridiculous.

The incidence where I believe we have not appreciated the government is the way they have handled the whole Satyam fiasco. The government to mind played its role from a distance but with unexpected firmness and foresight.

The government was obviously devastated by the revelations of Raju and it had to be red faced as its regulators had failed to find anything wrong with the fourth largest IT company in India. They absorbed shock as quickly as they could and got into firefighting mode straight away. Most of the time petty politics was kept aside though there were murmurs of collision between the Andhra government and Raju. Yes, certain things during the investigation were messed up as SEBI officials were not allowed to interrogate the brothers for quite sometime and actually had to move the court to get the permission.

But the government acted fast to appoint three prominent and respected persons, *viz.* Deepak Parekh, Kiran Karnik and Tarun Das as the directors on the board of the company with full powers to set right the company and also find a buyer for the company so that the business can go on and more importantly save the jobs of around 50,000 people working with it.

It was appreciated that the people in the company had no role to play in the entire fraud that was single handedly claimed to have been purported by Raju brothers themselves. The government also eschewed the temptation of taking over the company as used to be the case in India pre-liberalization era. The government this time was only willing to play the role of Friend, Philosopher and Guide's role. This is what a mature government should be doing. If a business fails sometimes you have to let it fail and allow the winding up of the company as quickly as possible so that the hurt could be minimized.

Having appointed an honourable Board the government stepped out of the way and gave all necessary authority to them. The Board also moved with great speed and was able to sell off the company to Tech Mahindra in a transparent manner, as is evidenced by the fact that none of the other bidders who lost the bid have accepted the verdict as fair. This is unprecedented in India. I do not remember this having happened any time. Most of the times we have seen frustrating delays in resolving many such cases of corporate failures. The government was happy to quote the law and allowed the red tepism without being pro-active as it should be.

So let's give the credit to the devil because this time it deserves it! This action also sets up a precedence that can be used effectively by the future governments in similar situations. This will definitely enhance our reputation in the international markets. Satyam episode tarnished our image internationally, but the quick resolve pushed through by the government has redeemed the situation to some extent. The customers of Satyam have not deserted the company wholesale as was feared immediately after the scam broke. Lot of the credit for this goes to the Devil.

So for once let's salute the Devil and give it its due! The Devil deserves it and we must applaud wholeheartedly and encourage the Devil to be innovative going forward. Though nobody has said it I believe that this action will turnout to be a great parting gift by this government. In India we do not know what needs to be celebrated and so end up celebrate things of not much relevance. This one action needs to be celebrated by all of us.

5. The Price of Financial Illiteracy

Why do we work? The primary reason is to make money. What everyone tries to do or at least that was the way it used to be in our times was to save part of what you earn for future and also to acquire assets that one aspires to possess. This seems to be conventional wisdom and as far as I am concerned the right thing to do. I see two things these days the young generation that is after money and does not seem to be bothered about savings. They spend more than they get at times and want everything in a hurry. To this end they are willing to take loans indiscriminately believing that their incomes will go on increasing and their EMI percentage to earnings will keep declining. We have seen many fall in this trap and suffer immensely. The second trend that also is evident is the financial illiteracy shown by many people who are above the age of 60. Now this generation was supposed to be a cautious one in terms of money!

Yesterday I came across a case of a man at that time 73 buying a pension product that will require him to pay ₹ 5 lakh per year for ten years! Did he believe that his income will keep coming for the next ten years? This is not the only investment that he has committed to. He seems to have made many such horrendous mistakes. If this is not the case of financial illiteracy then what is this?

I know people and gentleman above is one of them, who refuse to even entertain the thought of making a will. Secondly, it is simply astounding that their spouses do not know most of the investments that they have made. The reason given by most men is what do women understand about money? Such a terrible chauvinistic attitude. Women on the other hand say all my life I have not been involved anything like investments because my husband was handling everything and I was only sign the papers that he asked me to sign! Mind you these women are actually educated! I have seen people making investing on their single name without informing their partners. Worse I have come across cases where husbands have made investments in the name of their wives singly by signing their names themselves!

When these people fall ill or die suddenly the other members of the family then come to know about all this and are in utter shock. They do not know what to do with all this mess. There is no will, there is no nomination on most investments and they do not even know what is the magnitude of the mess that has been created, as they keep finding more and more dirt!

Why do people behave like this can be a subject of further study? But there are too many of them who fall into this category. This does not mean that I have not met or heard of sensible people who do the things right! I have fortunately come across many in this category as well.

I fervently hope that more and more people will realize that they do not know everything. When they will realize that they are actually illiterate financially? Do they also not hear of the cases where a lot of financial mess gets created? I am sure all of them have heard such stories but seems to believe that it will not happen to them because they are smarter and they also seem to believe that they are unlikely to die in a hurry and when the times comes to say good bye they will have enough time to put everything in order! What arrogance is this?

I appeal to all to make sure that all your investments are in joint names and you must put all your shares in de-mat account. Whatever you invest make sure that your partners and your children know what you are doing. If you are doing something that you do not want to tell your dear and near ones then you do not love them enough for sure. Make sure that you maintain a record of all your investments in a safe place and your partner and children know where to look for it. Make a will not because your time is up but to make sure that your survivors do not suffer because of that. This will also be a way to make sure that do not get into acrimonious fights over your property and other assets. You owe it to yourself and also to your family.

6. The Success of Coal India IPO

The biggest IPO in the history of Indian stock markets has just been concluded successfully. The Government of India must be very pleased with the success of this mega IPO from a public sector company that is not widely known to retail investors. Why did this IPO succeed so spectacularly?

The first reason is that it was probably sensibly priced. On top of that retail investors were offered a 5 per cent discount. Since the issue was large and 50 per cent is reserved for retail investors this was very important and seems to have worked as the retail response was very encouraging in this offer. It will be interesting to see how many of the successful investors have sold out on listing. It would make sense as they got almost ₹ 100 per share profit on listing and some investors must have cashed out immediately. I am also interested in knowing how many will look at this investment as long-term one and hold on to the shares. I think this company has the potential to create value for investors who will stay invested long-term. With the modernization in the offing and the results from which come after 2-3 years the stock value is then likely to go up giving excellent return to the holders.

The most disappointing aspect in this offer was that there were very few takers for the reserved quota for the employees of the company itself. This was a big tragedy and the unions must be squarely blamed for this as they told their members to stay away from the offer. Many people who work in coal mines must obviously be illiterate or semi-literate, but it is very clear that even many educated ones also did not apply! I think the government should consider giving part of the compensation or bonus by way of shares to the employees of the company that is going public, because history will bear me out that in most PSU disinvestments the successful shareholders have made handsome gains. Also I think the time has come that part of the funds in provident funds must flow in the equity markets without delay. The unions protests must be firmly dealt with and 10 per cent corpus must be invested in stocks. They can make a start by investing these funds in the PSU issues to start with. This should please the leftist unions who believe that prominence of PSUs must be maintained. On the one hand they take this position on the other they ask their members are ill advised not to subscribe to the reserved quota, depriving them a chance of creating wealth for them.

We also saw a huge response from the international institutional investors to this issue. The appetite for good Indian paper is still there. US has decided to pump more money in their economy. A part of the money will inevitably flow to Indian markets. We should take advantage of this situation. The government has targeted to raise ₹ 40,000 crore this fiscal and has raised roughly half of that amount. We still have roughly four months before we come to the close of the current financial year and the government must go ahead and may be raise more money than they have targeted for. Yes, there are dangers in the American madness of printing more and more dollars and some day not only they but the entire world will pay a price and when that happens Indian markets will be impacted like in 08, but right now let us cash in on the madness.

Close on the successful offer of Coal India, comes the news of the follow on offer of Power Grid has got a great response, even though the offer price is very close to the existing market price. So the success of Coal India has been real in the sense that retail investors are probably willing to come back to the IPO market if the pricing is right. However, they would do better to stay away from the secondary markets as this is not the time to enter. The markets will have to correct from this level but due to excess global liquidity they may go up further. When will the correction come cannot be predicted by anyone.

So for the mean time let us celebrate the success of Coal India offer. It will be sensible for retail investors to consider investing in coming IPOs of government companies in the months to come. The fall out of this will be that the government may increase its disinvestment target for the next fiscal in the coming budget. And if they continue to price these offers sensibly then it is a chance of middle-class Indians to create wealth for themselves.

7. Benefits of Economic Slowdown

(Please keep in mind that this was written in March '09. Many things are still relevant)

That the Indian economy has slowed down is clear to anyone. Is the slow down really bad considering the scorching growth rates of the past five years? We need time to consolidate.

It is always observed that a lot of things go wrong during the boom years and are neglected because the growth is strong and hence the arrogance that everything must be right. The sub-prime crisis or the complete terror unleashed by the derivatives of all sorts is the result of this arrogant perception that if growth rates are good everything in the system is ok. This is a terrible assumption.

So I think a slowdown is actually welcome as it will bring us down from our artificially propped up high horses. An economy growing at around 6 per cent is not a very bad thing at all. Yes we need to grow at 10 per cent to make a serious dent on poverty is true, but it is more important to make sure that we do not grow at rates that will bring more trouble called euphoria!.

I believe that the industry uses slowdowns as an excuse to get more concessions from the government and the governments falls prey to these. When things improve it becomes difficult to withdraw these concessions. The industry does not offer anything to society when the things are going well. Will the industry offer to takeover government run schools for example and run them? Will they build schools and run them, appoint good teachers and pay their salaries? I bet they will ask for more tax breaks for this! Right now they want AS-11 to be kept in abeyance for two years. How can accounting standards be changed like this. What will they ask for once IFRS is enforced? There is no need to even discuss this. Companies must report their accounts as per all the accounting standards issued. Banks also want concessions so that they can hide their losses on Treasury.

The real action that is required is that to stimulate demand the companies must reduce the prices of their products. We have seen that in spite of the cut in excise duties to 8 per cent from 16 per cent not all this benefit has been passed on to the consumer, and neither has the government initiated any action against these companies. Interestingly no political party including the Left, have not made an issue out of this! Is the industry sharing this profit to finance the political parties for elections?

The real estate companies have ripped the buyers for past several years. By all accounts they are still making good profits. However they are refusing or resisting price reduction. Most middle-class families in urban India want 1 BHK flats. For several years now the builders have refused to build these, now some of them are announcing schemes which will have only 1 BHK flats. It is necessary that all builders must be forced by regulation to build affordable houses for the common people, in every scheme of theirs. Companies like DLF are lobbying and saying that the interest rates on housing loans need to be brought down to stimulates demand. This is a scary argument. First and foremost the price of the house has to be affordable; the question of interest rates arises only after that. The interest rates are much lower than they were in the 90s and the incomes have increased substantially. I therefore believe that interest rates are not the main reason. Prospective buyers are convinced that they can get a better price if they postpone their buying decision.

In a difficult economic year it is natural that the government must play a pro-active role. But to give concessions across the board by worsening its own finances is surely not the right way to do it. The deficit of the government is very high and will mean that the government is going to be a big borrower in the markets this year. Large government deficits are worse than slim corporate bottom lines and low Sensex.

Companies, who are suffering because of wrong strategies, need to fight out the bad days with the same enthusiasm as they showed in the booming markets. Slowdowns are also good because they help the market to weed out bad companies and save resources. These times are also good because it will force companies to look inwards and try to weed out the inefficiencies that creep in during the good times along with arrogance. I remember that HUL's top line growth was minimal in early years of this decade. However, their bottom line growth in the same period was quite robust! They obviously were able to achieve this by tightening the inefficiencies that they discovered internally. The stock markets hammered the stock down, where as I thought a company that is able to do this needs to be rewarded as this removal of inefficiencies will actually increase shareholders value in the long run! This same arrogance leads them to over ambitious strategies. They also are forced to look at their manpower costs. I have seen companies paying vulgar salaries to management students as starting salaries. They were competing with each other to offer ridiculous salaries. I do not know what they were expecting in return. I asked this question to some HR persons and their standard answer was we have to pay the market price to get good people. My question was how do you know these people will deliver was normally met with a shrug of shoulders which is so typical of them. It also meant it is not my money-so why should I bother! The beneficiaries of this scenario were the management institutes as they boasted of 100 per cent placement at ever-increasing average salaries, and increased their intake and fees every year.

I recently asked some marketing and sales persons in a FMCG company why their company has not passed on the benefits of excise cuts to their customers. Their answer was our profits were under pressure when input costs were going up in the previous years and we need to compensate for it. I then asked them what they will expect their company to do if the market leader HUL passes on these benefits. Their response was then we will also do it! I was trying to argue the point that since they are not the market leaders does it not make more sense for them to reduce prices and go for higher market share? This in turn will increase their profits in any case. My second argument was that since you call your company an ethical company and endlessly talk about customer satisfaction — is it correct not to pass on tax cuts to the customers? I have no problem when companies increase prices when input costs go up, but I have a problem when the same companies try and find every excuse that they can think of to not cut the prices. The best way to address demand recession would be to cut prices and induce demand. The government has gone and cut taxes on goods but the manufacturers are unwilling to sacrifice their margins and still claim that they are going through tough times and they need to be rescued by the government. If they are not willing to sacrifice anything then they have no right to ask the government to pick the tab to protect their bottom lines. We can see this in prices of not FMCG companies, but also in white goods and electronic goods. Prices are increased when the companies want, but with cut in taxes and the decline in input costs they must reduce prices to spur demand for their goods.

There is too much importance attached to profit margin to sales ratios. In a bad year what is more important to see is whether the companies have increased sales and profits in absolute terms and not in percentage terms. In year like this the sales may actually fall and so will the profits. A drop in profit margin is bad if the profit has gone down, in spite of sales going up; when profit has gone up and percentage has dropped in a bad market it is a very good achievement.

Most of the car manufacturers have been trying to be too cleaver. When steel and other prices of inputs were increasing they were increasing the prices. Whenever the government cut the excise they cut the prices for the customers, only to roll them back after a few days. Maruti, Hyundai, Honda and all others have done this. Bajaj Auto to mind is a peculiar case. Before the split of the company almost 50 per cent of their PAT used to come from other income, which was income earned on their treasury. Now they are losing sales every month even as Hero Honda' sales are increasing every month. Now any right minded person would think that they should cut prices and try increase volumes to improve profits. Have they done this? Obviously, not. Do not blame slowdowns and the government for your sales declining. Mr. Bajaj both senior and junior need to look inwards before they speak. All these companies will do well to revisit the books. The Goal and Goal II and draw some lessons from it, if they have forgotten.

Slowdowns are great because the markets come back to their senses and with them bring investors back to earth. This includes mutual funds as well. They were busy floating a plethora of schemes which have made investors poor. This in spite of the fact that only about 30 per cent of their assets under management are in equities! Merchant bankers are other culprits. They were selling IPO's happily with unsustainable premiums. The fiasco of withdrawal of IPO's of EMAAR-MGF and Wockhardt Hospital amply bears this out, coming as they did on the top of the biggest catastrophe called Reliance Power Ltd. The farce of bonus issue of this company never should have been allowed.

This has also shown the hollowness of Credit Rating Agencies. International CRAs have not been made to pay the price they need to pay for their role in the sub-prime crisis.

The government has reduced the prices of petrol and diesel by almost ₹ 10 per liter, because the international prices of crude have come down.. We are forgetting that the high crude priced never reflected in the street prices as the government doled out huge subsidies. These subsidies must be recovered. For this the prices of products should have been kept intact till the subsidies were recovered. Some price reduction in diesel prices is probably justified as our mass transport and goods transport depends on this fuel. The kerosene prices ought to be increased, insulating BPL families by providing cheap fuel through PDS.

It is time that our people learn to pay for what they use. I have asked many people, since the inflation rate had climbed to around 13 per cent last year, what sacrifices have they had to make? Did they alter their lifestyles? About 95 per cent people said that they did not sacrifice anything at all. May be they tightened their budgets a little on eating out and tried to control their fuel costs. The people that I spoke to belonged to the middle- and higher middle-class. The poor will obviously be more affected, but those who have low purchasing power will always suffer due to inflation, especially when food prices increase. But food prices must be increased to pay remunerative prices to the farmers. The MSP that the government pays to the farmers has gone up by almost 70 per cent in the last five years, however the subsidies to agriculture sector have also increased manifold. This is unacceptable. If you increase prices then correspondingly subsidies must come down.

What the government should do according to me is as follows:

Continue to spend money on infrastructure projects. Expedite all projects; put more people and machinery on the sites. Concentrate on roads, railways and power. This will have impact on employment and also on cement and steel sector.

Make massive investments in irrigation facilities. Invest in clod storages across the country. Encourage food processing. Involve private sector in all these activities. Employ local people wherever possible. Farmers must be made stakeholders in food processing. The cooperative sugar factories with all their short comings have helped remove poverty. The model for food processing need not be in the cooperative sector. The management must be professional, but the farmers must be shareholders and must get a share in profits.

Make it mandatory for housing societies and apartments to install solar water heating systems. Financing for this should provided by banks. These societies should also be forced to implement water harvesting systems. Both these measures will create employment for urban poor.

Every family below the poverty line should be provided free solar cookers and solar lanterns and should be trained to use these effectively. After doing this increase the price of kerosene supplied.

A massive programme must be launched to treat sewage in all cities. These plants should produce biogas that should be supplied to BPL families for cooking. The manure that this will produce should be given at cost price to the marginal farmers. The clean water instead of being released in the rivers should be used for watering plants in the municipal gardens, etc.

With the slowdown in job markets we may see the emergence of new entrepreneurs. This will be a very good thing for the economy in the long run. Entrepreneurs will create job opportunities and will create wealth by investing in productive assets. The way to reduce poverty is to encourage entrepreneurship by imparting training to people so that they can become economically independent.

These and such other measures will make the governments popular. It will create employment locally. The benefits of liberalization will go down with such initiatives.

8. Why should Companies be Allowed to Withdraw their IPOs after they Open?

Last week the IPO of Galaxy Surfactants withdrew it due to poor response. In 2008 Wockhardt Hospitals as well as EMAAR-MGF had done likewise. Why should this be allowed?

All IPOs are graded before launch and the rating agencies give their grades according to the methodology that they have. If the grade is 3 and above then it is said that the issue is worth investing in. All projects for which money is being raised have to be evaluated either by the lead merchant banker or the bankers that are going to finance the project. All this is done while filing the prospectus with SEBI.

Most IPOs go for underwriting. If an issue is underwritten then even if the public response is not good the company can still get the funds from the underwriters. This should satisfy the company as it will get the money for its project. The purpose of underwriting is to see to it that the issue goes through even if the public response is not good.

We have a situation here where company launches IPO that does not attract investors. The lead managers and underwriters then seem to prevail upon the issuing company to withdraw the issue. I am told the company law allows this and SEBI also allows this.

We have also seen that the issuing companies have been allowed to change the price band after the opening of the offer for subscription. It has also been seen that companies have been allowed to extend the subscription period.

I believe that this practice should be stopped. I am told that in India we practice soft underwriting. This allows withdrawal of an issue after it opens for subscription. This practice only protects the underwriters as well as lead managers to the issue.

ANNEXURE-II

IPO

What are the different kinds of issues which can be made by an Indian company in India?

Primarily, issues made by an Indian company can be classified as Public, Rights, Bonus and Private Placement. While right issues by a listed company and public issues involve a detailed procedure, bonus issues and private placements are relatively simpler. The classification of issues is as illustrated below:

(*a*) Public issue

(*i*) **Initial Public Offer (IPO)**

(*ii*) **Further Public Offer (FPO)**

(*b*) Rights issue

(*c*) Bonus issue

(*d*) Private placement

(*i*) **Preferential issue**

(*ii*) **Qualified institutional placement**

(a) Public issue: When an issue/offer of securities is made to new investors for becoming part of shareholders' family of the issuers it is called a public issue. Public issue can be further classified into initial public offer (IPO) and further public offer (FPO). The significant features of each type of public issue are illustrated below:

(i) Initial public offer (IPO): When an unlisted company makes either a fresh issue of securities or offers its existing securities for sale or both for the first time to the public, it is called an IPO. This paves way for listing and trading of the issuer's securities in the stock exchanges.

(ii) Further public offer (FPO) or Follow on offer: When an already listed company makes either a fresh issue of securities to the public or an offer for sale to the public, it is called a FPO.

(b) Rights issue (RI): When an issue of securities is made by an issuer to its shareholders existing as on a particular date fixed by the issuer (*i.e.*, record date), it is called an rights issue. The rights are offered in a particular ratio to the number of securities held as on the record date.

(c) Bonus issue: When an issuer makes an issue of securities to its existing shareholders as on a record date, without any consideration from them, it is called a bonus issue. The shares are issued out of the company's free reserve or share premium account in a particular ratio to the number of securities held on a record date.

(d) Private placement: When an issuer makes an issue of securities to a select group of persons not exceeding 49, and which is neither a rights issue nor a public issue, it is called a private placement. Private placement of shares or convertible securities by listed issuer can be of two types:

(i) Preferential allotment: When a listed issuer issues shares or convertible securities, to a select group of persons in terms of provisions of Chapter XIII of SEBI (DIP) guidelines, it is called a preferential allotment. The issuer is required to comply with various provisions which *inter alia* include pricing, disclosures in the notice, lock-in, etc., in addition to the requirements specified in the Companies Act.

(ii) **Qualified institutions placement (QIP):** When a listed issuer issues equity shares or securities convertible into equity shares to Qualified Institutions Buyers only in terms of provisions of Chapter XIIIA of SEBI (DIP) guidelines, it is called a QIP.

An unlisted issuer making a public issue, *i.e.*, (making an IPO) is required to satisfy the following provisions:

Entry Norm I (Commonly Known as "Profitability Route")

The issuer company shall meet the following requirements:

(*a*) Net tangible assets of at least ₹ 3 crore in each of the preceding three full years.

(*b*) Distributable profits in at least three of the immediately preceding five years.

(*c*) Net worth of at least ₹ 1 crore in each of the preceding three full years.

(*d*) If the company has changed its name within the last one year, at least 50% revenue for the preceding one year should be from the activity suggested by the new name.

(*e*) The issue size does not exceed five times the pre-issue net worth as per the audited balance sheet of the last financial year. To provide sufficient flexibility and also to ensure that genuine companies do not suffer on account of rigidity of the parameters, SEBI has provided two other alternative routes to the companies not satisfying any of the above conditions, for accessing the primary market, as under:

Entry Norm II (Commonly Known as "QIB Route")

(*a*) Issue shall be through book-building route, with at least 50% to be mandatory allotted to the Qualified Institutional Buyers (QIBs).

(*b*) The minimum post-issue face value capital shall be ₹ 10 crore or there shall be a compulsory market making for at least two years.

Entry Norm III (Commonly Known as "Appraisal Route")

(*a*) The "project" is appraised and participated to the extent of 15% by Financial Institutions/ Scheduled Commercial Banks of which at least 10% comes from the appraiser(s).

(*b*) The minimum post-issue face value capital shall be ₹ 10 crore or there shall be a compulsory market making for at least two years. In addition to satisfying the aforesaid entry norms, the issuer company shall also satisfy the criteria of having at least 1,000 prospective allottees in its issue.

A listed issuer making a public issue (FPO) is required to satisfy the following requirements:

(*a*) If the company has changed its name within the last one year, at least 50% revenue for the preceding one year should be from the activity suggested by the new name.

(*b*) The issue size does not exceed five times the pre-issue net worth as per the audited balance sheet of the last financial year.

Any listed company not fulfilling these conditions shall be eligible to make a public issue by complying with QIB Route or Appraisal Route as specified for IPOs.

(*iii*) **Certain category of entities which are exempted from the aforesaid entry norms, are as under:**

(*a*) Private Sector Banks

(*b*) Public Sector Banks

(*c*) An infrastructure company whose project has been appraised by a Public Financial Institution or IDFC or IL&FS or a bank which was earlier a PFI and not less than 5 per cent of the project cost is financed by any of these institutions.

An issuer making a public issue is required to *inter alia* comply with the following provisions mentioned in the guidelines:

Minimum Promoter's Contribution and Lock-in: In a public issue by an unlisted issuer, the promoters shall contribute not less than 20 per cent of the post-issue capital which should be locked-in for a period of three years. "Lock-in" indicates a freeze on the shares. The remaining pre-issue capital should also be locked-in for a period of one year from the date of listing. In case of public issue by a listed issuer [*i.e.*, FPO], the promoters shall contribute not less than 20 per cent of the post-issue capital or 20 per cent of the issue size. This provision ensures that promoters of the company have some minimum stake in the company for a minimum period after the issue or after the project for which funds have been raised from the public is commenced.

IPO Grading: IPO grading is the grade assigned by a credit rating agency registered with SEBI, to the initial public offering (IPO) of equity shares or other convertible securities. The grade represents a relative assessment of the fundamentals of the IPO in relation to the other listed equity securities. Disclosure of "IPO Grades", so obtained is mandatory for companies coming out with an IPO. For more details on IPO grading please refer to the sub-section on "IPO Grading".

4. Pricing of an Issue

(a) Who fixes the price of securities in an issue?

Indian primary market ushered in an era of free pricing in 1992. SEBI does not play any role in price fixation. The issuer in consultation with the merchant banker on the basis of market demand decides the price. The offer document contains full disclosures of the parameters which are taken into account by merchant banker and the issuer for deciding the price. The parameters include EPS, PE multiple, return on net worth and comparison of these parameters with peer group companies.

(b) What is the difference between "Fixed price issue" and "Book built issue"?

On the basis of pricing, an issue can be further classified into fixed price issue or book built issue.

Fixed Price Issue: When the issuer at the outset decides the issue price and mentions it in the offer document, it is commonly known as "Fixed price issue".

Book Built Issue: When the price of an issue is discovered on the basis of demand received from the prospective investors at various price levels, it is called "Book built issue". For more explanation on book built issues please refer to the section titled **"Understanding book-building"**.

◆ Understanding Book-building

What is Book-building?

Book-building is a process of price discovery. The issuer discloses a price band or floor price before opening of the issue of the securities offered. On the basis of the demands received at various price levels within the price band specified by the issuer, Book Running Lead Manager (BRLM) in close consultation with the issuer arrives at a price at which the security offered by the issuer, can be issued.

What is a price band?

The price band is a band of price within which investors can bid. The spread between the floor and the cap of the price band shall not be more than 20%. The price band can be revised. If revised, the bidding period shall be extended for a further period of three days, subject to the total bidding period not exceeding thirteen days.

How does Book-building work?

Book-building is a process of price discovery. A floor price or price band within which the bids can move is disclosed at least two working days before opening of the issue in case of an IPO and at least one day before opening of the issue in case of an FPO. The applicants bid for the shares quoting the price and the quantity that they would like to bid at.

After the bidding process is complete, the 'cut-off' price is arrived at based on the demand of securities. The basis of allotment is then finalized and allotment/refund is undertaken. The final prospectus with all the details including the final issue price and the issue size is filed with ROC, thus completing the issue process. Only the retail investors have the option of bidding at 'cut-off'.

How does "cut-off" option works for investors?

"Cut-off" option is available for only retail individual investors, *i.e.*, investors who are applying for securities worth up to ₹ 1,00,000 only. Such investors are required to tick the cut-off option which indicates their willingness to subscribe to shares at any price discovered within the price band. Unlike price bids (where a specific price is indicated) which can be invalid, if price indicated by applicant is lower than the price discovered, the cut-off bids always remain valid for the purpose of allotment.

Can I change/revise my bid?

Yes, you can change or revise the quantity or price in the bid using the form for changing/revising the bid that is available along with the application form. However, the entire process of changing or revising the bids shall be completed within the date of closure of the issue.

Can I cancel my bid?

Yes, you can cancel your bid anytime before the finalization of the basis of allotment by approaching/writing/making an application to the registrar to the issue.

◆ Takeover Code

Who is an 'Acquirer'?

Acquirer means any person who, whether by himself, or through, or with persons acting in concert with him, directly or indirectly, acquires or agrees to acquire shares or voting rights in, or control over a target company. An acquirer can be a natural person, a corporate entity or any other legal entity.

What is meant by persons acting in concert or 'PAC' in the context of SAST Regulations, 2011?

PACs are individual(s)/company (ies) or any other legal entity (ies) who, with a common objective or purpose of acquisition of shares or voting rights in, or exercise of control over the target company, pursuant to an agreement or understanding, formal or informal, directly or indirectly cooperate for acquisition of shares or voting rights in, or exercise of control over the target company.

SAST Regulations, 2011 define various categories of persons who are deemed to be acting in concert with other persons in the same category, unless the contrary is established.

◈ What is a 'Target Company'?

The company/body corporate or corporation whose equity shares are listed in a stock exchange and in which a change of shareholding or control is proposed by an acquirer, is referred to as the 'Target Company'.

What are the threshold limits for acquisition of shares/voting rights, beyond which an obligation to make an open offer is triggered?

- Acquisition of 25 per cent or more shares or voting rights: An acquirer, who (along with PACs, if any) holds less than 25 per cent shares or voting rights in a target company and agrees to acquire shares or acquires shares which along with his/PAC's existing shareholding would entitle him to exercise 25 per cent or more shares or voting rights in a target company, will need to make an open offer before acquiring such additional shares.
- Acquisition of more than 5 per cent shares or voting rights in a financial year:

An acquirer who (along with PACs, if any) holds 25 per cent or more but less than the maximum permissible non-public shareholding in a target company, can acquire additional shares in the target company as would entitle him to exercise more than 5 per cent of the voting rights in any financial year ending March 31, only after making an open offer.

◈ Buyback of Shares

1. Listed companies are required to intimate the stock exchange of general meetings and resolutions passed thereof. Hence, information on companies proposing to buy-back shares may be obtained from the stock exchanges.
2. When buyback offer document or public announcement is filed with SEBI, SEBI issues a press release and the offer document is put on the SEBI website under primary market page under the head "buyback".

How does one tender one's shares for buyback, in the tender offer method?

The company will send you a tender/offer form. You will have to fill up the form as per the instructions of the company and enclose the documents asked for, by the company.

How does one participate in the buyback in case one does not receive the tender/offer form?

You can make an application on plain paper stating your folio number, name, address, number of shares held, share certificate number, distinctive numbers, number of shares tendered, together with the original share certificate and tender the same at the collection centres/ registrars, as mentioned in the public announcement.

Can you tender your shares for buyback if you are not a registered shareholder?

Yes, provided you submit the duly executed transfer deed for transfer of shares in your name, along with the offer form and other relevant documents as required for transfer, if any. The same should be sent to the registrar to the buyback offer.

What is the manner in which the company decides the acceptances from each shareholders?

In case the shares of the company are tradable compulsorily in de-mat segment, the acceptances from any investor shall be on a proportionate basis irrespective of the number of shares tendered in the buyback, and irrespective of whether shares are in physical or de-mat form.

If the shares are not in compulsory de-mat segment, first the entire shares tendered being less than the minimum market lot shall be accepted in full. Thereafter, the acceptances will be on proportionate basis in a manner to ensure that the acceptances are in market lot. In such a case, a draw of lots shall be done, as in the case of public issues.

When will the shareholder receive intimation about acceptance of his shares?

The company is required to send intimation to the tenderers within 15 days from the closure of the offer.

When will the shareholder receive the consideration/the share certificate?

The company is required to send the above, within 21 days from the closure of the buyback offer.

◆ Delisting of Shares by Companies

1. What is meant by delisting of securities?

The term "delisting" of securities means permanent removal of securities of a listed company from a stock exchange. As a consequence of delisting, the securities of that company would no longer be traded at that stock exchange.

2. What is the difference between voluntary delisting and compulsory delisting?

Compulsory delisting refers to permanent removal of securities of a listed company from a stock exchange as a penalizing measure at the behest of the stock exchange for not making submissions/comply with various requirements set out in the listing agreement within the timeframes prescribed. In voluntary delisting, a listed company decides on its own to permanently remove its securities from a stock exchange.

3. What is the exit opportunity available for investors in case a company gets delisted?

SEBI (Delisting of Securities) Guidelines, 2003 provide an exit mechanism, whereby the exit price for voluntary delisting of securities is determined by the promoter of the concerned company which desires to get delisted, in accordance to book-building process. The offer price has a floor price, which is average of 26 weeks average of traded price quoted on the stock exchange where the shares of the company are most frequently traded preceding 26 weeks from the date public announcement is made. There is no ceiling on the maximum price.

In case of infrequently traded securities, the offer price is as per Regulation 20(5) of SEBI (Substantial Acquisition and Takeover) Regulations. For this purpose, infrequently traded securities is determined in the manner as provided in Regulation 20(5) of SEBI (Substantial Acquisition and Takeover) Regulations.

4. Does a company listed at BSE/NSE have to provide exit offer to shareholders in case it delists from stock exchanges other than BSE and NSE?

No, the company does not have to provide exit offer to shareholders because it continues to be listed on the BSE/NSE which have nationwide reach and shareholders can exit any time they decide to so by way of selling shares in NSE/BSE.

CONSENT ORDERS

◆ On Consent Orders and Compounding of Offences

1. What is a Consent Order?

Consent order means an order settling administrative or civil proceedings between the regulator and a person (Party) who may *prima facie* be found to have violated securities laws. It may settle all issues or reserve an issue or claim, but it must precisely state what issues or claims are being reserved. A consent order may or may not include a determination that a violation has occurred.

2. What is Compounding of Offence?

Compounding is a process whereby an accused pays compounding charges in lieu of undergoing consequences of prosecution.

3. What are the Administrative/Civil Enforcement Actions?

Administrative/Civil enforcement actions include issuing directions, suspension or cancellation of certificate of registration, imposition of monetary penalty, pursuing suits and appeals in Courts and Securities Appellate Tribunal (SAT).

4. What is Prosecution?

Filing of criminal complaints before various criminal courts by SEBI for violation of provisions of securities laws which may lead to imprisonment and/or fine.

5. What is the Objective of Consent Order?

Consent order provides flexibility of wider array of enforcement and remedial actions which will achieve the twin goals of an appropriate sanction, remedy and deterrance without resorting to litigation, lengthy proceedings and consequent delays.

6. What is the Objective of Compounding of Offence?

Compounding of offence allows the accused to avoid a lengthy process of criminal prosecution, which would save cost, time, mental agony, etc., in return for payment of compounding charges.

7. Does SEBI have Power to Pass Consent Orders?

The Parliament of India has recognised SEBI's powers to pass an order with consent of the parties. This will of the Parliament is clear from the words of Section 15T of the SEBI Act, 1992. Section 15T(2) of the SEBI Act reads as under:

"15T(2). No appeal shall lie to the Securities Appellate Tribunal from an order made (*a*) by the Board on and after the commencement of the Securities Laws (Second Amendment) Act, 1999;

(*b*) by an adjudicating officer, with the consent of the parties."

Thus, the Parliament in its wisdom has recognized that SEBI and its authorized delegate have power to pass consent orders. Similarly, courts have well recognized inherent powers to settle a case before them on an application made by the parties.

8. Is Compounding of an Offence Permitted?

Section 24A of SEBI Act permits compounding of offences by the court where prosecution proceedings are pending.

9. What Kind of Offences/Cases can be Compounded or Consented?

Consent orders can be passed in respect of all types of enforcement or remedial actions including administrative proceedings and civil actions, e.g., proceedings under Sections 11, 11A(1)(b), 11B and 11D of SEBI Act or under Enquiry Proceedings Regulations or Adjudication Rules or equivalent proceedings under the Securities Contracts (Regulation) Act, 1956, Depositories Act, 1996 and other civil matters pending before SAT/courts. Compounding of offence can cover appropriate prosecution cases filed by SEBI before the criminal courts.

10. Who can Seek Settlement of Proceedings Through Consent Order and Compounding?

Any person who is notified that a proceeding may or will be initiated/instituted against him/her, or any party to a proceeding already initiated/instituted, may, at any time, propose in writing for settlement.

11. What Factors will be Taken into Consideration for the Purpose of Passing Consent Order/Compounding of Offence?

Following factors, which are only indicative, may be taken into consideration for the purpose of passing consent orders and also in the context of compounding of offences under the respective statute:

1. Whether violation is intentional.
2. Party's conduct in the investigation and disclosure of full facts.
3. Gravity of charge, *i.e.*, charge like fraud, market manipulation or insider trading.
4. History of non-compliance. Good track record of the violator, *i.e.*, it had not been found guilty of similar or serious violations in the past.
5. Whether there were circumstances beyond the control of the party.
6. Violation is technical and/or minor in nature and whether violation warrants penalty.
7. Consideration of the amount of investors' harm or party's gain.
8. Processes which have been introduced since the violation to minimize future violations/ lapses.
9. Compliance schedule proposed by the party.
10. Economic benefits accruing to a party from delayed or avoided compliance.
11. Conditions where necessary to deter future non-compliance by the same or another party.

12. Satisfaction of claim of investors regarding payment of money due to them or delivery of securities to them.
13. Compliance of the civil enforcement action by the accused.
14. Party has undergone any other regulatory enforcement action for the same violation.
15. Any other factors necessary in the facts and circumstances of the case.

12. At What Stage can Consent Orders be Passed?

Consent order can be passed at any stage where probable cause of violation has been found. In the event of a serious and intentional violation, the process cannot be completed till the fact finding process is completed whether by way of investigation or otherwise.

13. How will a Person Propose to Consent or Compound a Violation/Offence?

A person can make an application proposing administrative/civil consent by writing to the 'Division of Regulatory Action, Enforcement Department' at SEBI's Mumbai address. Where compounding is proposed by a party, such application may be made to the court and a copy can be addressed to the "Division of Prosecution, Enforcement Department" at SEBI's Mumbai address. (addresses given at the bottom of this document).

14. At What Stage Compounding of Offence can Take Place?

At any stage after filing criminal complaint by SEBI. Where a criminal complaint has not yet been filed but is envisaged, the process for consent orders will be followed rather than the one for compounding.

15. What are the Principal Terms and Conditions of Consent Order and Compounding of Offence?

Consent orders are passed by Competent Authority/SAT/Court where proceedings are pending, subject to the party taking remedial action and on such further consent terms including consent bars or consent penalties as the Competent Authority/SAT/Court where proceedings are pending, may find appropriate in the facts and circumstances of the case. Consent orders can be passed either: (*a*) admitting guilt, or (*b*) without admitting or denying guilt. Where an order is passed without admitting or denying guilt, such person shall never represent subsequently that he/she is not guilty. In the event such a representation is made, the enforcement process may be reopened. Similar appropriate terms will be sought by SEBI from Court where the prosecution is pending.

16. What is the Process for Passing Consent Orders/Compounding of Offences?

When the proposal of settlement is submitted by the party, it will be examined by a high powered committee headed by a retired High Court Judge. Where the committee finds the terms for passing a consent order inadequate, it may ask the party to revise the consent terms. Thereafter, the committee will submit its views/recommendations to the Adjudicating Officer/ Competent Authority where proceedings are pending for passing consent order. The above procedure and factors and waivers shall be applied for considering the proposals of composition of offences under the SEBI Act, SCRA and the Depositories Act, 1996, wherever applicable. Any party who wishes to compound an offence shall file an appropriate application before the Court where complaint is pending with a copy addressed to the Prosecution Division, Enforcement Department of SEBI's Mumbai office which will forward the application/request to be placed before the highpowered committee. The terms of compounding as recommended by the committee and approved by the competent authority would be placed before the Court by the prosecution division by way of written submissions or application, as appropriate, for passing orders as the Court deems fit. Where a matter is pending before SAT/Court, the same consent process will be undertaken and the draft consent terms recommended by the committee and approved by the competent authority will be filed before the SAT/Court. The SAT/Court may, if found fit, pass an order in terms of the consent terms and subject to such further terms as the SAT/Court may find appropriate in the facts and circumstances of the case.

17. Will SEBI Obtain Waivers while Passing the Consent Order?

Yes, while considering the proposal of the party, SEBI will obtain a waiver from the party of taking any legal proceedings against SEBI concerning any of the issues covered by the consent order. The party shall waive:

1. all hearings pursuant to the statutory provisions under which the proceeding is to be or has been instituted;
2. the filing of proposed findings of fact and conclusions of law;
3. proceedings before the Board or any officer;
4. all post-hearing procedures; and
5. Appeal/review before/by SAT/Court.

By submitting an offer of settlement the party shall further waive:

(*a*) such provisions of the regulations or other requirements of law as may be construed to prevent any officer of SEBI from participating in the preparation of, or advising the competent authority as to, any order, opinion, finding of fact, or conclusion of law to be entered pursuant to the offer; and

(*b*) any right to claim bias or pre-judgement by SEBI based on the consideration of or discussions concerning settlement of all or any part of the internal proceeding.

In addition, if the party violates the consent order subsequently, the party shall waive a plea of limitation for reopening the case. Similar appropriate waivers will be sought by SEBI from the accused before Court where the prosecution is pending.

18. When Will Final Acceptance of any Offer of Settlement/Compounding come into Effect?

The final acceptance of any offer of settlement/compounding will come into effect only upon the Competent Authority/SAT/Court passing the consent order/compounding order.

19. What Will be the Procedure after Passing Consent Orders?

The consent order will be published through press release and would be put on SEBI website. In cases where a party undertakes compliances, it has to comply with the same as per agreed schedule.

20. Whether the Party has to Pay any Compounding/Settlement Charges for Mitigating the Violation?

Yes. Depending upon the facts and circumustances of the case, gravity of alleged violation, interest of investors and the securities market and deterrent effect, amount payable by a party will be decided. In pending prosecution cases and cases pending before SAT/Courts, the party is also liable to pay legal expenses incurred by SEBI.

21. Whether SEBI can Consent, if the Enforcement Order was Already Passed and Appeal is Pending before Securities Appellate Tribunal/Court?

Where a matter is already in SAT/Court, the same consent process will be undertaken and the draft consent terms will be filed before the SAT/Court with an appropriate prayer to consider the terms of the consent and subject to such further terms as the SAT/Court may find appropriate in the facts and circumstances of the case.

22. What will be the Remedies Available with SEBI, if the Consent Order is Violated by a Party?

Failure to obey consent orders would invite appropriate action, including for violating SEBI orders, besides revival of the pending action. In this context any proceeding which had been kept in abeyance pending the consent process will begin from such stage at which it was suspended.

23. What will be the Consequences of Non-acceptance?

If SEBI rejects the offer of settlement, the person making the offer shall be notified of the same and the offer of settlement shall be deemed to be withdrawn. The rejected offer shall not constitute a part of the record in any proceeding against the person making the offer, provided, however, that rejection of an offer of settlement does not affect the continued validity of waivers. SEBI and the party will be free to resort to legal recourse as may be available to them under law and neither SEBI nor the party would be entitled to use any information relating to the settlement process in such proceedings. In cases where SEBI is not inclined to accept settlement/compounding of offence, SEBI would file its objections before SAT/Court for consideration.

Source: SEBI website.